THE SETTING AND THE ACTION

The people who lived beside it, deriving sustenance, called it Chesapeok—the mother of waters. They fished and they hunted, thinning the forest with the fires that drove the game toward the waiting line of men. The women cleared garden patches to plant corn, beans, and various gourd crops. All lived in small bands, often fiercely at war with one another—their lives and forms of self-esteem very closely bound up with readiness for such warfare.

Then came the navigators who called themselves English. With the aid of charts, they brought their ships over in what by their calendar was the year of the Lord 1607. They made Chesapeake into a bay upon a map of a land they had called Virginia. They claimed to possess it all in the name of their king. The waters of Powhatan and Pamaunk became the rivers James and York. Rappahannock and Potomac kept ancient names, but they too became entries upon the map.

The English lodged among the earlier inhabitants and kept themselves alive only with the help of those peoples—until they discovered that they could grow rich, as they accounted wealth, by planting and harvesting a drug plant, the sot-weed, tobacco. Then commenced more than two centuries of conscripting labor to make the crop. The marking of maps upon the ground soon began in earnest as surveys divided the land into properties.

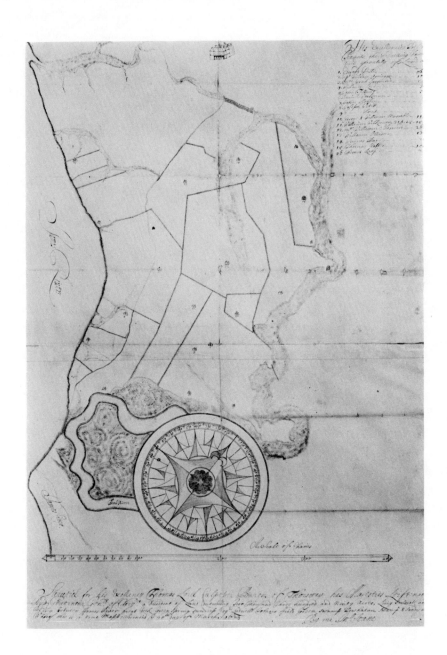

At first the English huddled together in wattle-and-daub huts behind tall palisades, but as the original inhabitants were driven back by the newcomers and killed off by imported diseases, strong liquors, and broken hearts, the invaders boldly set up homes in the midst of the territories they had staked out. They brought nails across the seas, and making use of an abundance of timber unknown for centuries in the island from which they had come, they learned to frame, wall, and roof "Virginia houses" of beams and boards. Boundaries enclosed boundaries, according to notions of the fitness of things that they had also brought with them. Thus counties and parishes were laid out. Courthouses and churches arose, put together at first from materials hewn from the forest.

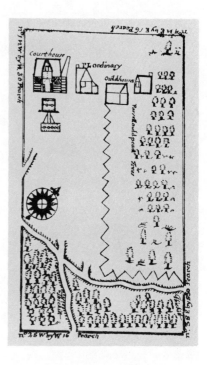

Some of the English, being owners of land and lords of labor, consolidated an eminence above the rest. When, after a time, they found there was a shortage of their own island people who were willing to enter into bondage for a term of years in order to be carried to a continent of supposed opportunity, the would-be masters supplied themselves with captives from Africa instead. Thus another people came to live and work on the Chesapeake shores.

The wealth produced by African slaves for life, whose children too were defined as slaves, further enhanced the mastery of the great men among the English. Such masters began to have big brick mansions built as monuments for the lineages they sought to perpetuate.

They had also established a new seat of government called Williamsburg, for a liberator king. This place was endowed with a college, where youths might learn to be English Christian gentlemen. Other edifices enhanced the new center of authority: a dignified house of

worship, a governor's "palace," and a "capitol" for the making of laws and the doing of justice. In the counties and in the parishes also the great men began setting up fine brick courthouses and churches as emblems of the rule they sought to exercise and of the divinity legitimating that rule. Yet the order that imposing buildings began to proclaim after a century of planting tobacco did not long remain unquestioned. Within half a century of its apparent consolidation the system would be overturned.

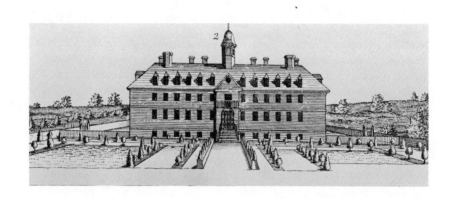

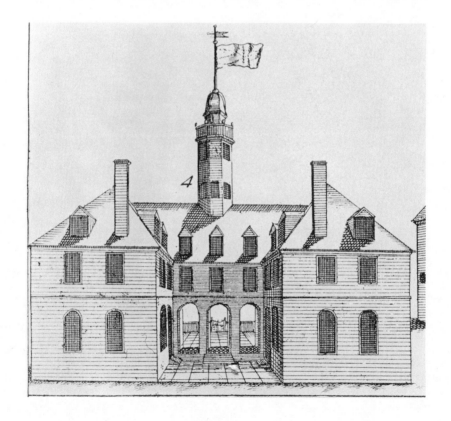

First, from the North came stern-faced men who fostered ideas of divinity that were not expressed in elegant, ornamented churches where the greater presided over the lesser members—and where even the furnishings expressed a downward flow of governance. If the new sense of ultimate meaning was embodied in buildings at all, it was in rough meetinghouses that were stark without, and within revealed a denial of all worldly pretension. The forms of action associated with such meetinghouses were as rich as the settings were simple. Africans and their offspring, as well as the descendants of the English, were drawn to them in growing numbers.

At about the same time patriot leaders came forward and questioned the dominion of the rulers of England. This dominion had been accepted in principle, if not always in practice, from the time of the first seaborne settlement on the Chesapeake shore. Disturbing questions then arose as to who the descendants of the English now were, and in what way they should be governed by the customs of their forefathers. At courthouse meetings the patriots rallied the owners of the land, and striking at trade with England, they urged resolutions that all should make do without the supplies of manufactured goods that had lately been ordered in quantities exceeding the value of the crops exported.

Within a decade the patriots rose up in arms to defend their own redefinition of the nature of the connection with the parent island—to defend it against another redefinition that confronted them from across the ocean. Defiantly they discarded the style of dress worn by soldiers of their king and donned hunting shirts in the fashion of the ancient inhabitants whom they had displaced. After more than a year of fighting they declared the bonds of ancestral loyalty severed.

Riflemen.

When the bitter, devastating war was over, both masters and slaves found themselves in a world subtly but decisively changed. The shores of the Chesapeake were now left behind by the hordes of people of all conditions who were moving or being moved westward to possess the lands beyond the mountains. Parish churches, no longer centers of whole communities, began to fall into disrepair. The new meetinghouses, with their strict rules and their recurrent mass gatherings for emotional release, symbolized a different kind of religious association—one that took in only a part of the people. The stern-faced preachers persuaded their followers to adopt stricter morals. Al-

though not all descendants of the English changed accordingly, their houses were generally less open places for convivial assembly and more frequently became closed domestic refuges for individual withdrawal. The descendants of the Africans, by contrast, took the new forms of worship and made them the core of a profoundly collective way of being. Meanwhile the courthouses were incorporated as the base of a new system of government under which the sons of free settlers all along the widening margin of the great continent agreed to rule themselves in a way they were assured was distinctively American.

THE TRANSFORMATION OF
VIRGINIA

THE TRANSFORMATION OF

VIRGINIA

1740–1790

BY RHYS ISAAC

PUBLISHED FOR THE INSTITUTE OF

EARLY AMERICAN HISTORY AND CULTURE

WILLIAMSBURG, VIRGINIA

BY THE UNIVERSITY OF NORTH CAROLINA PRESS

CHAPEL HILL

The Institute of
Early American History and Culture
is sponsored jointly by
The College of William and Mary
and The Colonial Williamsburg Foundation.

Manufactured in the United States of America

Library of Congress Cataloging in Publication Data
Issac, Rhys.
The transformation of Virginia.

Includes bibliographical references and index.
1. Virginia—Social life and customs—Colonial
period, ca. 1600-1775.   2. Virginia—Civilization.
1. Title
F229.18   975.5'02   81-10393
ISBN 0-8078-1489-X   AACR2
ISBN 0-8078-4116-1 pbk.
First printing, April 1982
Second printing, August 1983
Third printing, March 1984
Fourth printing, October 1984

The cost of editorial work on this volume
was assisted by a grant from the
Commonwealth of Virginia Fund for Excellence.

First

for Colleen

who has so long allowed recalcitrant slaves,
proud men on horseback,
and gaunt prophets pointing skyward
to parade through her life

Then

for

Edwyn & Frances
Glynn & Alison
Meg & Lyn

who have been willing to argue with me always.

CONTENTS

THE TRANSFORMATION OF

VIRGINIA

Virginia c. 1775.
Adapted from the map of Virginia religious congregations
in Lester J. Cappon et al., eds.,

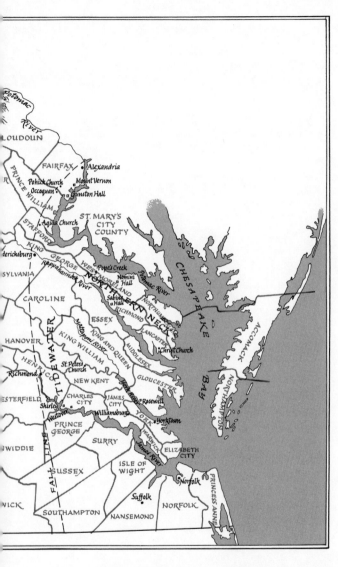

Atlas of Early American History: The Revolutionary Era,
1760–1790 (Princeton, N.J., 1975), 39.
Drawn by Richard J. Stinely.

INTRODUCTION

Anthropologists cross frontiers to explore communities other than their own. Social historians cross time spans to study earlier periods. Whether one moves away from oneself in cultural space or in historical time, one does not go far before one is in a world where the taken-for-granted must cease to be so. Translation then becomes necessary. Ways must be found of attaining an understanding of the meanings that the inhabitants of other worlds have given to their own everyday customs.

The chapters of this work are a series of linked studies of changing expressions of the meaning of life, traced through half a century of religious and political revolution in Virginia. No claim is made that hitherto unknown facts or sources have been discovered, although here the reader will find that the rich records of popular religious upsurge, previously left as the preserve of denominational historians, have been given the same importance as the records of the struggle for independence. The intention has been to review in social-cultural context the double revolution in religious and political thought and feeling that took place in the second half of the eighteenth century. If this work has a distinctive contribution to make, it lies in the results of a search for means of access to the alien mentalities of a past people. Considerable effort has gone into experimenting with strategies of presentation that would serve to explicate ways of life. Devices appropriated from both art and social science were found to afford the most serviceable mirrors of reality. The theater supplies a concept of dramaturgy, suggesting a way of looking at the important communications included in patterns of action. Social life, in its routines as well as in its convulsive processes of change, is viewed as a complex set of performances. Not only words but also settings, costumes, and gestures all carry their messages in the incessant exchanges of interaction. The authority system can be seen expressed in the assignment of roles. Crucial power struggles occur over the definitions of the situation—the "scenes" to be enacted, their meanings, and the forms of action appropriate to them.

This book is composite in character. Themes of religion and the roles assigned to an ecclesiastical establishment have provided the main thread of continuity. Yet the intention has been neither to write religious history nor to present the story of a church, but rather to decipher important beliefs, values, and aspirations in a society where the religious institutions that had provided a focus for authority in the community were challenged and ultimately overthrown. In subject matter this book ranges from the hoeing of hills for the planting of tobacco to niceties concerning the degree of orthodoxy requisite for election to the rectorship of the most desirable parish. In order of writing it includes a collection of essays published at different times, but with certain interpretations now radically revised.

The work is divided into three parts, each with a different intention. The first part attempts to characterize the ways of life that had taken shape in Virginia by the second quarter of the eighteenth century, focusing on religion, learning, and authority as topics of central concern. The second part consists of a series of closeup analyses of particular episodes, intended to reveal something of stress and change as they appeared in passages of action and exchanges of words. The studies most important for the development of the theme of this work (chapters 7, 8, 11, and 12) deal with popular movements, their impact, and their implications for systems of authority in society. Chapters 9 and 10 deal with the higher culture of the ruling gentry, reviewing disturbances manifested at that level in consequence of popular challenges to the traditional order. (Those who may not wish to involve themselves in the intricacies of disputed symbols for the legitimation of authority at a time of upheaval can pass over these chapters and yet stay with the main argument of the book.) Part II is followed by an Afterview that seeks glimpses of some of the differences in the ways the inhabitants of old Virginia experienced their world after the decades of religious and political upheaval. Part I and the Afterview, although as systematic as could be managed, are necessarily based on selections from selective research; the episode studies, on the other hand, more in accordance with the requirements of the historian's craft, are closely bounded in time and place and are based as far as possible on a thorough reading of all directly related sources. Since the incorporation into the text of extended discussion of concept would distract attention from the past peoples whose ways of life this book seeks to reconstruct, A Discourse on the Method offers a fuller explication of the methodology employed. It is necessarily technical and can be omitted by readers not concerned with such theoretical issues.

In sum, my purpose is twofold. First, it has been to develop in myself, and to communicate in this book, an understanding of the generations of people of all races and religions who lived during the revolutionary decades in the distinct cultural region between the Chesapeake Bay and the Blue Ridge. My second purpose arose from the first. It has been to seek concepts and methods for gaining an understanding of past people and so to contribute a mite to humanistic historical social science.

Note: Since pictorial representations surviving from the past provide us with vital documents for reconstructing vanished ways of life, I have included notes "About the Illustrations" at the end of the volume (pages 415–421). These notes amplify the information given in the text and in the captions to the illustrations.

I

TRADITIONAL WAYS OF LIFE

FIGURE 1.

1

PROSPECTS OF VIRGINIA
Overviews of the Landscape

Water and trees—trees and water. These are the features that now dominate the impressions of a traveler in Tidewater Virginia. In some parts the woods are so dense that one can see but a few yards into them. Elsewhere they thin out, and standing water marks the edge of a swamp. The lay of the land is better revealed in those places where the road crosses or runs alongside one of the great rivers. There, oaks and pines stand thick along the banks, almost down to the high-water mark. From the air the terrain is even more fully revealed, and the eye can take in a total pattern of dense green or black forest, lighter-colored swamps, and the silver arms and fingers of the sea that reach far into the land spread out below. Moving to the west, in the region between the rocky falls and the heaving lines of the Blue Ridge, the land is a series of rolling hills, and the river inlets become fast-flowing streams. Journeying through this Piedmont region, one still finds dense woods, but as the roads top the crests, the eye enjoys views of lovely valleys and is carried across sweeps of pasture or cornfields.

The twentieth-century traveler sees these distinctive Chesapeake terrains and automatically assimilates them into that romantic set of landscape images that we all carry around with us. We are conventionally appalled by urban sprawl, charmed by unspoiled countryside, and enraptured by untamed wilderness. If the traveler is also a historian or an antiquity-minded tourist, he or she will be led to reflect—especially by the view from the air—upon the ways in which the forested, river-dissected terrain worked to shape the emergent Anglo- and Afro-Virginian society. Such travelers will also be moved by the landmarks of the past—an ancient family seat, an old church or meeting-house, a courthouse village, a tavern where Lafayette is declared to have biv-ouacked his little army, or just a succession of magically evocative names. These are deeply satisfying journeys. Yet in order to recover the realities of a remote past and to appreciate its ethos, we have to transcend our romantic views of the terrain and strive to recover something of the sense of it that its possessors had, each in their own generation. For the purposes of this study, it is the meanings that the eighteenth-century inhabitants attached to their en-vironment that are to be sought out.

The perceptions a people has of its world are not usually formed or ex-pressed by statistics, yet such information is invaluable to observers seeking to understand the conditions that shape experiences. In 1700 the colony of Virginia had a total population of about 60,000, distributed on the shores of the Chesapeake and the three "necks," or peninsulas, between the great rivers that open off the bay itself (see figure IV). The Indians being almost gone, the population was sharply divided between the 85–90 percent who were free or servant Anglo-Virginians and the 10–15 percent who were Afro-Virginian slaves. The total population was growing at a rate of more than 20 percent each decade; it would reach 90,000 by 1720 and 230,000 by 1750. The white contribution to expansion came largely from a surplus of births over deaths. The blacks were increasing naturally also, but at a slower rate, so that their rising proportion in relation to the whole—more than 40 percent by 1750—derived in large part from the continued importation of slaves from Africa at a rate of approximately 1,000 per annum. The population growth was matched by an extension of settlement from the Tidewater into the Piedmont west of the Fall Line, where layers of hard rock create rapids that impede fur-ther navigation of ocean-going ships. The society expanded by replicating its basic units in the new areas. Scattered fields and households continued to be included within a network of parish and county lines. Parishes and counties were smaller and more densely settled in the Tidewater, larger and sparser in the west. In 1726 there were fifty-five parishes, ranging in size from ten miles square to thirty or more miles in length by ten in width. The twenty-eight counties varied in dimension but were mostly of a size to contain two par-ishes. Population density was from twenty to thirty per square mile, reducing as one looked farther to the west. By 1750 there would be seventy-one parishes and forty-five counties. Settlement had already advanced as far as the Blue Ridge, while immigrants from Pennsylvania were moving into the valley beyond.[1]

So much for a demographic mapmaker's view of Virginia. Landscape, however, is not merely measured physical terrain—it is that terrain interpreted by the eye, or one might say, experienced in life. A concept of social or experiential landscape provides the perspective used here to sketch a view of the society and way of life that had taken shape on the shores of the Chesapeake by the second quarter of the eighteenth century.

The development of a moderately secure "Virginia" identity and the emergence of an easy acceptance of the colony's distinctive landscape can be traced in the contrast between the essays of two gentlemen—essays that were published twenty years apart during the first quarter of the eighteenth century. In 1705 a book entitled *The History and Present State of Virginia* appeared in London. Its author was Robert Beverley, a first-generation native of the colony. For him, as for most of his predecessors in the nascent literary tradition of Virginia, the most striking aspect of the region was its natural endowment: "The Country is in a very happy Situation, between the extreams of Heat and Cold. . . . Certainly it must be a happy Climate, since it is very near of the same Latitude with the Land of Promise. Besides, As *Judaea* was full of Rivers . . . So is *Virginia*. Had that fertility of Soil? So has *Virginia*, equal to any land in the known World." Phrases like "the extream fruitfulness of that Country" recur in Beverley's descriptions. He praised Virginia as a region where "the clearness and brightness of the Sky, add new vigour," and where the inhabitants "enjoy all the benefits of a warm Sun, and by their shady Groves, are protected from its Inconvenience. . . . Their Eyes are ravished with the Beauties of naked Nature. Their Ears are Serenaded with the perpetual murmur of Brooks. . . . Their Taste is regaled with the most delicious Fruits. . . . And then their smell is refreshed with an eternal fragrancy of Flowers."[2]

Beverley's perception of the bounteousness of nature in Virginia was conditioned by a deep-seated identification with two visionary landscape images that pervade his descriptive commentaries. One of these was drawn from Scripture, reinforced by Classical preoccupations with an arcadian Golden Age located in a timeless past. The other was based on an idealized picture of the English countryside that he longed to see replicated in Virginia but found to be in marked contrast with reality.[3]

Beverley evoked the past and timeless landscape in a set of recurrent allusions: "Almost all the Year round, the Levels and Vales are beautified with Flowers of one Kind or other, which make their Woods as fragrant as a *Garden*." "A *Garden* is no where sooner made than there, either for Fruits, or Flowers." Even the chapter "*Of the Recreations, and Pastimes used in Virginia*" begins with the observation that "for their Recreation, the Plantations, Orchards, and *Gardens* constantly afford 'em fragrant and delightful Walks." Beverley constantly interpreted the landscape by analogy to Eden, using human archetypes to give primary meaning to the scene. The dominant image of the Indians in the book is of a "harmless people" who have lived "happy . . . in their simple State of Nature, and in their enjoyment of Plenty, *without the Curse of Labour*." Food gathering for them was "diversion," and "the bare planting of a little Corn, and Melons . . . took up only a few Days in the Summer." Furthermore, he stressed, "they claim no property in Lands, [which] . . . are in Common to a whole Nation. Every one Hunts and Fishes. . . . Their labour in tending Corn, Pompions, Melons, &c. is not so great, that they need quarrel for room" (see figure I).[4]

By 1705, however, the Indians were already a vanishing people in Virginia. Only their sorry remnants could be listed in Beverley's book. The future of the land clearly lay with the invaders, whose occupation of the New World garden Beverley narrated dispassionately. He presented the triumph of his countrymen neither as an atrocity story nor as an epic of conquest. The author condemned not the violence of the intrusion but the failure of the settlers to take advantage of the "Liberality of Nature" to create an apotheosis of the English landscape in their new home. Because of the arrival of the Europeans, "the Indians," Beverley sadly recorded, "have lost their Felicity, as well as their Innocence." The English had "taken away great part of their Country." They had "introduc'd Drunkenness and Luxury amongst them," which had "multiply'd their Wants, and put them upon desiring a thousand things, they never dreamt of before." Nevertheless, what was "unpardonable" in Robert Beverley's eyes was the "Laziness" of the invaders, which kept them from engaging in handicrafts and the industrious cultivation of wholesome crops. Closely associated with this moral failure was the way "Ambition" had led many a settler to dream of being "Lord of a vast, tho' unimprov'd Territory"—an aspiration fostered by "the Advantage of the many Rivers, which

afforded a commodious Road for Shipping at every Man's Door." The consequence, Beverley noted, was to make "the Country fall into such an unhappy
Settlement . . . that to this Day they have not any one Place of Cohabita-
tion among them, that may reasonably bear the Name of a Town." The total
neglect of crafts was so general that in a land "over-run with Wood," where
flax, wool, furs, and leather could be plentifully produced, "they have all
their Wooden Ware from *England*," as well as their clothing, hats, and shoes.
For Robert Beverley "Virginia" had yet to acquire definitive shape. A garden,
in which every sense is charmed, was an appropriate habitation for "natural"
men, but for the English, "improvements" were requisite.[5]

   In 1724 the Reverend Mr. Hugh Jones, with the customary modest dis-
claimers of that age, offered another literary Virginia landscape, entitled simply *The Present State of Virginia*. Jones was not native born but had come out
from England to minister in a parish. His book is pervaded by the recognition
that a distinctive way of life, with its own "temper . . . and manners," had
come into being. He understood that it was necessary for English law, the
English church, and immigrants from England, such as himself, to adapt to
the different circumstances.[6]

   What Mr. Jones found and described was a *colony*. Having gotten some
theological and geographical preliminaries out of the way, he briskly sketched
the mechanics of the maritime tobacco trade that governed the disposition of
elements in the landscape and largely dominated the outlook of the gentry
elite. "The Country of Virginia" is revealed to be "about a thousand leagues
[3,000 miles]" clear sailing from England, and to be oriented to the anchorages
all along the tide-washed shores of the four principal rivers, "for the con-
veniency of which most houses are built near some landing-place; so that any
thing may be delivered to a gentleman there from London, Bristol, etc. with
less trouble and cost, than to one living five miles in the country in England."
Jones deftly indicated the personal bonds of association that were part of the
consignment system with the added note that the recipient would "pay no
freight for goods from London," but that he was "in gratitude engaged to
freight tobacco upon the [same] ship" for its return voyage. The pattern of
settlement that followed from this way of securing a living was portrayed
without the condemnation that had recurred in Beverley's descriptions:

   Thus neither the interest nor inclinations of the Virginians induce
   them to cohabit in towns; so that they are not forward in . . . the

making of particular places, every plantation affording the owner the provision of a little market; wherefore they most commonly build upon some convenient . . . neck of land in their own plantation, though towns are laid out and established [by law] in each county. . . . The whole country is a perfect forest, except where the woods are cleared for plantations.

Jones also registered approval for the ordered hierarchy that now showed clearly in the arrangement of settlements: "The gentlemen's seats are of late built for the most part of good brick . . . commodious, and capacious; . . . the common planters[*] live in pretty timber houses . . . ; with timber also are built houses for the overseers. . . . The Negros live in small cottages called quarters, in about six in a gang, under the direction of an overseer."[8]

Hugh Jones had found a community that had a patterned existence of its own, although as a colony it was dependent for its prosperity on the export of a staple to the parent society and on returns received in manufactured articles. Material reliance entailed also cultural and psychological dependence. With goods came tastes, standards, and a whole set of assumptions about the proper ways of ordering life.

The main features of the thriving colonialism that Jones discovered may be reduced to two: easy access from the sea along natural waterways that ran deep into the country itself; and the disposition of the leading inhabitants to exploit the situation by settling strategically "near some landing place." Jones saw clearly how maritime trade stimulated and sustained the clearing of fields for cultivation of the staple and the construction of networks of roads, bridges, and ferries for the tobacco to be hauled to the warehouses and stores near the rivers, where it could be exchanged for English goods. (The great gentlemen's tobacco would usually be sent directly to England, and the returns consigned the same way.) Jones was further impressed by signs of civility in the courthouses set up in each county, where affairs were regulated and disputes settled

---

* Throughout the 18th century the word "planter" was used in two senses. English commentators frequently employed it to designate those who lived in the "plantations" ("colonials," we might say). Among Virginians themselves the term meant a person who lived by growing crops, but who was not entitled to be accorded the dignity of a gentleman. "Planters" were thus men who bent their backs and hardened their hands in the fields. That usage, the opposite of general 19th- and 20th-century signification, is retained throughout this book—otherwise the meaning of important quotations would be reversed.[7]

according to forms only slightly modified from English law. The dignity and
decorum evident in the seat of government at Williamsburg was a further reassurance of the colony's progress. The replication in the Virginia General
Assembly of the outlines of the English Parliament suggested a due deference
to the authority of Westminster. Finally, the delimitation of parishes, the
building of handsome brick churches, and the maintenance of a beneficed
clergy, all at public expense, set a seal of loyalty on this "happy retreat of true
Britons and true churchmen." Although he found the virtual absence of
towns and the endless woods unfamiliar, Jones recognized in churches and
courthouses, mansions and provincial government buildings, clear evidences
of the civilized "improvements" that Beverley a short time before had found
lacking.[9]

2

SHAPES IN THE LANDSCAPE
The Arrangement of Social Space *

From being a raw settlement—a beachhead of uncertain prospects, opened by the parent country on an alien continent—Virginia had become an established province. An understanding of this social world as it presented itself to its own diverse inhabitants requires a distinctive strategy. Robert Beverley and the Reverend Mr. Hugh Jones were literary landscape artists offering elaborate and explicit interpretations of the scene they surveyed. Because they were writing for publication, their perceptions were more intensely shaped by long study and close attention to the conventions of high culture than would have been true of more provincial gentlemen. Can we also recover to any degree the landscapes experienced by the ordinary Virginia squire and his lady? Or by the yeoman and his wife? Or—most elusive—by the slave man and woman?

Fortunately, we do have the means of getting at the sense of environment shared by plain folk who have not left explicit statements such as the word pictures provided by Beverley and Jones. The term "landscape" referred originally to artists' renditions of terrain, but it has a well-established extension to the creative achievements of those who give studied form to gardens or town

---

* This chapter and those that follow in Part I aim at a view of patterns of life in Virginia during the second quarter of the 18th century, centering approximately on the year 1740—that is, after the Tobacco Act of 1730 had confirmed the dominance of the gentry but before the rise of evangelical popular dissent (to be analyzed in Part II) had begun to challenge the hegemony of the elite. Where sources are meager or absent and do not indicate fundamental change in a particular facet of life, however, evidence from after 1750 is admitted without apology.

plans. It can thus be usefully applied to any terrain or living space that has been subjected to the requirements of a conscious or unconscious design. Shaping environment for use in accordance with ideas of well-being is a universal trait of human behavior. Comparatively abundant evidence survives concerning the "landscaping" activities of the inhabitants of old Virginia—on both macro and micro scales.

A society necessarily leaves marks of use upon the terrain it occupies. These marks are meaningful signs not only of the particular relations of a people to environment but also of the distribution and control of access to essential resources. Incised upon a society's living space appears a text for the inhabitants—which he who runs may read—of social relations in their world. Moving more slowly, anthropologists for present societies, and historical ethnographers for past ones, must seek to interpret such texts—both to understand the relations of production inscribed upon the land and to decipher as much as they can of the meanings that such relations assumed for those who were part of them.

POSSESSING THE LAND

"It is the business of the Surveyor," wrote Robert Beverley, "to take care, that the Bounds of his Survey be plainly marked, either by natural Boundaries, or else by chopping Notches in the Trees." Already Beverley had noted that the Indians "claim no property in Lands, . . . [which] are in Common to a whole Nation." The most decisive act of the invaders in reshaping the configuration of the Chesapeake landscape was the imposition of the lines of exclusive property rights. This was not a once-only demarcation, since every three years the vestries that governed the parishes commissioned a number of the worthies from each precinct to "procession" all the property lines in the presence of witnesses and to make a formal return that recorded the fulfillment of this duty.[1] The surviving precinct returns are themselves little memorials to ancient rituals, expressive of the sacred importance attached to ownership of the land. A document from Christ Church Parish in Lancaster County, written ceremoniously with flourishes, illustrates the procedures:

> We the subscribers, being appointed have processiond every particular
> persons land within our precinct In obedience to an order of vestry
> Dated in June 1727 as In manner following vizt.
>   Beginning November the 13th at a corner old pine or chestnut Stake
> Standing on the bayside a Dividing line between the said Cox and
> Kelley to a Corner pine Standing on Tabs Creek Including Coxes then
> up the said Creek to a Corner Spruce pine.[2]

The persistence of other ancient rituals further communicated the mystique
surrounding the possession of land. Transference of ownership, for example,
was often accompanied by the symbolic giving of "Twigg & Turf," taken from
"the Land and premises" themselves, in the so-called "Livery of Seizen."[3]

The establishment and maintenance of lines of property in land not only
marked a fundamental distinction between English and Indian ways of life
but also inscribed upon the landscape the gradations and divisions that were
developing within the expanding colonial society. It would be misleading to
stress property in land as a principle of merely private rights. The system
of land grants was designed not to scatter individuals but to impose upon
the terrain a pattern of collective occupation—albeit one very different
from that which Beverley celebrated as characteristic of the Indians in their
"towns." In the formative years of the colony, entitlement to land was assigned on the basis of "head rights." Fifty acres of land were allowed for each
man, woman, or child, servant or slave, whom the claimant was considered
to have imported, bearing the cost of transportation across the ocean. Extensive grants of land thus went to those rich and influential men who stood at
the center of large clusters of dependents bound to work at their bidding. The
workers were not employees on wages, but bond servants who lived under
their master's roof (or an annex of it) and ate his "meat." He was deemed a
father-king over them, and they were liable to the fearful legal penalties for
petit treason should they strike him down. A Virginia legal manual sums up
the nature of the crime and its pains thus: "I. Where a Servant kills his Master. . . . II. Where the Wife kills her Husband. . . . The son killing his Father . . . is guilty of Petit Treason *if he receives Meat, Drink, or Wages.*" In
short, the manner of apportioning territory imprinted upon the landscape
the great cultural metaphor of patriarchy. The identification of both God and
the king as fathers not only incorporated experience from everyday life into

the highest levels of cosmology but also sanctified the authority of the head of each household.[4]

The role of patriarch was fairly widely distributed in the society, though mostly on a small, unlordly scale. In a sample Tidewater county (Lancaster), whose landholdings at mid-century have been analyzed and published, about half of the three hundred identifiable adult white males owned land. Only one-quarter owned the 100- to 200-acre tract necessary to support a family comfortably under existing systems of agricultural exploitation. Two-thirds of the landowners had working slaves, but only one-tenth had the ten or more that might make for the beginnings of affluence and the possibility of asserting genteel rank. Three men—2 percent of the white adult males—had more than twenty slaves and unchallengeable status as gentlemen.[5]

Patriarchy was not the only formative pattern of social organization evident in the way the terrain was occupied. The principle of money was also powerful in giving shape to the colonial landscape. In its purest form the wealth of the patriarch consists primarily of the accumulated obligations of dependents to show submission, render service, and supply needs. Money, by contrast, is a form of wealth that operates very differently. It is impersonal, being designed to establish a universal scale of values that transcends the particularities of ties between persons; and, unlike the personal obligations contributing to patriarchy, it is in essence composed of discrete units. Money not only expresses obligation in precise amounts but also instills the idea of obligation as calculable debt rather than as forms of service and submission.

The pervasiveness of the cash nexus in the social world that the English established on the shores of the Chesapeake can be clearly seen in the way the essential supports of the patriarchal household were saleable. Headrights, landownership, and the labor of bond servants were all convertible into money by unrestricted sale. Furthermore, the desire to acquire land and to set labor to work upon it was, especially in the early years, directed not to the creation of ongoing patriarchal systems of personal relationships but to the raising of a tobacco crop that could be exchanged at a cash value.[6] Nevertheless, despite the profound differences between "money" and "patriarchy" as principles of organization, the two systems were closely intertwined in the society that was taking shape. A man's (or, in the longer perspective, a lineage's) eminence in the social landscape depended on the size of the group of dependents bound to work his land for him in the patriarchal mode; but the viability of that social unit and the value of the land depended on their strategic location for the purposes of the money-oriented tobacco export trade. *

FIELDS AND SEASONS

The marking out and shaping of the domains enclosed by boundary lines was largely determined by the requirements of tobacco cultivation as it had come to be practiced. A late colonial treatise on agriculture explains why very large tracts of land were needed for tobacco cultivation:

> First, that the planter may have a sure prospect of increasing his cul-
> ture on fresh land [cleared as old fields were exhausted]; secondly, that
> the lumber may be a winter employment for his slaves and afford casks
> for his crops. Thirdly, that he may be able to keep vast stocks of cattle
> for raising provisions in plenty, by ranging in the woods; and where
> the lands are not fresh, the necessity is yet greater, as they must yield
> much manure for replenishing the worn-out fields. This want of land is
> such, that they reckon a planter should have 50 acres of land for every
> working hand.[8]

Only four or five acres per hand could be cultivated at any one time in tobacco and the food staple, Indian corn. For this reason woodland comprised a large part of even long-settled holdings.

---

* The operation of money as an idea in a complex of ideas, rather than as a material substance, was particularly evident in Virginia for a number of reasons. It was highlighted by the opposition between the saleability of all forms of property and the urge to maintain familial social units rooted in the soil that supported them. This feeling about land was variously reflected in the special laws relating to "real" property; in such rituals as "livery of seizin"; and in the recurrent practice of binding a lineage to a particular territory through "entails." Another circumstance that highlighted the character of money as a cultural metaphor was the absence of a circulating medium of fixed value. The tobacco, tobacco notes, and Spanish, French, and Portuguese coins that were current fluctuated in value relative to each other and to sterling, which, though it was the most prestigious form of money, did not appear in the colony save as the "bills of exchange" that transferred personal credits accumulated in Great Britain. Even the coins that circulated— pistoles, pieces of eight, joes, and moidores—were not officially rated according to the marks upon their faces but were assigned a value in pounds, shillings, and pence, "current money of

Within this comprehensive agrarian setting, the fields that tobacco cultivation created had a distinctive form. The Reverend Mr. Jones's account supplies vivid images:

> When a tract of land is seated, they clear it by felling the trees about a yard from the ground, lest they should shoot again. What wood they have occasion for they carry off, and burn the rest, or let it lie and rot upon the ground.
>
> The land between the logs and stumps they how [hoe] up, planting tobacco there in the spring, inclosing it with a slight fence of cleft rails. This will last for tobacco some years, if the land be good. . . .
>
> Land when tired is forced to bear tobacco by penning their cattle upon it; but cowpen tobacco tastes strong. . . .
>
> When land is tired of tobacco, it will bear Indian corn, or English wheat . . . with wonderful increase.
>
> Tobacco and Indian corn are planted in hills as hops, and secured by wormfences, which are made of rails supporting one another very firmly in a particular [zig-zag] manner.

Sometimes the trees were not felled but merely girdled, so that planting in the roughly hoed ground would take place beneath the gaunt spread of leafless limbs (see figure VII).[9]

Virginians' perceptions of their landscape were conditioned by the rhythms of work that sustained production in the fields. Neither the African-descended slaves nor the hard-handed "planters" have left descriptions of their rounds of toil. Yet a great deal can be learned about the tasks and life experiences of those who worked in the crops from the record kept by a gentleman who was a diligent plantation owner-manager seated in Richmond County, on the northern shore of the Rappahannock River. Colonel Landon Carter's diary (from the year 1766, for example) traces the congested succession of arduous tasks as well as the hazards, cares, and anxieties that faced those concerned with the cultivation of the fields. From Carter's diary entries one can sense how demanding the cultivation of tobacco was. Common knowledge (and even calculation) dictated that the yield would be closely proportioned to the

Virginia." Those pounds, shillings, and pence had no tangible form but were simply a money of account, used for reckoning the values of exchanges of goods, services, coins, and paper notes.[7]

intensity of the labor applied to the fields. Yet the diary also brings twentieth-century readers into touch with the eighteenth-century agriculturalist's keenly felt dependence on the vagaries of climate and weather and reveals one pattern of response to this dependence—a posture of supplication and fatalistic submission toward God, who alone governed natural forces. "That man . . . must be a very foolish boaster," declared the colonel, reviewing the farmer's fortunes, "who shall think that he either can or does make anything but by Almighty permission."[10]

Corn and tobacco were the twin staffs of life. Corn pone was bread, and tobacco was literally money. Livestock was also necessary, since the availability of meat made the difference between a mean and a satisfying diet; dung was needed where lands were "worn"; and animal power was required to draw plows and carts. In 1766 Colonel Carter supervised closely the operations of some five quarters located near his mansion at Sabine Hall—Mangorike, the Fork, Davis's, Jammy's, and his own "home" fields. We may follow the succession of seasonal tasks, cares, and anxieties surrounding the raising of crops and livestock at the Fork quarter, where an old slave, Jack Lubbar, was foreman over a number of others. The diary enables us to glimpse the landscape as it existed for most Virginians, not in Hugh Jones's maplike perspective, but as a pattern of surrounding woods, fields, worm fences, threshing floors, barns, and tobacco houses—all known as the inhabitants were known, by particular names and by shared associations.

The work had no beginning and no end. Before the making of one tobacco crop was completed, preparations for the next year's planting were under way. An account of the seasonal fieldwork may nevertheless start with the sowing of the tobacco seeds in February. The seeds were sown in carefully prepared beds, which despite the frosts, snow, and sleety rains, had to be "hoed up again and laid off, raked and ready." Through March and April the soil had to be plowed—often in the same bleak weather conditions—for the sowing of wheat, while broad fields had to be prepared for the setting of corn and the transplanting of tobacco seedlings. The soil—a "heavy stiff white Clay" in many places—had to be hoed up into "hills" about three feet apart. This hard labor—sometimes performed in sweltering heat—would be called for intermittently until at least the middle of June. At the same time, Carter's old lands had to be fertilized with dung, which had first to be turned in the cattle pens and then carted out—"a long and troublesome job," since the winter-starved horses and oxen found the struggle through the mire almost too much for them. Meanwhile, during all of March and April the tobacco seedbeds would require close tending. The young plants had to be covered and uncovered with straw or bundles of brush to protect them first from frost and then from the voracious tobacco fly, which could, in bad years like 1755 and 1758, decimate the colony's crop and so plunge the society into crisis. "[April 25] Plants fine in the fork meadow. I gave orders if the flye came in them to float them off [by flooding] as it can be done in a few hours."

When spring rains had rendered the lands "miry to hoe or even ride on," the workers were busy in earnest, piling up "hills" to receive the tobacco seedlings or corn grains: "[April] 29, Tuesday. Plants at the Fork quarter very fine. I must ditch the patches now to drain off the too great moisture. . . . We shall finish planting corn there tomorrow." A spring landscape of muddy fields can be pictured: men and women moving through the mire, bending over about six thousand times a day, making holes in the crowns of the hills "with their fingers or a small stick" for the reception of the corn seeds. Soon this process at the Fork fields would have to be repeated with "near as much trouble as at the first planting," for on May 4, when the colonel "rode out to . . . fork quarter," he found that "the birds had pulled up the corn" and that in another place of which he had had great expectations the corn had been "all rooted up this day" by livestock, even though he had "yesterday given particular charge about it and indeed ordered the fence to be made more secure by the Cow yard rails close by." With a gleam of insight into the antagonistic feelings of many of the human figures in this landscape toward the dominant one, Landon Carter went on to note: "but the more particular we are in our charges and the fonder we show ourselves of anything[,] the more careless will our slaves be."[11]

Replanting corn was still in progress on May 21, "owing to lazy people," the colonel thought. By May 23 the workers had turned some seven or eight thousand hills for the reception of tobacco plants. Four days later the hands at the quarter were still busy with this work, "burying Dung and hoeing hills for next season." (A "season" was a spell of rain needed to make the soil ready for the reception of seedlings.) When it came on the night of May 30, the workers at all the quarters went out the next day and "planted and made good about 95,000 hills." The diary entry for May 26 suggests that Carter expected each field hand to set more than a thousand seedlings in the waiting hills in the course of a day's backbreaking labor.

There were times when the squire (and no doubt his humbler neighbors) had been hopeful about the crops. On April 30 he had written: "This day I uncovered my fork meadow plants. It is a fine patch not overweedy"; and again on May 16: "Plants flourish well at the fork." By early June, however, the urgent need to give close attention to a variety of crops gave rise to a different view of the scene: "[June] 10. . . . My Crop of Corn and Peas at the fork near ruined with weeds. I must give over I fear a part of the tobacco and clean out corn and pease. Meadow still to mow later than ever." As the summer advanced, these routine anxieties and dilemmas were compounded by a spell of too much rain. Earlier Carter had feared that the summer would be too dry, as the six previous ones had been: "God be merciful to us, we shall all perish with such an other drye disasterous year. . . . What then will not 7 do? This is my 7th drye year." By the beginning of July, however, he was in a quandary as he surveyed waterlogged fields:

> A rain came on this day . . . prodigeous plenty in about 2 hours. I dread the effects of it. This is a certain instance that man knows not which is best for him. My missing tobacco crop and my new wed [weeded] as well as grassy cornfields want rain; but my Wheat Oats and flax want none in my opinion; however let us hope for the best, and it may be we shall be convinced rain is best . . . but we are as fainty in our hearts as we are defective in our Judgments.

Soon, repeated days of "violent rain" had flooded the land, turning the farmers' doubts to desperation. "Every field is a sea," and "our very tobacco though but young is in many places drowned and so miry we cannot stick a first plant in those hills or worm" (i.e., go from plant to plant removing caterpillars). The workers nevertheless had to be out in the mire within two days, "holling [hoeing?] the weeds from things" and planting again what the waters had washed out. A dry spell renewed the battle with the weeds that flourished in the wet soil. By July 10 Colonel Carter and his neighbors could see only gloomy prospects as they looked out on their lands: "From our preceding drye years we did expect that this moist year would be a good crop year, but as yet I see reason to think otherwise. . . . The corn first merely choked with weeds which cannot be killed any way. . . . The tobacco not growing, very weedy and miry. Add to this a glut of all sorts of worms." When heavy rains resumed, all the growers in the area must have shared Landon Carter's feelings as he looked sadly at "my low grounds in ponds, and my hillsides knee deep [in mire] so that the Corn is there in danger. . . . God have mercy upon us or we perish for bread."

August brought relief from floods—even a touch of drought ("Every thing burn't up"). But then came a plague of worms, "destroying all the Tobacco before them," so that, although the squire saw all his people out in the hot sun picking off and destroying the pests, he doubted the sufficiency of their efforts. Finally, on the evening of August 26 the field hands "began to cut tobacco." We may picture this new phase of the work, and its setting, from Hugh Jones's description: "They cut it down about six or eight leaves on a stalk, which they carry into airy tobacco houses; after it is withered a little in the sun, . . . it is hung to dry on sticks." When the processing began, the scene of work shifted to the tall tobacco houses of rough-hewn timber, where tier upon tier of sharp-pointed stakes, each heavy with newly cut plants, had to be raised and hung from the beams.

The arduous work of cutting, carrying, and passing up from hand to hand continued until after October 13, by which time a frost had heralded the end of summer, and winter wheat had been sown in plowed fields "at the fork." Barley, rye, and clover had already been planted before October 23, when the tedious work of "stripping" commenced. Those engaged in processing the tobacco at this stage were required to "strike it, or take it down, then cover it up in bulk [to sweat] . . . [then] to stem it (that is pull the leaves from the stalk) or strip it (that is take out the great fibres) and tie it up in hands [bundles] . . . and so by degrees prize or press it with proper engines into great hogsheads." These tasks were often assigned at night, as overtime.[12]

The corn, which was also the product of much clearing, hilling, planting, and weeding, would mostly be stored in cornhouses or lofts. As the staple diet of those who worked the fields, it sooner or later had to be husked and ground, either in the traditional manner with a pestle and hollow-stump mortar, or by being taken to one of the water mills on the runs and creeks. Meanwhile the tobacco would be carried down a creek in a light boat, or loaded in a cart, or when made up in a hogshead (a huge cask standing four feet high with a diameter of two and a half feet, weighing between 1,000 and 1,300 pounds), it might be rolled by hand or drawn by a horse, the barrel itself acting as a single great wheel. Ultimately it went to a public warehouse, where an official inspector certified it as "merchantable," or in some cases, ordered it to be burned as trash. (Tobacco was usually stored at the warehouse

FIGURE 2.
The young Colonel Landon Carter

FIGURE 3.
Hanging, stripping, and prizing the tobacco crop

after approval. The certificates issued by the inspectors were known as "tobacco notes" and changed hands like money, until the current holder finally
consigned the hogshead named on the certificate to a ship's captain for export.) In the case of the common planter, a large part of his crop was already
owed—in return for an advance of supplies of clothing, tools, and other imported goods—either to the gentleman whose house dominated the neighborhood waterfront, or increasingly as the century progressed, to the agent
("factor") of a Glasgow trading house. Dependence on credit reduced the impersonal now-and-done-with quality inherent in cash transactions, sustaining
in its place a network of continuing, face-to-face personal relationships.[13]

The urge to establish credits and the need to clear debts at home and abroad were the great motors that drove Anglo-Virginians on and underlay the constant need to expand the territory on which their way of life was laid out. The movement of tobacco, corn, goods, and people along the roads traced upon the landscape the community's lines of connection. Fields, quarters, and houses were linked to stores, water mills, and wharves as well as to such places of assembly as taverns ("ordinaries"), courthouses, and churches. Public authority was as much concerned with maintaining the highways that joined such centers as it was with securing the boundaries of landed property. The starting points, courses, and destinations of the roads were like diagrams of the needs, influence, and power of persons of importance in each neighborhood. The gentlemen justices of the county courts—by and large the occupants of the great houses established near the landing places—directed the laying out of the roads and the location of bridges. They appointed the road surveyors and imposed fines on those surveyors who neglected the upkeep of their assigned sections of highway. The same groups of county gentry also regulated the important centers of service and exchange to which the roads led: they licensed both the water mills that turned corn into meal and the "ordinaries" that were placed at crossroads, ferries, courthouses, and other facilities. Most important, they nominated the tobacco inspectors, whose decisions determined whether a grower's crop was cash or trash. Finally, the great gentlemen advised the colonial legislature on the siting of the warehouses and ferries as well as of the churches and courthouses.

HOMEPLACES: QUARTERS AND HOUSES

Isolated habitations, each in the midst of its cluster of field clearings, were the main points of human concentration in a settlement pattern that generally did not include towns or even villages. Two distinctive kinds of dwelling place, expressing sharply contrasting life-styles, were established by each of the two great cultural traditions—the African and the English—that had been brought to the New World.

Descriptions of the slaves' dwelling places are rare and invariably reveal more about the observer than the observed. The Reverend Mr. Jones passed quickly over this feature in the landscape, fastening on the masters' concerns and noting only that "the Negroes live in small cottages called quarters, in about six in a gang," and that an overseer was often located nearby to supervise the occupants' tasks. Edward Kimber, an English traveler who passed through the Chesapeake region in the 1740s, was more informative when he explained that "a Negro Quarter is a Number of Huts . . . built at some Distance from the Mansion-House; where the Negroes reside with their Wives and Families, and cultivate, at vacant Times, the little Spots allow'd them." Equating the huts with "Hovels" and going on to express contempt for these "true Pictures of Slavery, which begets Indolence and Nastiness," Kimber was more concerned to deplore what he saw as deprivation than to interpret the signs of a different way of life. He has had many successors.[14]

Taken for granted at that time—and easily overlooked in the record since— was the distinctive configuration of these dwellings, whose meanness was almost the only feature observers noted. The Anglo-Saxon house typically provided a home for only one married pair—the patriarch and his wife. The Anglo-Virginian arrangement intensified this pattern by withdrawing the household from the communal village setting often found in England, thus heightening the distinction between "family" and community. The slave settlements imprinted quite a different shape on the landscape. The word "quarter" had a triple meaning. It could refer to a "Barreck"—similar to that depicted in a diary reference to "Negroe quarters 20 by 16 [feet]" to accommodate, we can only guess, four to six adults; it could designate a unit of production (as in "Fork Quarter"); or it could apply to the locality where the slaves lived, as in Kimber's description of "a Number of Huts." The design of the "huts" or slave "cabins" may have come from West Africa and no doubt often housed a married pair of slaves and their offspring. Almost equally often, however, these structures housed unmarried persons or a single parent and children—the other parent being on a different plantation. In the 1730s and 1740s more than half the slaves in Virginia lived in clusterings of over ten people. Whatever the varying details of house occupancy, therefore, we may be sure that the general pattern was quite different from that prevailing at the plantation house. The quarter was a composite communal living space, encompassing a plurality of married pairs and parent-child combinations as well as unmarried slaves.[15]

It cannot be assumed that the form of the slave quarters was simply the result of deprivation caused by the parsimony of the masters. Indeed Kimber's condemnation of the slaves' "Nastiness" suggests a dim recognition that Afro-Virginians might have actively preferred to live in close physical proximity to large numbers of their own kind—a preference that had become highly repugnant to the sensibilities of English gentlemen by the eighteenth century. Certainly a clear indication of the initiative that slaves themselves took in shaping their own living space is given in a diary entry dating from some thirty years after Kimber's visit. Describing a Sunday walk to a place a little away from a great white residence, the writer noted that he "saw a number of Negroes very busy at framing together a small House." He remarked that "Sundays they commonly spend in fishing making Potatoes &c [digging up their small Lots of ground allow'd by their Master], building & patching their Quarters or rather Cabins." The blacks evidently fitted their surroundings to their own needs.[16]

The communalism of the slaves was especially apparent in the ways they came together to join in distinctively African forms of celebration. An English observer from the 1770s conveyed a strong sense of the impulse that drew attendance at such gatherings:

> Instead of retiring to rest, as might naturally be concluded he [the slave] would be glad to do, he generally sets out from home, and walks six or seven miles in the night, be the weather ever so sultry, to a negroe dance, in which he performs with astonishing agility, and the most vigorous exertions, keeping time and cadence, most exactly, with the music of a banjor (a large hollow instrument with three strings), and a quaqua (somewhat resembling a drum), until he exhausts himself, and scarcely has time, or strength, to return home before the hour he is called forth to toil next morning.[17]

THE COMMON PLANTER'S PLACE

Great men took up strategically sited land along the river fronts, building their houses near the landing places. Their domination of the export of the tobacco staple enabled them to found or consolidate the great fortunes that, through control of credit, secured them extensive power in colonial society. The dwellings of the humbler yeomen and tenants tended to be removed from the main waterways, so that the great majority of the total population lived amid fields and trees along the lesser creeks.

The humbler "Virginia house" was a one- or one-and-a-half-story frame dwelling with two rooms on the ground floor and a chimney on the gable at one or both ends. It was covered with unpainted riven clapboards, made by splitting four-foot lengths of the oak timber that was so plentiful in the country. Conflicting accounts of the "statements" made by these buildings have been transmitted to us by eighteenth-century commentators. Where settlement was well established the "common planters" might, no doubt, "live in pretty timber houses, neater than the farm houses are generally in England," as Mr. Jones affirmed. Too often, however, the dwellings, like the fields, must have borne the marks of the constant need of tobacco growers to relocate. A later observer noted that "the houses here are almost all of wood, covered with the same; the roof with shingles, the sides and ends with thin boards, and not always lathed and plaistered within; only those of the better sort are finished in that manner, and painted on the outside. The chimneys are sometimes of brick, but more commonly of wood, coated on the inside with clay. The windows of the best sort have glass in them; the rest have none, and only wooden shutters" (see figure 13).[18]

Even the poor, ill-equipped houses were built according to an exacting set of design conventions. A recent rigorous analysis of old Virginia farm buildings has shown that a strictly coded "grammar" of folk architecture had developed as regional culture matured. Plain persons' houses were constructed with precisely shaped timber upon ground plans characterized by controlled combinations of squares and divisions of squares of fixed size. Implicit rules governed the placement of doors, windows, and chimneys in these structures. The form and manner of construction, and the austere decoration applied to the finished lines, have all been interpreted as expressing a sharp sense of the need to define boundaries between "culture" and "nature."[19]

The humbler habitations probably ranged in form and degree of finish from disciplined rectangularity to makeshift irregularity. The evidence suggests that, considering farmhouses and their settings together, the overall impression was not one of extreme orderliness. The common planters of Virginia generally—not just of the frontier—were repeatedly declared slovens in agriculture, a charge supported not only by accounts of their neglectful treatment of cereal crops but also by the records of their methods of clearing and cultivating tobacco fields. The natural abundance of well-watered land, where horses, cattle, and hogs could range freely in the woods, did not encourage intensive use of space and did not instill a compulsion to control the environment strictly. The appearance of the orchards, found wherever there were houses, may be considered in this light. Travelers noted that the orchards flourished, but they implied no careful ordering of the landscape when they observed that Virginians "plant them . . . in the worst of their ground in order to Improve it, their Cattle and Swine feeding under [the trees]." The common practice was, indeed, to shake down the fruit for the livestock. "The Fruit-Trees are wonderfully quick of growth," noted Robert Beverley, "so that in six or seven years time from the Planting, a Man may bring an Orchard to bear in great plenty, from which he may make store of good Cyder, or distill great quantities of Brandy. . . . Yet they have very few, that take any care at all for an Orchard; nay, many . . . let them go to ruine, and expose the Trees to be torn, and barked by the Catle." The custom of permitting passersby of all ranks to refresh themselves with orchard fruit was certainly in accord with the proverbial hospitality of the planters, but it also reveals that boundaries were not jealously maintained. [20]

The best and most durable of the yeomen's houses may have been squared statements of formality, but their larger settings were not. Worm fences, being zig-zag stacks of split young tree trunks, lacked the rectilinear precision of posts and rails. "Making Virginia fences" became a proverb for inebriation. Altogether it seems clear that the small plantations of Virginia at this time rarely attained a close integration of human habitation with a clearly shaped and organized farm landscape (see figures IV and VI). [21]

THE GENTLEMAN'S SEAT

By the second quarter of the eighteenth century the distribution, siting, and external appearance of the principal plantation centers, or "great houses," had come to be elaborate, overt expressions of social values.

A large main building with a profusion of separate structures around it was
the most distinctive feature of these countryseats. William Hugh Grove, an
English gentleman who came to Virginia in 1732, recorded clearly his first
impressions:

> I went by ship up the [York] river, which has pleasant Seats on the
> Bank which Shew Like little villages, for having Kitchins, Dayry
> houses, Barns, Stables, Store houses, and some of them 2 or 3 Negro
> Quarters all Separate from Each other but near the mansion
> houses. . . . [They] make a shew to the river of 7 or 8 distinct Tene-
> ments, tho all belong to one family. . . . I sailed up the [Mattaponi]
> which divide[s] King and Queen County from King William. . . . The
> North side . . . is Thick seated with gentry on its Banks with in a Mile
> or at most 2 mile from Each other. . . . Most of These have pleasant
> Gardens and the Prospect of the River render them very pleasant [and]
> equall to the Thames from London to Richmond, supposing the Towns
> omitted.[22]

The design of the houses was evidently explained to Grove as being particularly suited to the Chesapeake climate. He noted that "the Manner of Building is much alike" and that "they have a broad Stayrcase with a passage thro
the house in the middle[,] which is the Summer hall and Draws the air."
Some houses had two rooms on each side of the passage; others, of more traditional design, had only one, "and the Windows opposite each other" for
ventilation.[23]

A French traveler in 1686 had seen a great plantation as "a rather large
village"; the Englishman in 1732 saw it as a "little" one; another Frenchman
fifty years later remarked that the Byrds' seat at Westover, seen from across
the river, "with its different annexes, has the appearance of a small town and
forms a most delightful prospect." There was, however, an evolution—a for-
malization—occurring in the style of the great houses, which these observers
did not comment on. It was a development they did not find remarkable,
since it served to replicate in the colony certain established European architectural norms that were expressive of social position. From early in the eighteenth century the main residences that stood at the centers of the sprawling
domains of Virginia gentlemen were being fashioned as declarations of the

=York River. looking N W. up to West Point=

FIGURE 4.
"Gentlemen . . . love to build near the water"

owners' status, not only by sheer scale but also by means of elaborately contrived formal relationships. Calculated proportion and rigidly controlled symmetry became mandatory (see figure VIII and figure 7).[24]

The manner in which the new anglicized Classical conventions were introduced into the colony is itself revealing of the dynamics of innovation in
a maturing colonial society that was inevitably a cultural province of the
mother country. The new idiom that became the standard mode of grand architectural expression made its first and most influential appearance in the
governor's house—instantly styled "the Palace"—in Williamsburg. Construction of the palace began in 1706 and was finished under the direction of Governor Alexander Spotswood, by about 1720. Spotswood had produced a fine

example of a mansion in a style later called "Georgian." At the political and cultural capital of a province whose great houses were surrounded by clusters of dependencies, he had shown how the basic layout could be given formal balance by the addition of adjoining "offices" symmetrically arranged on each side of the central block. The formal setting was completed with enclosed gardens and finely wrought gates (see figure 5).[25]

All of the many great houses built in the ensuing decades—indeed, through the eighteenth century and beyond—were conceived upon Spotswood's fundamental plan. The great Virginia gentry families were establishing a colonial tradition parallel to (and continuously interconnected with) an ongoing cultural development in England. The new style of building conveyed a whole

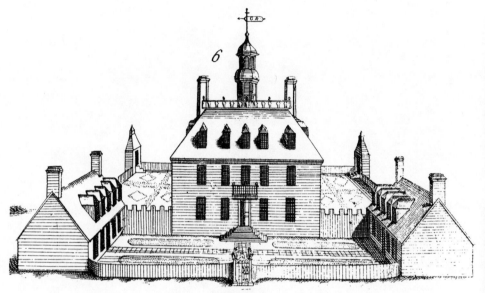

FIGURE 5.
Governor's residence

set of social values and assumptions through attention to mathematical proportion and through the invariable usage of a three-part design. A strong
sense of gradations of dominance and submission was expressed in the elevation of a central unit by means of balanced, subordinated lateral elements.

Members of the Virginia gentry liked to think of their estates as rural re-
treats from a world of unworthy striving, where, as one declared in a biblical
phrase echoed by many others, "we sit securely under our Vines and our Fig
Trees." They identified their countryseats with Roman villas such as Horace's
Sabine farm, from which Colonel Landon Carter took the name of his newly
built countryseat, Sabine Hall. This imagery served to intensify the ideal of
the great house, with its symmetrically retained dependencies, as a self-sufficient rural community. Rule over slave-supported plantations encouraged in
the Virginia gentry a deep response to the symbolism of rank that the three-
part structures so strongly expressed. The prominence of an elevated center,
or "head," to which all other parts, or "members," were subordinate silently

reinforced the dignity and claims to obedience of the gentleman who was styled "the head" of the household.[26]

The timing of the first of these architectural pronouncements of social order and their frequent restatement in a series of great houses was not fortuitous. English settlement in Virginia had been turbulent and prone to violence from its beginnings. Only in the last decades of the seventeenth century, with the first emergence of a powerful native gentry, was social authority on traditional English lines becoming effective. From about 1700 onward, ownership of large numbers of slaves supplied a secure foundation for the wealth and status of the elite. The construction of the great houses was a part of the consolidation of this gentry dominance—a process that by the fourth decade of the eighteenth century in turn inaugurated a stable political authority in Virginia to a degree that was exceptional among the British colonies in America.[27]

The Classical form of the great houses continued to communicate established social values for well over a century. A serene sense of the hierarchical authority that the plantation house was intended to assert is conveyed in an item of folk art of uncertain date, now held in the collections of the New York Metropolitan Museum of Art (see figure 6). A mansion of late eighteenth-century design rides supreme above tiered ranks of dependencies leading down to a waterfront and river, where a three-masted ship signifies the maritime orientation of this little social world. Allusion to the idealized rural retreat celebrated in the literary tradition is sustained by the copious grape vine that entwines one of the trees. Together the trees and vine make the whole scene a sylvan enclosure.[28]

The vine was a Mediterranean symbol. Latin imagery could readily merge with that of the Hebrew Scriptures. Beside this picture we may set a famous Virginia idyll penned by William Byrd II in 1726, just as he was about to undertake the building of Westover, one of the most beautifully sited and executed of the great Tidewater houses:

> I have a large Family of my own, and my Doors are open to Every
> Body, yet I have no Bills to pay, and half-a-Crown will rest undisturbed
> in my Pocket for many Moons together. Like one of the Patriarchs, I
> have my Flocks and my Herds, my Bond-men and Bond-women, and
> every Soart of trade amongst my own Servants, so that I live in a kind

FIGURE 6.
Plantation as idyll

of Independence on every one but Providence. However this Soart of
Life is without expence, yet it is attended with a great deal of trouble.
I must take care to keep all my people to their Duty, to set all the
Springs in motion and to make every one draw his equal Share to carry
the Machine forward.[29]

The ambivalence of the system is nicely revealed in this fantasy. Byrd's
commentary opens with an explicit opposition between "money" and "patriarchy." Coin was scarce, and with food and fuel produced within the plantation, cash transactions played a comparatively small part in the daily life of
early eighteenth-century Virginians. Yet money—mostly in the form of credits entered in the books of a tobacco merchant—was the lifeblood of the
plantation, great or small. Credit gone, William Byrd would have found that
necessary supplies of clothing and implements for the use of his bondmen and

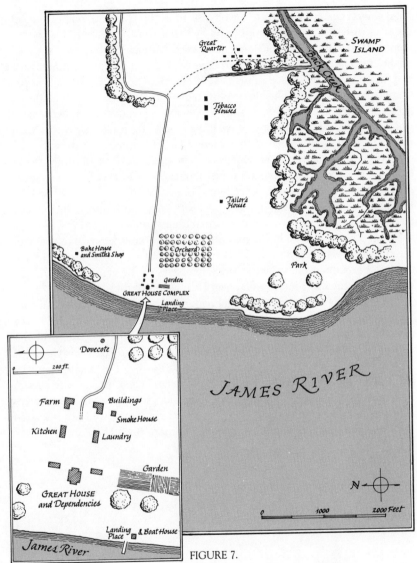

FIGURE 7.
Plan of a great house, riverfront, and quarter, 1742

bondwomen ceased to arrive. Cut off also from the elaborate refinements of dress, furnishings, transportation, and diet that were the essential accoutrements of his rank, he would have lost, with his financial credit, his social credibility. His slaves would probably have started to run off in great numbers, and his own debts would certainly have been called in, forcing the sale at the sheriff's "outcry" of his valuable property. For all its fancifulness the plantation gentleman's idyll did resonate values deeply embodied in the way settlement was organized. The scattering of dwellings, isolating each Anglo-Virginian married couple in the midst of their own tract of land, reveals patriarchy as a great organizing principle, at least equal to money, in the landscape. Byrd's idealized vision further illuminates the significance of Robert Beverley's reference to "the Ambition each had of being Lord of a vast . . . territory." By 1726 that ambition was increasingly associated with an aspiration to be surrounded by dependents whose permanent personal obligation supported the status of the head of the household. The master's identity became deeply involved with the successful regulation of the slaves' activities. Byrd's imagery, then, elucidates the metaphor embodied in the symmetries of the great house and extended over the even more widespread habitations of the slaves.

The slave quarters registered an ambivalence different from that which contraposed money and patriarchalism. These living places were included in the patriarchal structure but not wholly co-opted by it. While the assigned habitations of white attendants might be incorporated into the tightly ordered design at the center, those of the blacks could not be. The Virginia gentleman, although dependent on the labor and deference of his slaves to sustain his exalted role, tacitly recognized that they had a social system of their own. The communal living pattern of the quarter's clustered dwellings inscribed the mark of a distinctive culture upon the plantation world.

3

FIGURES IN THE LANDSCAPE
People and Environment

Houses and fields, roads and stores, were all parts of a shaped landscape that took its meaning from the arrangement of human figures. The bearing and demeanor of persons also expressed relationships to environment. Dress, diet, and medicine reveal the more intimate perceptions that peoples had of their own bodies and of their place in nature.

Clothes defined status as clearly as did the location and style of habitation. "A *periwig*, in those days," wrote the aging Reverend Mr. Devereux Jarratt, reminiscing about his boyhood as a farmer-artisan's son in the 1730s, "was a distinguishing badge of *gentle folk*—and when I saw a man riding the road, near our house, with a wig on, it would so alarm my fears . . . that, I dare say, I would run off, as for my life." [*] Symbols and practical necessities were combined in the conventions of dress. A periwig and lace-ruffled cuffs proclaimed freedom from manual work in field or workshop; the plain attire of the common planter, by contrast, admitted subjection to the necessities of such labor. Jarratt recalled that his own plowman's "whole dress and apparel consisted in a pair of coarse breeches, one or two oznaburgs shirts, a pair of

[*] Jarratt's autobiography will be quoted extensively in the following chapters as a unique firsthand description of what it was like to grow up as a yeoman's son. The account has two evident, partly contradictory, biases. On the one hand the old man idealized traditional forms of deference and regretted that they had lost legitimacy during the Revolution; on the other hand he rejected and condemned the religion and morality of the pre-Revolutionary order, viewing it from the standpoint of a convert to evangelicalism. The facts of Jarratt's descriptions that can be checked prove accurate.

shoes and stockings [as a boy he had gone barefoot in summer], an old felt hat, [and] a bear skin *coat*." Such attire qualified the wearers for "the Epithet of Buckskins, alluding to their Leather Breeches, and the Jackets of some of the Common People; which is all over Virginia, as great a Reproach as in England, to call a Man Oaf, or Clown, or Lubberkin."[1]

The gentry did not always wear the full formal regalia expected of their English counterparts, whose style they followed in so many things. William Hugh Grove observed in 1732 that "in Summertime even the gentry goe Many in White Holland [linen] Wast Coat & drawers and a thin Cap on their heads and Thread stockings. The Ladyes Strait laced in thin Silk or Linnen." He noted, however, that in winter they dressed "mostly as in England and affected London Dress and wayes." Edward Kimber, visiting from England some ten years later, evidently in the summer, also observed that "except some of the very elevated Sort, few Persons wear Perukes, so that you would imagine they were all sick, or going to bed: Common People wear Woollen and Yarn Caps; but the better ones wear white Holland or cotton. Thus they travel fifty Miles from Home." Although Kimber noted that the Virginia fashion was "cooler," he still considered the relaxation of formality "very ridiculous." Conscious adaptation to climate was opening a cultural rift between the colony and its parent society.[2]

Slaves "had Coarse Shirts and . . . Drawers given [to] them"—two pairs per annum. The material was osnaburg, a coarse canvas cloth, of which the young Jarratt's clothing had also been made. As in the case of the common planter's son, shoes were only given as winter wear.[3]

Travelers were struck by the varied diet that was the boast of Virginians. In season, the abundance of meat, game, fish, and greens supplemented the staples of hominy, mush, pone, and hoe-cake, all made from Indian corn. "The Gentry at Their Tables," reported Grove, "have commonly 5 dishes or plates, of which Pigg meat and greens is generally one, and Tame fowl another. Beef, Mutton, Veal and Lamb make another. Pudding, often in the mid[dle], makes the 5th. Venison, Wild fowl, or fish a 4th. Smal[l] beer made of molasses, with Madera Wine [and] English Beer [is] their Liquor. . . . They have good Cyder but will not keep it, but drink [it] by pailfulls never Workt." This appears to be a description of the table for dinner—usually taken between two and three in the afternoon—but another traveler asserted that "the same, with some small Addition" might appear at supper (taken at about eight-thirty in the evening), followed by "a good hearty Cup to precede a Bed of Down." In the same way, "their Breakfast Tables [8:30–9:30 A.M.] have generally the cold Remains of the former Day, hash'd or fricasseed; Coffee, Tea, Chocolate, Venison-Pasty, Punch, and Beer, or Cyder, upon one Board." Travelers at mid-century tended to exaggerate, depicting an idealized land of plenty, but the gentry who kept these tables undoubtedly had the means to supply themselves copiously with field produce as well as with the fish and game that slaves were sent out to procure. The privileged foods of the wealthy, and also an easy familiarity with the common fare, can be seen in Robert Beverley's observation that "the Bread in Gentlemen's Houses, is generally made of Wheat, but some rather choose the Pone, which is the Bread made of *Indian Meal.*"[4]

Some of the natural abundance of woodland and rivers must have enhanced the diet of the less well placed, but the basic fare for them was Indian corn—a staple particularly vulnerable to periodic drought. "Only a Peck of Corn [2 gallons] & a Pint of Salt a Week" (with a pound of meat for some) was the official ration of the slaves at Nomini Hall, Robert Carter's great house. Slaves added to such fare what potatoes, greens, fruit, and chickens they could raise at their quarters, plus those supplies they could extract from granaries and storehouses. It appears that the timing of the slaves' meals might have been similar to that of the masters. Certainly the Honorable Robert Carter had at Nomini Hall "a large good Bell of upwards of 60 Lb. which may be heard some miles, & . . . is always rung at meal Times" to regulate breaks for eating. The disapproving account of a traveler, however, suggests that the slaves' day had a distinctive rhythm. For all the melodramatic overstatement, an essential contrast with the masters' basic routine is drawn, and the consistency of unremitting toil with monotonous diet is revealed:

> He [the slave] is called up in the morning at day break, and is seldom allowed time enough to swallow three mouthfuls of hominy, or hoe-cake, but is driven out immediately to the field to hard labour; at which he continues, without intermission, until noon; and it is observed as a singular circumstance, that they always carry out a piece of fire with them, and kindle one just by their work, let the weather be ever so hot and sultry. About noon is the time he eats his dinner, and he is seldom allowed an hour for that purpose. His meal consists of

hommi:ny and salt, and, if his master be a man of humanity, he has a little fat, skimmed milk, rusty bacon, or salt herring to relish his homminy, or hoe-cake . . . twice a week. . . . They then return to severe labour, which continues in the field until dusk. . . . It is late at night [if there is work to be done in the tobacco houses] before he returns to his second scanty meal.[5]

The hard-handed common planter's daily fare was regulated by necessity, not by a calculated and imposed parsimony. Devereux Jarratt described graphically the circumstances of his yeoman-artisan parents, revealing how diet was consciously associated with the ordered ranking of society.

They always had plenty of plain food . . . wholesome and good, suitable to their humble station. . . . Our food was altogether the produce of the farm or plantation, except a little sugar, which was rarely used. . . . We made no use of tea or coffee for breakfast, or at any other time; nor did I know a single family that made any use of them. Meat, bread and milk was the ordinary food of all my acquaintance. I suppose the *richer sort* might make use of *those* and other luxuries, but to such people I had no access.[6]

Analysis of thousands of inventories in which all the contents of householders' dwellings were carefully listed when they died reveals that tea and the apparatus for the ceremonial drinking of it were indeed found only at the topmost levels of society. At the very bottom an increasing number of tobacco growers in the eighteenth century were managing to provide for variations in the extremely monotonous diet of boiled mush to which simple folk had formerly been limited. Roasting spits and frying pans had by 1740 become more usual in humble stocks of equipment alongside the ubiquitous iron pots.[7]

BODY AND CLIMATE

Diet was not only interwoven with social status, but it was also part of every individual's relationship to the cosmos. No aspect of eighteenth-century life requires more imaginative effort if we are to grasp its implications; no effort

brings us more clearly to a view of the distinctive landscape of this past world
as its inhabitants experienced it. Although ideas were changing, people of
European culture lived in the mid-eighteenth century with a stock of basic
concepts derived from a cosmology that posited a direct nexus between the
microcosm of the human body and the macrocosm of the physical universe
that contained it. The interpenetration of these systems was formulated the-
oretically in the notion that the functioning of the body and its temperament
were governed by four humors, each corresponding to one of the elements
that composed the cosmos. There was blood, corresponding to air and tending toward heat and moisture; phlegm, corresponding to water and tending
toward wet and cold; yellow or green bile (choler), corresponding to fire and
tending toward heat and dryness; and black bile (whence the word "melancholy"), corresponding to earth and tending toward cold and dryness. The
health of the body depended upon the maintenance of balance in these humors. An excess of blood would make a body feverish and a temperament too
sanguine; while too much phlegm could lead to coldness and dullness; and so
on with bilious and melancholic disorders. As outlined here this mode of
thought seems bookish and abstract, but for persons in the eighteenth century, constant reading of climate and weather in these terms, constant attention to proper diet as this system defined it, and constant application of the
violent remedies it prescribed, made it an inescapable part of daily existence
and a pervasive conditioner of life experience.[8]

Virginia's climate—indeed its essential character—was continually interpreted with reference to humors. "The Natural Temperature of the In-
ha[bit]ed part of the Country, is hot and moist," declared Robert Beverley,
and he went on to attribute "this Moisture . . . [to] the abundance of low
Grounds, Marshes, Creeks, and Rivers, which are every where among the
lower Settlements." He protested, however, the healthiness of this temper-
ate climate for those who would live temperately within it. Hugh Jones followed him closely but was less certain that the effects of the climate could be
averted. "At the sudden changes of the weather, from heat to cold, people are
apt to take cold . . . which with abundance of damps and mists from the
water, and by eating too plentifully of some delicious fruits, makes the people
subject to feavers and agues, which is the country distemper, a severe fit of
which (called a seasoning) most expect, some time after their arrival in that
climate." Robert Beverley's further exploration of the consequences of this

situation reveals the intimate relationship assumed to exist between the human body system and the environment: "When these Damps, Colds, and Disorders, affect the Body more gently, and do not seize People violently at first; then . . . these small Disorders are suffer'd to go on, until . . . the Body is overrun with obstinate scorbutick Humours. And this in a more fierce, and virulent Degree, I take to be the Yaws."[9]

Such views were not confined to the educated elite. The young Devereux Jarratt, when he moved from his plowman's work on an inland plantation, naturally attributed the sudden deterioration in his health not to mosquitoes and malaria microorganisms but to the qualities of the new location where he now lived, "on the banks of James River, and between two bold creeks . . . which ran into the river above and below the house." He found that he "was violently attacked with a quotidian ague, which, in a little while, changed to a tertian, and, at last, terminated in a *quartan*, which followed [him] eight or nine months."[10]

The same diary that gave us day-by-day glimpses of the seasonal tasks in the fields gives a close-up view of continual attempts to regulate the body in accordance with humoral theory. As physical causes were assumed to govern health, so the physical manifestations of the body—its eliminations and effluxions— were observed with an inevitable fascination; so also harsh physical attacks were made upon the disordered system to restore its balance. The violence of these assaults must have made humoral medicine a dramatic part of the consciousness of every person in this age. Like other heads of households, Colonel Landon Carter had to administer physic. Unlike most, he had a spirit of scientific inquiry and kept careful records of symptoms and doses. That his view of the nature of the processes at work, though reinforced by very extensive reading in medical texts, was not confined to himself is suggested by his irritation with his slave assistant, Nassau—"the best bleeder" in the county— who so far identified with the work as to claim that "on every recovery it is his doings." Slaves, as well as common planter neighbors, not only sought treatment in accordance with humoral theory but adhered to varying prescriptions in its terms. Even the numerous folk remedies that were available as alternatives did not necessarily contradict the theory of humors.[11]

The assumed relationship of climate, diet, and the balance of humors in the study of the body's emissions is clearly seen in the following case record:

[July 1766] 24. . . . My daughter Judy the 17th of this month went to the great race, when it seems it was a most improper time being her Lunar period; From whence nothing could stop her going to a dance at her uncle Beale's; and there in a very hot night she danced. . . . The next day she came home very sick . . . no vomit would be taken for particular reasons which at last I would, know . . . no feaver as I was informed. Yesterday she came down stairs very hungry. . . . I then said she must take a vomit. . . . [T]his day of her own accord she got one from Tom [a house slave] and took it being 3 spoonfulls Ipecacuana wine . . . and brought off much dark green bile and other. I was told she was easy. I ordered some thin broth to ease the passage of some of the bile downward, but it seems she drank some toast and beer. I do suppose cold as well as windy. . . . She vomited both yellow and green bile, and it seems took a clyster [medication by the rectum] for no motion had happened downwards; her sickness returned again as the Clyster brought off nothing, and I do suppose I shall have her on my hands, by her obstinacy and Secrecy. She does bear ungovernable the whole summer through, eating extravagantly and late at night of cucumbers and all sorts of bilious trash.[12]

The human body, perceived as a system of balanced humors, had a central place in the whole world view. The conception extended upward into modes of understanding temperament and behavior, as in the case of Landon Carter finding he was compelled by his family "to accommodate their humours." At a higher level still this medical model was transferred to the workings of society—the body politic. The well-known preoccupation with balance as essential to preserving virtue in the community certainly owed as much to physiological theory as to Newtonian mechanics—indeed the sense of a sharp distinction between the organic and the inanimate belongs to the twentieth century, not to the eighteenth. The words "constitution" and "corruption" had a strong medical-theological reference long before they came to be secular-political in connotation. The body politic was really thought to be as subject to aging, infirmity, and decay as was the human body; the preoccupation with "recurrence to fundamental principles" had reference to physicians' procedures in restoring balance to a disturbed system.[13]

FIGURE 8.
Memento mori: The body corruptible

Perceptions of the human body extended outward also from the social world to the order of nature. They were applied automatically to animal creation, so that Landon Carter can be discovered bleeding and dosing a sick cow "upon a full perswasion that this disorder in the Cattle was somehow occasioned by a thick visid blood perhaps made acrid by an ill temperated bile." Beyond such obvious application, however, lay the pervasive assumption that the cosmos was a vast body system. "There is a phylosophy," noted our diarist, "that with me accounts for the rain after burning this marsh. It [the marsh] is of 2,000 or 3,000 acres very rank in its captail sedge and of course must through [throw] up abundance of smoke which . . . by inveloping the common rising moisture of earth must at last condense and descend in rain." The movement of the aqueous element, or cosmic humor, was in turn related to the celestial bodies. Thus on January 7, 1770, the colonel declared: "I believe we are still under the watery effects of the late Comet." The passage that follows, although mutilated in the manuscript, clearly conveys Carter's wish that the great Newton might have turned his mind to the puzzling relationship between "excessive seasons of . . . moisture" and "an emission of a fiery nature."[14]

The flux in the great system naturally influenced the balance of humors in the microcosm. Thus in the midst of a bout of sickness in the family that was ascribed to an excess of bile, the colonel observed that "the clouds that have hung as it were in the Horizon from the West to the North for·3 days, now discover their sharpness by a steady . . . gale." He expressed the hope that it would be "a great service" to his household "if it releives us by clearing off the Epidemic disorder[s] of a most bilious nature." Such had been "the Putred biliousness of the season" that half his work force was disabled.[15]

It is important that we be reminded of the pervasive sense of unity between the environment and the intimate self that humoral medicine expressed, for this theory supplied essential metaphors for the understanding of religion as well as society and politics. Inescapable dependence on "Almighty permission" for the making of crops helped sustain what we would call a religious— though not necessarily a pietist—world view. Similar reinforcement came from awareness of the physical frailty of fallen human nature, especially when that awareness was constantly intensified by close study of the loathsome marks of the body's corruptibility. As long as this mode of consciousness remained strong, the most intimate experiences carried implicit theological references: the corruptibility of the flesh was a consequence of the Fall; and the meaning of infirmity in this life was partly given by knowledge of the coming resurrection, when the body would be "incorruptible." One's own body was an ever-present metaphor of Christian cosmology and eschatology.[16]

TRAVELING THROUGH THE LANDSCAPE

How would Virginians of different ranks have experienced their surroundings as they went through them, heading out from home along the ways that connected places?

The slave would most likely slip away through the trees. He might go to set traps in the woods. Whether conducted on his own or on his master's behalf, this was a free-ranging activity. Frequently he would be going visiting. Although the law forbade him to be off the plantation without carrying a letter of permission from his master, enforcement was infrequent and erratic. Still, at any time he could be called upon to show his "pass." The landscape through which his way took him was marked by the signs that the masters possessed it according to the same system that classified the slave himself as property: boundary trees, fenced fields, tobacco houses, carriage roads. There was, however, another set of marks, most visible to the slave—signs of the occupancy of his own people—places with associations arising from the opportunities the slaves seized within a system that denied them the right to possess. Perhaps the way took him past his own garden lot or those of others, where he and his fellows were allowed to supplement their meager rations, easing the master's provision expenses.

Slaves worked long hours—Sundays, Christmas, Easter, and Whitsun being the only daylight time allocated to their own use—yet they were in the habit of taking night hours for their special forms of association. Their landscapes were crisscrossed by the trails that led to scenes of communal activities. The paths to these assemblies took participants through a realm of nature closely linked to that of human life—perhaps animated by spirits, certainly manipulable to human ends by means of ritual formulas. The paths must also have passed visible landmarks formed by the forceful, albeit clandestine, assertion of officially suppressed personalities. Here would stand a cornhouse, perhaps, that was from time to time illicitly opened, by the loosening of boards in the gable end, to supplement the rations of hungry families. Those who could provide in this way stood tall in the quarters, making the scenes of their exploits the more notable. Such providers might trade their loot for the much-sought-after liquor that was so valuable for celebrations. Beyond the storehouses and granaries, but well marked in the memory, were the places deep in the woods where the slaves might slaughter and barbecue the semi-wild hogs that bore on their ears and rumps the marks of a master's claim to possession. The scattering of settlement through a wooded countryside that enabled the Anglo-Virginian masters to space their property boundaries widely also allowed the covert activities of the blacks to maintain an alternative territorial system. The endless repertoire of trickster tales, adapted from a common matrix of African folklore, celebrated and gave fuller meaning to landmarks that derived from slave opportunism.[17]

Where a sense of security or the need to head for a river crossing led the slave to follow the road, he would have to be ready to make an exaggerated show of submissiveness to any white person he encountered. He probably knew more about aspects of some of these persons' households than they knew themselves. Meetings with other slaves would take a varied course. We do not know how status systems within the black community governed social exchange. Certainly if either party were of African birth, much would depend on the degree of fluency he or she had attained in the "Plantation-Creole" speech that was the language of the blacks.[18]

The common planter or his son, riding out, would see the landscape differently—from a vantage point some three feet higher, for a start. Leaving his own fields behind he would follow the sandy road along the higher ground through mixed woodland and savanna. Stones were so few in the Tidewater region that a poorer man's horse was certain to be without shoes. Where the road turned down toward a creek or river crossing, enclosed fields would again appear. The condition of these fields was a familiar statement of a neighbor's prospects; of his character and standing; of the size of his labor force; and of his ability to keep his workers to their tasks. Coming to a sudden loop in the road, circling a crop of tall tobacco or corn plants, he would be reminded of a contest of petitions and neighbors' counterpetitions before the county court a year or so back, all to determine whether the highway might be turned so that the owner of the land could clear and plant a single field and not have it

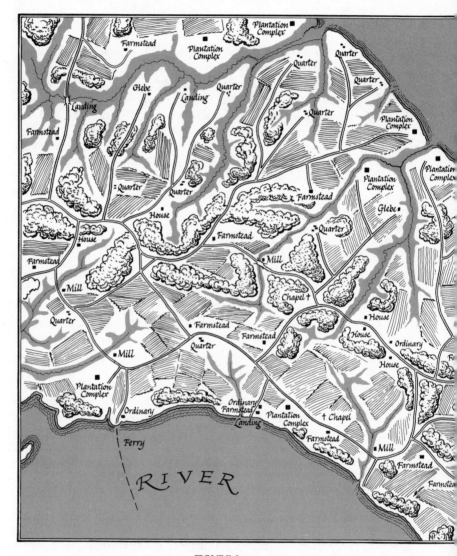

FIGURE 9.
*A Tidewater landscape shaped by use: fields, woodlands,
dwellings, mills, roads, and community centers*

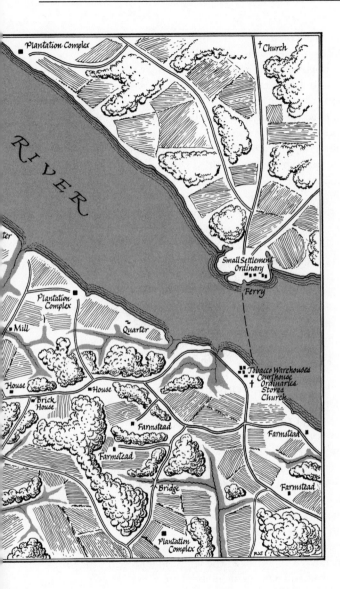

Plantation Complex

† Church

RIVER

ter

Plantation
Complex

Mill

Quarter

Small Settlement
Ordinary
Ferry

House

House

Brick
House

Tobacco Warehouses
Courthouse
Ordinaries
Stores
Church

Farmstead

Farmstead

Farmstead

Farmstead

Bridge

Farmstead

Plantation
Complex

RJS

bisected by the road. On encounter with a gentleman, riding out in his chaise or sulky, there would be a deferential raising of the hat, met by an answering salutation. If our horseman was a yeoman of substance he would see his worthiness reflected in the respect with which the gentleman returned his greeting. When it came to election time—or perhaps a jury-tried civil suit— the gentleman might need his neighbor's goodwill for himself, for his cousin, or for one of his friends. Both parties would remember the exchange of civilities—or lack of them. The situation of the common planter was complex: at home he was master of his own domain, entitled to a measure of true Virginia pride in his independence, yet even if he held broad acres and half a dozen slaves, he was probably in debt to a wealthy neighbor—or might in the event of a bad year need to seek the support of a loan or a surety bond. He could not lightly dispense with the goodwill and esteem of the gentry.[19]

The gentleman, when he rode out leaving his great house, would receive in the obligatory marks of deep respect and submission from those who worked in his fields a reinforcement of his habitual sense of exalted rank. He would know himself to be a man with few equals—above other men. Even if he thought he detected something lacking in some of the obeisances of certain of his inferiors, the resentment he would feel served to remind him afresh of his true entitlements. Leaving his own domains, he would see the same fields as the other passers on the road, but he might consciously or unconsciously direct his judgment on the state of them to considerations of whether he would extend credit to the yeoman whose prospects were there displayed, or call in an existing loan, or lend his influence to have a debt suit in process delayed. At the sudden loop in the road he might remember not only the "turning" dispute but the influences that had resolved it. Likewise, a mile farther on at the "branch," or "run," where the road now ran across a broad dam wall, he knew just why the court had agreed to settle on this particular owner the license to construct a water mill here. Through his own kinfolk connections he had had a hand in the matter himself. Humble planters on the road showed in their manner of greeting the respect they knew was owed to both his own person and to his lineage.

What if the slave, the planter, or the gentleman had brought his wife along? How might each have experienced the landscape through which their way took them? Slave women knew the fields as laborers on the same terms as did the men. On this account they probably had considerable freedom of movement. Many had husbands on different plantations. For the wives and daughters of common planters—except perhaps the very poorest, who must raise crops—the home was the center of work, while the fields, though familiar, were the terrain of men and slaves. Journeys would be undertaken less frequently—and for a more limited range of purposes—church attendance, a marriage, a christening feast, or a housewarming party. Women—even widows who controlled property—did not, it seems, go into stores to make their own purchases. Those were places where men gathered, drank, swore, and even boxed or wrestled among themselves. For the ladies of genteel families, riding out for social calls or to visit the sick was not unusual. They would be attended by servants, with gentlemen of the household escorting, if possible. The need these ladies felt to protect themselves from the sun, dust, and other contaminations of the public highway was expressed by the manner in which "when they ride out they tye a white handkerchief over their Head and face." Philip Fithian, the tutor from New Jersey who came to Robert Carter's Nomini Hall in 1773, was at first "distress'd whenever [he] saw a Lady, for [he] thought She had the Tooth-Ach!"[20]

The landscape of eighteenth-century Virginians was complex and experiences of it diverse, contingent on rank and condition. Upon the fields depended the welfare of all. Houses stood among the untidy scatter of these fields, yet the occupants were not isolated by drudgery and distance. Virginians of every degree were drawn along the roads toward great places that were marked by potent forms of action.

4

CHURCH AND HOME
Celebrations of Life's Meanings

Churches were the important centers for community assembly, dispersed at the most frequent intervals in the countryside. The parishes of the established religion were sometimes, in the western part of the colony, coterminous with counties, but usually they were considerably smaller. In both cases the parish would have a number of houses of worship—churches and "chapels of ease." Each person, except those who formally dissented (and they were very few in the settled parts before mid-century), was deemed a member of "the Church of England as by law established." All were required to attend divine service at least once in four weeks, under penalty of a fine of five shillings or fifty pounds of tobacco, for failure to comply. It was important, therefore, that no part of the parish be too far from one or another of its churches. Central location and accessibility by road were the prime considerations for the siting of these edifices. Thus a church often stood alone in a cleared area near some crossroads at the center of its parish precinct.

The churches were generally plain structures. In the early eighteenth century they were oblong in form. Rarely did they have steeples or belfries. (In the absence of town or even village settlement too few of the parishioners would have lived within the sound of the bells.) Formerly churches had been constructed of wood, but by 1720—as a further indication of the social consolidation that the great houses expressed—they were built of brick. The courses were sometimes elaborately contrived in such a way that blue-glazed "headers" alternated with light red "stretchers" in "Flemish bond" to form a

FIGURE 10.
Churches stood alone at convenient crossroads

checkerboard effect. Doors were handsomely picked out by the use of softer bricks rubbed into the pleasing forms of moldings that showed a contrasting deep, rich color. The tall windows were elegantly arched and designed to let light freely into these temples of rational religion.

In the 1730s a new church design was introduced. Its rapid spread is a clear sign that those who dominated decision making at the parish level thought it appropriate. The first of these new-fashioned edifices, Christ Church in Lancaster County, has somehow survived the triumph of the sectaries and escaped the ravages of three wars that have laid waste parts of Virginia. With nearly all of its woodwork and most of its original glass intact, it stands in its wall-enclosed green among the trees on the northern shore of the Rappahannock River, lovingly restored as a silent reminder of the religious observances and the social exchanges that it was built to contain.

As the churchgoers approached, they came upon the familiar bulk of this

Greek-cross church, which presented from each side the face of one of its four
tall gabled ends, carrying high the steep-pitched shingle roof. Fine rubbed
brickwork dignified the plain lines of the great doors and windows. The common planters rode up, mounted astride; the gentry and their families came in
coaches and six, with older sons and household retinue possibly riding escort.
Before the start of the service the surroundings of the church "look'd like the
Out-Skirts of a Country Horse Fair." The advance gathering was important.
Philip Fithian, whose Presbyterian upbringing in New Jersey filled him with
Sabbatarian disapproval, noted that there were

> three grand divisions of time at the Church on Sundays, Viz. before
> Service giving & receiving letters of business, reading Advertisements,
> consulting about the price of Tobacco, Grain &c. & settling either the
> lineage, Age, or qualities of favourite Horses. 2. In the Church at
> Service, prayrs read over in haste, a Sermon seldom under & never
> over twenty minutes, but always made up of sound morality, or deep
> studied Metaphysicks. 3. After Service is over three quarters of an
> hour spent in strolling round the Church among the Crowd, . . .
> [when one might be] invited by several different Gentlemen home with
> them to dinner.

The combination of ordered service and animated conversation produced
at the church a blend of formality and informality—of convivial engagement and structured relationship—that recurs in accounts of Virginia social
gatherings.[1]

Those who were completely at ease on these community Sunday mornings,
when the affairs of the world pressed in around the setting for divine service,
have not left records of their untroubled feelings. Yet a note to Sir Peyton
Skipwith from one of his agents shows how freely the very secular could be
associated with the religious. Without revealing any sense of incongruity, the
writer informed the baronet that a blood stallion of his had been taken to
church so that the people might look the proud creature over with a view to
having him cover their mares. Similarly, young Ben Carter, anxious to have
Fithian take him to New Jersey, begged the tutor "to acquaint him with the
manners of the People in regard to Religion, and he swears he can suit himself to any serious, or formal visage." It is evident that Virginians, whatever
their rank, generally did not affect postures of grave piety and that on Sunday

at church they took for granted the close proximity of the profane to the sacred.[2]

Concerns of the world, brought to the church door as a matter of course, were not so readily abandoned in order to cross its threshold into the more hallowed time and space set apart for worship. "It is not the Custom for Gentlemen to go into Church til Service is beginning, when they enter in a Body." Pride of rank accompanied the gentry even as they took their places within, so that we may picture them tramping booted to their pews at the front. Their exit was made "in the same manner"; women and humbler men waited to leave until the gentlemen had gone.[3]

Entering Christ Church, Lancaster County (and other churches following its design), one is suddenly in a lofty, light-filled, enclosed space. The high-vaulted interior would certainly be the largest "room" or hall that most parishioners ever entered. The intended effect was not—as with the form of Gothic churches—to channel the devotions of the faithful through the clergy and the sanctuary to the heavens, but rather, in the Protestant spirit, to make the community-congregation worshipfully present to itself.

The architectural plan maximized the visibility to the assembled community of a numerous emulative gentry. In the center the four arms of the Greek cross united to form a large focal space. Great oak-walled pews reserved for magistrates and leading families stood at the front of each arm of the church, delimiting the central area. High within the space thus defined stood the pulpit under its grand, ornately canopied sounding board, or "tester." The pulpit was the obvious point of attention in the design, symbolizing, again in the Protestant spirit, the central importance of the explication of the Word of God. Only a clergyman who had been examined, ordained, and licensed by a bishop, successor to the Apostles, could mount the elevated rostrum to unfold the divine mysteries. In tiered hierarchy beneath the pulpit were the desk from which the scriptural lessons were read, and the clerk's desk from which the parson's lay assistant "lined out" the psalms for communal intonation. Behind pulpit and desks, and hence symbolically and dramaturgically in the lowest position, was the gallery that a small number of slaves would enter by a steep narrow stairway just inside the south door.

On the far side of the central space stood the altar. Above it on the end wall, the words of the Ten Commandments and the Apostles' Creed shone out in gold lettering from black tablets, keeping the people mindful of the

FIGURE 11.
The pulpit dominated the great enclosed space of the church

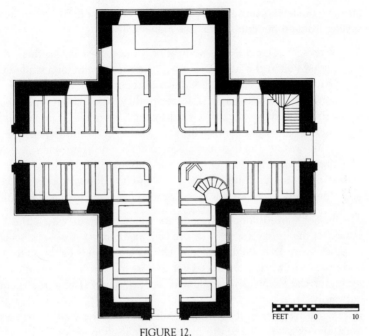

FIGURE 12.
Christ Church: The seating plan

cosmic framework within which their community was contained and of the moral absolutes to which it was subject.

The services conducted in such churches were in harmony with their settings. The New Jersey tutor's brusque deprecation of the form of the devotions should not be the final word. Worship consisted almost entirely of reading the services from the Book of Common Prayer, whose use was sanctioned by law. The mode was thus liturgical and alien to Presbyterian sensibilities. We of the antiformalistic twentieth century are likewise ill attuned to appreciate the meanings that could be conveyed through the weekly repetition of set words, with appointed variations marking the seasons of the year and the rotations of the ecclesiastical calendar. The appeal these rituals had is best revealed to us in the pronouncements of a late seventeenth-century English bishop who defended the liturgy against the criticism to which it was already subject from proponents of creative individualism:

> Whatsoever good things we hear only once, or now and then, though perhaps upon the hearing of them, they may swim for a while in our brains, yet they seldom sink down into our hearts, so as to move and sway the affections, as it is necessary they should do in order to our being edified by them; whereas by a set form of public devotions rightly composed, we are continually put in mind of all things necessary for us to know or do, so that it is always done by the same words and expressions, which, by their constant use, will imprint the things themselves so firmly in our minds, that . . . they will still occur upon all occasions, which cannot but be very much for our Christian edification.

The bishop's words not only indicate the manner in which the familiar phrases of the liturgy might be savored but also convey powerful resonances of a traditional ordered community, in which persons were expected to aspire to become inwardly what the social constraints of their lives (including the intoning of the formulas of the prayer book responses) required them to be outwardly.[4]

The seating plans of the Virginia churches—accentuated by the manner of entry and exit—exhibited the community to itself in ranked order. The form and tone of the liturgy reinforced the demonstration inherent in the physical setting. The services of the Book of Common Prayer had been given their vernacular shape in the sixteenth century and expressed strongly an ethos of English Christian gentility. The appointed set of words, read in the midst of a community ranged in order of precedence, continuously evoked postures of deference and submission. Liturgy and church plan thus readily combined to offer a powerful representation of a structured, hierarchical community. The ceremonial of the county court—as will be seen—asserted similar, complementary values and relationships. Church and courthouse, each in its proper way, exhibited symbols and formulas expressing the orientation of the local community to the larger social world.[5]

The words and forms of action at church clearly asserted the hierarchical nature of things, confirming definitions of authority within the rural community itself. The appeal of these proceedings for the gentry can readily be imagined. With a greater effort of the imagination it can be recognized that the services also offered satisfactions to humbler persons to the extent that they had internalized the view of the world that the liturgy and seating plan represented. Such persons might take pleasure in admiring the magnificence of the great and in deferentially receiving attentions bestowed on them from above. "Condescension" was, in the eighteenth century, a praiseworthy quality for persons of rank.

The institutional organization of the church also served to reinforce claims to authority from above and its acceptance from below. Each parish was ruled by a vestry of twelve gentlemen presided over by the minister. These worthies (who filled their own vacancies by co-option) regulated church affairs, annually imposing whatever taxes they considered necessary to pay the parson's salary, to meet incidental costs, and to repair, extend, or build de novo great and expensively furnished churches. The levies might occasion murmurings from parishioners, but the vestries also exercised patronage over lesser men, since the relief of the poor was entrusted to them. They could choose to ease—or not to ease—a person's declining years. It lay with them to decide whether to lighten the burden assumed by poor but self-sufficient householders who had to undertake the care of an aged or infirm relative.[6]

RELIGION AND LIFE EXPERIENCES

Christian formulas were scattered throughout the daily routines of Anglo-Virginians. Before dinner it was usual "to 'say Grace' as they call it; which is always express'd by the People in the following words, 'God bless us in what we are to receive'—& after Dinner, 'God make us thankful for his mercies.'" The best account we have of a child's growing up in a humble household before mid-century stresses the worthiness of the parents without suggesting unusual piety, yet it was recalled that "they taught . . . short prayers" and made their children "very perfect in repeating the *Church Catechism*." Any child— perhaps a majority of white boys—who had instruction in reading, had the Bible for his reader. Landon Carter's dependence for a good crop upon the contingencies of nature was reflected in a resigned, fatalistic supplication to God. The world of the Old Testament was one that eighteenth-century Virginians could readily identify with. In a famous passage, quoted above, Wil-

FIGURE 13.
*Hierarchy in buildings: great house, church, courthouse,
planter's house, and slave cabin*

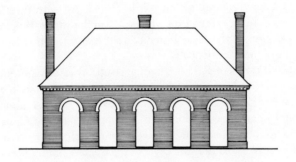

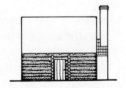

liam Byrd compared himself to "one of the Patriarchs" with their "flocks . . . Herds . . . Bond-men and Bond-women." Similarly, the simple field-and-orchard metaphors of the New Testament parables referred to a recognizable world of immediate experience.[7]

Although all ranks of Anglo-Virginians subconsciously assumed a correspondence between Judaeo-Christian cosmology and the familiar rounds of daily life, they did not find it necessary to exhibit the assumption in pious routine. Family prayers were unusual in Chesapeake society. Custom and the law required attendance once in four weeks at church, but neither were strict concerning regularity, so that the cycle of the week—an important rhythm of life in Virginia—was marked more certainly by a seventh day of rest and conviviality than by prayerful devotions. "Generally . . . by five o'clock on Saturday every Face (especially the Negroes) looks festive and cheerful—All the lower class of People, & the Servants, & the Slaves, consider [Sunday] . . . as a Day of Pleasure & amusement, and spend it in such Diversions as they severally choose."[8]

Many slaves came or were sent to the religious observances of their masters. Yet the specific religious beliefs that prevailed at the quarters are difficult to ascertain. The fixed formalities of Anglican liturgical worship and the didacticism of much of the preaching could not readily be assimilated to African modes of proclaiming the meaning of life.[9]

RITES OF PASSAGE

The Reverend Mr. Hugh Jones gives a very revealing account of how the Christian religion was woven into the great events of the lives of Anglo-Virginians. As an Anglican of moderate temperament, Jones—unlike dissenting commentators—understood and accepted the customary forms and usages that prevailed in the Old Dominion. He reserved his occasional mild strictures for some of the colonial departures from English practice. Certainly he found the total absence of a bishop to be a serious truncation of the ritual forms of the Church. Since parishioners lacked means for "confirmation" as communicants, many were reluctant to present themselves for the sacrament, at least until the approach of death established a greater sense of urgency. The churches themselves could not be considered consecrated, and Jones proposed a substitute ceremony whereby there might be "some solemn dedication prescribed for setting . . . [churches] apart for sacred uses; which would," he hoped, "make people behave themselves with greater reverence than they usually do, and have a greater value for the house of God and holy things." [10]

Hugh Jones noted also, significantly, that Virginians insisted on having certain rituals performed in their homes rather than in churches, as English usage would have required:

> It is customary to bury in gardens or orchards, where whole families lye interred together, in a spot generally handsomly enclosed, planted with evergreens, and the graves kept decently. Hence . . . arises the occasion of preaching funeral sermons in houses, where at funerals are assembled a great congregation of neighbours and friends; and if you insist upon having the sermon and ceremony at church, they'll say they will be without it, unless performed *after their usual custom.* In houses also there is occasion, from humour, custom sometimes, from necessity most frequently, to baptize children and *church* women. . . . In houses also they most commonly marry, without regard to the time of day or season of the year. [11]

The definition of sacred space—its location at the church—had become confused, reaching almost the point of caricature with the removal of the churching of women to the home! It has been common to attribute these developments to the scattered settlement pattern and the distances arising from it, despite the notorious propensity of Virginians of all races and ranks to travel far to points of assembly when they were inclined to do so. As Jones noted, custom rather than expediency was already being argued in defense of the preference for services at the dwelling place. Custom, even when it arises originally from necessity, shapes experience. For colony-born Anglo-Virginians, rites of passage within the home were simply the taken-for-granted shape of things. Sacred significance attached to these rites, being no longer confined within the church, was transferred to the home and was there associated with the gathering of neighbors to share in the event. Christian forms were not set aside. The ceremonies of the Church were carried out as far as possible in the prescribed manner. (The law required marriage in all cases to be solemnized by a minister of the Established Church; custom dictated that "most of the middling people" would have a funeral sermon, though it cost them a very substantial forty-shilling fee.)

The transference of rites of passage from church to home meant, however, that specifically Christian ceremonies had come to be closely surrounded, and even overshadowed, by social rituals and forms of celebration that persons in the Anglo-Virginian tradition would have defined (if forced to distinguish) as secular rather than religious. Yet these social enactments were important and contributed powerfully to the aura of the house.

Afro-Virginians cannot have been caught in the subtle tensions between church-centered, "sacred" celebrations and home-centered, "profane" forms. For them the English Christian distinctions between the "religious" and the "secular" would probably have had little meaning. Although we can discover almost nothing of the symbols that the slaves used to represent ultimate value and meaning, we know that their primary modes of expression were song and dance, with exemplary tales perhaps playing a secondary role. A basic African cultural "grammar" appears to have transcended the great diversities of language and specific customs that confronted the captive migrants as they began to coalesce into a distinct society upon the North American seaboard. This is a case where the medium was indeed the essence of the message. Clearly, during the formative decades of the eighteenth century the slaves were able to keep alive distinctive African expressive styles and sensibilities. (In no other way could these features have survived strongly enough to be recorded by nineteenth- and twentieth-century folklorists and narrative collectors.) Spontaneous performances of song were the rule, invariably accompanied by rhythmic body movement and usually in the form of a litany between leaders and their communal choruses.[12]

HOUSE, HOST, AND HOSPITALITY

Residences were highly significant places in the social landscape. The ideal of the home as a center of private domesticity was not familiar to Anglo-Virginians in the mid-eighteenth century. They lived or aspired to live in the constant presence of servants and guests. Their houses were the sacrosanct settings for hospitality and for the open celebration of the major events of life and death. Jones had lamented the absence of forms for the "solemn dedication" of churches; he could have gone on to note that an appropriate ritual did exist for homes. Early in his stay in Virginia Fithian became aware that "whenever any *person* or *Family* move into a House, or repair a house they have been living in before, they make a *Ball* & give a supper . . . in compliance with Custom, to invite . . . Neighbours, and dance, and be merry." Indeed, most of the dominant values of the culture were fused together in the display of hospitality, which was one of the supreme obligations that society laid upon heads of households. In 1705 Robert Beverley had written:

> The Inhabitants are very Courteous to Travellers. . . . A Stranger has no more to do, but to inquire upon the Road, where any Gentleman or good House-keeper Lives, and there he may depend upon being received with Hospitality. This good Nature is so general . . . that the Gentry when they go abroad, order their Principal Servant to entertain all Visitors. . . . And the poor Planters, who have but one Bed, will very often sit up, or lie upon a Form or Couch all Night, to make room for a weary Traveller. . . . If there happen to be a Churl, that either out of Covetousness, or Ill-nature, won't comply with this generous Custom, he has a mark of Infamy set upon him, and is abhorr'd by all.

This observation was repeated in varied form throughout the colonial period, and often in a context that shows that the extending of hospitality was not only an obligation but also a source of intense gratification—almost an inner compulsion. The stress on hospitality arose from and contributed to the sacred importance attached to the house. A man's homeplace—his plantation and house—were special extensions of the self.[13]

Myths of southern hospitality at stately mansions must not be allowed to obscure the larger context in which the gentry's displays of magnificence occurred. The living quarters of the great majority of persons in the middle of the eighteenth century were still cramped and confined, yet changes were already taking place that had important long-term implications for the transformation of psyches, and so of religion and ideology. For this reason the evolution of household interiors from the turn of the seventeenth century to the 1750s will briefly be traced. *

The seventeenth-century "Virginia house" (as documents of the period designated such structures) was a one-story frame dwelling with two rooms on the ground floor. The whole structure (very often including the roof) was covered with unpainted clapboards split out of four-foot lengths of oak. Chimneys were set outside the gables at one or both ends. In the roof, attics usually afforded additional space. They could be entered by a stair or ladder from one of the rooms below. Typically the entranceway led directly into the main living room with its focal hearth, so that the house was a comparatively open structure for both inhabitants and visitors. Even the great houses of the gentry were organized in such a way that access to the inner parts was through a "hall" in which most domestic activity was concentrated (see figure 14).[14]

Crowding people into a single room—sometimes as small as ten by twelve feet—made for a communal style of life. With so little specialization of space there could be only minimum differentiation of functions. Persons growing up in such an environment would not develop a sense of segregated self with a need for privacy. The physical congestion was further intensified by the extreme paucity of furniture. A recent analysis of inventories shows that more than half the households in the society owned personal property worth £60 or less. At this level of existence no more than one in four families had a table to sit at. About a third of the households had chairs or benches, but only one in seven of such families owned both. It is necessary to look well up the social scale before such possessions became the rule rather than the exception. Beds as we know them—let alone bedrooms—were not available to most households. In fewer than one-seventh of the inventories worth less than £60 did even a single bedstead raise the most privileged persons in the house off the floor. The small numbers of mattresses and blankets listed in inventories

* The discussion that follows is based on published and unpublished papers by members of the St. Mary's City Commission sponsored by the State of Maryland. The studies cited are concentrated mostly on St. Mary's County—a typical Tidewater tobacco-growing region in colonial times. Errors are undoubtedly introduced by generalizing from partially completed research on one small area. Such errors are nonetheless minimal beside those that would be implicit in leaving readers to imagine styles of life in early Chesapeake society on the basis of ethnocentric assumptions about how Anglo-Saxons live, compounded by the impressions that historical museums convey.

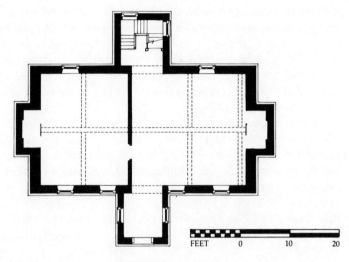

FIGURE 14.
*Ground-floor plan of a grand seventeenth-century
hall-parlor house*

make it clear that most people shared sleeping space, lying two or three together. And nights were long, since most houses had no candles or lamps and
could rely only on the light from the fire in the hearth after the day's end.[15]

Thus the inhabitants of the seventeenth-century Chesapeake world have
been aptly characterized as "squatters or leaners." They rested slumped on the
floor, or crouched on the boxes and chests that were the only ubiquitous items
of furniture. They held their food bowls in one hand when they ate, using a
spoon with the other. Nearly all persons, whatever their rank, lacked knives
and forks until after 1700. Although the well-to-do had more space, more
furniture, and greater quantities of superior equipment, as late as the 1680s
their houses and possessions were not organized to sustain a life-style qualita-
tively different from that of their poorer neighbors.[16]

By the mid-eighteenth century an important series of changes had begun
and was still continuing. First, distinct gentry families emerged and came to
be more and more set apart by an increasingly refined way of life. This refinement was expressed in architecture, since the great houses had passageways

with rooms opening off them to create segregated spaces for special persons
and functions. Such movement away from communality was most dramatically signaled in the custom of "dining," with its reserved space, its linen-
covered table, and its fashionably styled matching sets of plates, knives,
forks, and other eating accoutrements. At regular times select companies
gathered at this ritual center, and each member would be seated on a chair in
a carefully defined social space.[17]

For the middling and lower orders in Virginia society, changes came later.
Some poorer whites, together with the slaves, were still in a comparatively
unmodified "seventeenth-century" condition of life at the end of the eighteenth century. The houses of common folk remained small, with little provision for segregation of persons and activities. By mid-century, for all save the
very least fortunate, important modifications in household equipment had
been made. Social space and the boundaries of the person were being redefined. Bedsteads, tables, and chairs came to be the rule rather than the
exception. But even in the 1750s, the combination of tables and chairs was
found in only one-third of households with inventories that were valued at
less than £40—households that constituted about 30 percent of the total.
Knives and forks appeared in about the same proportion of inventories.[18]

Records have not been found that could support a direct analysis of customary behavior in the houses of humble tobacco growers. The patterns of
ceremony-oriented, rule-bound life in the great houses, however, can be studied. They will be reviewed here through the detailed observations recorded in
Philip Fithian's diary during the years 1773 and 1774.[19]

CEREMONIAL SPACE AT THE GREAT HOUSE

The young Fithian was greatly struck by the grandeur of Robert Carter's countryseat. The house stood on "a high spot of Ground," and being seventy-six
by forty-four feet (with a height of more than forty feet), it could be seen "at
the Distance of six Miles." It was not merely the size but the elegance that
impressed him. A strong sense of authority is communicated in Fithian's description of the elaborate but controlled facades and the careful setting of the

mansion itself in a great hundred-yard rectangle, with the corners defined by substantial one-and-a-half-story brick dependencies.[20]

Inside, the four principal rooms on the ground floor were "disposed of in the following manner. Below [the stairs?] is a dining Room . . . ; the second is a dining-Room for the Children; the third is Mr. Carters study; & the fourth is a Ball-Room thirty feet long." Significantly, Fithian omitted the hall from his count of rooms. The presence of the master in the hall when it was used to receive invited guests or as a cool summer living place might introduce an atmosphere of grave propriety, as on this occasion, noted by our diarist: "About ten [o'clock] an old Negro Man came with a complaint to Mr. Carter of the Overseer that he does not allow him his Peck of corn a Week. . . . We were sitting in the passage, he sat himself down on the Floor clasp'd his Hands together, with his face directly to Mr. *Carter*, & then began his Narration." More generally, however, when it was not the scene of encounter between persons with a high sense of their dignity, the hall—significantly styled "the passage"—was the area of least formality in the house. Fithian gave two revealing glimpses of the comparative freedom of this space. In the first he showed "*Dennis*, a [slave] Boy of about twelve Years old, one of the Waiters at Table . . . standing in the front Door" at the entrance to the hall, evidently taking his ease, when in a sudden gust, the door, "which is vastly huge & heavy," slammed to and took off the end of his middle finger. In the other scene children were bickering as Fithian "was passing through the Hall from Breakfast—[and] the Nurse, a short stump of a [white woman] . . . call'd to [him], & begg'd [him] to close the Quarrel."[21]

The way in which the partitioning of interior spaces and the specialization of functions created greater refinement is clearly demonstrated in the use of the dining room that opened off the hall beneath the stairs. The dinner table was the center for the most highly formalized behavior in gentry houses. Decorum was enhanced by the setting aside of a separate chamber for the meals of young persons, who had not yet learned to conform to studied rituals. Fithian's note that the dining room was "where we usually sit" indicates some relaxation of strictness. Yet his whole account of the routines at Nomini Hall suggests that such use served less to vulgarize the room than to heighten the formality of social intercourse for those who were included in the circle that sat and conversed in this sanctum.[22]

Even more than the select seclusion of the room, the ceremonial character of the meals—especially dinner—marked off the table as sacrosanct within the time and space of daily domestic life. The dinner table was not only the center of ritual of the gentry household; it was also the very focus of that hospitality whose hallowed importance has already been stressed. (Guests were so much the expected thing that their absence would occasionally elicit a journal entry: "no company.") To the Honorable Robert Carter's table came not only the heads of neighboring houses and their families, "by particular invitation," but also, as they had cause to call on the master, a succession of persons in more or less client station, such as clerks, estate stewards, head overseers, and tobacco inspectors. A continual series of essential exchanges took place here—obligations incurred and returned. Tokens of social esteem, or simply of recognition, were given by the great and received by the less exalted. The tables of the honored guests would in turn be graced by the colonel himself; the patronized clients would be expected to make their returns in other, less honorific, ways.[23]

Bells, rung at stated hours, proclaimed the times of assembly at the highest table. Those who were eligible to attend were obligated to do so, as Fithian learned when, because his "Head was not dress'd, & [he] was too lazy to change . . . clothes," he decided he would not go. "Mrs Carter . . . in the evening lash'd [him] severely . . . said [he] was rude, & censurable." The form of proceedings proclaimed the dominance of the master, whose role Fithian characterized as director of the "ceremonies at Table." He would "say Grace"; he "must carve—Drink the Health—and talk"; and he performed the offices of magnanimous hospitality: "Sir—This is a fine Sheeps-Head [fish], Mr Stadly shall I help you?—Or would you prefer a *Bass* or a *Perch*?— Or perhaps you will rather help yourself to some picked *Crab*." Since formality extended its constraints to the table talk, the master also conducted that, leading in with topics suitable for polite discourse. Thus on Wednesday, June 8, 1774, "Mr *Carter* . . . introduced . . . a conversation on Philosophy, on Eclipses; the manner of viewing them; Thence to Telescopes, & the information which they afforded us of the Solar System; Whether the planets be actually inhabited &c." On another occasion he opened with an observation "that many of the most just, & nervous [i.e., delicate] sentiments are contain'd in Songs & small Sketches of Poetry; but being attended with *Frippery Folly* or *Indecency* they are many times look'd over." Likewise the social awareness of the young was to be formed in a polite conversational mold. When they were being given orders "concerning their conduct" during the course of a great Christmas entertainment held at a neighboring gentleman's house, they were told to bring back "an Account of all the company at the Ball." The patriarch exercised less comprehensive control, however, when his peers were present. An analysis of the dinner table conversation topics reported in the diary shows that honored guests, less subject to the control of the grave gentleman, introduced a more trivial, anecdotal tone.[24]

At the conclusion of dinner (taken about three o'clock in the afternoon) came a series of toasts. It seems these were always loyal toasts—to the king, the governor, and in time the Continental Congress—sometimes followed by one to "absent Friends." (Even when the colonel and the tutor dined alone, this first group of toasts was de rigueur.) Then usually followed (after the ladies' withdrawal?) the gallantry of each gentleman "giving" the health of a lady whom he chose to name. Supper (taken at about nine o'clock) was also followed by toasts if there was company, and might be no less formal than dinner.

Two scenes depicted in Fithian's diary entries describe companies gathered for dancing at the hall: "Half after eight we were rung in to Supper; The room looked luminous and splendid; four very large candles burning on the table where we supp'd, three others in different parts of the Room; a gay, sociable Assembly, & four well instructed waiters!" On another occasion Fithian recorded that "the Company danced after candle-light a Minuet round, . . . when we were Rung to Supper[.] after Supper we sit til twelve drinking loyal Toasts."[25]

The exclusive social authority that all this highly formal display was calculated to engender is revealed in the predicament of a man from a circle slightly below that of the gentry, who found himself patronized at the colonel's table twice during July 1774. According to Fithian he lacked refined style and became very self-conscious about it:

> Dined with us one—one—Mr.—Mr.—I forget his name—I know his trade tho': An Inspector [of Tobacco]—He is rather Dull, & seems unacquainted with company[,] for when he would, at Table, drink our Health, he held the Glass of Porter fast with both his Hands, and then gave an insignificant nod to each one at Table, in Hast, & with fear, &

then drank like an Ox—The Good Inspector, at the second toast, after having seen a little our Manner[:] "Gentlemen & Ladies (but there was none in Womans Cloathing at Table except Mrs. Carter) The King"—I thought that during the Course of the Toasts he was better pleased with the Liquor than with the manner in which at this Time he was obliged to use it.

A few days later the inspector showed yet more unfamiliarity with bon ton when the company "had after Dinner, *Lime Punch* & *Madaira*; but he chose & had a Bowl of *Grogg* [rum and water]"![26]

When the house was the setting for a large-scale celebration of the greatness of its family and the magnanimity of its head, the precise lines of formality were inevitably trampled by the press of numbers gathered at the house. Unfortunately no grand rite of passage was celebrated at Nomini Hall while Fithian was there, but he was able to observe one day of a splendid four-day ball that Squire Lee held at his family seat in January 1774. The tutor's account reveals how the festivities, which more than seventy guests attended, involved throwing open the whole ground floor of the great house. (It can be inferred from known custom that the bedchambers upstairs and in the dependencies would have been reserved for those who had traveled the greatest distances.) The refinement of segregating different activities and functions could not be maintained, although an effort was made to retain polite tone in spite of irrepressible exuberance among many of the assembled visitors:

> As soon as I had handed the Ladies out, I was saluted by Parson *Smith*; I was introduced into a small Room where a number of Gentlemen were playing Cards . . . to lay off my Boots[,] Riding-Coat &c—Next I was directed to the Dining-Room to see Young Mr. *Lee*; He introduced me to his Father. . . . The Ladies dined first, when some Good order was preserved; when they rose, each nimblest Fellow dined first—The Dinner was as elegant as could be well expected when so great an Assembly was to be kept for so long a time. . . . About Seven the Ladies & Gentlemen begun to dance in the Ball-Room—first Minuets one Round; Second Giggs; third Reels, And last of All Country-Dances. . . . The Music was a French-Horn and two Violins—The Ladies were Dressed Gay, and splendid, & when dancing their Silks &

Brocades rustled and trailed behind them!—But all did not join in the Dance for there were parties in Rooms made up, some at Cards; some drinking for Pleasure; some toasting the Sons of america; some singing "Liberty Songs" as they call'd them, in which six, eight, ten or more would put their Heads near together and roar.[27]

Adaptation to climate and perhaps to the social leveling of a new settlement led to another manner of celebrating the hospitality of the head of the household and his homeplace—one that avoided encroaching on the formalities of the house or imposing the decorum proper to domestic space upon the gathering. From late July until the end of summer the Carters of Nomini Hall and their gentleman tutor were frequently invited to attend "fish feasts" or "barbecues" upon the banks of the river. We shall see that outdoor entertainments might be even freer from restraint among common planters and slaves.[28]

HUMBLE DWELLINGS

The ceremonies that made the tobacco inspector feel so ill at ease were made possible by the leisured affluence that the ruling gentry enjoyed. Persons who had to work in the fields from dawn to dusk could not always sit at table for their dinner, let alone dress their heads. (In the earlier decades of the century many did not possess a table to sit at.) Of necessity, then, less formality prevailed at the common planters' houses and the slaves' quarters. This is not to say that there were no rules, no customary ritual forms—although no account has been found describing what these were. (Perhaps we get a hint of one in the inspector's way of drinking the health of the company, giving a "nod to each one at the Table" in a fashion that seemed "insignificant," or pointless, to the well-bred tutor from New Jersey.)

The humble "Virginia house," with its two rooms downstairs, was extremely restricted as to space for social gatherings. As described in one of the few accounts we have of festivities at a common planter's homeplace, entertainment necessarily flowed out of doors when it occurred on a large scale. A simple wooden Tidewater farmhouse, amid its orchards and outbuildings, was

made ready for the celebration of the return visit of a younger brother who
some two years before had gone west to teach school. Many years later that
brother, Devereux Jarratt, remembered seeing, as he rode up, great "numbers,
both within and without doors." Outside "the tankard [of hard cider] went
briskly round, while the sound of music and dancing, was heard within."[29]

Little is known of the rituals with which slaves marked life's important mo-
ments. Uncomprehending white observers characterized the celebrations
they saw among the slaves as completely informal—"Rude and uncultivated
. . . irregular and grotesque" were the words used by one traveler. A remarkable painting survives, however, that enables speculative interpretation to go
a little further (see figure 15).[30]

Though the action takes place out of doors, dress and demeanor give a certain degree of formality to an enactment that also involves vigorous bodily
movement. At the center of the picture are three slaves engaged in an Afro-
American dance. Surrounding them is a circle of nine persons whose faces
register joy—though not without signs of a sense of the dignity and importance of the action. Lacking knowledge of the meanings expressed in the
grouping of the figures, in the objects that they hold, and in the manner of
their movement, one can only guess at the nature of the occasion. More definite conclusions can be drawn from close attention to the setting in which
the artist has shown the action. One of the most powerful statements implicit
in the disposition of the elements of the picture is the distance registered between the slaves and the imposing, symmetrically extended great house to
which they evidently "belong." Also notable is the location of the action—
the slaves are gathered at a quarter, in the space enclosed by a cluster of their
own houses.

CELEBRATION: THE DANCE

When a householder opened the resources of his plantation to guests, the
opportunities for self-assertion, display, and conviviality were at their greatest. For the gentry, a birthday, the Christmas season, or mere inclination provided sufficient reason to engage in lavish ostentation; for humbler people,

cause for celebration was more likely to be a christening, a wedding, a home-coming, or a funeral.

The social circle was most complete at celebrations of house and of family rites of passage. Young and old, men and women, assembled together. Danc-ing was at the center of the action and was evidently one of the most mean-ingful expressions of the soul of this entire people: "*Virginians* are of genuine Blood—They will dance or die!" It was inevitable, given the significance at-tached to this activity, and given the proud, self-assertive values of the so-ciety, that dancing should be vigorous and competitive. Performances were closely watched, and consensual judgments speedily became known.[31]

As one explores the dancing of Virginians of diverse ranks, and the pas-sions and values it expressed, one has an opportunity to enter more deeply into the world of those whom historians have arrogantly called "the inarticu-late." * Most is known about activities in elite circles, but the evidence sug-gests that despite a self-conscious emphasis among the grandees on high, even courtly, styles, continuities connected the performances of the gentry with those of common farmers and slaves.

In the great houses attention was given to the formal instruction of young ladies and gentlemen in polite forms of dancing. Often lessons were con-ducted by teachers who came from Europe. The College of William and Mary was promoting such accomplishments well before its academic faculty was complete. The principal dances taught were the minuet and the by-then for-malized and fashionable country dances and reels. Fithian noted the strict-ness of the teacher who held classes in the great houses of the Northern Neck

---

* Historical understanding has too long been enthralled by the assumptions, preferences, and definitions of intellectuals—a high priesthood of which historians themselves form a part. In highly literate milieus the assumption is unquestioned that significant communication is con-veyed by words, especially by written words, and above all by printed words. Yet one may ask: How many people in our own society—among the elite even—arrive at articulate verbal state-ments of the meaning of their own lives? For all persons such statements are most often implied in patterns of behavior. In face-to-face oral cultures like that of 18th-century Virginia, action in a social context assumes an even more important place in the total process of communication. Scholars' predilections have long placed undue emphasis in early American history on New En-gland, with its great output of printed sermon commentary about society and the nature of things. In Virginia it was not in words but in vivid dance forms that the meaning of life was most fully expressed. Historians must seek to "read" these kinds of statements also.

FIGURE 15.
Celebration at the quarter

on the eve of the Revolution, and the accuracy of the pupils' performances. Yet he saw the same pupils engage in more vigorous, less-refined plebeian dancing when they were out of school. Similarly, Andrew Burnaby, staying among the Virginians for a year in 1759–1760, observed that they were "immoderately fond of dancing," but that "they discover great want of taste and elegance. . . . Towards the close of an evening, when the company are pretty well tired with country dances, it is usual to dance jiggs; a practice originally borrowed, I am informed, from the Negroes. These dances are without any method or regularity: a gentleman and lady stand up, and dance about the room, one of them retiring, the other pursuing, then perhaps meeting, in an irregular fantastical manner." The jigs might not even be confined to the latter part of the evening. Nicholas Cresswell, describing a Twelfth Night ball in Alexandria in 1775, was struck by the aspirations to high style expressed in the dress and coiffure of the ladies. He also noted the general fondness for dancing, and the failure, as it seemed to him, to "perform it with the greatest elegance": "Betwixt the Country dances they have what I call everlasting jigs. A couple gets up and begins to dance . . . (to some Negro tune) others comes and cuts them out, and these dances always last as long as the Fiddler can play. This is sociable, but I think it looks more like a Bacchanalian dance than one in a polite assembly." [32]

The form of the jig gives a strong sense of the consistency of the culture. Even in the most convivial activities a palpable element of contest was subtly incorporated. The company formed a circle, observing and informally adjudicating the performances in the center. A kind of challenge and response was rendered explicit (and extended to include females) in the "cutting out" ritual—which would certainly have been controlled by the judgment of the onlookers. Even the pitting of the fiddler against dancers in a test of endurance carried intimations of contest.

Fithian had been impressed by the strict formality of gentry dancing lessons, but his diary also casts light on the processes by which African influences competed with European courtliness in giving expressive content to Virginia dancing. The New Jersey tutor recorded an episode involving the Honorable Robert Carter's son Benjamin and his nephew Harry: "This Evening [Sunday] the Negroes collected themselves into the School-Room & began to play the *Fiddle*, & dance. . . . I went among them, *Ben & Harry* were of the company—*Harry* was dancing with his Coat off—I dispersed them however immediately." We see for an instant how the dance might function repeatedly as a common medium of expression, linking persons at opposite extremes of the social hierarchy. Such communication of tone and feeling was not confined to impromptu occasions. Slaves were present as attendants at the grandest balls, able to observe the performances of the gentry for later adaptation or satirization. The musicians at the assemblies in the great houses were usually blacks, who were thus certain to introduce in covert ways their own conception of the dance into the most modish proceedings.[33]

An English traveler just off a ship on the Potomac observed the interaction of cultures in a situation where African traditions clearly predominated. On May 29, 1774, Nicholas Cresswell recorded that he

> went to see a Negro Ball. Sundays being the only days . . . [they] have to themselves, they generally meet together and amuse them-selves with Dancing to the Banjo . . . a Gourd . . . with only four strings. . . . Some of them sing to it. . . . In their songs they generally relate the usage they have received from their Masters or Mistresses in a very satirical stile. . . . Their dancing is most violent exercise. . . . They all appear to be exceedingly happy at these merry-makings.[34]

Dancing certainly marked important entertainments at the homes of com-mon planters, yet the records permit only tantalizing glimpses. The reminis-cences of converts to radical evangelical religion make clear how significant this activity was as an intense form of social engagement and as an expression of attachment to worldly pleasure. Understandably, however, the pious memoirs do not describe carefully the sinful pastimes that they mention only to deplore. Travelers' reports of family entertainments have not been found, but we have vivid pen sketches of outdoor festivities. In July 1774 Nicholas Cresswell witnessed "what they call a reaping frolic" while he was ashore on the Maryland side of the Potomac. "This is a Harvest Feast," he noted. "The people [were] very merry, Dancing without either Shoes or Stockings and the Girls without stays." On another occasion he went to a barbecue, also on the shores of the Potomac: "These Barbecues are Hogs, roasted whole. This was under a large Tree. A great number of young people met together with a Fid-dle and Banjo played by two Negroes, with Plenty of Toddy, which both Men and Women seem to be very fond of. I believe they have danced and drunk till there are few sober people amongst them." The fiddle and the banjo appearing together give a hint of cultural fusion. The "banjar" was still an African gourd instrument; for Anglo-Virginians "a sweet Fiddle," played by "a worthy good tempered Man," was an emblem of "distinguished . . . social Virtues."[35]

Behind the "bacchanalian dance," and in the "irregular, fantastical manner" of the movements, was intensity of purpose. For many of the participants the stakes were high. In a comparatively open society, where land was plentiful and easily became exhausted and where much of the wealth, in the form of slaves, was mobile, the making of a good match was one of the surest ways to establish or secure a "fortune" (as it was called). A number of activities might enable young men to prove their prowess, but dancing was at the center of those community gatherings where men and women were most directly visible to each other and able to perform accordingly. Indeed, Virginia dancing—especially the jig, with its vigorous alternating pursuit and retreat—was a stylized representation of bold, active courtship on the part of both sexes. One visitor thought courtship, and others' keen observation of it, was "the principal business in Virginia."[36]

The workings of these processes can be seen most clearly in the reminiscences of another convert to strict evangelical piety. James Ireland was a penniless schoolmaster who emigrated from Scotland and had almost no family connections. He settled in a part of Frederick County where "balls, dancing and chanting to the sound of the violin, was the most prevailing practice." In his autobiography he recalled how, dancing being his "darling idol, and being esteemed by all who ever saw [him] perform upon the floor, a most complete dancer," he not only acquired "the confidence and esteem of . . . young ladies" but also emerged as the protégé of a grand gentleman. In addition, he became the favorite companion of the "heads of tolerably numerous families" with whom he was actively engaged in "swearing, drinking and frolicking, [as well as] horse racing." Had he not suddenly become converted to evangelical religion, and so been led to renounce the conviviality at which he excelled, he would evidently have been on his way to a good marriage and advancement within gentry society. Small wonder, then, that performance in the dance was watched so intently and assessed so publicly—or that young men might vie to be designated leader of the ball. Activities, exciting in themselves and with such high stakes, could not but project compelling images of what the good life was about—images that would be internalized by young onlookers, and so, by entering powerfully into their socialization and character formation, be carried forward through their lives to sustain the pattern of cultural values.[37]

5

OCCASIONS
Court Days, Race Meetings, Militia Musters, and Elections

The times when Virginians came together from their dispersed plantations had a very distinctive quality. Communal assembly was intermittent rather than continuous, and it was oriented more toward a striving for advantage in various forms of contest than toward peaceful exchange and sharing.

COURT DAY

In the eighteenth-century Virginia landscape, the courthouse occupied a unique place. It can be pictured in its physical setting—usually an isolated brick structure with a simple round-arched, loggia-style porch on the front. Not uncommonly it stood at a crossroads in the midst of woods and fields, since most counties were without towns, and central location was the prime consideration in choosing a site. The courthouse, however, was never quite solitary, for it was invariably accompanied by supporting buildings—always at least one ordinary (i.e., tavern), a lockup, and often a store. A typical county seat is evoked by a passage in William Byrd's droll account of his travels to visit some iron mines and the outlying quarters of his vast estates. He had passed the night at the house of the clerk of the newly formed Caroline County court. (The holder of this much-sought-after office was assured

FIGURE 16.
A courthouse, its green under snow

of influence and income. Byrd noted, for example, that his host, Major Ben
Robinson, was reformed from the "gaming and idleness" that had plunged
him into debt, and that by means of the perquisites of his post, "in a quarrel-
some county [he] will soon be able to clear his old scores.") Riding ten miles
inland, away from Major Robinson's seat on the Rappahannock River, Byrd
reached the Caroline courthouse, where he noted that "Colonel Armistead
and Colonel Will Beverley have each of 'em erected an ordinary well supplied
with wine and other polite liquors for the worshipful bench. Besides these,

there is a rum ordinary for persons of a more vulgar taste. Such liberal supplies of strong drink often make Justice nod and drop the scales out of her hands."[1]

It was a cluster of almost deserted buildings that called from William Byrd this wry comment on what it would be like on court days. Only when it came together did the scattered community attain full existence. In the monthly concourse at the courthouse the male part of Virginia county society became visible to its members in a manner similar to that observed at the parish church. We may obtain a glimpse of a courthouse gathering suddenly illuminated one Thursday in July 1768. A brief notice in the *Virginia Gazette* tells how:

> Last Sussex court day at night, a flash of lightning struck near the end of the court house of that county, killed two horses (the property of one Ehren Horn, a German) and three hogs, and also struck two trees. There were upwards of an hundred people in and about the ordinary, within thirty yards of where the mischief was done. The poor man that owned the horses was indemnified upon the spot, by the generous contribution of the Gentlemen who attended that court.

Court day had drawn so large a multitude that more than one hundred persons remained at the ordinary after dark. The horse trader, Ehren Horn, was no doubt one of a number of dealers and peddlers who had come to offer their goods for sale—a custom that gave court days the aspect of a country fair. The gentlemen in attendance displayed that liberality proper to their rank by compensating the unfortunate man's losses. Earlier in the day some of these same gentlemen had conducted the court, lending their personal authority to what was nearly the sum and substance of government at the time—adjudicating disputes, recording transactions, and distributing small favors to the fortunate.[2]

A great deal besides the court proceedings drew the county's inhabitants together on court day, but the sessions in the courthouse were at the center of all activity. A society dominated by landholders, jealous of their independence and litigious in the defense of their boundaries and entitlements, could not but attach great importance to the arena in which conflicts over matters of this kind were joined and their issue determined. The importance of the arbitrator's function conferred considerable dignity on those who exercised it.

We must picture the gentlemen justices, bewigged and dressed in their fine coats and waistcoats, seated on the raised "bench"—His Majesty's commissioners engaged in the communal dispensation of "justice." A ceremonial enveloped their hearings. To the twentieth-century observer incessant oath taking is its most striking feature. Periodically the county's commission of the peace was renewed, and the court would then publicly reconstitute itself by an elaborate, carefully recorded round in which a junior justice would administer the oaths of office to the senior justice present, who would then duly swear in all the rest. No justice or militia officer could act until he had qualified himself by taking the oaths in open court. He promised to execute his office faithfully, swore allegiance to the king, and finally "repeated and subscribed the Test." This last was an explicit expression of detestation for the papist doctrine of transubstantiation, and so frequently served to reaffirm the official identity of white Virginians as Protestant Englishmen.[3]

Legal transactions—the deeds that secured the all-important properties, boundaries, and entitlements of the county's inhabitants—could be admitted to the record only after they had been read in court and acknowledged by the voices of parties and witnesses. This was a society with a low level of literacy skills. The legal system was based on written instruments, but in the courts it was nevertheless essential for the written record to be rendered viva voce. In a world where oral culture was strong and custom ruled, the acts of authority were spoken aloud and so assimilated into the fund of necessary community knowledge accessible to all.[4] The continual calling and swearing of juries may be explained in part by this need. When free persons arraigned for felony were sent to the General Court in Williamsburg for trial, society paid not only for the witnesses to attend but also for a jury of twelve "venire men," as they were called, to come from the "vicinage" of the crime to judge the facts. Quite explicitly, then, the community's fund of knowledge and received wisdom was incorporated in formal proceedings. In the county courts juries were frequently impaneled and sworn not only to determine causes and assess damages but also to go into the fields in boundary suits with a surveyor, both to adjudicate the way the line was to be run and to be witnesses to its settlement, adding the outcome to the communal store of information. The same applied to the semiannual calling of "twenty-four of the most capable freeholders" as grand juries to translate the community's knowledge of wrongdoings into recorded indictments: for bearing a bastard child; for swearing profane oaths; for being absent overlong from a parish church; or (in the case of court-appointed surveyors) for neglecting to keep the county's roads passable.[5]

Free persons and indentured servants indicted for felony were tried in the General Court at Williamsburg if the justices found sufficient evidence to warrant a trial. Only slaves were tried in county courts for capital offenses. Solemnity surrounded even these summary hearings, however. The justices would meet on a specially appointed day to constitute themselves as a court of oyer and terminer by having the governor's commission read aloud and then swearing the prescribed oaths. Duly constituted, the court would try for his life (without jury) a slave who had been accused, perhaps, of breaking into a storehouse to steal hams, bolts of cloth, or other commodities. If the judges found him guilty and set the value of the stolen goods higher than five shillings, he would be sentenced to hang near the courthouse—a yet more awful ceremony that would take place within a few days. If the court saw fit to set the value of the theft at less than five shillings, the slave was eligible for "Benefit of Clergy"—he would then be "burnt in the Hand . . . in open Court," lashed, and released. It was "usual upon such occasion" for the condemned person, as sentence was passed and the hot iron brought forth, to cry out, "God save the King." Public stigmatization by branding was yet another ritual for memorization, appropriate to a community in which oral culture and traditions were still vigorous. All present must remember the occasion— its victim was no longer eligible for "benefit of clergy" if he should ever again be convicted of a felony.[6]

It would be hard to overemphasize the importance of the ceremonial at the center of the coming together on court day. In the cultural context of the time it served not only to make the community a witness to important decisions and transactions but also to teach men the very nature and forms of government. Anglo-Virginians had no written constitution; they could only conceive of law and authority in their society as extensions and adaptations of English custom. (Modern Americans are so dependent on the idea of a constitution as a document that they readily misconstrue colonial charters, and even governor's "instructions" in the case of Virginia, as instruments functioning in the manner of written fundamental law.) There were no elementary textbooks on "government"—and not many schools to teach from them had they been available—and few, even among the more literate gentry, would have studied learned volumes giving systematic explication of the English customary "constitution." For most men the primary mode of comprehending the organization of authority was through participation in courthouse proceedings. The oaths and rituals were so many formulas, diagrams, or models, declaring the nature of government and its laws. The executions were fearful demonstrations of the consequences of putting oneself outside the protection of those laws.

The importance of the court was not merely confined to the solemn figuration of a symbolic order. Its communication of the symbols of power would necessarily have been feeble had it not itself commanded real and impressive powers. The monthly work of the court was routine enough—mostly cases of debt recovery. Nevertheless, routine as such cases were, a great deal could be at stake for members of the community. If one looks at the inventories of goods attached by the sheriff in small-debt cases, and if one considers how grave were the consequences of the enforced sale of an entire household stock, one may gain an impression of the weight of the law and its magistrates on the lives of simple countryfolk. The disposition of the cases was determined by juries impaneled by the sheriff from among the freeholders present in the courthouse, in the yard, or in the nearby ordinary. Thus the community participated to a large extent in the settling of its disputes, yet it could make all the difference to defendants if, through the intercession of a well-disposed member of the bench, they could get a postponement of the hearing of their cases. The justices indeed disposed a great many favors, none of which was likely to lead to spectacular wealth, but all of which might be of vital assistance to a man battling to overcome financial difficulties or striving to better himself in the world. The bench of magistrates issued the licenses for the establishment of water mills in the county, they licensed and supervised the conduct of ordinaries, they arranged the contracts for the construction of bridges, jails, and other public works, and they submitted recommendations for the governor's annual appointment of the inspectors in charge of the tobacco warehouses, where all tobacco had to be certified as of standard for the market. The post of tobacco inspector was one of real power, and the consideration it necessarily commanded could only enhance the respect enjoyed by the members of the bench, who were the patrons in making or continuing the inspectors' appointments.[7]

The court was central to the organization of society. Its functions went deeper than the conduct of business and the distribution of patronage. The court was the guardian of the Law, and the Law defined rights and obligations. Rights meant property—above all in land and slaves. Obligations meant, essentially, the monetary regulation of relationships between landowners (as in trespass cases) and of relationships that arose from trade in the produce of land (mainly debts and credits). The connections linking the patriarchal household units of plantation society to the maritime exchange system were formalized and secured in court. At the sessions of the county commissioners a powerful form of high culture—the Law—met with a compelling local need—security of property. Without security of property there could be no effective independence of persons, a supreme value in this age. In the courthouse, the royal arms and the form of justice in the king's name expressed the descent of authority from above. In addition, the character of the justices as leading landowners of their county represented the patriarchal property system and affirmed the basis of English law in the needs and consent of the governed.[8]

THE ORDINARY

By looking at the taverns, where the out-of-court activity centered, we can most readily sense the texture of community life. No detailed accounts survive of the nature of the action in and around these public houses, but passages can be found in travelers' journals that give intimations of the tone. These accounts suggest that in addition to buying and selling, borrowing and lending, patrons participated in continual play at cards and other games of skill or hazard. Dice, billiard tables, and decks of cards were standard equipment in the ordinaries. Strong impressions of the tavern ethos are conveyed in the journal of a French traveler who could only evade engagement in games for high stakes by persistent firmness, and who observed that "at night, [there was] Carousing and Drinking In one Chamber and box and Dice in another, which Continues till morning Commonly." The style of action is revealed in his observation that "there is not a publick house in virginia but have their tables all baterd with the boxes, which shows the Extravagant Disposition of the planters." The stranger's comment evokes an image of rough play, with men raising fists to slam down dice and containers as they make their throws.[9]

The same observer also drew attention to the extravagant ways of talking that were characteristic of such places. He found himself at an ordinary in Hanover County in the company of a militia major, who said "freely he'l sooner Die than pay a farthing [of the Stamp Tax], and is shure that all his Countrymen will do the Same." Another traveler recorded a prolonged battle of wits between himself and "a number of colone[l]s, captains, esquires &c, who had met [at an inn in Goochland County] for public business." Interspersed with loud guffaws, whereby the challengers shared their delight at their respective triumphs, were lines that indicated their skill in pressing provocation beyond permitted limits, and then seeming to step back half a pace, to within acceptable bounds. "*Esq. U:* You lie, Sir; I mean on the bed." To which the applauded answer from the butt of the humor was: "And you lie, Sir; I mean under a mistake." Since gentlemen sometimes wore their swords in the ordinaries, despite laws to the contrary, aggressive banter could have fatal consequences. Restraint and decorum were, however, reinforced by the etiquette of the table—including the ceremonious giving of toasts— which evidently prevailed as much in the chambers of the ordinaries where gentlemen drank and dined as in the dining rooms of the great houses.[10]

Self-assertive style, and values centering on manly prowess pervaded the interaction of men as equals in this society. Everywhere, in play and in talk, amid conviviality would be emulation, rivalry, and boastful challenge, which not infrequently erupted into ugly violence among common planters, as affronted pride demanded satisfaction in bouts of boxing or wrestling. Bystanders would form a ring and enforce the customary rules. The causes for which Virginia males could come to blows were recorded by a visitor to the country. It might be that one "has in a merry hour called [another] a *Lubber* . . . or a *Buckskin*, or a *Scotchman* . . . or offered him a dram without first wiping the mouth of the Bottle." Custom permitted the fight to be carried on with "Kicking, Scratching . . . Biting . . . Throttling, Gouging [the eyes], Dismembering [the genitals]," all of which "generally is attended with a crowd of People." An Englishman, commenting with distaste, remarked that a code of honor applied nonetheless. It was common for contestants to agree in ad-

FIGURE 17.
Shared pastimes cut across but did not level social distinctions

vance whether to limit modes of attack, and "that whatever terms are specified . . . let the conflict be ever so severe, they never infringe [their agree-
ment]." He also noted, however, that although gouging had become so
widespread that it was forbidden by a specific act of Assembly, the practice
continued, and that he had "seen a fellow, reckoned a great adept in gouging,
who constantly kept the nails of both his thumbs and second fingers very long
and pointed . . . [and] hardened them every evening in a candle." A New
England traveler, the horrified witness of a fight in the crowded precinct of
Hanover courthouse, was relieved to see the eye of a hard-pressed combatant
saved by his timely bawling out: "King's cruse!"—a sign that he yielded the
contest.[11]

Virginia society had started as a violent assemblage of rough male immigrants coming from England to seek their fortunes and smashing their way
into Indian territory. By the second quarter of the eighteenth century life
took on a more settled character as a roughly even balance of the sexes was
reached and a cultivated elite emerged. Yet the very dominance of that elite
was consolidated by their command of the labor of numerous imported Africans and their descendants. A system of chattel slavery, and the physical
severity necessary to maintain it, lay at the base of this society. Nevertheless,
the connections between conquest and slavery and the violence of the society
can easily be exaggerated. Slavery was then only one extreme in a whole
spectrum of harsh labor systems that existed throughout the Atlantic world.
Everywhere poverty and the brutal quality of the struggle for survival conditioned a ready acquiescence—even a delight—in the violent infliction of
pain and suffering. This aspect of everyday experience in Virginia (as in other
parts of the eighteenth-century world) can most clearly be seen in a number
of popular sports that were closely associated with gatherings of the countryfolk at the courthouse and the ordinaries.[12]

HORSE RACES

The "quarter race" was the Virginia sport par excellence. A distinctive form
of horse racing had evolved in the Chesapeake region during the seventeenth

century that clearly indicated the prevailing taste for strong self-assertion and aggressive contest. The race was a violent duel that tested not only the speed of the horses but also the daring and combative skill of the riders. A straight quarter-mile track ran from starting to finishing post. Sometimes it was hedged in; other times the lines of boisterous spectators served to define its limits. Contestants might ride among this throng, clearing the ground with long whips. At the start the two riders were accustomed to jockey for position, and when the starter's signal sent them hurtling at full gallop down the narrow track, each might be free (depending on agreed rules) to use whip, knee, or elbow to dismount his opponent or drive him off the track. The end of the race would be greeted with "a tornado of applause from the winner's party . . . more especially if the horses had happened to jostle and one of the riders been thrown off with a broken leg." These race meetings customarily adjourned to the nearby ordinary, where participants were further entertained by bouts of the ferocious wrestling already described.[13]

These events were keenly followed and had intense meaning, for the riders in the quarter races were known to the spectators in terms of their family histories, life stories, and individual character traits. Riders and spectators would have to continue to live together in a world shaped by their own dramatic performances. Furthermore, Virginians depended on their horses and attached great importance to them. Observers repeatedly commented during the eighteenth century that common planters would "spend the morning in ranging several miles in the woods to find and catch their horses only to ride two or three miles to church, to the courthouse, or to a horse-race." The apparent illogicality of this is readily resolved when we consider how essential it was to be proudly mounted when one entered the stages of significant action in the social landscape. The role of the steed as an adjunct to virile self-presentation is revealed in the endless conversations the gentry had about their horses, in which they expressed the closest identification with the animals. Philip Fithian, the New Jersey tutor, sometimes felt that he heard nothing but "Loud disputes concerning the Excellence of each others Colts . . . their Fathers, Mothers (for so they call the Dams) Brothers, Sisters, Uncles, Aunts, Nephews, Nieces and Cousins to the fourth Degree!" The preference for a genealogical vocabulary that assimilated horses into the world of human relationships, and the rejection of one that removed them from it, achieved

its ultimate caricature in a note in the old register of Blissland Parish, New
Kent County, that "Fearnought colt of Lucky by Kg. Herod was foal'd in May,
1785."[14]

The heavy betting that accompanied the horse races intensified the spectators' involvement with the contestants. A letter of 1754, containing a report
of an acute shortage of coin in the colony, incidentally throws light on the
manner in which the wagering was negotiated. Persons evidently went about
hawking aloud the odds they would give to any that would take them: "It is a
rare thing to see a dollar, and at public places where great monied men will
bet on cock fights, horse races, etc., the noises is not now as it used to be—
'one pistol[e] to 2!' or '3 pistoles to one!'—it is now common [to] cry '2
cows and calves to one!' or '3 to one!' or sometimes '4 hogsheads tobacco to
one!'" These were high stakes. Four hogsheads of tobacco were more than the
whole cash crop a poor family could expect to earn in a year, and betting was
not confined to "great monied men." In April 1752 the governor exhorted
the gentlemen of the legislature to exert themselves to curb the growing evil
and its associated vices when they returned to their counties: "I . . . recom-
mend to you, as far as possible, to discourage Gaming, Swearing, and immod-
erate Drinking, particularly at the County Courts. The first of these Crimes, I
am informed, has been pretty general in this Country, and is now much prac-
tised among the lower Class of our People: I mean Tradesmen and inferior
Planters, who . . . follow the Examples of their Superiors." He urged them to
enforce recently renewed laws designed to curb "excessive and deceitful Gaming" and to suppress "ordinaries where gaming . . . is permitted." In vain!
Sovereign custom had long since legitimated the gambling ways of Virginians
of all ranks.[15]

As the eighteenth century wore on and the polite traditions and high style
of the great established families matured, course racing was introduced in imitation of English fashion. By the 1750s it tended to overshadow the indige-
nous quarter race in the long-settled Tidewater region. The course race was a
more formalized affair. Combat by proxy gave it dramatic form: jockeys riding
thoroughbred horses represented the competing gentlemen owners. Unlike
the sudden-death quarter races, these trials were drawn-out events, lasting
through three five-mile heats. Several horses might be run simultaneously,
but it was difficult to find many entrants able to match champions that had
been bred and trained to stay the distances. This meant that the new-style

race often remained a duel between two challengers. Fithian, our wide-eyed northern commentator, gave a sketch of such an event:

> Rode this morning to Richmond Court-house, where two Horses run for a purse of 500 Pounds; besides small Betts almost enumerable. One of the Horses, belonged to Colonel John Taylor, and is called *Yorick*— the other to Dr. Flood, and is called *Gift*—The Assembly was remarkably numerous, beyond my expectation and exceeding polite in general. The Horses started precisely at five minutes after three; the Course was one Mile in Circumference, they performed the first Round in two minutes, [the] third in two minutes & a-half, *Yorick* came out the fifth time round about 40 Rod before *Gift*.[16]

Once a year at Fredericksburg and at Williamsburg special races were conducted that lasted the best part of a week. Lavish events of high significance, these contests were also the occasions for great fairs, with such added excitements as "Puppet shows, roape dancings &ca." The increased expense and magnificence of such grand race meetings, and the extended geographical area from which participants were drawn, introduced greater social distance, even segregation between ranks, than was characteristic of the more intimate courthouse-yard quarter races. This development toward class exclusiveness was offset by the increasing involvement of the gentry in another violent, absorbing, and very popular form of contest.[17]

COCKPITS

In 1724 Hugh Jones had described cockfighting (along with horse racing) as a ruling passion of the "common planters." If it was then more particularly a vulgar pastime, it soon ceased to be beneath the attention of gentlemen. When William Byrd came to Mr. Secretary John Carter's great house, Shirley, in March 1740, he found the master "gone to the cock-fight." Betting in this sport too was heavy and no doubt grew more so as it came under genteel patronage. The diary of Robert Wormeley Carter, oldest son of Landon Carter of Sabine Hall, shows him to have traveled in May 1768 all the way from the Northern Neck to Chesterfield County, south of the James, in order to witness and bet upon the matching of some sixty cocks in a "main" to be determined between Colonel Edward Carter and Colonel Anthony Thornton. He entered his losses as £21.16.3. and noted that this was "pretty considerable considering my situation & the present scarcity of cash."[18]

The cocks fought individual duels to the death; the "main" prize went to the side that had won the greatest number of such matches by day's end. Details concerning these contests have not been found for the first half of the eighteenth century, but graphic accounts were left by travelers during the Revolutionary period. Elkanah Watson, a visiting Yankee entrepreneur, described how he went with a gentleman to a meeting in Southampton County:

> The roads, as we approached the scene, were alive with carriages, horses, and pedestrians, black and white, hastening to the point of attraction. Several houses formed a spacious square, in the center of which was arranged a large cock-pit; surrounded by many genteel people, promiscuously mingled with the vulgar and debased. Exceedingly beautiful cocks were produced, armed with long, sharp, steel-pointed gaffs, which were firmly attached to their natural spurs. The moment the birds were dropped, bets ran high. The little heroes appeared trained to the business, and not the least disconcerted by the crowd or shouting. They stepped about with great apparent pride and dignity; advancing nearer and nearer, they flew upon each other . . . the cruel and fatal gaffs being driven in to their bodies, and, at times, directly through their heads. Frequently one, or both, were struck dead at the first blow, but they often fought after being repeatedly pierced, as long as they were able to crawl, and in the agonies of death would often make abortive efforts to raise their heads and strike their antagonists.

Baron von Closen, who gave a sketch of the curved "gaffs" or "steel spurs" (likening them to a shoemaker's awl), said he had seen some "very dextrous [fighting cocks] who played with this instrument with the greatest daring and skill." No direct evidence suggests that Virginians bestowed on their birds the kind of close personal identification that they often gave to their horses, but the baron did note that champion cocks "often win a reputation for fifty miles or more." The marquis de Chastellux, unexpectedly finding a "numerous assembly in . . . a deserted spot" (Willis's Ordinary in Louisa County), learned that the people had gathered specially for a cockfight. He noted that "when the principal promoters of this diversion [probably gentry] propose to match their champions, they take care to announce it to the public, and although there are neither posts nor regular conveyances, this important news spreads with such facility that planters come from thirty or forty miles around, some with cocks, but all with money for betting, which is sometimes very considerable." He recalled the passionate interest aroused: "While the bettors urged the cocks on to battle, a child of fifteen, who was near . . . leaped for joy and cried, 'Oh! it is a charming diversion!'"[19]

The excitement engendered by the mortal combat between the birds extended to all ranks of society. Philip Fithian recorded the keen engagement of slaves. "Easter Monday," he entered in his diary, "a general holiday; Negroes now are all disbanded till Wednesday morning & are at Cock Fights through the County." On the following Sunday he observed "before Breakfast . . . a Ring of Negroes at the Stable, fighting Cocks." As this form of contest was taken under the patronage of the gentry, it too became more elaborate. From the 1750s onward, newspaper notices repeatedly advertised great matches between counties. Festival holidays in the Church calendar—Easter and Whitsun—were frequently the times designated for these stirring events. It came to be expected that ladies would attend, and a ball was sometimes promised for the evening. The culmination of these grand plays was a two-day battle held in Williamsburg in May 1773 between the "upland" and "lowland" gentlemen.[20]

The development of gentry magnificence in the patronage of sport is a revealing indicator of changes in life-styles and the balance of wealth within the society, but it should not obscure the persistence of older customs. Local quarter races and cockfights on the courthouse green continued to furnish country people with opportunities to engage in these absorbing pastimes, despite the connotation of backward rusticity that such forms of entertainment acquired as the century advanced. In the fall of 1736 the newspaper announced a forthcoming festive meeting arranged in Hanover County by "some merry dispos'd Gentlemen." The communal ethos expected to prevail at the occasion is evident from the announcements. Festivities would include a "neat Hunting-Saddle, . . . to be run for (the Quarter). . . . A fine *Cremona* Fiddle to be plaid for, by any Number of Country Fiddlers, (Mr. *Langford*'s Scholars excepted.) With divers other considerable Prizes, for Dancing,

Singing . . . Wrestling &c . . . [and] a fine Pair of Silk Stockings to be given
to the *handsomest Maid* upon the Green, to be judg'd of by the Company"—
strongly guided, no doubt, by the inclinations of the same "merry dispos'd
Gentlemen." [21]

Intensely shared interests of this kind, cutting across but not leveling social
distinctions, serve to transmit images of what life is really about. The gentry,
having the means and the assurance to patronize sport and to be seen playing
grandly for the highest stakes, were well placed to ensure that their superior
social status was confirmed among the many who took part in these exciting
activities. In a community setting where many of the participants could identify each other as personalities or as members of known families—and thus
were bound to observe the proper formalities of deference and condescension—the congested intimacy of collective engagement only served to confirm social ranking. In this respect the operations of a face-to-face, rank-
structured society differ radically from those of an impersonal "class" society,
where such mingling is distasteful partly because it does introduce confusions
of relationship. [22]

MUSTER FIELD

The forms of patronage and conviviality most evident on the gala occasions
when the squires, yeomen, tenants, overseers, and slaves gathered at race-
track, cockpit, or fairground were apparent at another place of assembly—the
muster field. The militia muster, like court day proceedings, was closely regulated by law. This meant that a blend of formality and intimacy, similar to
that observed at the church and the courthouse, prevailed on the field also.
The structure of the militia and the patterns of its infrequent comings together
can be seen as a microcosm of male-dominated Anglo-Virginian society.

By 1757 the Virginia militia statute had assumed definite form. In its rules
the legislators had instinctively embodied an idealization of the social order
that the muster tended to reinforce. Expectations and anxieties concerning
relationships between different ranks and races were all closely woven together in the law. The statute may be profitably analyzed to bring out the
images it subtly communicated. The first clause, introduced to remedy the

defects of an earlier law, is illuminating: it declared that henceforth "every county-lieutenant, colonel, . . . and other inferior officer, in the militia of this colony, shall be . . . resident in the county of which he is . . . commissioned." This simple requirement pertained to the essence of authority in traditional Virginia society. Power was decentralized, being located in the dense regional networks of gentry families that vied with each other at the county and parish levels. Authority was social in character; it could not be exercised impersonally in the name of an office or a commission. In this world of personal relationships capacity to mobilize the gentry, the freeholders, and the tenants could only be realized by a gentleman of known estate, living in close connection with the leading families of the county.[23]

The militia act is suffused with the sense that society is a ranked system of dignity, honor, and obligation. This may be seen in the careful listing of those whose high standing or sacred learning rendered their mustering among the freeholders inappropriate—unless they were commissioned officers. It is seen even more clearly in the graduated scale of compensation that the exempted dignitaries were required to make to their county in the form of equipment for a specified number of soldiers. A carefully differentiated scale also appeared in the fines instituted for failure to comply with the mustering requirements of the act—from twenty pounds for a county commander in chief to three shillings for an ordinary militiaman.[24]

Certain categories of humble persons were also exempt—both from mustering and from supplying equipment. The inclusion of millers, miners, and iron founders in these categories safeguarded the economic enterprises of the well-to-do. Internal security and the property rights of landed gentlemen were simultaneously protected in the exemption from mustering of "any person being bona fide an overseer over four servants or slaves . . . receiving a share of the crop or wages for his care." ("Imported servants" were not even to be included in the county enlistments, while the requirement that only "male *persons*" be listed for service implicitly excluded slaves, who were, in law, nonpersons.) The attraction of the muster field as a place of resort was clearly indicated by the provision imposing a severe twenty-shilling fine on overseers and millers who attended despite their exemption.[25]

A reminder of the harsh racist aspect of this society comes early in the statute with the provision that "free mulattoes, negroes and Indians . . . shall appear without arms, and may be employed as drummers, trumpeters, . . . or in such other servile labor as they shall be directed to perform." The concluding section of the act—the patrolling clause—brought to light the lurking apprehensions of white Virginians concerning the society they were embodying themselves to defend. The county lieutenant was

> required some time before the tenth day of June yearly, to appoint an
> officer and . . . men of the militia, . . . not exceeding four, once in
> every month or oftener if thereto required to patrol and visit all negroe
> quarters, and other places suspected of entertaining unlawful assem-
> blies of slaves, servants, or other disorderly persons . . . or any other
> strolling about . . . without a pass . . . and to carry them before the
> next justice of the peace, who if he shall see cause, is to order every
> such slave, servant, stroller, or other disorderly person . . . to receive
> any number of lashes, not exceeding twenty, on his or her bare back
> well laid on.[26]

This provision does not reveal the practical means by which the blacks were kept in subjection so much as it affords a glimpse of a symbolic enactment of force. The regulation expressed the fears of the masters and their determination to dominate by violence. Once a month the slave quarters were to be visited by a patrol of not more than five men. More practical perhaps was the measure enacted in 1726 that had established patrols to avert the "great danger [that] may happen to the inhabitants of this dominion, from the unlawful concourse of negros, during the Christmas, Easter, and Whitsuntide holidays, wherein they are usually exempted from labour." Monthly patrols, however, would be a frequently recurrent show of force— perhaps more impressive to blacks; certainly more consoling to fearful masters.[27]

The statute set up a model of what a militia should be and should do. Against this may be set another view of the militia—that of Edward Kimber, the traveler in the colonies whose observations were published in the *London Magazine* in July 1746:

> To behold the Musters of their Militia, would induce a Man to nause-
> ate a Sash and hold a Sword forever in Derision. Diversity of Weapons
> and Dresses, Unsizeableness of the Men, and Want of the least Grain
> of Discipline in their Officers or them, make the whole Scene little
> better than Dryden has expressed it—

And raw in fields the rude militia swarms;
Mouths without hands, maintain'd at vast expence,
In peace a charge, in war a weak defence:
Stout, once a year they march, a blust'ring band,
And ever, but in times of need, at hand;
Of seeming arms, they make a short essay,
Then hasten to get drunk, the bus'ness of the day.[28]

Corroboration of Kimber's description—but without his sneer—may be drawn from the testimony of a neighbor of a militia officer. In 1756 a witness reported of a certain Captain Wager in Elizabeth City County that

for many Years past [he] hath kept an hospitable House, and freely entertained all Persons that came there, as well Strangers as Free-holders. That at the Muster of his Company, after the Exercise was over, he usually treated them with Punch, and they would after that come before his Door and fire Guns in Token of their Gratitude, and then he would give them Punch 'til they dispersed, and that this has been a frequent Practice for several Years.[29]

On the one hand, there is the decorum prescribed by the statute—county society mustered in order, armed as required, and acting under authority; on the other, there are scenes of confusion or, at least, opportunities for drunken exuberance. Between the contemptuous judgments readily made by an out-side observer and the idealization contained in formal rules, it is necessary to seek signs of the successful communication of the shared understandings that sustained social order. One must begin by recognizing that the militia did pro-vide both an important means of formalizing authority in society and assem-blies at which the male fraternity of warriors might get drunk together.

William Byrd's *Secret Diary* contains the most direct accounts of the actual workings of the militia. A visit of the governor in September 1710, to install Byrd as a county lieutenant or commander in chief, provided an uncom-mon occasion for effective display of the descent of authority from above. On September 22 Colonel Byrd rode with Governor Nicholson into Henrico County:

Colonel Randolph with a troop met us at Pleasant's mill and con-ducted us to his plantation, where all the men were drawn up in good

order. The Governor was pleased with them and exercised them for
two or three hours together. He presented me likewise to them to be
their commander-in-chief [and they] received me with an huzzah.
About 3 o'clock they went to Colonel Randolph's house and had a
dinner and several of the officers dined with us and my hogshead of
punch entertained all the people and made them drunk and fighting all
the evening, but without much mischief.

Important exchanges, establishing and reinforcing social bonds, were made
at this special muster. Byrd, presented by the governor, laid claim to commanding authority, and the huzzah endorsed this claim; in return the great
gentleman set a seal on the allegiance of his men by showing his "liberality"
in standing up a hogshead of liquor for their entertainment. The pattern of
conviviality after the muster usually involved segregated activities for officers
and men, but the rule was not inflexible. On the previous night in Charles
City County, according to Byrd's account, after the muster "as many of the
officers as could sit at the table stayed to dine with the Governor, and the rest
went to take part of the hogshead in the churchyard."[30]

At a routine muster across the river there was less ceremony: "I caused the
troops to be exercised by each captain and they performed but indifferently
for which I reproved them. [Massot] . . . was drunk and rude to his captain,
for which I broke his head in two places. When all was over we went to dine
with Captain Jefferson. . . . Most of the company went home with John Boll-
ing and got drunk."[31]

The posture of magnanimous gentry presiding over and patronizing—even
participating in—the pastime of the enlisted men is described in the account
of the next day when Byrd, escorted by several of his captains from the
Southside, recrossed the James River to the next muster. They found that the
major had already exercised his companies. Byrd recorded: "Then I ordered
the men to be drawn in single [file] along the path where the men were to run
for the prize, and John Hatcher, one of Captain Randolph's men, won the
pistol. Then I caused the men to be drawn into a square to see the men play
at cudgels and Dick O-l-n won the sword, and of the wrestling Will Kennon
[an officer] won the gun."[32]

William Byrd's emotions were very much involved in his role as militia officer. Phrases such as "Everybody showed me abundance of respect" recur in his

diary. Mutual gratification is evident in the ceremonies of deference: "I could not persuade the officers to return but all went with me to . . . the ferryboat." "I thanked them all for the honor they had done me." "Will Randolph's troop waited on me to church and within a quarter of a mile of the church three more troops met me in good order and I took their courtesy very kindly." Evidently the colonel's standing as commander contributed significantly to his sense of personal identity.[33]

Being mustered together under authority and treated by the gentlemen officers were important reinforcements of the bonds of society, but like most expressions of community in the scattered agrarian world of eighteenth-century Virginia these gatherings were intermittent. By contrast the identification of leading persons by militia rank was continuous and ubiquitous. Edward Kimber, the previously quoted English traveler, noted: "Wherever you travel in Maryland (as also in Virginia and Carolina) your Ears are constantly astonished at the Number of Colonels, Majors, and Captains that you hear mentioned: In short, the whole Country seems at first to you a Retreat of Heroes." So general was this usage that we must suppose that titles of militia rank supplied important signs of status in society at large. Colonel William Byrd II was not singular in allowing his persona to become deeply engaged in his role as a commander of county militia.[34]

The commitment of the leaders of this society to the militia and their roles in it is not hard to understand. It was in accord with a powerful current in eighteenth-century Anglo-American ideology. The arms-bearing English yeomanry and gentry were so closely associated with the farmer-soldiers of the venerated early Roman Republic that Edward Gibbon could solemnly remark about his writing of the famous *Decline and Fall* that "the captain of Hampshire militia had not been useless to the historian of the Roman Empire." The internal pressures to which contemporary Virginia society was subject, with its base in the enforced repression of a growing population of enslaved blacks, ensured that such identification with the role of citizen as armed man was reinforced in the colony.[35]

A preoccupation with self-defense, as well as important divisions within white society, can be seen very clearly in the correspondence of William Gooch, lieutenant governor of Virginia from 1727 to 1749. In rapid succession after his arrival Gooch faced a series of alarms: African runaways establishing a settlement in the west in 1727; a real or imaginary slave conspiracy

in Norfolk and Princess Anne counties in August 1730; and a wave of disturbances during 1732 in the Northern Neck, following the enforcement of
Gooch's favorite project, the tobacco inspection act of 1730. Finding in the
armed freeholders the only means for defense of the social order, Gooch
"thought it proper to look narrowly into the state of the Militia" and decided
that "to no purpose are Men obliged to provide themselves with Arms and
Ammunition and to attend the Musters at stated times . . . if when they are
got together scarce one Officer knows how to form . . . or instruct them." He
sought, with the Council's assent, to remedy this general incompetence by
appointing "a very active and understanding Man," at £150 per annum, as
adjutant to supervise military training.[36]

In the alarm raised by a rumored slave rebellion in August and September
1730, Gooch declared that with "the speedy Appointment of Party's of the
Militia sent out to Patrole [he was] in hopes by keeping the Militia to their
Duty, to deter [the slaves] from any . . . unlawful Meetings." Nevertheless,
there are intimations of serious discontent on the part of the men because the
service kept them away from their crops. By 1740 Gooch had revised his assessment of the causes of the weakness of the militia. Reporting on an act
authorizing £2,000 to be spent in equipping the forces of the counties, he
explained: "The Officers of the Militia have always been so sensible of the
Incapacity of the poorer sort of people to provide themselves with arms, that
they have neglected to hold their annual meetings. Because they would not
[then] be under the necessity of fining them,. . . . as the Law required." He
noted that he had failed in 1736 to get the General Assembly to establish a
fund for buying arms for the poorer planters. Soon he was expressing the hope
that by instilling discipline and deference the adjutant would work a general
social improvement: "The ordinary people want a good deal of polishing
and on that account these regular Exercises will be of great benefit to the
country."[37]

ELECTION DAY

The supreme authority in Virginia was the General Assembly, consisting of
the governor (or his lieutenant), the Council (appointed by the crown from

among the heads of great landed families), and the House of Burgesses (composed of two elected members from each county). Regard for the principle of representation made the elected House a sacrosanct center of authority in the province. Elections occurred comparatively infrequently, however, only when the governor chose to dissolve the Assembly and call a new one, or when a member's death or resignation created a vacancy. On the governor's order the office of the secretary of the colony would issue appropriate writs directed to the county sheriff (a position customarily occupied by the gentlemen justices in rotation), who then appointed a day for the election, opened and closed the poll at will, determined the result, and made return accordingly.

The courthouse was prepared for election day by setting up a polling table either inside the building or out in the yard. Each candidate secured the services of a clerk to enter on a sheet the name of each freeholder who came and spoke aloud his vote for the candidate who had employed the clerk "to take his poll." A decided element of confrontation was introduced into the action by the presence of the candidates, who were seated at the table during the time of polling. An account from late in the century is suggestive of both the form of the contest and the manner in which it was integrated into the patterns of favor and obligation characteristic of a face-to-face agrarian society. The election was held to fill a single vacancy. The candidates, John Marshall and John Clopton, were at the table when the voters came up. The sheriff asked:

> "Mr. Blair, who do you vote for?" "John Marshall," said he; and thereupon the future Chief Justice of the United States replied, "Your vote is appreciated, Mr. Blair." As the next voter approached the sheriff inquired: "Who do you vote for, Mr. Buchanan?" "For John Clopton," he answered; and Clopton, at the other end of the table, responded: "Mr. Buchanan, I shall treasure that vote in my memory. It will be regarded as a feather in my cap for ever." [38]

Mr. Blair and Mr. Buchanan were gentlemen of consequence (ministers of religion, in fact) whose votes were valuable tokens of esteem and likely to influence the choices of their inferiors. For humbler men, voting was less an opportunity to confer a favor than a chance to show gratitude or to secure the goodwill of a powerful neighbor.

A report of an election in Accomack County shows how the relationship of gentry to common folk was expressed in the custom of treating voters. The

seating of Edmund Scarburgh as burgess was contested because he had, before
the election, given

> strong Liquors to the People . . . once at a Race, and the other Time
> at a Muster; and did, on the Day of Election, cause strong Liquor to be
> brought in a Cart, near the Court-house Door, where many People
> drank thereof, whilst the Polls of the Election were taking; and one
> Man, in particular, said, *Give me a Drink, and I will go and vote for Col.*
> Scarburgh, . . . and Drink was accordingly given him out of the said
> Cart, where several People were merry with Drink: But it doth not
> appear, whether that Person voted for the said *Scarburgh*, or not.[39]

Colonel Scarburgh's election was upheld by the House, for he had not
done anything unusual. A code controlled conduct at the polls, but (as James
Madison was later to discover to his cost) candidates could not get elected
unless they paid handsomely to treat the voters. The militia was one of the
readiest channels for the social exchanges involved in the custom of treating.
A single example will suffice as illustration. Testimony concerning a disputed
Lunenburg County election of 1758 revealed that both of the candidates who
were returned as elected had worked to enhance their standing with their
own and others' militia companies by plying them with rum. The House upheld the election of Mr. Read because, with genteel decorum, he had not
solicited votes for himself. "It appears . . . that after it was publicly known
. . . that the Writ [for the election] was issued . . . one *Memican Hunt* gave a
Treat on Behalf of Mr. *Read* to a Company of Militia he formerly had commanded, with Mr. *Read's* Knowledge, but not at his Request, and invited Mr.
Read's Friends to partake thereof." Mr. Marrable was in every way less dis-
creet. He postponed until after the election the fulfillment of a promise to
treat Captain Williams's militia company, expressing the fear that otherwise
"it would vacate his Election." But, hard pressed by opposition, he was soon
treating all around the county, and on "the Morning of the Election Liquor
was distributed to the Company of Mr *Marrable* by his Orders, but with this
Caution, To take care they should not intoxicate themselves, least a Riot
might ensue at the Election, because he wanted a fair Poll, and every Candidate to stand or fall by his own interest; and Mr Marrable declared he ex-
pended seven Weathers [wethers], and thirty Gallons of Rum on that Occasion." Nevertheless, it seems that it was not so much on account of the

mighty barbecue that Marrable was unseated. He evidently lacked the support among the ruling gentry that had enabled Mr. Read to stand by while
others treated on his behalf. This weakness drove Marrable to a further step,
probably the decisive one in invalidating his election. He wrote a letter "to
Mr David *Caldwell*, a Man of great Interest in the County, strongly solliciting
his Interest." Marrable actually offered a bond of £500 in an attempt to have
the county divided along certain lines. Such political trafficking was disapproved of—probably the more so when employed to offset weak personal connections among the county gentry.[40]

"Treating" was not simply a way of buying support. The paternalistic dominance of the gentry was expressed in their acceptance of an obligation to
show "liberality" toward their poorer neighbors. The candidates confirmed
their characters as magnanimous gentlemen when they stood treat to all
voters, regardless of how they voted. This claim of a candidate to general respect was further attested by the readiness of fellow leaders in county society
to preside over treats on his behalf. For the most part, without a large measure of such gentry support a candidate could not possibly carry an election.

"Interest" is the key to understanding the electoral process. The word is
rich in the connotations of an entire social system based on personal relationships—kinship, neighborhood, favors exchanged, patronage given, and deference returned. Once the world in which gentlemen had a measurable "interest" is evoked, even such a familiar word as "friend" must be reinterpreted.
A "friend" was a person, whether of higher, lower, or equal station, related by
the expectation of a mutual exchange of services. In short, one's "friends"
were one's "interest." The militia and election systems were integral to this
social order—and ready instruments of it.[41]

In the county communities that made up Virginia, the formal occasions,
reinforced by the accompanying informal activities, served to establish and
maintain crucial identities and relationships. The muster defined most clearly
the qualities and obligations of free manhood, the fundamental status that
conferred full membership in society. The court embodied law and property,
establishing genteel proprietors as the upholders of these twin pillars of the
social order. Elections provided for the endorsement of the most eminent of
the gentlemen to attend the legislature at the center of the province as custodians and revisers of the body of laws itself. These institutions all displayed

principles of descending authority—from those whose rank and accomplishments fitted them for rule, to those whose circumstances and limited understanding ordained that they should be ruled. Elections and even treating, however, signified that the government of free men required their own participation and consent.

6

TEXTURES OF COMMUNITY
Mobility, Learning, Gentility, and Authority

Fields, houses, and quarters have been viewed—shapes cut in a forested landscape. There have been glimpses of the dancing at reaping frolics, at Christmastime, and on the slaves' day of rest. We have looked in on recurrent occasions: the sociable weekly gatherings in the churchyards; the reading aloud of the liturgy from the heavy octavo prayer books on raised desks in the high-windowed churches; and the pronouncement of judgments from raised benches in the finely styled brick courthouses. Forms of contest have been discernible everywhere—but most expressly at racetracks, polling tables, muster fields, and taverns. All of these situations convey impressions of people and their ways of life. Yet the study of landscapes with figures and the analysis of dramatic actions in particular settings still leave questions to be answered about the society as a whole—its distribution of power and the kinds of total life experiences that it afforded its members.

EXPERIENCE OF COMMUNITY

Judaeo-Christian cosmology provided an encompassing framework for Anglo-Virginians' perceptions of everyday life—the work in fields and orchards, the way of understanding health and sickness. Yet the Virginia parish was no simple, traditional Christian village sustained by a strong sense of continuity between the past and the present. Considered from day to day, week to week, month to month, participation in community in Virginia was distinctly intermittent, a characteristic of life in the Chesapeake that was amplified by the very high mobility of much of the population.

Tobacco culture was land greedy and involved those who were sustained by it in a constant western movement to clear new areas. The result was a dispersal of the bonds of society over wide distances, transcending the narrower bounds of locality. The social experience of Virginians, then, was marked by a sharp dichotomy. On the one hand the long settlement of eastern regions had built up communities of interlocked families; on the other hand all these families were likely to have members, or entire branches, settled away to the west. Many men would be compelled to abandon worn holdings that were reduced in size by successive divisions between heirs.

The reminiscences of Devereux Jarratt have already served to illustrate the appearance, diet, and domestic celebrations of humble persons in the 1730s and 1740s, when he was growing up. The old clergyman's autobiography is both charged with censorious judgments on traditional Anglican religious life and colored by the idealizations of order and respect that age is apt to impose upon memories of childhood years. Nevertheless the recollections provide direct insights, unique for the eighteenth century, into poor Virginians' alternating experiences of community and transience through the course of their lives.

Jarratt was born in 1733, the youngest of four, in New Kent County, where his father's father had settled long previously, taking up some 1,200 acres of frontier land. Two of his grandfather's three offspring married and settled in this locality. His autobiography describes growing up in a world of familiar neighbors and kinfolk. Devereux's two older brothers settled and made their life careers as planter-artisans (like their father) in this setting, so that when their young sibling was left an orphan in their care, he did not have to migrate to an unfamiliar community. The break came—as must commonly have been the case—when Jarratt found himself approaching manhood with a meager patrimony (£25 in cash, but no land) and a substantial ambition to better himself in the world. His first step in this direction shows how the ties of Virginia neighborhoods might extend beyond the local boundaries that the more mobile members of the community had crossed.

The ambitious youth had applied himself to the study of practical arithmetic:

> I was so well skilled in the *Division of Crops*, the *Rule of Three*, and
> *Practice*, that, you may be sure, the fame of my learning sounded far.
> One *Jacob Moon*, living in Albemarle county, about one hundred miles
> [west] from New Kent, had also heard how learned I was. He, being a
> native of New Kent, and perhaps, prejudiced in favour of his old
> county folk, sent me word that he should be glad to employ me as a
> schoolmaster.

The affective bonds of the old home community continued to pull at the
youngster once he had made the move west—as they evidently had done on
Jacob Moon. In the new environment Jarratt was laid low by the "quotidian ague" (malaria). He recalled that he "frequently wept, at the thought
of . . . being in a land of strangers, at a great distance from the place of [his]
nativity, and . . . nearest relations." After a few years away he returned to the
scene of his childhood, where he found that his visit was made much of: "My
brothers and their wives, and all the black people on the plantation seemed
overjoyed at my coming. The pleasure of seeing each other was mutual, and
our congratulations are not easily described. Nothing was thought too good
for me, which their houses afforded, and they wished to entertain me, in the
most agreeable manner." This last meant not only opening cellars that "in the
season of autumn . . . were generally stored with good, sound cider," but also
calling in neighbors and kinfolk for "frolic and dance." Eventually time and
continued social and geographical mobility largely detached Devereux Jarratt
from these connections, yet it is clear that an idealization of the values and
relationships of folk neighborhood retained a powerful influence over his consciousness to the end of his life.[1]

The variety of dwellings made a pattern in the landscape that emphasized
the dichotomized experiences of community and dispersal that confronted
Virginians in their daily lives. Great houses were built, and they endured as
monuments of family pride in the older settled parts, although their continuing magnificence would come to be increasingly dependent on the surpluses that slaves produced in the newly carved-out quarters farther to the
west. The members of these dispersed "households" were constantly coming
and going between old settlements and new productive units. (The masters

and their families had, furthermore, a widespread web of kin and connection so that the colony was—at their own level—almost their parish.) Humbler houses, standing amid the fields that sustained them, were much less involved in such movement, but their occupation by one particular family was far more likely to be transient. The great houses with their family burying grounds beside them came, then, to be set apart as monuments of a precious continuity of generations to which few of the neighboring small plantations, and perhaps none of the slave quarters, could aspire.[2]

SOCIAL MOBILITY

Rank was not defined in old Virginia simply by wealth. Yet there was a direct connection between status and the ownership of sufficient property to support a great household. It was this close association that most impressed an acerbic Scots tutor, James Reid, who felt himself to be very much an observer from outside the charmed circle:

> If a [man] . . . has Money, Negroes and Land enough he is a compleat Gentleman. These . . . hide all his deffects, usher him into (what they call) the best of company, and draws upon him the smiles of the fair Sex. His madness then passes for wit, his extravagance for flow of spirit, his insolence for bravery, and his cowardice for wisdom. . . . Learning and good sense; religion and refined Morals . . . have nothing to do in the composition. These are qualifications only proper for a dull, plodding, thoughtfull fellow, who . . . cannot appear in polite company for want of Negroes: Nor at horseraces and Cock matches for want of skill in those . . . heroic exercises.[3]

This view of the Virginia gentry, as the crass winners in a ruthless social gambling game, was extreme—a harsh caricature—but it was not without insight.

Display and overt self-assertion were manifest wherever Virginians gathered together. Even the prevailing convivial style became a medium for contest as "each one endeavoured to display his talent in wit, to the best advantage." Men were drawn great distances to be where the action was. Gambling, whether with money or reputation, was inseparable from the ubiquitous competition in politics and high living, as well as in gaming more narrowly defined. Wagers on the outcome of contests only made commitment and its consequences more explicit.[4]

"Deep Play" is a concept of irrationality applied by Jeremy Bentham to gambling for stakes so high that the possible returns from winning cannot outweigh the destructive consequences that flow from losing the play. Yet people cannot keep away from such contests. "They play away and play it all away," the hard-working, thrifty Colonel Landon Carter agonized in the diary that he designed his gaming son should read one day when his father was dead. Important Virginia social values were asserted in forms of deep play, where persons, closely watched by all the company, would make bids for acceptance at high valuation. To be forced to cry out "King's cruse" to save the sight of one's eye (or one's manhood itself) in a bout of wrestling; to be unhorsed and rolled in the dust at the start of a quarter race; to see one's lovingly groomed champion cock, with half a year's income wagered upon him, pierced through the head by the first deft blow of his opponent's gaff; to be "cut out," without a murmur of protest from the watching circle, before one had fairly got into the step of the jig—in short, to lose in a world where personal prowess was of great consequence—would mean a momentary taste of annihilation. In this pre-humanitarian age, where chattel slavery was an unquestioned fact of life, people came to these events as much for the excitement of seeing some laid low by defeat, as they did for the pleasure of exulting in identification with the winners.[5]

Generally, then, this society must be understood as an almost paradoxical compound of close neighborhood ties and the incessant mobility of restless striving. It was a system in which networks of personal relationships had a functional—indeed structural—importance they no longer have in our urbanized scheme of things. It was also a success culture sharply dividing the winners from the losers. (This aspect of competition was profoundly reinforced by the demand, as a matter of course, that slaves assume the posture of uncontesting losers. Much of the assertiveness of white men in this society, their demonstrations of combative independence, stemmed from the importance of demonstrating before all the world that one was not a socially immobilized, apparently humbled slave.) A perpetual struggle for advantage was constantly wrenching against the confines of settled community and the fixities of hereditary land tenure.

VALUES AND RELIGION

A strong correspondence is to be expected between a society's ways of doing things and the outlook on the world prevalent in its midst. One might predict that traditional Virginia culture, oriented to the achievement of success and lacking intensely restrictive community horizons, would be characterized by worldliness of outlook. Measurement of these variables would be difficult, if not impossible, but impressions, supported by the testimony of many witnesses, suggest that such was indeed the case, and that the tone in old Virginia was highly secular. General involvement in display of prowess meant that religious piety was considered appropriate only for the old and for those approaching death. An Anglican minister noted that "generally speaking, none went to the *table* [for communion], except a few of the more aged," and James Ireland remembered of his youth that, "comparing [his] present pleasures" with "confused ideas of the happiness of heaven," he had felt that he would not have foregone the former for the sake of the latter. He therefore "determined to pursue" worldly engagements until he "arrived to such an advance in years that [his] nature would . . . enjoy no further relish." He persuaded himself that "a merciful God . . . would accept of a few days or weeks of [his] sincere repenting."[6]

Institutionalized religion found its principal expression in services as appointed in the Book of Common Prayer. But churchgoing in colonial Virginia had more to do with expressing the dominance of the gentry than with inculcating piety or forming devout personalities. The intended congruence between Virginia Anglicanism and the ethos of the ruling elite is neatly suggested in the way the Reverend Mr. Hugh Jones described what was expected of the clergy in the colony:

> Neither would they have meer scholars and stoicks, or zealots too rigid
> in outward appearance, as they would be without loose and licentious

profligates; . . . And as in words and actions they should be neither too reserved nor too extravagant; so in principles should they be neither too high or too low: The Virginians being neither favourers of popery . . . nor of presbytery. . . . They must be such as can converse and know more than bare philosophy and speculative ethicks, and have studied men and business . . . as well as books; they may . . . be facetious and good-humoured, without too much freedom and licentiousness.[7]

Wanted, a parson who can carry his religion, as he should his liquor, like a gentleman!

LITERACY AND ORAL CULTURE

Although erudition was not required of him, the rector of the parish was one of the specially commissioned custodians of "higher culture." The importance of having gentlemen in the rectories arose from the qualities attributed to a gentleman in this society, and in particular from the connection between status and education. In a world where illiteracy and semiliteracy were widespread, the culture of common folk was transmitted and sustained in ways very different from those that exist in an urbanized society where schooling is compulsory. Much of the specific content of the oral culture that migrant English tillers of the soil adapted and developed on the shores of the Chesapeake is as unknown as that of their eighteenth-century African counterparts, but enough traces exist to enable us to characterize the milieus of the large proportion of whites to whom books were effectively closed as direct sources of knowledge.

Language is, in all cultures, the primary form of communication, and thus words are the main elements used to construct knowledge of the world. Familiarity with writing has profound effects on a person's sense of the nature of words. Studies made possible by the tape recorder have shown that a great transition takes place in cultures—and so in consciousness—when high levels of literacy are established. Writing is a medium through which communication can take place without the always-demanding presence of others.

Proliferation of printed books over the centuries, for example, greatly encouraged private reading where previously reading aloud had prevailed. When private readers withdrew into a secluded realm where discourse reached them in solitude, modes of silent thought developed—thus was engendered "individualism." Where systems of printed communication are well established, impersonal media are the primary and continuing sources of knowledge about the world. Oral cultures and the residual oral subcultures of the unlettered, on the other hand, have no means to sustain communication apart from the personal interaction of the members of society, and therefore have fewer resources for introverted modes of silent thought. This contrast is probably one of the most important differences between "modern" and "premodern" social systems.[8]

Within an oral culture words can only be experienced in socially structured contexts where setting, dress, and demeanor are likely to ensure that communication reinforces existing relationships. It is partly for this reason that so much stress has been placed in the preceding chapters on dramatic scenarios and the dramaturgical forms of expression necessarily employed in face-to-face communities.

Virginia society in the eighteenth century—like that of much of Western Europe at the time—was under the influence of *both* the oral-dramatic *and* the script-typographic media of communication, each generating its distinctive sense of the nature of language and of the world itself. The presence of the written word was felt throughout the society—even slaves were required to carry "passes" (i.e., letters from their masters) before they could lawfully go off the plantation. Nevertheless, levels of literacy were not high. The best and most carefully corrected measurements of the ability of persons to write their own names show a close correlation between signature rate and social rank. Ratios between signed names and marks made in lieu of signatures indicate that the level of literacy among white males rose markedly, from 46 percent in the 1640s to 62 percent by about 1710. After that date literacy seems not to have altered much until some time in the nineteenth century. In the eighteenth century about two-thirds of the adult white males could sign; among females the signature rate was much lower. The internalization of the alphabet by Anglo-Virginians had stabilized at a low level. The direct influence of the written word remained comparatively weak. Persons with little or no literacy training could not attain effective access to knowledge through the print forms available at the time. Slaves who could forge a "pass" certainly feature in the records, but blacks who found the opportunity to acquire such skills must have been a tiny proportion of the whole population. In aggregate, then, some three out of every four persons whom a growing child in Virginia would have met were largely or entirely confined within the oral medium. Yeomen's offspring would have found a very minimal literacy fairly general in their world, but they would have continually encountered total or almost total illiteracy among slaves and women. The children of the gentry would have had their skills and sensibilities informed by a divided experience: they were confronted by books and the more literate speech of parents, neighboring gentlefolk, and teachers on the one hand, and by the altogether orally conditioned language usages of slaves, some servants, and other humbler Anglo-Virginians on the other.[9]

The social and cultural patterns surrounding developed literacy in Virginia were complex and multilayered. At one extreme, very little removed from the realm of the wholly oral, were the minimal skills that allowed the scrawling of an awkward note to a storekeeper or the painstaking decipherment of a recipe for a cure from a farrier's manual. At the other extreme was cosmopolitan, "polite" literature—the slow creation of more than two hundred years of the development of printing. Within this expansive realm "individualistic" personalities could come into existence free from the direct pressures of the immediate presence of others. Access to this realm was limited to the few who had the opportunity to immerse themselves intensively in the reading of books. Coexisting with this comparatively new world of silent literary communications was another cultural form that was ancient and in the process of being superseded but that still retained much of its power. "Speaking books" is a suitable term to convey the function of the highly important bodies of written words, such as the Bible and the common law reports (together with the extensive commentaries surrounding each), that derived from manuscript traditions in which the written word was closely tied to formal speech. The sacred texts had originated in oral performance settings, and their constant recitation in churches and lawcourts ensured their exalted authority in the word-of-mouth culture of common people. Within this tradition, "learning" consisted of the skills to interpret the Scriptures and other authoritative writings and to communicate to an audience the customary and indispensable knowledge that had been stored within these writings from ancient times.[10]

FROM FOLK TO GENTEEL CULTURE

Basic forms of oral culture, and some of the ways in which they interlocked with the valued wisdom contained in printed books, can best be traced in what has already been introduced as the only substantial Virginia account of the childhood and youth—the socialization—of a humble son of the soil. From the vantage point of the social eminence to which the Reverend Mr. Devereux Jarratt had climbed, he was moved in his declining years to look back on the world of his boyhood, and on the steps of his advancement. Jarratt's recollections of the processes by which he acquired, first, common literacy, and then access to higher learning, provide outlines of the relationship between popular culture—with its large oral component—and the authoritative realm of great books.

The young farm boy soon showed particular talents that, while exceptional, reveal the forms of verbal expression that contributed to the shaping of the outlook of the countryfolk among whom he grew up. Oral cultures are dominated by mnemonic formulas that enable their traditions to be remembered and thus to survive. Jarratt excelled in memory, and as he also had a "voice . . . remarkably tuneable, and soft, or sonorous; as the case required, . . . [he] could sing . . . with an air and grace, which excited attention and admiration," so that he was encouraged to learn "the longest *songs*" by ear. A version of "the old song of *Chevy Chase*" was evidently current in Tidewater Virginia, which the young Devereux "learned to repeat, and sing, by hearing it a few times only, though it contained near a hundred stanzas." The lad can have experienced little difficulty when his parents saw to it that he was "made . . . very perfect in repeating the *Church Catechism*," for he early found that "before [he] knew the letters of the alphabet, [he] could repeat a whole chapter in the Bible, at a few times hearing it read." From the "pregnancy of genius" thus revealed, the youngster was dubbed "*parson*." His mastery of Scripture evoked an archetypal symbolic figure.[11]

Low levels of literacy and an agrarian way of life evidently worked to sustain a vital English oral culture in Virginia during the eighteenth century. Yet that culture had for a thousand years been contained within a book-defined cosmology, bounded at critical points by the written word whose highest forms were Divinity and Law. The Bible was evidently the source of some of the most powerful oral performances that helped mold the consciousness and establish the promise of the little "parson." He heard it read aloud by the elders; he assimilated it through his ear; then he recited it aloud again. Catechism and Bible lessons were important interfaces where authoritative forms of the written word met oral culture and imprinted their shapes upon it.

In the world of farmers who grew tobacco for an export market, minimal literacy skills were a practical asset. "My parents," recalled the aged Jarratt, "neither sought nor expected any titles, honors, or great things, either for themselves or children. Their highest ambition was to teach their children to read, write, and understand the fundamental rules of arithmetic. . . . They wished us all to be brought up in some honest calling, that we might earn our bread, by the sweat of our brow, as they did." Thus at age eight or nine, young Devereux "was sent to an English school [i.e., not a Latin one] in the neighbourhood: and . . . continued to go to one teacher and other, as opportunity served, (though not without great interruptions)" until he was twelve or thirteen years old. "In this time," the boy whose ear and tongue had been so apt at mastering the stanzas of ballads and the sonorous phrases of the Authorized Version "learned to read in the Bible, (though but indifferently) and to write a sorry scrawl." In the confines of a schoolhouse—with its drudgeries of intermittent formal instruction—the promising virtuoso of oral performance became a clumsy tyro in the world of letters. At this point, long before he had developed any ease or mastery in the written medium, all schooling for Jarratt ceased. His case was not singular. The measurements (cited above) of men's and women's ability to sign their names to legal documents suggest that about half of his contemporaries among farm boys failed to get as far as he did. Few indeed went appreciably further—while their sisters were in general left incapable of forming letters at all.[12]

Both of Jarratt's parents had died by the time he was thirteen. Although the orphaned lad would later idealize his yeoman forebears' acceptance of their lot, he was unwilling to be a farmer or to learn the country carpenter's craft from his brothers.

I was not contented with the small degree of learning I had acquired, and wished for more knowledge, especially in figures. . . . To understand figures well, we reckoned the height of learning. Philosophy, Rhetoric, Logic, &c we never heard of. . . . *Arithmetic* was all and all. To acquire this, I borrowed a plain book, in manuscript, and while the horse, with which I harrowed or ploughed, was grazing an hour or two at noon, I frequently spent the time in application to that book.

At age nineteen the young field-worker was "called from the *ax* to the *quill*." (The use of these metaphors is itself evocative of a close-bounded world with its clearly discernible symbolic hierarchies of function.) His attainments in applied arithmetic won him such renown that he received the invitation—described above—to go and teach in Albemarle County, making his home with Jacob Moon, formerly of New Kent County. Yet it almost goes without saying that disappointment awaited the young hopeful in the west. Jacob Moon could not perform as well as he could promise, for he was but the overseer in charge of the Bremo quarters of Colonel Richard Cocke and so lacked the influence to gather many children under the new schoolmaster's care. Fees of £1 per child per year were the teacher's cash income, and only nine pupils attended his school.[13]

During the course of Jarratt's stay at Moon's house, "Mr. Whitefield's eight sermons, preached in *Glasgow*, were left, by some one," and since it was the first sermon book he "ever had seen, or, perhaps, heard of, [he] had the curiosity to look into it." But the young schoolmaster was still "a poor reader, and understood little of what [he] . . . read." Books and religion impinged only to a small degree on his awareness. The consciences of persons around him were unencumbered by formal piety. "The Sabbath day was usually spent in *sporting* and whether *this* was right or wrong, I believe, no one questioned."[14]

A belief that Moon's dwelling place on the banks of the upper James River was unhealthful drove Jarratt to move at the end of the year, although the school he was able to assemble in a more upland neighborhood would net him only £7 in the next twelve months. He was obliged to receive most of that sum in the form of lodging from his employers, "proportioning the time to the number of children, they sent." His first residence was "at the house of one Abraham Childers," and his recollections of that stay are a rare record of the tone of a humble farmhouse: "Here I wished to pitch my tent for the

whole year, as I found the manners of that family very much to the taste of my
. . . mind. I always had a great turn for *merriment, banter, buffoonery* and
such like. The members of the family had the same turn, consequently we
met the approbation of each other. As my ambition was always to excel in
every thing, I had a mind to, so I strove to excel in *these.*" These folk maintained a definite sense of propriety, and the youth occasionally met with re-
proofs. To Jarratt as a devout old man looking back on his unregenerate
youth, it seemed that the Childerses were "ungodly" people. Yet it is clear that
they had the same easily worn religion that he himself had been brought up
with. They had no deep sense of sin and no need for devotional reading, nor
for any intense forms of piety that might establish strict constraints on their
daily lives.[15]

A decisive change occurred in Jarratt's career at the conclusion of his al-
lotted time with the convivial Childers family. The authority that the gentry
derived from their superior command of book learning and refined manners
appears plainly in the narrative of the next stages in the young schoolmaster's
life:

> I went now to board with a gentleman, whose name was *Cannon.* He
> was a man of great possessions, in lands, slaves, &c. &c. As I had
> been always very shy of *gentlefolk* . . . imagine, how awkwardly, and
> with what confusion, I entered his house. . . . It was on a Sunday,
> P.M. when I first came to the house—an entire stranger, both to the
> gentleman and his lady. . . . The interview, on my part, was the more
> awkward as I knew not . . . what style was proper for accosting persons
> of their dignity. However I made bold to enter the door, and was
> viewed, in some measure, as a phenomenon. The gentleman took me
> . . . for the son of a very poor man, in the neighbourhood, but the
> lady, having some hint, I suppose, from the children, rectified the mis-
> take, and cried out, *it is the schoolmaster.*[16]

The rough-mannered retainer who had come to live in the "great house"
had another cause for trepidation, since he "had been told, that the lady . . .
was a *New-light,* and of sentiments so rigid and severe, that all levities of
every kind must be banished from her presence." Evangelical dissent was just
beginning its spectacular rise to prominence in Virginia. Jarratt therefore
now faced religious doctrines and a discipline that were entirely unfamiliar to

him. His mind became engaged in "some serious reflections . . . how to de-
mean [himself], in her presence," and his social ambition manifested itself in
"a *project* entirely new to [him] . . . *to act the hypocrite.*" He "had no intention
of being religious, but wished to appear so, in order to gain her good opinion." So the young man sat by while the lady "read a sermon, in *Flavel*, every
night." Sometimes in furtherance of his plan of winning favor, he would even
"ask her to read another . . . though [he] . . . understood not the tenth part
of what was read." At first, "when she was weary of reading," she would ask
him to read in his turn. "But so poor a hand did [he] make of the business,
that . . . she soon desisted asking." [17]

There came a night, however, when the conscience of the bored young
acolyte was "imprest"—or was it his ambition, in subtle form? "The text of
the sermon was, '*Then opened he their understanding.*' From which words were
pointed out, what new discoveries would open to the eye of the mind, by
means of spiritual illumination, &c." He was led to ponder his ignorance of
such things. He forsook sinful frivolity and embarked on the course of study
in divinity that in time elevated him to the genteel status of a parson in the
Church and earned him minor celebrity in the English Atlantic world as a
tract writer and correspondent of John Wesley. [18]

As yet Jarratt remained a poor schoolmaster. The patronage of a gentle-
woman (who was not at one with her husband in religious matters) was not
sufficient to spare him the vicissitudes to which his humble rank left him prey.
His second school dwindled, and he was forced to return to Moon's, where he
found that his new earnestness concerning the salvation of the soul met only
with rebuff:

> They *made light of it*—turned all off with a laugh—imputing the whole
> to *new-light cant.* . . . Moon and his wife, being *Church people,* as they
> said, could listen to nothing but what came through that channel. . . .
> I was myself . . . but little acquainted with the principles of the
> church. Nor did I understand the meaning of many scriptures, which I
> read, but I understood . . . that . . . except a man be *born again,* he
> cannot see the Kingdom of God. . . . This they did not deny, "We
> must all be *born again,*" said they, "but that is to be after we are dead."

The pursuit of higher learning was not encouraged in this easygoing ethos.
The ambitious young man had to seize opportunities as they chanced his way.

"[He] had not a single book in the world" and was too poor to order any. Fortunately for his purpose, pious tracts were to be found here and there, often little cared for, and so "by some means, [he] got hold of a little old book, in a smoky condition, which [he] found to be *Russel's* seven sermons." He borrowed it and read it again and again, but found himself still in need of some "help in understanding the scriptures." Jarratt's quest for a means to enter into the interpretation of the Bible shows the awed relationship of common people to the higher learning that towered dimly but authoritatively over them. He mentioned his need for "an expositer" of the Sacred Word to an acquaintance, who told him "of a very large book, belonging to a gentleman, about five or six miles distant across the river, *which* explained all the New Testament." After "living so long with Mr. Cannon, and [by] the resort of gentlemen to his house," Jarratt found that he "had worn off some of [his] clownish rusticity, and had become less shy of persons in the upper ranks of life." He therefore went more readily to secure a loan of this impressive book whose fame was spread so wide. It was a folio volume "called *Burkett* on the New Testament" and made the borrower "wonderfully pleased . . . because [he] found the *writer* to have been a minister of the Church." To the diligent study of this great authority the poor schoolmaster now devoted himself. He may be pictured at his pious labors: "As I had no candle, my custom was, in an evening, to sit down flat on the hearth, erect the volume on the end of a chest, which stood near, and, by the light of the fire, read till near midnight. . . . By these means . . . I soon became, what was called a good reader, and my relish for books and reading greatly increased." [19]

Some time later a return visit to his home neighborhood brought about a lapse from his newfound piety and asceticism. Back in the place where he had once been an awkward plowboy he now wore linen instead of osnaburg and had a veneer of culture. His command of genteel manners, combined with his virtuosity in the convivial style, was enough to secure him social advancement: "As I possest a great degree of vivacity, and was extremely jocose, my company was very acceptable . . . and courted by persons much my superior, in family and fortune." [20]

Jarratt's career was not to be consummated in the profane mode—perhaps by a marriage into a New Kent gentry family?—but was again deflected onto its former course when Mr. Cannon, now having a young son (in place of a daughter and a niece) to be educated, engaged him as a resident teacher at

£15 a year. Under this renewed influence he returned both to study and to evangelical piety. His patrons arranged for him to receive the Latin education that provided the indisputable cachet of gentility. With this qualification he was employed as a tutor at £40 per annum in the household of Mr. Thompson Swann and went on from there—again assisted by patrons—to be ordained by the bishop of London as a clergyman of the Church of England.

By the time Jarratt's studies raised him to a dignified station in the world, the association of learning and genteel rank had already been institutionalized in Virginia for more than fifty years. In 1690—just when the great plantation owners of Virginia were seeking to consolidate the social positions of their lineages—subscriptions were solicited from them to establish and endow a college where their sons could acquire a "liberal" education. The importance of this unprecedented investment in a collective venture was soon underscored by the decision to move the seat of government to the same locale. The College of William and Mary was a chartered foundation consisting of a corporate body of professors, mostly clergymen, under a president, who was invariably a minister. The college was tied to the Established Church by the statutory tests of conformity imposed upon its members. The faculty was under episcopal protection, since it was customary to alternate the chancellorship between the bishop of London and the archbishop of Canterbury. A more immediate surveillance was exercised by a board of visitors drawn from the great families of the James-York region and presided over by the governor of the colony. The Randolph family came to have a particular patronage and to use the chapel crypt as though it were their family vault.

At the time of its construction the college was equipped with the grandest buildings in the province—a status they did not lose throughout the colonial era—yet the institution did not become a renowned center of higher learning. Nor did its divinity school produce the numbers of native clergymen that had been predicted when royal patronage for the project was sought. Nevertheless the pious foundation was made to answer the main purpose of its Virginia sponsors. A Latin grammar school for the sons of the gentry was now maintained at public expense. Degree courses were rarely undertaken, since the college's most important function was as a provincial center where young gentlemen from the various parts of Virginia could simultaneously acquire higher accomplishments, knowledge of government affairs, and acquaintance with one another.

When it operated smoothly, the college was regarded with pride. It was complacently described in 1746 as "the Source from which so much real Happiness hath been derived to the People of this Colony." In the 1750s, when the institution came to be strife ridden, its troubles contributed (as will appear in later chapters) to a general anxiety among the leading gentry about the future of the rising generation of the elite in society.[21]

THE AUTHORITY OF THE GENTRY

The defining characteristics of gentility are elusive. At first glance being a gentleman resided in the fact itself—a claim made upon the world and accepted by the world. A complex of attributes and ways of conducting oneself were required to support the claim—deficiency in some would need to be balanced by a fuller measure of others. Appropriate demeanor, dress, manners, and conversational style were essential. These traits—especially if accompanied by a familiarity with the sources of sacred, Classical, or legal learning—gave a *presumption of gentility*, but the status of gentleman could be confirmed only if one unmistakably possessed the means of personal independence. In this slaveholding colony customary English valuation of manly independence was carried to very great heights.[22]

The quality that most nearly epitomized what was needed to make a gentleman was "liberality." This word was rich in connotations deriving from its Latin root: first and foremost, it denoted *freedom* from material necessity and the grubbing for subsistence that poverty entailed; second, it meant *freedom* from the servile subjection that the quest for satisfaction of material want imposed; third, it evoked *freedom* from the sordid subordination of considerations of honor and dignity to calculations of interest that lack of independence was presumed to involve; fourth, it was associated with *freedom* to elevate the mind by application to the authoritative books that contained the higher learning (as in the expression "liberal arts"). Ultimately the idea of "liberality" referred to a certain disposition in the soul that all these freedoms made possible—the disposition to undertake important responsibilities in the community at large. The "liberal" principles of a gentleman might be manifested in his accepting and fulfilling a commission to sit, without salary, sev-

eral days a month as justice on his county bench; or in his subscribing to in-
demnify a poor but worthy victim of misfortune—such as the horse trader
after lightning had struck at the courthouse. The same admired quality might
be revealed in the generous treating of humbler men who did their duty by
attending a muster or an election; and in a yet more down-to-earth vein, "liberality" might show itself in the breeding and racing of horses, or in the
mounting of a match of fighting cocks for the gratification of the many persons from all ranks who followed the sport.[23]

In the eighteenth-century world a man had to be either a master or a servant. State and corporate bureaucracies had not yet emerged to create broad,
impersonal spheres of salaried employment. The case of the yeoman—Jarratt's parents, for instance—makes it clear that not every master was a gentleman; but no dependent "servant" could ever be one. In England the rank
of gentleman was typically guaranteed by the ownership of broad acres of
land. In Virginia, where land was cheap and plentiful, the ownership of
slaves was essential. In both societies credit and connections won for substantial merchants the dignity of gentlemen. Social values in Virginia usually ensured that wealthy persons in trade would acquire both land and slaves. The
learning that gave access to one of the "liberal" professions also afforded a
title to gentility, but that title could only be secured by the accumulation of
an estate, or in the case of a clergyman, by establishment in a benefice. The
transformation of Devereux Jarratt from a plowboy into a gentleman was not
completely accomplished until his gentry patrons had elevated him to a parish pulpit. As rector he was assigned a role of authority in the community and
guaranteed a secure income. The entitlements of the parson, including his
stipend, were a species of freehold for life, and his parish could be sued at law
should it attempt to withhold them.[24]

The means that secured independence to the gentleman fixed the dependence of others upon him. Power—the capability of determining the actions,
even the destinies, of fellow members of society—is most generally institutionalized in the control of valued resources and the distribution of the prod-
ucts of labor. In Virginia the domination of masters over slaves was the fullest
manifestation of social power. The claims of the slave owners were limited
only by a few constraints: the difficulty of supervision, the interest of the master in preserving his property, and the real though tenuous barriers of customs
such as the right of slaves to be relieved of labor on Sundays and certain re-

ligious holidays. In a land of plenty, slaves were kept on short rations by masters relentlessly bent on collecting the surplus needed to sustain their own
proud display.

The distribution of power within the society of free men is much more difficult to define. The leading families had superior access to property in land,
either from prior purchase or from readier contacts in the secretary of the
colony's office and the King's Council, which controlled the land-grant process. Thus, these families had the power to exact a toll—in purchase price,
rent, or client obligation—from less-favored men. Yet the abundance of land
and its bounty served to ensure that competition between landowners kept
such tolls light. The low price of tobacco and the growers' heavy dependence
on imports made control of credit more important than land leasing as a basis
for the dominance of the wealthy. Studies have shown that debts owed by
humble neighbors might constitute a substantial proportion of the total assets
of a great gentleman, but the social and political implications of debt depen-
dency have not yet been explored. How many of those who were considered
to be men of "great interest" in their counties were creditors with a network
of debtors subject to their influence? Certainly the gentry's ability to secure
deference and compliance was reinforced by their share in the social power
that was inherent in the control of credit.[25]

All the different forms of gentry domination were subtly concentrated and
institutionalized in the system of local government. Seats on the county
courts and parish vestries were held by members of the ruling elite, who
served without salary and filled up their own vacancies by co-optation. They
thus simultaneously embodied "liberality" and the rightful rule of those whom
distinguished property, family, and learning set above the common folk.
Command of the law sustained this social supremacy of the gentry. "They
diligently search the Scriptures," wrote James Reid, our bitter Scottish satirist, "but the Scriptures which they search are the Laws of Virginia: for though
you may find innumerable families in which there is no Bible, yet you will not
find one without a Law-book." The exaggeration is palpable, but the observation behind it was certainly accurate. The law was the most valued branch of
higher learning in this society of assertive, litigious landowners, even though
lawyers tended to be suspect. The tendency was to emphasize the social authority of the gentlemen justices rather than the specialized authority of
professionals.[26]

The General Court, to which appeals went within Virginia, was the King's Council acting in a judicial capacity, and so was made up of great landowners not specially trained in law. It was presided over by a governor who was never drawn from among the gentlemen of the bar. At the county level the commissioning of squire justices, unsupervised by assizes of learned judges, encouraged the "determining of every thing by the Standard of Equity and good Conscience," as Robert Beverley described procedures. Beverley took pride in the way Virginia courts spurned "the impertinences of Form and Nicety." Colonel Landon Carter thought that issues should be decided rather by "Good reason and Justice" than by "Precedents" and sneered at the "Mechanical knowledge" of attorneys. In this the colonel was not disparaging law but expressing a true Virginia view of its nature. He was setting his face against the strict, literal application of what was to be found in law books and asserting a substantial role for the common sense judgments of men of affairs— gentlemen who would bring their experience of life and the wisdom of a generalized higher learning to bear on the cases before them. Indeed it was very much the gentleman's sense of right, rather than the technical interpretation of texts, that prevailed.[27]

The dispensing of common sense justice was effective in the courthouses of close county communities. Strength was derived from merging the prestige of learning with a communal consensus that was arrived at in each case with the aid of a jury drawn from the throng. Viewing the situation in this light, we can better understand the assurance with which the leaders among these gentlemen were able, during the crisis later in the century, to draft the outlines of a new rational order in the lapidary phrases of the Virginia Declaration of Rights, the Declaration of Independence, and the subsequent Bill of Rights.

The nature of jurisprudence in Virginia was very largely determined by the great continuities between the House of Burgesses, where statutes were drawn, and the local contexts where the laws were applied. The county courts conducted in the judicial mode a great deal of business that nowadays would be regarded as policy making. They administered their territories, acting as assessors and arbitrators on a great many issues that could not be encompassed within the "Mechanical" forms of pleading at law. A review of the journals of the House of Burgesses demonstrates how much the legislature served as a county court writ large. It received and settled claims against the public purse, and it regulated and arbitrated the location of ferries, tobacco-inspection warehouses, courthouses, and the boundaries of local jurisdictions. A count made from the journal of one session shows that over 30 percent of the entries can be classified as judicial or judicial-administrative, in the manner of county court arbitrations. About 25 percent of the entries related to the development of new facilities such as bridges and townships—many of which involved a substantial measure of arbitration with respect to explicit or implicit rival claims. The formal output of the Assembly—its statute roll—conceals this aspect of the work of the Burgesses. According to this record, only 6 percent of the laws could be classified as judicial-administrative, 34 percent as relating to the development of facilities, and 60 percent as other.[28]

The same cultural traditions that had made Parliament the highest court in the kingdom sustained a judicial mode of lawmaking in the colony. It is accordingly more appropriate to think of the forms of government that regulated the affairs of freemen in Virginia as authority rather than as "power." Justice, according to the ancient maxim, consists in giving to each his own. The state was perceived as having more to do with securing rights in a fixed order of things than with determining policy that would shape the future. The colonists, in keeping with "true whig" principles, exalted the authority of those whose rule consisted of judgments under law—judgments that were intended to restore balance. They dreaded the power of those who disposed of resources so as to disturb equilibrium. It followed from such a view of government that all offices of any importance would be reserved for gentlemen. The same persons were both lawgivers and law enforcers. Those who were to serve in either capacity had to be seen to have independence, learning, and liberality in order to fulfill their customary roles as expected.[29]

VIRGINIA ON THE EVE OF REVOLUTIONS

By the second quarter of the eighteenth century, the two great principles—patriarchy and money—that had governed the ordering of Virginia society from the time of first settlement had come to be associated with a developed system of social differentiation. The instruments that maintained the social order, such as the law and learning generally, had been refined. The elite had introduced more elaborate symbols, especially in architecture and ceremony, which legitimated distinctions of rank.

An enduring socioeconomic organizational structure had emerged, based on households of greatly varying size. In contrast to modern wage-labor economies or the prevalence of tenancy in contemporary England, established men—mostly proprietors—exercised direct command over the labor of their "families" of dependents. Not employees, but slaves, children, and wives (in the case of poor planters) were deployed to assist the masters in raising the crops that fed everyone and provided payments for imported necessities and amenities. The patriarchal system of social grouping and control was, however, cleft by the chasm that separated the English traditions of the masters from the Afro-Virginian culture of the bondsmen on whose labor the preeminence of substantial households rested. Race slavery engendered a jealousy of their own independence among white proprietors that reinforced formal patriarchalism. The layout and location of dwellings proclaimed the centers of the large productive units; carefully processioned boundaries defined the limits between each one and the next. At the same time courthouses, roads, stores, warehouses, and wharves revealed key points in the network that directed and controlled all-important money credits. Behavior at these centers of community declared a set of social values expressed in unending challenge and response. Proud display provoked counter-assertions—overtly in the keenly followed contest pastimes, and implicitly in the patterns of interaction that continually called forth rival demonstrations of prowess.

Regard for rules did not eliminate violence from social life but helped to contain it. Even in the ferocious wrestling bouts, great importance was attached to the observance of conditions agreed upon in advance. The needs of the propertied members of society ensured respect for law. Association with institutionalized divinity helped to give law a sacrosanct character. The parochial organization—maintained at considerable cost, under legal sanctions—expressed a concept of inclusive community in which all members shared in a corporate responsibility to maintain worship and to receive instruction in duties that were at once religious and social. The raised benches in the courthouses and the magistrates' pews at the front of the churches gave formal pre-

cedence and authority to the leading gentlemen who headed great households, commanded large credits, and had an assumed familiarity with the
books in which the essentials of law and divinity were stored.

After 1740 this order, only just settling into its newly built Classical mansions, courthouses, and churches of brick, began to undergo radical changes.
Important alterations took place in the economic system. Revolutions in
church and state were brought about by intense popular movements, which
will be the subject of studies in the second part of this work.

The emergence of preeminent families with a distinctive life-style had established a native gentry in Virginia by 1700. Resources continued to be concentrated under the control of these leading families throughout the next
century and beyond. The enforcement of the tobacco inspection acts of the
1730s—against much opposition—asserted and confirmed the domination of
the great slave owners. In the middle decades of the eighteenth century, however, the steady expansion of Glasgow merchant houses brought about a massive diversion in the flow of credit. Under the consignment system, gentlemen tobacco growers had freighted their own crops and those of poor and
dependent neighbors directly to a dealer in England, who sold it on commission. In response to orders the same dealer had returned goods of all kinds
that he bought and charged against the credits entered on his books. The
Scots interlopers, much resented yet highly successful, operated differently.
Instead of receiving and returning consignments, they sent out employees to
establish trading stores in many places throughout the colony. At such outposts these "factors" sold imported goods on credit at a high markup. In exchange they took tobacco, which they shipped to Glasgow, where it was disposed of—largely on the expanding Continental market—for the merchants'
profit. This newer system reduced the role of colonial gentlemen as interme-
diaries between small growers and overseas markets.

The loss of control of credit and the consequent reduction in direct social
power available to the squires after mid-century probably facilitated a growing
collective rejection of the requirement that all persons attend an established
parish church—a place of worship where ritual forms served so well to affirm
the cultural hegemony of the gentry. From 1740 onward diverse movements,
all with growing popular support, challenged traditional assumptions about
the nature of religion and its role in sustaining ordered community. In the

1760s and 1770s a "patriot" movement gathered support for the redefinition of customary relationships between the colony and its parent society and culture. In the ensuing turmoil the official consensus that governed social values was shattered, and conceptions of lawful authority were revolutionized.

II

MOVEMENTS AND EVENTS

The gentry dominance so subtly expressed in the great churches raised at community expense was hardly consolidated before it began to be subverted. In the fabric of the traditional order the ecclesiastical establishment proved to be the least durable strand. Signs of the unraveling of the threads of social authority that wove parish and county together started to appear in a small way in the 1740s and 1750s. A related set of disputes gives a view of the early responses of members of the gentry and of the clergy to the problems of authority that popular movements of religious dissent created.

7

THE PARSON, THE SQUIRE—AND
THE UPSTART DISSENTER

In April 1747 the Reverend Mr. William Kay brought an action before the General Court in an attempt to save himself from being turned out of Lunenburg Parish, Richmond County, where he had been minister for some years. The evicted parson's account of his difficulties is eloquent concerning the attitudes involved:

> I found to my sorrow, that I had one wealthy, Great, powerful Colonel named Landon Carter, a leading Man in my Vestry, whom I could not reasonably please or oblige. . . . I soon perceived that he wanted to extort more mean, low, and humble obedience, than I thought consistent with the office of a Clergyman, all his houts and insults I little noticed, until he publicly declared that I preached against him (which I did not), cursed and attempted to beat me, saying my Sermon was aimed at him, because I preached against pride. I replied that I was glad he applied it, for it was against every one that was proud. After this he was my implacable Enemy and swore Revenge, that if he ever got a majority in Vestry against me, he would turn me out of the parish and said he would do it, and not be accountable to the King, Bishop, Government or any Court of Judicature, and vowed he would clip the wings of the whole clergy, in this Colony.[1]

When the colonel was able to secure a majority in the vestry ("most of those," according to Mr. Kay, "his kindred relations, or such as were subject unto him"), an order was signed to discharge the parson and to "lock up the doors and Nail up the pulpits, Reading desks and windows of both Churches." The rector's glebe was leased out to lay tenants, who made depredations on his livestock. Significantly, it was these tenants, not the gentlemen of the vestry, whom the injured parson determined to challenge for his rights. The case was a protracted one, since the General Court had difficulty in deciding whether a minister who was received into a parish without being formally inducted had security of tenure. After two years the court decided in the clergyman's favor and awarded him £30 damages on April 21, 1749, but the parson's rights were once again jeopardized by the arbitrariness of the influential squire. Although a standing rule prohibited appeals to the Privy Council in cases involving less than £300, Landon Carter was able to secure permission from London for an appeal. Secretary Thomas Nelson tried to dissuade him from proceeding, but the colonel noted in his diary: "I told him neither should I be Scared out of my right. I claimed it as a Subject of Great Britain. It was an order of the King in Council to an inferior Court." In May 1753, however, Carter lost the appeal, and the colonial General Court decided in October of the same year to award the parson £200 for arrears of salary. Meanwhile sympathizers had helped Kay to secure a new parish and so end the dispute.[2]

THE PARSONS' CAUSE

Relations between Church and State in Virginia are best understood as dealings between parson and squire—between the clergy and the vestrymen who were the lay governors of the parish churches. The position of the parson was a weak one, since he was usually an immigrant without a local family basis of support. He depended for authority solely on his official status, and unlike the incumbent of an English proprietary church, he did not enjoy the formal protection of a great patron. From the start, the incoming rector of a Virginia parish had to seek alliances, ingratiating himself with powerful persons and kin groups, or else face isolation. The temper of the Virginia gentry did not make them respecters of weakness or reticent about filling a power vacuum. If the minister contemplated defying the leading men in his little world, then he might stand in need of the warning given to George Fisher and his companions as they voyaged out from England to establish themselves in Virginia:

> John Randolph, in speaking of the disposition of the Virginians very freely cautioned us against disobliging or offending any person of note in the Colony . . . ; for says he, either by blood or marriage, we are almost all related, or so connected in our interests, that whoever of a Stranger presumes to offend any one of us will infallibly find an enemy of the whole, nor, right nor wrong, do we ever forsake him, till by one means or other, his ruin is accomplished.[3]

The parson's dependence on the goodwill of the gentry of his parish was apt to engender a sense of insecurity and to be a source of endemic conflict. In a slaveholding society personal independence was a supreme value, and a man forced into client status was inevitably degraded. Members of the clergy, therefore, were understandably anxious about issues relating to tenure and guaranteed income. The ministers sensed a disparity between their actual status and the dignity to which they felt their sacred office and expected proficiency in higher learning entitled them.

The dispute between the vestrymen and the Reverend Mr. Kay had repercussions beyond parochial boundaries. By highlighting the uncertain legal rights of the parsons, it served in the first instance to induce the colonial General Assembly to take steps to regularize the clergy's position. In May 1749 the Assembly enacted an amended version of the old "Act for the better Support of the Clergy." Under the revised statute, a minister was given legal tenure from the time of his reception into a parish, even if the vestry did not present him to the governor for formal induction. The parsons came to look upon this law as their charter of independence and to guard jealously against encroachments upon it.[4]

A mood of militancy became apparent among the clergy. Their new assertiveness in turn engendered ill feeling and fanned flames of anticlericalism. Both sentiments were carried to an extreme when the Virginia General Assembly, for the second time within four years, passed an act (known as the Twopenny Act) that effectively curtailed the value of the salaries that the statute of 1749 had entitled the ministers to receive. A meeting of parsons in Williamsburg appealed to the authorities in England to have this measure disallowed. Their complaints, together with English elaborations of them—all highly disparaging to the ruling gentry of a colony that prided itself on loyalty to Church and King—were soon published in Virginia. Colonels Landon Carter and Richard Bland, both staunch churchmen, rushed into print to defend the Assembly and denounce the machinations of the priesthood. The laymen charged the parsons with avarice and deceit in the manner of their appeal. Their disloyalty in calling the acts of the representatives of the people of Virginia into question before the imperial authorities was clearly what gave deepest offense. The Privy Council upheld the appeal and disallowed the Twopenny Act in 1759, but by that time the law, enacted as a temporary expedient, had already expired. The clergy could only turn the token victory into an actual one by bringing lawsuits to recover the damages they had sustained during the time the allegedly null and void act had been enforced. Four such suits in four different courts—all proved unsuccessful. The Parsons' Cause, as the suits came to be called, did keep resentment alive, however— and gave young Patrick Henry his debut as a popular orator.[5]

SOURCES OF DISCORD

Seen as an anticipation of the Revolutionary struggle over the nature and distribution of jurisdiction within the British dominions, the Twopenny Act conflict has assumed considerable constitutional significance. Considered in its immediate context, however, the Parsons' Cause is best understood as the culmination of a series of clashes between increasingly anticlerical squires and increasingly assertive clergymen. The sharpest anticlerical polemics came, ironically, from two devout orthodox churchmen, Colonels Carter and Bland. Why did the parsons come to be highly defensive of their legal rights and clamorous for a more dignified establishment? Why did they meet with sharp reproof from those who might have been expected, at least in principle, to give them support?

The increased assertiveness of the clergy arose in part from the nature of things in a developing colonial society. In raw, early stages, settlements can only appear as outposts of the mother country—improvisations and makeshift arrangements seem appropriate enough. But as a colony matures, refines its forms, and becomes a province rather than an outpost, so its inhabitants will feel a more urgent need to make up a full complement of the institutions found in the parent society that supplies the model for a completed whole. The clergy's striving in the 1750s reveals a persistent desire to escape from the merely ad hoc status of individual ministers hired by scattered colonial communities. They aspired not only to win secure possession of their livings but also to gain recognition for themselves as a corporate body. They hoped that by frequent conventions the whole society, as well as the parsons, should become "acquainted with the dignity and the duties of their Sacred office." To accomplish this it seemed essential that their annual salaries be converted as far as possible into an inviolable legal right of property, analogous to the tithes of beneficed clergymen in England. Only then could the Virginia clergy feel themselves securely contained within an established church endowed with the proper forms. The Assembly's claim to a right to adjust the salaries from time to time as it saw fit, was anathema. If the parsons acquiesced, they would "become dependants," no better than "mere servants to the House of Burgesses to be ranked with their doorkeepers for bread." The clergy viewed this as a total surrender of their aspirations to formalized authority. It meant no less than *"giving up a legal establishment."* [6]

The more strident claims of the clerical militants threatened to encroach upon ways of doing things to which the colonial squires had long grown accustomed. Indignant anticlerical responses expressed their resentment. An awkward dilemma faced these colonial Englishmen, adding to their irascibility. They were attached to the ecclesiastical controls that were theirs by custom. Yet their intense pride in their Anglican loyalty, consciously contrasted with dissenting traditions to the north, made resistance on church issues embarrassing. The mid-century conflicts between parsons and squires are thus intelligible as manifestations of an evolutionary phase through which maturing Virginia society was passing. There were also certain immediate reasons why the clergy were anxious to enhance their dignity at this time, and why stalwart churchmen strove to keep them under lay control.

Social disquiet was arising in Virginia by mid-century from a variety of causes, but the most dramatic signs of change appeared in the sphere of religion. A movement of dissent from the Church of England itself was commencing in the 1740s. In some places common people were departing from the established churches into congregations of their own making. The parish community at the base of the barely consolidated traditional order was beginning to fracture. The rise of dissent represented a serious threat to the system of authority. The nature and extent of the anxiety produced in Virginia by the Great Awakening—that astonishing religious revival that reached every region of colonial America—must be examined before we can understand the sudden intensification of anticlericalism.

The first signs of the coming disturbance in traditionally Anglican parts of Virginia appeared in Hanover County in about 1743 when numbers of ordinary people led by Samuel Morris, a "Bricklayer," began reading religious tracts and absenting themselves from church. The group grew, and was inspired by readings from George Whitefield's sermons. (The great evangelical preacher, a breakaway assistant of John Wesley, had preached in Williamsburg in 1739, during his first tour of the colonies.) The pious gatherings soon reached such a size that a meetinghouse was built to accommodate them. Disaffection from the Church seems to have been sufficiently general that "when the Report of these Sermons and the Effects occasioned by reading them was spread Abroad," Samuel Morris was invited to travel and conduct meetings "at a considerable Distance." The movement took a new direction in the middle of 1743 when emissaries from Hanover persuaded the Reverend William Robinson, a New Side Presbyterian missionary among the Scotch-Irish in southwest Virginia, to come and preach. * From then on the Hanover group identified themselves as Presbyterians, rather than Anglicans, and periodic visits from revivalist preachers occasioned mass meetings that created considerable commotion. At these gatherings the preachers reportedly had a way of "speaking pretty freely of the degeneracy of the [Church of England] clergy." Their followers displayed similar disconcerting tendencies; one even suggested that the bishop of London might be "an unconverted man." [7]

While the Hanover group remained isolated, it evidently did not excite much attention, although the county court had called upon some of its members to give an account of themselves, and fines had been imposed for nonattendance at church. So uncertain were these "dissenters" of their own identity before they were enlisted as Presbyterians that when asked to declare to what denomination they belonged, they had hesitated, as Samuel Morris later recalled, until, "recollecting that *Luther* was a noted Reformer, and that

---

* The "New Side" was an evangelical faction fervently committed to "rebirth" and to a requirement that ministers show strong evidence of "conversion" in addition to learning and moral rectitude.

his Doctrines were agreable to our Sentiments, . . . we declared our selves *Lutherans.*" [8]

When New Side preachers began attracting large crowds, however, the Reverend Mr. Patrick Henry, Sr., an Anglican rector of St. Paul's Parish, Hanover County, called on authorities in Williamsburg for aid. He denounced itinerancy and the subversive doctrine "that a true Christian may know whether a Minister be converted or not by hearing him preach or pray." The Reverend Mr. William Dawson, as the bishop of London's commissary, had already sought legal assistance from Benjamin Waller, clerk of the General Court. Waller had advised him in a letter of January 30, 1744/1745, that "rigor should be used, not so much to reclaim a persone Enthusiastic . . . as to deter other unthinking Mortals, whose strongest Passion is often Fear [of hellfire]." The gravest offense of which "those Simple Wretches" were guilty, "who vainly imagine they in their Folly have formed a new Light," was the "depraving and despising [of] the Common Prayer." * As itinerants the preachers were "liable to be bound to their good Behaviour & treated as Vagabonds by a Justice of the Peace." Waller pointed out that if the dissenting ministers wished to benefit from the Act of Toleration, they must seek licenses. His letter, although showing alarm at the appearance of the New Lights, was cautious concerning the possibilities of repression and concluded significantly by urging Dawson to put the Church's own house in order. [9]

Lieutenant Governor William Gooch, acting at the request of the Council, was more resolute. He denounced to the grand jury in April 1745 "certain false teachers that are lately crept into this government." The grand jury indicted one of the preachers, the Reverend John Roan, for "vilifying the Established Religion," but the charge was not sustained. Dissenting laymen were, however, called to Williamsburg for trial, and some were fined for unlawful assembly. The readiness of the grand jury to charge the dissenters with extravagant utterances indicates the manner in which alarm encouraged fantasy. On April 3, 1747, the governor and Council issued a stiff proclamation calling for "all Itinerant Preachers" to be restrained. [10]

Few editions of the *Virginia Gazette* survive to give fuller evidence concerning opinion in a wider circle of the gentry, but the extant numbers and

---

* The word "enthusiastic" then had similar connotations to "fanatic" now. The term "New Light" was sneeringly applied to those whose belief in conversion implied direct communication from God.

some indirect evidence do show clearly that the elite were expressing alarm and indignation. On October 31, 1745, approving reference was made to a letter published in February, which exposed "our modern *New Light*, and the Propagators of it" and likened itinerants to "*those who have turn'd the World upside down*." In 1748 Samuel Davies complained about satires in the newspaper against persons who abandoned vicious living to become "New Lights."[11]

The conduct of the dissenting preachers that the upholders of traditional order deplored most was their traveling about as "itinerants." Encapsulated within this pejorative epithet was a whole view of authority and society. All members of the community were required to be under a spiritual guardian who needed proper authorization to exercise his function. Itinerancy was anathema because it negated these conditions. The preachers "who make it their Study to screw up the People to the greatest heights of religious Phrenzy, and then leave them in that wild state" removed persons from the control of the old authorities without bringing them under a new one. More subversive yet were "Assemblies, especially of the common People, upon a pretended religious Account; convened sometimes by merely Lay Enthusiasts." Governor Gooch took exception to "false teachers . . . who, without order or license, or producing any testimonial of their education or sect, . . . lead the innocent and ignorant people into all kinds of delusion." The symbolic importance of the license is thus revealed. Self-appointed teachers were regarded with abhorrence, while a commission from some recognized sect, or a degree from a college, would confer a measure of the proper authority that the spiritual function required. In February 1745 the Reverend Mr. Patrick Henry, contemplating the impending arrival in Hanover County of a new contingent of preachers, exclaimed, "I wish they could be prevented, or, at least be oblig'd to show their credentials."[12]

Reactions were conditioned by considerations of social authority rather than religious doctrine as such. It would be hard to find any more striking evidence of contrasting perceptions of the varieties of dissenters than the markedly different attitude that leading Anglican churchmen expressed toward settled communities of foreign Protestants from that expressed toward "itinerants." Only a few months after he wrote a letter denouncing the New Light missionary Samuel Davies as an avaricious upstart, Thomas Lee sent a letter to the Board of Trade advocating that exemptions from Church taxes be granted to foreign Protestants who might settle in the west. Thus the formation of Lutheran and Reformed Church communities under their own framework of authority encountered little opposition in Virginia. Governor Gooch's assurances of toleration to the Scotch-Irish Presbyterians in 1738 must be seen as part of the same policy. The difference between such readily accommodated autonomous religious societies and the spirit of the Great Awakening in the 1740s is made even clearer by the behavior of certain settled dissenting ministers when they found themselves challenged by New Light or Moravian preachers. A few of them appealed to the Anglican central authorities, asking that the intruding itinerants be suppressed.[13]

The advent of Samuel Davies as settled minister to the congregation of Presbyterians in Hanover County hardly improved the situation. He was sent because the New York Synod recognized that the converts would be given no peace " 'till they were an organized Congregation, and had a Minister qualified, and their Meeting-Houses licens'd, according to Law." Yet the regularization that the new minister did achieve in April 1747 by securing a license for himself and four meetinghouses in Hanover and neighboring counties was soon offset by the alarm that his success as a preacher aroused. After granting licenses for three additional meetinghouses in Goochland, Caroline, and Louisa counties, the Council determined to check the progress of disaffection by curbing Davies's activities. A license for a meetinghouse granted by the New Kent County court on April 12, 1750, was soon revoked by the General Court. It is noteworthy that the move toward greater restraint came at a time when the provincial government, headed by Thomas Lee, president of the Council, temporarily lacked an English governor and was entirely in the hands of Virginians.[14]

A long struggle ensued over the issue of licenses, and it became clear that the Council was determined to confine the dissenters within bounds. Immediately after the New Kent license had been annulled, President Lee informed the Board of Trade that he thought the liberty sought by Davies to extend his preaching activities was "not within the words or intent of the Toleration [Act], and gives great uneasiness to the Clergy and the people." While the bishop of London supported the Council's endeavors, the Lords of Trade, never very sensitive to the needs of uneasy colonial ruling groups, gave cold comfort. They advised that "a free Exercise of Religion is so valuable a branch of true liberty, and so essential to the enriching and improving of a Trading

Nation, it should ever be held sacred in His Majesty's Colonies." They urged
the Council to do nothing "which can in the least affect that great point,"
although they might "admonish Mr. Davies to make a proper use of that indulgence which our Laws so wisely grant." The Council placed its own interpretation on these seemingly unambiguous instructions and continued to re-
fuse new licenses to Samuel Davies pending further advice from England. In
the meantime Peyton Randolph, the Virginia attorney general, prepared a
statement that revealed a determination to retain restrictions.[15]

Toleration was a shibboleth in the eighteenth-century Anglo-American
world; it was unthinkable to question it in the open. Virginia traditionalists
such as the attorney general, however, took the view that toleration implied
only a respect for the status quo—a right of persons to continue practicing
the doctrine with which they had been nurtured, not a right to disturb existing social arrangements by embracing and propagating new beliefs. Peyton
Randolph made this clear when he advised that

> there ought not to be more than one House licensed for one Preacher
> . . . [since] the People within the Bounds of a County, will sufficiently
> employ a Preacher, and it will give great Encouragement to fall off
> f[ro]m the established Church if they [the preachers] are permitted to
> range and raise Contributions over the whole Country. . . . Besides it
> tends to sow Dissention & Confusion among the People, & can only
> be calculated to put Money into the Pocket of the Teacher, whose
> Interest does not deserve so much Respect.[16]

Samuel Davies, being aware of the forces arrayed against him, moved cau-
tiously. He advised against fruitless petitioning and even withdrew from pre-
carious positions under threat. He too appealed overseas, calling on the
Dissenting Deputies in London for help. They advised him that the Act of
Toleration placed no restriction on the number of meetinghouses that could
be licensed, or on the movement of preachers from meetinghouse to meetinghouse; but in common with many in Virginia, the deputies doubted whether
the act was in force in the colony beyond the clauses enumerated in the Virginia law of 1699.[17]

Prevailing uncertainty concerning the law undoubtedly contributed to the
anxiety surrounding the rise of dissent in the 1750s. If the Act of Toleration
was not binding in the colony, then questions of acute public concern seemed

to be effectively outside the law. Indeed, the opinion of the attorney general quoted above, although given as legal advice, consisted of policy recommendations turning on considerations of expediency. Here is another instance of the helplessness of colonial elites threatened as a result of the ill-defined outlines of their incomplete institutions. The legal status of toleration in Virginia remained uncertain until resolved by the revolutionary Declaration of Rights in 1776. Although official attempts to restrict the Presbyterians seem to have been abandoned after 1759, no formal ruling was made in their favor, and the Baptists, whose spectacular rise came in the 1760s, had to face yet more intense harassment.[18]

The House of Burgesses was largely inactive on the question of dissent, making it difficult to ascertain the attitudes of the leading country gentlemen. It seems probable that the lower house, like the county courts, was more permissive than the Council. Yet the House was not unconcerned. In 1752 it ruled that the two members returned for Hanover County had not been duly elected because they had given bonds (written guarantees with a monetary penalty attached) to voters not to create a new Anglican parish in the county. It appears from Landon Carter's diary that it was not the giving of bonds that was the principal source of offense, but the intervention of "dissenters" in Church affairs. Carter recorded that "Mr. Waller argued that the bonds given to Church of England men would be of no consequence but to new Light men they were." The House went on to order "That the said Writing and Bond, . . . given by the sitting Members, be immediately torn, and thrown under the Table." Another sign of the House's concern at the spread of religious dissent occurred the following year when the Burgesses voted their thanks to the Reverend Mr. William Stith for a sermon he had preached before them and ordered that the sermon be printed. Since the House did not often give such an order, it is notable that Stith's sermon was directed against the New Lights and was a pointed statement of "rational" (as opposed to "enthusiastic") religion and social conservatism. It was a direct rebuttal of propositions supposedly held by Samuel Davies concerning the small number of the elect destined for salvation. The explicit purpose of Stith's sermon was "to vindicate GOD's Ways to Man, . . . and to reconcile the Gospel to the Dictates of natural Justice," by showing that not only the virtuous pagans but also the ignorant poor who did their duty in their station would be saved.[19]

The legend of Samuel Davies has come to include the belief that his outspoken patriotism during the French and Indian War transformed attitudes toward Presbyterians. No positive evidence supports this interpretation, and in view of the known prejudices of the Virginia gentry against New Lights, it seems most improbable. The initial reverses of the war produced signs of a crisis of morale among Virginians—a loss of confidence in their own virtue and martial prowess. Although colonial authorities themselves issued public reproaches in an attempt to arouse a new spirit, it must be supposed that such denunciations of prevailing apathy and irreligion when coming from a dissenting minister served mainly to increase resentment toward the New Lights. When Peyton Randolph finally raised a company of gentlemen volunteers and marched them to the frontier in order to set an example for the common people, we may be sure that he was attempting to offset rather than to emulate the actions of the volunteer companies from Louisa and Hanover counties, whose Christian piety Presbyterian preachers had so pointedly contrasted with the shortcomings of recruits from traditional Anglican society. Samuel Davies was becoming a figure of some eminence in the Anglo-American world of dissenters, but since he was known for his perseverance under persecution and for his missionary work among the unconverted slaves, Davies's fame was Virginia's notoriety.[20]

The spread of New Side Presbyterianism and the defection of the common people from the Established Church in settled parts of Virginia evidently continued to arouse anxiety throughout the 1750s and on into the early 1760s. As late as 1764 the rector of a parish in the Northern Neck, to which the movement had spread, was moved to preach a sermon exposing "the tenets of the Seceders . . . called New-lights, or Moon-lights." The evidence suggests that Presbyterianism only came to acquire a measure of respectability in the eyes of the gentry when its role as the vehicle of popular disaffection was overtaken (as will be described in the next chapter) by the Separate Baptists.[21]

RECRIMINATIONS: A HOUSE DIVIDED

The emotions stirred in the running conflicts between the parsons of the establishment and the squires of the vestries and the Assembly can be explicitly connected to the beginnings of the rise of dissent, for there was remarkable agreement on the essential cause of the falling away from the Anglican communion. The leading dissenters were almost brutal in their assertions that it lay above all in the established clergy's laxity in both morals and doctrine. Members of the Church of England clearly shared this view, although they usually preferred to express it less bluntly. The clericalist movement that emerged in the 1750s derived its meaning from a desire to enhance the quality, by improving the status, of the clergy. Nowhere was this more boldly declared than in the petition that John Camm and Thomas Warrington— later militants in the Parsons' Cause litigation—brought before the House of Burgesses on May 15, 1757. They expressed concern at low standards and urged increased salaries as a means of attracting better ministers. The connection between concern over poor conditions of service and anxiety at the inroads made by dissent was made explicit in a petition to the bishop of London against the first Twopenny Act. This document complained of the deterioration of conditions that the act would surely produce and asserted that "the people here are not like to be long without instructors, because certain Dissenting teachers amongst us cannot but be thought ready & eager enough to succeed the Established Clergy." The same anxiety is revealed in a letter from the bishop's commissary, the Reverend Mr. Thomas Dawson, dated July 9, 1757. Dawson referred to the conflict over the deprivation of a delinquent minister and lamented that "this present distracted & unsettled state of our Church & Clergy" should be a "matter no doubt of great joy & triumph to the Newlights." In September 1759 the Reverend Mr. James Craig, coming young and fresh to the difficult task of sustaining the Anglican church in Lunenburg County on the southern frontier, wrote thus: "And sorry I am to say, That if the Clergy in the *Establishment* had acquitted themselves, as they ought to have done, we would have had no Occasion at this Time to use . . . any . . . Expedients to curb or expell Enthusiasm & Superstition." [22]

Few of the clergy chose to be as outspoken as Craig, and one may suppose that he was in part echoing the views of concerned gentlemen in his parish. Certainly the laity were not reticent. In one of the earliest documents relating to the Great Awakening in Virginia, Benjamin Waller concluded his advice to William Dawson (on the means of preventing the spread of dissent) by suggesting that "the immoral & almost scandalous Lives" led by some of the ministers of the establishment "gives the Enemy too much Occasion of reproach. . . . If therefore the Heads of the Churches would join pious Examples to gentle & charitable Persuasions, these poor Souls who are lead astray by every blast of vain Doctrine . . . would be more wrought upon than by Severity which they will call Persecution for Conscience Sake." Even more pointed was an anonymous letter to the bishop of London, dated February 1, 1754, protesting: "My zeal for religion as profess'd in the Church of Engl[an]d (of which I am a member), prompts me to add that it is easy to determine whether the interest of the Church or that of the dissenters, is most likely to prevail here, where the former is promoted by some of the weakest & most worthless men; and the latter by men of sufficient learning adorned with piety & virtue." [23]

In his pamphlet entitled *A Letter to the Right Reverend Father in God*, Landon Carter elaborated a similar point of view without sparing any praise for the New Lights. Meeting the bishop's strictures on the recent rise of religious dissent in Virginia, he stated: "It was the Disrespect to some few of the Clergy that occasioned the Dissension. . . . Whilst *Faith* and *Works* went Hand in Hand, in Instances of pastoral Care, even *Whitfield* did but hum and buzz, and die away like the Insect of the Day; but, when . . . Faith had nothing to distinguish it from the *Emptiness of Sound* in the Preacher, a *Davies* was then able to collect his Admirers." [24]

While everyone agreed on the diagnosis of the malady, few concurred on the prescription for remedying it. The ministers sought to improve their standing as "Gentlemen, Christians and Clergymen," so that by having sufficient social authority they might reverse the movement away from the Church. Laymen like Landon Carter, on the other hand, called for disinterested devotion from the clergy, if not apostolic poverty. Reform, he maintained, must begin with the clergy's own morals, for only "if anyone would find out a Cullender to separate the bad [parsons] from the Good," would Carter "Join with the Petitioners" for higher salaries. The squire clearly wished to confirm the subordinate status of the clergy, demanding that they accept a discipline imposed by lay authorities. This would ensure that "those of the Clergy, who had fled to the Calling, as the dernier Resort for a Livelihood . . . either accommodated their Behaviour . . . or became really Men of pious Dispositions." By such measures alone, Carter argued, would "the People, who are ever strongly acted on by Example," be retained within the Church. "Is the Church deserted?" he asked the bishop of London. "Secure the Virtue and Decency of the Ministry . . . check the vicious Practice . . .

by which the Church is often disgraced with meanness . . . you will then see the wandering Flocks gathered to their former Folds."[25]

Neither of these rival prescriptions could be dispensed to the ailing Church in the circumstances of the time. Nor could they have worked a cure, since they were addressed to the institutional symptoms rather than to the causes of cultural revolt.

The Established Church was an integral part of the fabric of colonial Virginia society and its system of authority. The crisis of the Church and the helplessness of its adherents therefore had broad implications. Helplessness breeds resentment and recrimination, so that a house threatened is frequently a house divided. The Church of England in Virginia conformed to this pattern. The clergy were the most directly threatened, and it is humanly understandable that, reviled by their adversaries and resented by their own laity, numbers of them should have sought strength in a jealous corporate unity and in appeals overseas. Intensified anticlericalism was an equally understandable consequence of the gentry's exasperation with a ministry that, although unable to retain the allegiance of the common people to the establishment, sought increased remuneration and privileges.

In the end the conflict led to no triumphs. Both parties sustained damaging defeats—the anticlericals in the disallowance of the Twopenny acts, the clergy in the odium of unpopular and unsuccessful litigation. The Virginia legislature was restricted in its right to regulate affairs relating to the clergy; but the clergy discovered that the crown was helpless to support them effectively against hostile local pressures. The affair revealed, indeed, the predicament of the Virginia gentry. Confronted by disturbing movements of subversive tendency, they could not defend their interests by closer alliance of church and state because the ultimate levers of legitimate authority and patronage in these spheres lay overseas and outside their control.

The commotions created by the rise of a new sect soon drew attention away from the Hanover dissenters and their Presbyterian missionaries. In 1754 Shubal Stearns, the apostle of the militant Separate Baptists, came from Connecticut through the backcountry to North Carolina. His emissaries and those they recruited found ready followers in Virginia. A strong, truly popular movement developed in the 1760s.

8

POPULAR UPSURGE
The Challenge of the Baptists

An intense struggle for allegiance had developed in the Virginia countryside during the decade before the Revolution. Two eyewitness accounts may open to us the nature of the conflict. First, a scene vividly remembered and described by the Reverend James Ireland etches in profile the postures of the contestants. As a young man Ireland, who was a propertyless schoolmaster of genteel origin, had cut a considerable figure in Frederick County society. His success had arisen largely from his prowess at dancing and his exuberant facility as a satiric wit. Then, like many other young men at this time (*ca.* 1768), he became "awakened to a sense of [his] guilty state" and withdrew from the convivialities of gentry society. An older friend and patron of Ireland's, hearing that his young protégé could not be expected at a forthcoming assembly, sensed the challenge to his way of life that was implicit in Ireland's withdrawal. He swore instantly that "there could not be a dance in the settlement without [their young friend] being there, and if they would leave it to him, he would convert [him], and that to the dance, on Monday; and they would see [Jemmy] lead the ball that day." Frederick County, for all its geographical spread, was a close community. Young James learned that his patron would call, and dreaded the coming test of strength:

> When I viewed him riding up, I never beheld such a display of pride in any man, . . . arising from his deportment, attitude and jesture; he rode a lofty elegant horse . . . his countenance appeared to me as bold and daring as satan himself, and with a commanding authority [he]

called upon me, if I were there to come out, which I accordingly did,
with a fearful and timorous heart. But O! how quickly can God level
pride. . . . For no sooner did he behold my disconsolate looks, emaci-
ated countenance and solemn aspect, than he . . . was riveted to the
beast he rode on. . . . As soon as he could articulate a little his eyes
fixed upon me, and his first address was this; "In the name of the Lord,
what is the matter with you?"[1]

The evident overdramatization in this account is most revealing for it displays
the tormented convert's heightened awareness of the contrast between the
social world he was leaving and the one he was entering.

The confrontation between evangelicalism and the traditional order in
Virginia had begun with the Hanover Awakening in the 1740s, but it entered
into its fiercest and most bitter phase as the New Light Separate Baptists
moved into the longer-settled parts of Virginia in the years after 1765. The
social conflict was not over the distribution of political power or of economic
wealth, but over the ways of men and the ways of God. By the postures of the
antagonists we may see how the sides were drawn. On the one hand there was
a mounted gentleman of the world with "commanding authority," and on the
other hand there was a guilt-humbled God-possessed youth with "disconsolate looks . . . and solemn aspect."

A second scene—this time in the Tidewater—reveals the characteristic
responses of the forces arrayed. A 1771 diary entry gives a description of the
disturbance of a Baptist meeting by some gentlemen and their followers intent on upholding the cause of the Established Church:

Brother Waller Informed us . . . [that] about 2 Weeks ago on the Sabbath day Down in Caroline County he Introduced the Worship of God
by Singing[.] . . . While he was Singing the Parson of the Parish [who
had ridden up with his clerk, the sheriff, and some others] would Keep
Running the End of his Horsewhip in [Waller's] Mouth, Laying his
Whip across the Hym Book, &c. When done Singing [Waller] proceeded to Prayer. In it he was Violently Jerked off of the Stage, [they]
Caught him by the Back part of his Neck[,] Beat his head against the
ground, some Times Up[,] Sometimes down, they Carried him through
a Gate that stood some Considerable Distance, where a Gentleman
[the sheriff] Give him . . . Twenty Lashes with his Horse Whip. . . .

Then B[rother] Waller was Released, Went Back Singing praise to
God, Mounted the Stage & preached with a Great Deal of Liberty.[2]

Violence of this kind had become a recurrent feature of social and religious
life in Tidewater and Piedmont. The questions that arise are: What kind of
conflict was this? What was it that aroused such antagonism? What manner
of man, what manner of movement, was it that found liberty in endurance
under the lash?

The remainder of the narrative gives fuller understanding of the meaning
of "liberty" and of the true character of this encounter. Asked "if his Nature
did not Interfere in the time of the Violent persecution, when whiping, &c.,"
Waller "answer'd that the Lord stood by him . . . & pour'd his Love into his
Soul without measure, & the Bretheren & Sisters Round him Singing praises
. . . so that he Could Scarcely feel the stripes . . . Rejoicing . . . that he was
Worthy to Suffer for his Dear Lord & Master."[3]

Again contrasted postures appear: on the one hand there was forceful, indeed brutal, response to the implicit challenge of religious dissidence; while
on the other hand can be seen an acceptance of suffering sustained by shared
emotions that gave release—"liberty." Both sides were, of course, engaged in
combat, yet their modes of conducting themselves were diametrically opposite. If we are to understand the struggle that had developed within Virginia society, we must look as deeply as possible into the divergent styles of
life—at the conflicting visions of what life should be—that are reflected in
this episode.

Opposites are intimately linked not only by the societal context in which
they occur but also by the very antagonism that orients them to each other.
The strength of the fascination that accompanied hostility to the New Lights
is evident from the numerous accounts of men who were at first drawn to
Baptist meetings to make violent opposition, and at a later time, or even
then and there, came "under conviction" and experienced conversion.[4]

THE APPEARANCE OF A COUNTERCULTURE

The social world of the Baptists seems so striking a negative image of gentry-
dominated milieus that it must be considered to have been shaped to a large

extent in reaction to the dominant culture. Of course evangelical counterculture was no more exclusively the growth of Virginia soil than was the style of
life of the country gentleman. In this study we are looking at particular provincial variants of a confrontation that had already arisen in metropolitan
society (evident in the "Methodism" of the Wesleys and George Whitefield)
and had already created considerable disturbances in other provinces. It was
from New England that the first Separate Baptist missionaries came to Virginia, bringing their vision of an austere way of life that eschewed the refinements of gentility and the customary indulgences of traditional popular culture. Significantly, the intrusive movement of radical religious dissent did not
initially take hold in places where it would have had to oppose a mature establishment in full strength. The first Separate Baptist churches were formed
in southern and Piedmont Virginia where institutions, although present as
patterns of expected development, were not yet underpinned by generations
of great-family dominance, as they were in the Tidewater. Nevertheless, during the tumultuous 1760s and 1770s the values and organization of the rebels
in religion were inexorably carried from the peripheral to the longer-settled
regions.[5]

Contemporaries were struck by the contrast between the challenging gaiety
of traditional Virginia formal exchange and the solemn fellowship of the Baptists, who addressed each other as "Brother" and "Sister" and were perceived
as "the most melancholy people" who "cannot meet a man upon the road,
but they must ram a text of Scripture down his throat." The finery of a gentleman who might ride forth in a gold-laced hat, sporting a gleaming Masonic
medal, must be contrasted with the strict dress of the Separate Baptist, who
"cut off" his hair and explicitly renounced such "superfluous forms and Modes
of Dressing . . . [as] cock't hatts."[6]

The Baptists' appearance was austere, to be sure, but we shall not understand the deep appeal of the evangelical movement, or the nature and full
extent of its pointed negation of the style and vision of the gentry-oriented
social world, unless we look into the rich offerings beneath this somber exterior. Converts were proffered some escape from the harsh realities of disease, debt, overindulgence and deprivation, violence and fear of sudden
death, that were the common lot of small farmers. They could seek refuge in
a close, supportive, and orderly community, "a congregation of faithful persons, called out of the world by divine grace, who mutually agree to live to-

gether, and execute gospel discipline among them." To obtain entrance into this fellowship, a candidate related experiences of profound personal importance, which would certainly be heard with respect, however humble the candidate's station. There was community resonance for deep feelings, since despite their sober face to the outside world, the Baptists encouraged in their religious practice a sharing of emotion to an extent that would have elicited crushing ridicule in gentry-dominated society. Personal testimonies of the experiences of simple folk have not come down to us from that time, but the records clearly show the central importance given to narrations of the workings of grace upon the souls of the candidates for admission. A communal reliving of conversion, the decisive event in the lives of all the members, is evoked by such recurrent phrases in the church books as: "And a Doore was opened to receive Experiances." The Baptist search for deep fellow feeling must be set in contrast to the formal distance and rivalry in the social exchanges of the traditional system.[7]

The supportive relationship that fellowship in faith and experience could engender appears to have played an important part in the spread of the movement. For example, about the year 1760 Peter Cornwell of Fauquier County sought out in the backcountry one Hays of pious repute, whom he settled on his own land for the sake of godly companionship. "Interviews between these two families were frequent, and their conversation religious and devout; in so much that it began to be talked of abroad as a very strange thing. Many came to see them, to whom they related what God did for their souls . . . to the spreading of seriousness through the whole neighbourhood."[8]

A concomitant of fellowship in deep emotions was comparative equality. Democracy is an ideal, and nothing suggests that the pre-Revolutionary Baptists espoused it as such. Yet it is certain that these people, who called one another brothers and sisters, believed that the only authority in their church was the meeting together of those in fellowship. They conducted their affairs on a footing of equality so different from the explicit preoccupation with rank and precedence that characterized the world from which they had been called. Important Baptist church elections generally required unanimity and might be held up by the doubts of a few. The number of preachers who were raised from obscurity to play an epic role in the Virginia of their day is a clear indication of the opportunities for personal fulfillment that the movement opened up to men who would otherwise have found no avenue for public achievement. The following of the early Virginia Separate Baptist movement was accurately reputed to be composed of the poor and unlearned. Only isolated converts were made among the gentry, but many among the slaves.[9]

The cohesive brotherhood of the Baptists must be understood as an explicit rejection of the formalism of traditional community organization. Fithian's diary contains an account of an Anglican parish congregation that dispersed without any act of worship when a storm prevented the attendance of both parson and clerk. This stands in contrast to the report of the Baptist David Thomas that "when no minister . . . is expected, our people meet notwithstanding, and spend . . . time in praying, singing, reading, and in religious conversation."[10]

The popular style and appeal of the Baptist church found its most powerful and visible expression in the richness of its rituals, again a total contrast to the Prayer Book reading of the colonial Church of England, where even congregational singing appears to have been rare. The most prominent and moving rite practiced by the sect was the adult baptism by which candidates were publicly sealed into fellowship. A scrap of Daniel Fristoe's journal for June 15–16, 1771, survives as a singular contemporary description of a participant's experience:

> (Being sunday) about 2000 people came together; after preaching, [I] heard others that proposed to be baptized. . . . Then went to the water where I preached and baptized 29 persons. . . . When I had finished we went to a field and making a circle in the center, there laid hands on the persons baptized. The multitude stood round weeping, but when we sang *Come we that love the lord* & they were so affected that they lifted up their hands and faces towards heaven and discovered such chearful countenances in the midst of flowing tears as I had never seen before.[11]

The emotional appeal at a popular level can even now be sensed in Fristoe's account, but it must be noted that the scene was also a vivid representation of *a* community within and apart from *the* community. One must try to see the closed circle for the laying on of hands through the eyes of persons who had been raised in Tidewater or Piedmont Virginia with the expectation that they would always have a monistic parish community that encompassed all the inhabitants within its measured liturgical celebrations. The antagonism and violence that the Baptists aroused then also become intelligible.

The celebration of the Lord's Supper frequently followed baptism and was a further open enactment of closed community. An idea of the importance attached to such public display is given by David Thomas's justification of it:

> Should we forbid even the worst of men, from viewing the solemn representation of his [the LORD JESUS CHRIST's] dying agonies? May not the sight of this mournful tragedy, have a tendency to alarm stupid creatures . . . when GOD himself is held forth . . . trembling, falling, bleeding, yea, expiring under the intollerable pressure of that wrath due to [sin]. . . . And therefore, this ordinance should not be put under a bushel, but on a candlestick, that all may enjoy the illumination.[12]

Furthermore, the potency attributed to the ordinances can be seen through the eyes of the abashed young John Taylor who, hanging back from baptism, heard the professions of seven candidates, judged them not saved, and then watched them go "into the water, and from thence," as he thought, "seal their own damnation at the Lord's table." He left the meeting "with awful horror of mind."[13]

More intimate, and evidently vital for these tight little religious associations, were the rites of fellowship. The forms are elusive, but a ritual abundance is suggested in the brief note made by Morgan Edwards concerning Falls Creek: "In this church are admitted, Evangelists, Ruling Elders, deaconesses, laying on of hands, feasts of charity, anointing the sick, kiss of charity, washing feet, right hand of fellowship, and devoting children." Far from being mere formal observances, these and other rites, such as the ordaining of "apostles" to "pervade the churches," were keenly experimented with to determine their efficacy.[14]

Preaching itself was as much a form of ritual as a means of verbal instruction. Persons commonly came under conviction or obtained ecstatic release "under preaching," thus establishing a special relationship between the neophyte and his or her "father in the Gospel." Nowhere was the incantatory character of the preaching more apparent than in the mass assemblies of the Virginia Separate Baptist Association. The pastors would preach to the peo-

ple along the way to the meeting place and back; thousands would gather for
the Sunday specially set aside for worship and preaching. Then the close, independent congregational communities found themselves merged in a great
and swelling collective. The varieties of physical manifestations, such as crying out and falling down, that were frequently brought on by the stylized
emotionalism of popular evangelical preaching are too well known to require
description.[15]

Virginia Baptist sermons from the 1770s have not survived, perhaps another sign that the preachers did not consider their purely verbal content to
be of the first importance. The Reverend James Ireland's account of his early
ministry (he was ordained in 1769) reveals the recurrence of the dominant
themes expected to lead those who were not hardened into repentance: "I
began first to preach . . . our awful apostasy by the fall; the necessity of repentance unto life, and of faith in the Lord Jesus Christ. . . . Our helpless
incapacity to extricate ourselves therefrom I stated and urged."[16]

As "seriousness" spread, with fear of hellfire and concern for salvation, it
was small wonder that a gentleman from Loudoun County should find to his
alarm "that the *Anabaptists* . . . growing very numerous . . . seem to be increasing in afluence [influence?]; and . . . quite destroying pleasure in the
Country; for they encourage ardent Pray'r; strong & constant faith, & an in-
tire Banishment of *Gaming, Dancing,* & Sabbath-Day Diversions." That the
Baptists were drawing increasing numbers away from the dominant to the in-
surgent culture was radical enough, but the implications of solemnity, austerity, and stern sobriety were more radical still, for such demeanor called
into question the propriety of the occasions and modes of display and association traditionally so important in maintaining the bonds of Virginia's geo-
graphically diffuse society. Against the system in which proud men were
joined in rivalry and convivial excess was set a reproachful model of an order
in which God-humbled men would seek a deep sharing of emotion while re-
pudiating indulgence of the flesh. Yet the Baptist movement, although it
must be understood as a revolt against the traditional system, was not primarily negative. Behind it can be discerned an impulse toward a tighter, more
effective system of values to be established and maintained within the ranks
of the common folk. Evangelicalism can be seen as a popular response to a
mounting sense of social disorder. Whether alarm at encroaching evil was
expressed in the moralization of gentlemen patriots or in the thundering of

Baptist preachers against sin, it was directed against those forms of conviviality that provided such an important medium for customary definition and assertion of the self.[17]

As the conversion experience was at the heart of the popular evangelical movement, so a sense of a great burden of guilt was at the heart of the conversion experience. Popular perceptions of disorder in society—and hence by individuals in themselves—came now to be articulated in the metaphor of "sin." The movement was largely spread by revolt from within, not by "agitators" from without. Commonly the first visit of itinerant preachers to a neighborhood was brought about through the invitation of a group of penitents already formed and actively meeting together. Thus the "spread of seriousness" and alarm at the sinful hurly-burly of the traditional world tended to precede the creation of an emotional mass movement "under preaching." A further indication of the importance of order/disorder preoccupations as the ruling idea behind the spread of the new vision was the insistence on "works." Conversion could ultimately be validated among church members only by a radical reform of conduct. The Baptist church books reveal close concern for the disciplinary supervision of such changes. Censure, ritual excommunication, and moving expressions of penitence were invoked as means to deal with persistent problems like drunkenness. Quarreling, slandering, and disputes over property were other endemic transgressions that the churches patiently and endlessly sought to control within their own communities.[18]

With its base in slavery, the plantation world was one in which contest readily turned into unruly aggression. An episode in the life of one of the great Baptist preachers, John Waller (formerly "Swearing Jack"), illustrates the prevailing violence and the relationship between classes. Waller and some gentry companions were riding on the road when a drunken butcher addressed them in a manner they considered insolent. One of the gentlemen had a horse trained to rear and "paw what was before him," which he then had it do to frighten the butcher. The man was struck by the hooves and died soon after. Tried for manslaughter, the company of gentlemen were acquitted because the court declared itself uncertain whether the injury had indeed caused the butcher's death. The episode may have helped prepare Waller for conversion into a radically opposed social world.[19]

The new sect's concern for ordered self-control revealed itself most clearly in its members' attitude toward physical aggression. Traditional society expected a free man to "resent" insult and showed approval if he did. Yet in the Baptist community a man might even come forward to confess and ask forgiveness for "Geting angry Tho in Just Defence of himself in Despute." The monthly meeting of one church was informed of an incident involving its clerk, Rawley Hazard. He had been approached on his own land, addressed in "Very Scurrilous language," and then assaulted. When the church members heard that he "did defend himself against this sd Violence, that both the Assailant and Defendent was much hurt," they voted, seeming to make no allowances for the provocation, that the minister "do Admonish Brother Rawley Hazard in the presents of the Church . . . saying that his defence was Irregular."[20]

The recurrent use of the words "order," "orderly," and "disorderly" in the Baptist records reveals a preoccupation with establishing a tighter regulation of everyday life. "Is it orderly?" was the usual introduction to the queries concerning right conduct that were frequently brought forward for resolution at monthly meetings.[21]

The evangelicals' determination to impose controls within the "loose" society that they sensed around them was supremely expressed in their strict Sabbath-day observance. This concern is constantly manifested in autobiographies, apologetics, and church books. It appears that the Virginia method of keeping the Sabbath with "sport, merriment, and dissipation" readily served to symbolize the general disorder perceived in society. Conversely, cosmic order was affirmed and held up as a model for society by setting aside all worldly pursuits on the Lord's Day while men expressed their reverence for their Maker and Redeemer.[22]

By their "seriousness"; by their abstinence from convivial pastimes; and by the discipline with which these observances were maintained—in a word, by their insistence on strict purity—the Baptists marked out sharp boundaries segregating themselves as individuals and as church groups from the world. Yet their ways combined opposite aspirations regarding social relations. On the one hand they were heedless of how they disrupted traditional society, acknowledging that they not only sowed discord among neighbors but also turned slaves from their masters, children from their parents, wives from their husbands, since "our SAVIOUR told his disciples, that, he 'came not to send peace on earth but rather division.'" On the other hand, they created tight supportive communities "of persons, called by the Gospel out of the world," seeking "to live together as brethren." Bound up with the Baptists' urge to break down community at one level and rebuild it at another were the contrasting experiences through which many of the white converts passed. In the first place they underwent radical individualization as each was "awakened" to a sense of his or her sinfulness and faced alone the meaning of God's judgment. After "conviction" of sin, segregation of the self from "the world," and the lone ecstasy of conversion, however, the initiates received the comfort of close fellowship. Only the social validation of the individual works of grace, brought about through acceptance of testimony in the meetings, preserved converts (and then only partially) from being beset by doubts about the validity of the assurances of salvation they had received in solitude. Experiences polarized between individual isolation and intimate togetherness were replicated in the double character that Baptist church societies assumed. * On the one hand each society was a divinely ordained corporate community fostering the work of grace. Yet, on the other hand, according to individualistic principles, each was "a voluntary assembly, or company . . . associated, or connected of their own accord for the exercises of religion." [23]

It was a particular mark of the Baptists' radicalism, and without doubt the most significant aspect of their quest for means of moral regulation located among the people, that they included the slaves as "brothers" and "sisters" in their close communities. When the Baptists sealed the slaves unto eternal life, leading them in white robes into the water and then back to receive the bread and wine, the white preachers were also laying upon their black converts a responsibility to maintain godly conduct, and demanding that they internalize strict Protestant Christian values and norms. The dissenters were seeking to extend orderly moral community to the quarters, where hitherto there had seemed to be none. The slaves were members and therefore subject to church discipline. The incidence of excommunication of slaves for the sin

---

* Increasing "individualism" in the social and cultural system of England and America may well constitute an underlying "cause" of the rise of evangelicalism. The ambivalence of the movement—combining experiences of isolation and of communality—could be read as both involvement in and reaction against profound shifts in values and patterns of life. The relationship of "evangelical" individualism to a spectrum of other cultural indicators of the same trend is reviewed in the concluding chapter, or Afterview. (It should be noted that an added stress on the ambivalence between communitarianism and individualism constitutes the principal interpretive revision made to this chapter since its original publication as an article.)

of adultery points to the desire of the Baptists to introduce among the slaves their own ideal standards of conduct concerning marital relationships. The white Baptist perception of the slaves' mores can be sensed in the recurrent phrase that was often given as the sole reason for excommunication: "disorderly walk." [24]

Cultural differences between white and black converts, however, could not be removed merely by discipline. The success of the Baptists among the slaves was spectacular and inspired a good deal of the hostility of gentlemen in the legislature who sought to curb the expansion of the movement. It is nevertheless misleading to refer to this success in terms that imply that whites simply brought evangelicalism to blacks. We know that "a large number of blacks, belonging chiefly to the large estate of Colonel [William] Byrd," near the North Carolina border, were among the first converts that the Separate Baptists made in Virginia, and that "the breaking up of Byrd's quarters scattered these blacks into various parts." The result was that "through their labors in the different neighborhoods into which they fell many persons were brought to the knowledge of the truth." Perhaps the receptiveness of slaves to the new conception of religion helped open the whole society for its propagation. That is not to say, however, that "conversion" had the same meaning for blacks as for whites. It seems that Afro-American evangelicalism, taking root in the profoundly communal ethos of the quarter, did not typically involve its adherents in an isolating experience of awakening to a deep sense of guilt and sinfulness. Black religion, unlike its white counterpart, was not polarized between individualism and communitarianism but was centered much more unambiguously in collective celebration. [25]

CONFRONTATIONS

When the Virginia Baptist movement is understood as a rejection of the style of life for which the gentry set the pattern and as a search for different models of proper conduct, it can be seen why the main battleground was not the estate or the great house, but the small planter's house and the slave quarter. It was generally charged that the Baptists were "continual fomenters of discord." Similarly, the only reported complaint against the first preachers to be imprisoned was that they entered "private houses . . . making dissensions." It was in lowly dwellings that the most intense struggles took place between a style of life modeled on that of the leisured gentry and the style embodied in evangelicalism. In humbler, more straitened households a popular culture oriented to proud self-assertion and almost hedonistic values was necessarily less securely established than among the more affluent gentry. For this reason, an anxious aggressiveness was manifest in anti-New Light feeling and action among the common planters.[26]

With the rise of the Separate Baptists, the effrontery of the New Side Presbyterian itinerants in preaching without licenses seemed as nothing compared to the overturning of deference and respect that was proclaimed in the evangelicals' readiness to send out the humblest of men, including slaves, to expound Scripture, declaring them qualified by a "gift" of the Holy Spirit. The Baptist following may have amounted to as much as 10 percent of the population by 1772. More alarming for those wedded to the traditional system was the movement's rate of growth. In 1769 only seven Separate Baptist churches were constituted in Virginia, with no more than three of them located in the longer-settled regions north of the James. By October 1774 the number had climbed to fifty-four in all—twenty-four north of the river.[27]

Even during their most rapid advance the Baptists did not make a bid for control of the political system—still less did they seek a leveling of society or redistribution of worldly wealth. It was clearly a mark of the strength of the gentry's hegemony and of the rigidities of the social hierarchy that had slavery at its base that the evangelical revolt should have been so restricted in scope. Yet the Baptists' Sabbatarianism and anxiety over individual salvation effectively redefined morality and human relationships. Among the lesser folk, Baptist church leaders and organization introduced more popular focuses of authority and sought to impose a radically different and more inclusive model for the maintenance of order in society. Within the context of traditional conceptions of community and the forms of deference expected to sustain it, such a regrouping necessarily constituted a genuine challenge.

The beginnings of a cultural disjunction between gentry and sections of the lower orders where hitherto there had been a continuum, posed a serious threat to the traditional leaders of the community. Their response was characteristic. The popular emotional style, the encouragement given to men of little learning to "exercise their gifts" in preaching, and the preponderance of

humble folk in the movement gave the proud gentry their readiest defense—
contempt and ridicule. The stereotype of the Baptists as "an ignorant" and
"contemptible class of the people," a "poor and illiterate sect" that "none of
the rich or learned ever join," became generally accepted. References in the
Virginia Gazette to "ignorant enthusiasts" were common. It even published,
without protest, a heartless satire detailing "A Receipt to make an ANABAP-
TIST PREACHER": "Take the Herbs of Hypocrisy and Ambition, . . . of the
Seed of Dissention and Discord one Ounce, . . . [and] one Pint of the Spirit
of Self-Conceitedness."[28]

Morgan Edwards, a college-educated Baptist minister from the North, recorded an encounter with some gentlemen at an inn in Goochland County.
He noted the moderation of the gentry in this area, yet their arrogant scorn
for dissenters in general, and for Baptists in particular, is unmistakable from
the dialogue reported. Since Edwards had just come from Georgia, they began with ribald jests about "Mr Whitefield's children . . . by the squaw" and
continued as follows:

> *Esq[uire] U:* Pray are you not a clergyman? . . .
> *Capt. L:* Of the church of England I presume?
> *Nor[thern] M[inister]:* No, Sir; I am a clergyman of better church than
> that; for she is a persecutor.
> *Omnes:* Ha! Ha! Ha! . . .
> *Esq. U:* Then you are one of the fleabitten clergy?
> *N.M.:* Are there fleas in this bed, Sir?
> *Esq. U:* I ask, if you are a clergyman of the itchy true blue kirk of
> Scotland? . . .
> *Capt. L.* (whispers): He is ashamed to own her for fear you should
> scratch him, "Squire."
> [*When they have discovered that this educated man, who shows such address
> in fencing with words, is a Baptist minister, they discuss the subject
> bibulously among themselves:*]
> *Esq. U:* He is no baptist. . . . I take him to be one of the Georgia
> lawyers.
> *Mr. G:* For my part I believe him to be a baptist minister. There are
> some clever fellows among them. . . .
> *Major W:* I confess they have often confounded me with their argu-

ments and texts of Scripture; and if any other people but the baptists professed their religion I would make it my religion before tomorrow.[29]

The class of folk who filled the Baptist churches were a great obstacle to gentry participation. Behind their ridicule and contempt lay incomprehension, and behind that, fear of this menacing, unintelligible movement. The only firsthand account we have of a meeting broken up by the arrest of the preachers tells how they "were carried before the . . . magistrate," who took them "one by one into a room and examined [their] pockets and wallets for firearms." He accused them of "carrying on a mutiny against the authority of the land." This sort of dark suspicion impelled David Thomas, in his printed defense of the Baptists, to protest several times that "we concern not ourselves with the government . . . we form no intrigues . . . nor make any attempts to alter the constitution of the kingdom to which as men we belong."[30]

Fear breeds fantasy. So it was that alarmed observers put a very crude interpretation on the emotional and even physical intimacy of this intrusive new society. Its members were associated with German Anabaptists, and a "historical" account of the erotic indulgences of that sect was published on the front page of the *Virginia Gazette*.[31]

Driven by uneasiness, although toughened by their instinctive contempt, some members of the establishment made direct moves to assert proper social authority and to outface the upstarts. Denunciations from parish pulpits were frequent. Debates were not uncommon, being sought by both sides. Ireland recalled vividly a clash that reveals the pride and presumption of the gentlemen who came forward in defense of the Church of England. Captain McClanagan's place was thronged with people, some of whom had come forty miles to hear John Pickett, a Baptist preacher of Fauquier County. The rector of a neighboring parish attended with some leading parishioners "who were as much prejudiced . . . as he was." "The parson had a chair brought for himself, which he placed three or four yards in front of Mr. Pickett . . . taking out his pen, ink and paper, to take down notes of what he conceived to be false doctrine." When Pickett had finished, "the Parson called him a schismatick, a broacher of false doctrines . . . [who] held up damnable errors that day." Pickett answered adequately (according to Ireland), but "when contradicted it would in a measure confuse him." So Ireland, who had been raised a gentleman, took it upon himself to sustain the Baptist cause. The parson immediately "wheeled about on his chair . . . and let out a broadside of his eloquence, with an expectation, no doubt, that he would confound me with the first fire." However, Ireland "gently laid hold of a chair, and placed . . . it close by him, determined to argue the point with him from end to end." The contest was long, and "both gentlemen and ladies," who had evidently seated themselves near the parson, "would repeatedly help him to scripture, in order to support his arguments." When the debate ended (as the narrator recalled) in the refutation of the clergyman, Ireland "addressed one of the gentlemen who had been so officious in helping his teacher; he was a magistrate. . . . 'Sir, as the dispute between the Parson and myself is ended, if you are disposed to argue the subject over again, I am willing to enter upon it with you.' He stretched out his arm straight before him, at that instant, and declared that I should not come nigher than that length." Ireland "concluded what the consequence would be [and] therefore made a peaceable retreat." Such scenes of action speak for themselves. They are the stuff of social structure, as of social conflict.[32]

Great popular movements cannot be outfaced, nor can they be stemmed by the ridicule, scorn, or scurrility of incomprehension. Moreover, they draw into themselves members of all sections of society. Although the milieus most open to the Baptists' proselytizing were the poor whites' plantations and the slaves' quarters, there were converts from the great houses too. Some of the gentry defectors, such as Samuel Harris, played a leading role in the movement. Members of the squirearchy were particularly disturbed by the realization that the contemptible sect was making inroads among themselves. The exchanges between Morgan Edwards and the gentlemen in the Goochland inn were confused by the breakdown of the stereotype of ignorance and poverty. Edwards's cultured facility reminded the squires that "there are some clever fellows among [the Baptists]. I heard one Jery Walker support a petition of theirs at the assembly in such a manner as surprised us all, and [made] our witts draw in their horns." The pride and assurance of the gentry were threatened by awareness that their own members might withdraw from their ranks and choose the other way. The vigorous response of Ireland's patron to the challenge implicit in his defection provides a striking example.[33]

The intensity of the conflict among the people and, increasingly, among the gentry, makes intelligible the growing frequency of violent clashes of the kind already illustrated. The violence was, however, one-sided and self-defeating. The episode of April 1771, when the parson brutally interfered with the devotions of the preacher who was then horsewhipped by the sheriff, must have produced a widespread shock of revulsion. Those who took part in such actions were not typical of either the Anglican clergy or the country gentlemen. The extreme responses of some, however, show the anxieties to which all were subject, and the excesses in question could only heighten the tension.[34]

The continuing upsurge of the New Lights rendered the social challenge increasingly urgent. The gentry were forced to maneuver between a partial revolution in values and organization among the common planters and their own unshaken attachment to the Established Church—an institution that had served to affirm and legitimate their dominance over the whole community.

The rise of the Separate Baptists was particularly alarming because it coincided with a general crisis of authority. In 1765 popular discontent in Virginia became focused on the Stamp Tax, and the colony's leaders were impelled into acts of defiance against the supremacy of the British Parliament. Americans were on the watch from then on, and whenever the claims of Westminster were reactivated, colonial defiance was renewed. Yet Virginia patriots were deeply committed to upholding the British constitution as they understood it and were engaged throughout the years of struggle in strenuous attempts to arrive at an institutional accommodation between their colony and the mother country. Questions of cultural identity became acute. A heated controversy that broke out in 1771 reveals the terms in which some highly literate Virginians saw the crisis facing their society. One can see both the forms of authority that they hoped might give shape to their world, and the contrasting shapes that impending disaster assumed in their minds.

9

WHITHER VIRGINIA?
Specters of Bishop and Sectary

On April 4, 1771, Purdie's *Virginia Gazette* printed an addendum to the ordinary notice advertising the annual meeting of subscribers to the Fund for the Relief of Widows and Orphans of the Clergy. The Reverend the Honorable Mr. James Horrocks, commissary of the bishop of London, appended a special request "that there may be a general Attendance of the Clergy and [that] the Meeting may be as full as possible." There can now be no doubt that this call was included in the hope that the colony's clergy might be precipitately induced to petition collectively that a colonial bishop be sent out. It is also clear that the notice's silence concerning the real purpose of the general meeting was designed to forestall public controversy and so to engineer a fait accompli.

On the appointed day (May 4) it was found that the obscure request had not elicited the desired response. Just over a dozen parsons assembled at the college and "when they began to consider the Affair, the greater Part determined to desire the Commissary to insert another Advertisement for a second Meeting, and likewise to mention the Business for which they were summoned." The commissary duly published a notice five days later. He called openly for a special meeting on June 4 to consider "the Expediency of an Application to proper Authority for an *American* Episcopate." [1]

When the day arrived, again only twelve reverend gentlemen (out of a possible one hundred) came to the college in answer to this call. We may picture them waiting for proceedings to begin, standing perhaps outside the great west door of the chapel in their broadcloth coats, their Geneva bands flutter-

FIGURE 18.
We may picture the clergymen gathering outside the
west door of the college chapel

ing in the breeze. The clergy has ceased to be central as a profession in our
society, and consequently such a scene is likely to convey no idea of the suspicion that an assembly of divines might have aroused in the minds of people
of that time.

The strength of anticlericalism in the eighteenth century can only be understood through an imaginative reconstruction of complex inner conflicts.
Orthodox Christian doctrine was still generally taught and accepted as the
basis for understanding the world, but there was also a mounting sense of the

incongruence of doctrine and experience in a society in the process of secularization. Increasing numbers more or less consciously undertook a profound reappraisal of the meaning of life that involved an intensifying search for purposes and for sources of authority contained within the human social order itself. Bitter blows were inevitably struck at the symbols and guardians of orthodoxy—the clergy and their hierarchies of authority.[2]

For aroused Virginians in 1771 these cultural tensions, general to the eighteenth-century Atlantic world, were necessarily heightened by the political passions of the time. The defenders of "American Liberty" had a dark and fearful sense of the workings of power in society. The world view that they and the leaders in the other colonies articulated was no abstract body of principles but a vivid set of images of the political systems of Europe and America. A highly dramatic version of history and a sense of mounting contemporary crisis were the principal components of their "true whig" ideology. They believed that the free "Gothick" institutions that the Germanic invaders established in place of the licentious and tyrannical Roman Empire had been steadily undermined for more than a thousand years by priestcraft and despotism. Only Britain, through the revered English constitution, had been able to preserve and perfect its pristine liberties, at the same time successfully extending them to the American colonies. Liberty, however, was a feminine principle—as was her inseparable companion, Virtue—and so they both were continual victims of the lust for domination that was natural to men. In the 1760s signs of corruption in the rulers of Britain began to cause serious disquiet. The Stamp Act showed that conspirators in the king's ministry could induce Parliament to impose measures that would reduce the American colonies to enslaved tributaries paying to support the cost of luxury and vice. This sense of crisis called forth a lurid rhetoric that alternated between dark forebodings of British oppression and shining imagery of the future belonging to a virtuous America.[3]

THE EPISCOPACY CONTROVERSY

By the time the dozen clergymen convened in June 1771 for their second meeting, a polemical exchange in the *Virginia Gazette* had already revealed the passions that would be aroused for and against the coming of a bishop.

When prayers and formalities were over, the meeting considered a motion to petition the king immediately. This being rejected, the members decided (with four opposed) to make an attempt to rally the absent brethren by appointing a committee to prepare and circulate a petition for the establishment of an American episcopate. If this petition secured the signatures of a majority of the clergy in the colony, it was to be sent to the bishop of London, who was to be asked to present it to the king. With the minority in outspoken disagreement, the session was stormy. The dissidents raised the specter of civil violence, foretelling rebellion and anarchy if a bishop were to be imposed on the colony. They exhorted the majority "to reflect upon the Disturbances occasioned by the Stamp Act, and the more recent Calamities of North Carolina. They were also advised to defer their Resolution till the Violence of popular Clamour was subsided, and, above all, to lay the Matter before the . . . General Assembly, . . . the best Judges of the Wants of this Country."[4]

Two of the four dissidents, Samuel Henley and Thomas Gwatkin (reverend professors newly arrived at The College of William and Mary), immediately published a protest that denounced the impropriety of a clique (eight out of about a hundred clergymen) attempting to act for the whole body. They declared that the refusal of the majority of the meeting to consult the Virginia General Assembly was "an Usurpation directly repugnant to the Rights of Mankind." The other two opponents of the successful resolution—the Reverend Messrs. Richard Hewitt and William Bland—published a second protest that was even more eloquent on the subject of injured rights.[5]

Henley and Gwatkin's protest "brought on a Severe Paper War" in which the lead was taken by opposed factions in the college. The Reverend Mr. John Camm, professor of divinity, "commenced Champion for a Bishop," while the Reverend Mr. Samuel Henley, professor of moral philosophy, continued outspoken in opposition.* Under the circumstances it was inevitable

---

* John Camm was a stubborn Yorkshireman who by 1771 had served more than 25 years as a rector in Virginia parishes, and more than 20 years as a professor at the college. He was an inveterate controversialist "whose Delight," wrote Lt. Gov. Francis Fauquier, "is to raise a Flame and to live in it."

Samuel Henley was only 25 when he was appointed to the college. He was born in rural Devonshire, had attended Caleb Ashworth's dissenting academy at Daventry from 1762 to 1766, and had ministered to a congregation of dissenters near Cambridge from 1766 to 1768. In Mar. of that

that personal rancor and point-scoring debate should form a major part of the exchanges between these men, but the controversy raised issues that had implications for the entire colony. The protagonists of the episcopate stressed the disordered state of the Anglican church in the face of a rising tide of popular religious dissent and urged the necessity of installing a bishop who could discipline and rally the clergy. The new episcopal jurisdiction (so the anxious were reassured) would comprehend only the clergy, not extend to the laity. The antagonists of the scheme directed their energies at denouncing the evil tendencies inherent in episcopacy, demonstrating the impossibility of curbing such tendencies effectively (especially during troubled times), and proving that a conspiracy against the liberties of America lurked behind the proposal.[7]

At the height of the controversy fear of priestly intrigue was intensified, when on June 20, 1771, the press announced that "this Day the Reverend and Honourable the Commissary [Horrocks], with his Lady, took Shipping for England . . . for the Recovery of their Healths." There were those who drew the conclusion "that Horrock's errand to England is to lay a Foundation for this [episcopal] Establishment, & that he expects to be the First Right Reverend Father of the American Church."[8]

In the middle of the summer of 1771 the circumstances and the terms of debate were suddenly and dramatically altered. On July 12 the House of Burgesses resolved nemine contradicente to thank the four protesters "for the wise and well timed Opposition they have made to the pernicious Project of a few mistaken Clergymen, for introducing an *American* Bishop; a Measure by which much Disturbance, great Anxiety, and Apprehension, would certainly

---

year he was formally received into the dissenting ministry at Crosby Square, London. Living in Cambridge in 1768 and 1769 Henley had cultivated the acquaintance of Latitudinarian divines, notably Rt. Rev. Edmund Law, bishop of Carlisle, and Rev. John Jebb (whose Unitarian teachings forced him to leave the ministry in 1775). These men were among those who wrote recommendations to the bishop of London on the young man's behalf in 1769, when he sought to be ordained a minister of the Church of England and to go as a professor to The College of William and Mary. While in Virginia Henley had his name entered on the books of Queens' College, Cambridge, so that he might take out a B.D. degree after 10 years.

Thomas Gwatkin was the son of a gentleman of the same name from Herefordshire. Born in 1741, he had matriculated at Jesus College, Oxford, in 1763 but did not proceed to a degree at that time. He was ordained in 1767 by Robert Terrick, bishop of London, then chancellor of The College of William and Mary, and was nominated as professor by the bishop in 1769.[6]

take Place among his Majesty's faithful *American* Subjects; and that Mr. *Richard Henry Lee*, and Mr. *Bland*, do acquaint them therewith." This strong intervention by the legislature produced a momentary lull in the debate.[9]

When the controversy resumed in the press, its content (apart from personal invective, which continued unabated) had a more theoretical, declaratory character, since the prospect of Virginia initiative toward securing a bishop now seemed remote. By the beginning of 1772 polemics in favor of episcopacy were becoming more and more labored and verbose while those opposed were increasingly given over to vituperation and scurrility. On March 12, 1772, Purdie and Dixon announced that on account of readers' complaints "of their being tired of the Dispute," they would publish no more on the subject.

BISHOPS AND FEAR OF TYRANNY

The gentry who read the *Gazette* had a limited appetite for clerical disputation; nevertheless, the resolution of the House of Burgesses showed unmistakably that matters of deep concern to society were at stake in the controversy. Doctrine may not have aroused much feeling in the gentry, but at a time when Baptist sectaries were spreading rapidly, questions of church allegiance did. Read in the context of both internal disturbances in Virginia and external pressures on the colony, the altercations reveal pervasive anxieties. Indeed the dispute was not just over the organization of the Church. At bottom, it was about the nature of legitimate authority and the direction in which society ought to develop.[10]

The controversy over a colonial bishop reveals many contemporary cultural assumptions about authority and the role of religious institutions in society, and illuminates issues that troubled and divided Virginians in these stormy times. Prominent in the polemics were such familiar concerns as alarm at any further extension of the imperial power, and a jealous anticlericalism. The episcopacy question was easily linked with the constitutional political struggle. Most of the polemicists wrote under pseudonyms that were themselves ideological placards. "Country Clergyman," one of the opening contributors to the newspaper exchanges, was quite explicit in identifying the proposal as "a Scheme to trample into the Earth the fair, the rising Plant of American Liberty." The author declared his desire "to have his Name enrolled in the List of that chosen Band of the Defenders of the Liberties of Mankind," although he only signed with a nom de plume. Two of the original clerical dissidents, Hewitt and Bland, did put their own names to a denunciation of the king's ministers, who would exercise the royal right of appointing any bishop who might be sent. The protesters were convinced that the "Ministry, whose Sentiments have ever appeared extremely hostile and inimical to the common Rights of Mankind," would be certain to send a bishop "who should never feel any Remorse in executing what they, in their Omnipotence, should command him."[11]

Virginia patriots voiced real alarm at the political uses to which a bishop might be put by a British government intent on curtailing American liberty, but their fears went deeper. Images of spiritual lordship were powerful symbols of authority and the social order—benign symbols for some, malign for a great many more. It is notable that expressions of anxiety that a bishop would be the agent of ministerial conspiracy were relatively few and were outweighed by a fear of bishops, who were, it was felt, by nature cruel usurpers. The terrifying prospect was placed before Virginians that "we shall soon be overwhelmed with the mighty Torrent of spiritual Tyranny . . . which of all Tyrannies . . . is the most to be dreaded." The anticipation of a colonial bishop could, even in Anglican Virginia, evoke visions of the soil "moistened with the blood of Americans."[12]

Some of this fear and hostility may in part be accounted for by the long-standing tradition of anticlericalism in the colony. A conception of priests as worldly extortioners was well established, and it was therefore no accident that the first shot in the newspaper war was a mock advertisement, signed "The Collector," that parodied the commissary's call for a convention and threatened to discontinue the collection of the salaries of the parish ministers. Such themes recurred throughout the debate and were reinforced by the contrasting depiction of an idealized clergy dedicated to Christian poverty and humility. If "*Rewards and Punishments are . . . the Springs of all Government*," asked Samuel Henley, "what Opinion ought we to entertain of the *Founder of our Faith*, who withheld from his Apostles those Incentives to Virtue, RICH LIVINGS, and rewarded them *only* with *empty* Promises of Heaven?" This line of irreverent irony reached its most daring extension in a query: "But if the Apostles were Bishops, pray what was Jesus Christ? *An Archbishop?*"[13]

The terrors associated with the very idea of a bishop are complex and difficult to explain. The imagery may have had roots in the religious rhetoric of the Protestant Reformation and the English Civil War, but eighteenth-century political controversy had certainly kept the passions alive. John Trenchard and Thomas Gordon's *Independent Whig*, for example, was a series of newspaper polemics that appeared in London in 1720 and 1721 and had a continuing circulation among colonial men of letters. Republished as a single volume, it formed a sustained two hundred-page tirade against the cruel pride of the "High Clergy" and their ways of ensnaring the ignorant multitudes in dark superstition. This classic of the English "commonwealth" tradition was secular in its inspiration and reinforced the anticlericalism implicit in an ideology that entered deeply into literate Americans' understanding of their situation.[14]

The embarrassing fact that bishops and apostolic succession were the distinguishing and legitimating features of the Church of England in relation to other British Protestant groups made some Virginians uncomfortable about the opposition to a colonial bishopric. William Nelson, Sr., president of the Council, expressed suitable caution at the outset: "We do not want Bishops; yet from our Principles I hardly think we should oppose such an Establishment." Colonel Richard Bland, a staunch churchman, resolved the perplexity and expressed a determination that was evidently generally felt: "I profess myself a sincere son of the established church, but I can embrace her Doctrines without approving of her Hierarchy, which I know to be a Relick of the Papal Incroachments upon the Common Law."[15]

It is, however, the positive arguments for the settlement of a bishop in Virginia that reveal most about the underlying patterns of thought. The protagonists of episcopacy were compelled by the great weight of adverse opinion to elaborate the fundamentals of their cause as persuasively and fully as they could. Their opponents, on the other hand, were conscious of addressing readers who mostly shared their own views, and could get by with much less explicit reasoning.

Those on the episcopal side had an evident orientation toward the forms of metropolitan society. An obvious argument for them was that the establishment in the colony of a bishop of the Church of England, far from being an infringement of Virginia's laws, was necessary in order to render the colonial constitution complete. John Camm, in his first contribution to the debate, expressed the view that the colonies were "in this, a happy Copy of the Parent Country, that Episcopal Government in the Church is interwoven with the Constitution of the State." "A Country Man," daring to reopen the case after the Burgesses' condemnation, sought justification by asserting that a bishop was "absolutely necessary to the preservation of the American church" and essential also to "the preservation of the present form of. civil government." "A Church of England Man" was even more emphatic: "We ought to consider that the Constitution of the Church of England is adopted by our own Laws . . . [and] is adapted to and interwoven with, that of the State; that they mutually strengthen each other, and must stand or fall together."[16]

ECCLESIASTICAL DISCIPLINE: A PERENNIAL PROBLEM

The polemicists' contentions about the interdependence of the church and state in Virginia's constitution were more than mere debating points. In order to understand the controversy in its immediate context, it is necessary to go back to a point in time just before the outbreak of the "paper war," when an impending court action threatened to bring to a crisis long-standing problems in the organization of the establishment. Attention was drawn to the problem that one of the basic institutions in the traditional system of authority—the parish—was without proper protection at law. It became altogether uncertain whether a rector whose conduct was habitually scandalous could be removed from his living by constitutional means. In English law, sentence of deprivation was customarily passed by a bishop's court.[17] This consideration probably contributed to the decision of Mr. Commissary Horrocks to organize a petition that favored the founding of a Virginia episcopate.[18]

The annual meeting of subscribers to the Benefit Fund for Widows of the Clergy had been advertised twice in the usual way during March 1771 before the fateful request of April 4 that there be a general attendance. A letter dated April 17 from the acting governor, William Nelson, to the secretary of state in England provides an essential clue to what was already afoot. Nelson sought legal advice concerning jurisdiction in matters of ecclesiastical discipline, explaining that "a cause hath lately been instituted against a Minister for immoralities." It had been arranged "by consent of the Parties" that the first matter to be dealt with when the General Court heard the suit in October was "the point of Jurisdiction." The legality of exercising discipline over the clergy in the absence of a bishop's court would certainly be the crucial issue.[19]

The case brought before the court was between "Goodwin et al., Vestrymen of the Upper Parish, Nansemond County," and the Reverend Mr. Patrick Lunan, who had been received into the parish on December 8, 1760, and had been the subject of repeated attempts at discipline since September 22, 1762. The testimony of the vestrymen gives valuable dramatic emphasis to a grave problem for the colony at large. The vestry deposition asserted

> that the said Patrick Lunan hath been accustomed to drink of spirituous liquors to excess . . . [that] he went into his Parish not like a Priest but ridiculously apparelled and thus attempted to Perform divine service but [was] so drunk that he could not go through with it . . . that he had frequently disappointed persons who were Brought to be baptised and came to be married, being too much inebriated to do those offices . . . that Patrick Lunan is a common disturber of His Majesty's Peace and is often Quarrelling and fighting . . . and that the said Patrick Lunan on the tenth day of July . . . [1767] and at divers other times exposed his private parts to view in Publick Company and Solicited negro and other women to commit the crime of Fornication and adultery with him . . . and at divers other days the said Patrick Lunan declared that he did not believe in the revealed Religion (meaning the christian religion) and that he did not care what religion he was of so he could get the Tobacco [payments] nor what became of his flock (meaning his congregation) so he got the fleece.[20]

The development of this case brought to light some of the doubt and anxiety that surrounded ecclesiastical law in Virginia. Three of the colony's ablest legal minds—George Wythe, Richard Bland, and Thomas Jefferson— were retained by the vestry, and when the case came up in October 1771, they all presented strong arguments in favor of the General Court's power to deprive parish ministers. The three arguments differed radically, however, and were in important respects mutually incompatible. After the legal counsel had been heard, it was "adjudged that the civil court possessed ecclesiastical jurisdiction in general, and that . . . [it] might proceed to . . . deprive the defendant, if there should be sufficient cause." Nevertheless, "on the importunity of the Attorney general, John Randolph, counsel for the defendant, a rehearing was granted," but no record survives of any further court proceedings on this case. We know only that four years later, on September 30, 1775, the vestry of the Upper Parish of Nansemond County was reduced to buying Patrick Lunan's resignation for £300.[21]

This affair had probably ignited the episcopacy debate; certainly it fueled the fires of controversy. There was no bishop to discipline the clergy in Virginia, and the General Court could not make itself effective as an alternative authority. The general awareness of the importance of this defect in the colony's constitution was clearly expressed on March 27, 1772, when the House of Burgesses ordered the preparation of a bill "to establish a Jurisdiction for superintending the Conduct of the Clergy, to be exercised by Clergymen, with an Appeal to a Court of Delegates."[22]

The sad case of the depraved and unrepentant, but irremovable, Patrick Lunan haunted the whole episcopacy controversy. Far from trying to gloss over the issue of delinquent clergymen, the advocates of the episcopate attempted to turn to their advantage the anticlerical prejudices that were reinforced by scandalous parsons. They argued that the seriousness of the problem necessitated the immediate completion of the constitution by the settlement of a bishop.[23]

The tightening of discipline was expected to have results of greater moment than simply imposing order and propriety within the parsonages. Alarmed churchmen—lay and clerical—believed that the current spread of dissent in Virginia stemmed from scandals to the Church occasioned by the laxity of many and the depravity of some of the established clergy. An advocate of episcopacy declared: "The greatest Advantage which the various Dissenters have to spread their Tenets is in Parishes that either lie long vacant

. . . or are ill supplied by the Incumbent." "A Country Farmer" presented
more dramatically his forebodings concerning the fate of the bishopless, and
therefore leaderless, Church in Virginia:

> But let us consider with what Neglect . . . we now indeed treat the
> best of Mothers [i.e., the Church], when many of our Temples stand
> for a whole Month together . . . with not so much as a Book opened.
> . . . But alas! She is now made a Bye-Word and a Hissing by Sects and
> Sectaries, who passing by, wagging their Heads, are ready to cry out,
> Behold! what Manner of Stones and Buildings are here! But the Day
> cometh, and now is at Hand, in which there shall not one Stone be
> left upon another that shall not be thrown down.

Neglectful and delinquent clergymen were powerful symbolic figures in a
society where rapid change in religious affiliation was disturbing traditional
relationships.[24]

THE MENACE OF THE "ANABAPTISTS"

Although the year of the episcopacy controversy coincided with a lull in imperial disputes, this was precisely the time in Virginia when conflict and confrontation with the challenging Separate Baptist movement was at its height.
The sect was expanding rapidly, its preachers were defying legal restrictions
and were moving with increasing success from the southwest frontier areas
into regions of long-established settlement. The dramatic rise of dissent
reached a climax with the first meeting of the newly formed Virginia Separate
Baptist Association at the Blue Run Church, Orange County, May 11–15,
1771. A contemporary diarist estimated the attendance as "4,000 or 5,000
souls for the preaching and exhorting on the Sunday." Among the delegates
to the association meeting, defiance of authority was rife. Many were strongly
in favor of censuring "every one that had obtained license" to preach (as was
then required by law).[25]

The quickly growing movement was given further prominence by the
strong hostility it aroused among traditionalist sections of the community,
and by the attempts of authority in some parts to repress it, using court pro-

ceedings or encouraging riotous disruptions. Such forms of harassment began about 1765, when the Separate Baptists were called on to preach in the Piedmont. The incidents became more frequent as the movement reached into Tidewater regions. Yet the records make it clear that violent resistance was self-defeating. The same was evidently true of the more peaceful legal processes. By the end of 1771 itinerant preachers in at least twenty cases had been bound over to keep the peace, and having refused to give bonds, were remanded to county jails. Often they preached through the bars of the prison to followers outside; and in one case the exasperated justices were reduced to building a wall around the jail to prevent such communication. Not infrequently the authorities, embarrassed at the prospect of an indefinite detention, chose to release the prisoners without having forced them to give bond.[26]

Not only did the Baptists maintain a zealous defiance, but they were also often "Aggressors, by Abusing the Minister[s] [of the Church of England] . . . and uttering many indecent and scandalous Invectives & Reflections against the Church." Facing repression from the civil authorities, some Baptists turned their denunciations in that direction also. "An Address to the Anabaptists Imprisoned in Caroline County . . . ," published in the *Virginia Gazette*, defended a gentleman who had done "the Duty of an active upright Magistrate" by committing preachers to jail as disturbers of the peace. The author took the Baptists to task because one of their "Champions" had written a note that dared to consign the justice to "perdition."[27]

Some contributors to the *Gazettes* saw the spread of Baptist revivalism as a revolt of the "Anabaptists" against the society itself. This theme persistently entered the episcopacy debate.[28] The later and more desperate appeals for the establishment of a bishop abounded in the imagery of chaos and disorder. Prayers were offered that Virginia be saved "From all Sedition and privy Conspiracy and Rebellion." This concern had been present even at the opening of the debate: "If you are so alarmed by the Fears of Disturbances from a few designing Clergymen," urged "A Country Gentleman," "turn your Eyes on the Disturbances raised, and raising by the many Dissenters, who preach in unlicensed Places." A "Virginia Colonel" was quoted by "A Country Man": "I think, said he, the indisposition of our people, and the opposition of some Clergymen, to episcopacy, prove that we are verging fast towards republicanism and puritanism: And this, to me, seems to be sufficient reason for the King's sending a Bishop amongst us, who I hope would, in some measure, contribute to check a spirit so adverse to our present happy form of government." [29]

IMAGES OF AUTHORITY AND SOCIAL ORDER

In light of the disquiet at the upsurge of sectarian revolt, the attraction of the episcopate for some of the Virginia clergy is understandable. They hoped that the presence of a bishop would at once raise the level of the Anglican clergy, discipline the unworthy, and reinforce the political establishment; in short, a colonial bishop would strengthen authority in what seemed a disintegrating social order. Yet proponents of the measure were aware of the general weakness of the whole existing authority structure in the face of the new forces, and they did not all believe the solution lay in a superficial disciplining of the clergy, or in the mere coercion of dissenters. There were those who fantasized that a bishop would benignly establish a pattern by which the process of popular disaffection would be checked, or possibly even reversed. Virginia would then develop into a fully realized Christian deferential society. The controversy rendered explicit certain basic presuppositions current in the Anglo-American world concerning the "legitimate Influence" of the "Example of Men of Rank and Fortune," in contrast to "that Disrespect and Contempt, which, from the Constitution of human Nature, we find inseparably to attend on Poverty and a Mean Appearance"—such as characterized a poorly paid clergy. "An American" expressed complete assurance that "a Man, endowed with such Riches and Powers as a Bishop ought to have," would thereby possess "both the Means to execute, and the Authority to enforce all his beneficent Councils and Designs." [30]

The arguments for a bishop encapsulated a particular conception of what Virginia society should be like. Toward the end of the controversy "Church of England Man," "An American," and "A Country Farmer" presented a series of similar visions revealing how a bishop would contribute to transforming Virginia into an idealized England. This aspiration was an extension of the belief that a spiritual governor over the Church was needed to complete Virginia's constitution. In October 1771 a contender expressed the view that,

"Where all the Members of a Society are upon a Level, as is notoriously the Case of the . . . Clergy in Virginia . . . there can be no Order or Discipline among them." The writer maintained that the offices of the hierarchy were not to be regarded as "Scarecrows or Bugbears" but "as so many handsome Provisions for our own Sons . . . like the Steps of a Ladder, to the Summit, a BISHOPRICK." "An American" developed this idea into a revealing social commentary, asserting that Virginia was a "poor illiterate Country" with a "College . . . that sat in Darkness" until illuminated by the "wise, noble, and truly patriotick Measures of our never to be forgotten [governor] Lord Botetourt, during his short Stay among us." He expressed the highest expectations for the benefits to be derived "from a constant Succession of good Bishops." In a letter of December 19, 1771, from "The Country Farmer," this vision of Virginia raised to enlightened piety by the benign operation of a bishop at the head of a ladder of preferment reached an apocalyptic extreme. Anticipating the encouragement of new Virginia candidates for orders, the author predicted:

> This great Variety of Competitors would create a laudable Emulation, which is the very Nurse of all Excellency, and it would soon make them [the candidates] recognize that Virtue and Ability are the only Scale by which they may reasonably hope to ascend safely to Interest and Preferment, and therefore would shape their Actions by this most exemplary Model. . . . I will be bold to prophesy that we shall never see this blessed and powerful Day of the Lord, in this our dark and benighted Land, until God's High Priest shall come and pull down the strong Holds in which Ignorance and Errour, Heresy and Schism, have so long intrenched themselves.

The bishop, distributing rewards to raise up an elite in society, was proffered as a panacea for the multitude of ills that seemed to be about to overwhelm the Old Dominion.[31]

The "Country Farmer's" exalted utterance depicted a kingdom of virtue, thus attempting to appropriate to the tory side of the controversy the shining ideal that inspired the American whigs. The ideas of "hierarchy," "scale," "preferment," "steps of a ladder," are the keys to a fundamental understanding of both sides in this debate. These metaphors reveal important orientations in the social thought of the time. The terminology used reveals that the opponents of a colonial bishopric had the same perception of the nature and workings of episcopacy as did its advocates, but that they rejected with horror a vision of society molded by such processes. The strongest pejorative directed at the supporters of the episcopate was that they sought to introduce "hierarchy." An opposition writer was aware, he said, that he would "draw down upon his Head all the Fire of the *Hierarchical* Heaven." A legalistic letter, signed "Churchman," characterized English history "from the conquest to the revolution" in terms of "the ambition, avarice, and tyranny, of the hierarchy." In the previously cited famous passage from a letter written by Richard Bland, what was singled out for condemnation as a "Relick of the Papal Incroachments on the Common Law" was *not* episcopacy but "Hierarchy." [32]

"None but a *Slave* will submit to *usurpation*, and he who submits to *hierarchical usurpation* is the most *abject of all slaves*," declaimed Samuel Henley. The source of this aversion lay deep in whig ideology, which maintained that hierarchy, by its nature, led to a chain of dependence, with a consequent loss of all prospect of virtuous life. If a gentleman lost his independence, he forfeited his quality of liberality. So far from being a "scale" on which men might rise by "Virtue and Ability," as envisaged by advocates of episcopacy, hierarchy was supposed by its opponents to be a means whereby the corrupt and power hungry would make themselves the instruments of despotism. An early opponent of a Virginia bishopric foresaw the introduction of "*Deans, Archdeacons, Vicars General, Chancellors, Commissaries, Prebendaries*, and a Thousand other subalternate Officers, who must all be maintained in a State suitable to their Ranks." The author feared lest "an ambitious Man, who is not content with Places and Preferments . . . beyond his Merit, may have a Chance to become a Metropolitan, and . . . overturn the Constitution." An image used in a radical libertarian oration delivered by a student at the college in 1772 reveals with striking clarity the fearful perceptions of social hierarchy that led anti-episcopal writers to invert the hopes entertained by its advocates. The student expressed horror at the possibility that "the Substance of Freedom may be attenuated into Shadow, and the Machine of State converted into *a Ladder for the ambitious*." [33]

The opponents of episcopacy, like its advocates, were expressing a view of what Virginia society ought to be like. They were opting determinedly for a social order different from the pyramidal English form with its tiered topmost part. In fact, they rejected the pattern that was the norm in the Atlantic world of their time. In keeping with a dissident tradition of admiration for the institutions of the ancient Roman Republic, they preferred a societal pyramid without an apex—one that would deny "ladders" to the ambitious and would have no "hierarchy" to bind the gentry with chains of dependence. "A Churchman" expressed anxiety because the introduction of even a limited episcopate made it "no difficult matter to forsee the introduction of ecclesiastical courts, and the speedy destruction of our laws limiting stipends, and placing the power of presentation to vacant parishes in our vestries." Where "The Country Farmer" had seen a "dark and benighted Land" waiting to be enlightened, "A Churchman" and others like him saw a simple society, ripe for corruption by hierarchy and ambition if it were not saved by virtuous self-denial. Thus Richard Henry Lee was moved to assert that "Neither Tythes nor Ecclesiastical courts will do in America[.] Our law Courts can never have weight or strength sufficient to encounter the latter." This ambitious, opportunity-seeking man of affairs had more reason than most to be aware of the hunger for remunerative and honorific office among leading members of the gentry in Virginia, where the prevailing system offered few avenues to exalted rank. A note of get-thee-behind-me-Satan pervades the gratuitous conclusion to Lee's instructions from Virginia concerning the education of his sons in England. He wrote that the "eldest may be conditioned for the Church here," and hastily added, "where we are determined to have no Bishops."[34]

Opposition to an American episcopate cannot be understood merely as political resistance to further incursions by the British power structure. Both the defense of colonial rights and the denunciations of tyrannical bishops drew their passion from strong reactions for or against a further importation of the dominant hierarchical social norms of the Atlantic world into the maturing colonial society. The rhetoric of the debate contained layers—concentric rings, as it were—of meaning. At the center lay a set of related assumptions, aspirations, and anxieties concerning the processes of social change at work in Virginia on the eve of the Revolution. Where the advocates of a bishop looked forward to an urgently needed strengthening of authority from above and to positive benefits from a hierarchical system, their opponents feared the threat of tyrannical inquisition and corrupting preferments, to which they felt especially vulnerable. The correspondence between positive and negative images is a clear indication that the men on both sides saw the church as a microcosm of society, and that they shared a framework of assumptions about how the world worked.

DIVIDED COUNSELS ON TOLERATION

The symmetry revealed in arguments and imagery should not obscure the manifestations of profound confusion, perplexity, and rancor that characterized the debate over an American bishopric. At a time when familiar social arrangements were undergoing rapid transformation, there could be no complacency among the gentry about the rejection of episcopacy—the proper institutional form of church polity—while they tenaciously maintained the establishment of the Church of England against growing pressures. The controversy was particularly disturbing to contemporaries because it highlighted contradictions between Virginia everyday values and English higher cultural forms.

A striking sign of the confusion of the times was the public and dramatic division among the clergy themselves. Not only did some clerics strongly oppose the proposed episcopate, but two of the most vociferous anticlericalists, Samuel Henley and Thomas Gwatkin, were themselves clergymen. One of these reverend professors from the college even contemplated "tossing the Bishop when he comes into the Sea." Furthermore, they or their associates went so far as to ask flippant questions that made light of the doctrine of apostolic succession—the Church's title to legitimacy. Expressions of this sort were unacceptable to some gentlemen who yet had no desire to see a bishop in Virginia. Protest against irreverence mounted, culminating in a letter from "An Episcopalian" printed in March 1772. The outraged author declared himself in no way interested in entering the original debate, but he protested against an offensive expression of levity, cited earlier in this chapter:

> When I find . . . you have made Use of some bold Assertions in
> Favour of Presbyterianism, I think myself and every Church of En-
> glandman deeply [interested]. . . . I . . . must . . . assure you that
> many sensible and good Men behold with Indignation your Attempts

to subvert the established Religion of their Country; and they hold you in the highest Contempt for that *profane Pertness* of Wit displayed in your Question, "if the Apostles were *Bishops*, pray what was Jesus Christ? An *Archbishop?*"[35]

Division and uncertainty were not confined to the affairs of the Church. Letters published in the *Gazettes* reveal that other institutions formerly regarded as sacrosanct were subject to question. The efficacy of the county courts and the qualifications of the justices were challenged; the social status of jurors was deplored; graver misgivings than ever surrounded the college; and by 1774 even the structure of authority in the militia was called into question.[36]

Public discussion of the competence and soundness of Virginia justices was particularly disturbing during this time of religious controversy, for it coincided with open challenges to the legality of current attempts at the judicial suppression of the Baptists. The confused state of the laws governing toleration intensified anxiety and dissension within the ruling group. These laws were in the same half-formed condition as those concerning church discipline—that is, they were an ad hoc mixture of particular provincial enactments and uncertain applications of English law. Two acts of the Virginia Assembly were invoked in this connection—first, a statute (14 Charles II c. iv) of 1662 that restricted the right to preach in the colony to those who had received "ordination from some Bishopp in England"; and second, a revised statute (4 Anne c. xxx) of 1705 that exempted Protestant dissenters from penalties for nonattendance at their parish churches (to which they were liable under Virginia law). Those qualified for exemption were defined by reference to an English statute of 1689 (1 William and Mary 18) —the famous Act of Toleration.[37] The 1705 law's references to the English statute were the sole, and somewhat tenuous, legislative grounds for arguing that the entire Act of Toleration was in force in Virginia. Nevertheless, the authorities in the colony had been licensing preachers and meetinghouses under the act since 1747, although they had at the same time introduced arbitrary variations from English law (mainly in the direction of tighter restriction) in order to meet local exigencies.[38]

The uncertainties in the law of toleration were already apparent when on March 17, 1758, Lancaster County court rescinded its earlier license for a Baptist meetinghouse on the grounds that it had been issued "unadvisedly and by surprize" and that the court was "now informed that no Act of Parliament relating thereto is binding in this Colony, and that there is an Act of Assembly [14 Charles II c. iv] now in force here w'ch forbids any person to preach, who has not rec'd. an Ordination from some Bishop in England." For more than a decade after that, however, the King's Council in Williamsburg continued the policy that has already been noted in relation to the ministry of Samuel Davies. In 1768 the president informed the king's attorney for Spotsylvania County, where preachers were held imprisoned, that "the act of toleration . . . has given them a right to apply, in a proper manner, for licensed houses, for the worship of God."[39] This view prevailed thereafter at the county level, and committals usually either bluntly specified "Preaching Contrary to Act of Parliament" or more elaborately spelled out that the accused had "preached the Gospel . . . not having Episcopal Ordination or being licensed . . . [under] the Act of Tolleration."[40]

By the latter part of 1771, however, when the confrontation with the itinerant preachers was at its height, doubts about the validity of the Act of Toleration in Virginia had come to be widespread. The author of "An Address to the Anabaptists Imprisoned in Caroline County . . . ," dated August 1771 and published February 20, 1772, declared that he was "one among the few Lawyers in the Country who think you are entitled to all the Benefit of that Act." He explained the doubts of those who took the opposite view: "Those Gentlemen who think the Toleration Act not in Force here, found their Opinion upon our having no Bishop."[41] A week after these revealing words had been penned, Purdie and Dixon's *Gazette* of August 22, 1771, published a forceful denial of the legality of proceedings under the act. The author, adopting the pseudonym "Timoleon," declared that if "the Dissenters have not religious Privileges allowed to them by Law, neither are they liable to be punished by any Law for their . . . Manner of Worship." He asserted that a justice who imprisoned "dissenting Teachers" exceeded his authority and so became "a Tyrant."[42]

The ruling gentry who so strongly resisted the coming of a bishop expressed sharply divergent views as to whether coercive or conciliatory measures should be applied to the growing problem of religious dissent. Many exhibited a strong urge to define a line that could be held determinedly against the alarming advances of the Baptists. The "Address to the Anabaptists" justified the firm handling of dissenters and offered a vigorous apology for religious establishment. The author defended the right of the legislature to fix limits to toleration and assured the imprisoned preachers that "as often as you break those Limits . . . you may expect to be proceeded against." Even stronger evidence of the prevailing desire to deal with dissent by the assertion of authority is to be found not in newspaper statements but in the exertions of magistrates and in the form of the toleration bill that the House of Burgesses adopted at the height of the crisis that had mounted during the fall of 1771.[43]

In February 1772 the harried Baptists petitioned the House of Burgesses for relief and also for clarification of the law governing religious dissent. Their plea represented a considerable moderation of the defiant posture of the Separate Baptists, whose association had only eight months before been on the verge of condemning any of its members who implicitly subordinated God's law to man's by seeking licenses to preach. The House of Burgesses now set out to take advantage of the opportunity to establish control that this appeal offered. Legislation was proposed that merely adapted the English Act of Toleration to the institutions of Virginia. Although the bill was subsequently amended to abolish mandatory subscription to certain of the Thirty-nine Articles, the changes did not altogether bring about a liberalization of the English act, since other amendments had been introduced that were redolent of the fears concerning the Baptists and the desire to subject the dissenters to restraint. To the English toleration act's prohibition of meeting behind locked doors the Burgesses added clauses banning worship at night and forbidding the inclusion of slaves without their masters' permission.[44]

After the House of Burgesses had approved this measure at a third reading, however, it voted that the bill should be printed for public consideration rather than being sent up to the Council for immediate enactment. The elected House was accustomed to being the proud arbiter of the good of the community. This rare abdication of its authority is a testimony to the doubts raised by religious conflict. The form and content of the bill nevertheless indicate that a majority in the House of Burgesses was inclined to seek a solution to the problem of increasing dissent by establishing a hard and fast line.[45]

Nearly two years later, in January 1774, the young James Madison (future president of the United States) was exultant about the progress of the American cause in the aftermath of the Boston Tea Party, but he despaired of Virginia on account of continued religious intolerance. He wrote that he had "nothing to brag of as to the State of Liberty" in his "Country," where "Poverty and Luxury prevail among all sorts" and "that diabolical Hell conceived principle of persecution rages." In April of the same year he still had little hope that a bill would pass that would ease the predicament of dissenters. In the previous session of the House "such incredible and extravagant stories" had been told "of the monstrous effects of the Enthusiasm prevalent among the Sectaries and so greedily swallowed by their Enemies," that even measures in favor of regulated freedom "lost footing." Burgesses "who pretend too much contempt to examine into their [the Baptists'] principles . . . and are too much devoted to the ecclesiastical establishment to hear of the Toleration of Dissentients" were likely to prevail once again. Madison's foreboding was correct inasmuch as the old regime in Virginia was never able to arrange a legal resolution of the toleration problem.[46]

One group of gentlemen, however, sharply opposed the enforced control that the majority in the legislature favored. Supporters of unrestricted religious liberty looked forward to an accommodation of the new religious forces in society. They envisaged a new moral order in which a different system of authority would make coercion redundant. We have no means of knowing precisely who wrote the letter signed "Timoleon" printed in Purdie and Dixon's *Gazette* of August 22, 1771, but the position taken up in this piece was one soon to be identified with members of a liberal set within the college. The letter not only asked "by what Authority have some dissenting Teachers been imprisoned in this Province," but also took issue with the whole policy of attempting to restrain the evangelists. "Is attempting to make the Ignorant and Wicked wiser and better a Breach of any Law? The Magistrate should approve of such Attempts, as there is great Need of both." The author, although tacitly accepting the general designation of the preachers as "a Pack of ignorant Enthusiasts," nevertheless denied that this was sufficient reason to imprison them. Going to the heart of the matter, he assailed the fundamental assumptions of the persecutors: "Many will scarcely believe that Society can subsist on any Foundation but a Sameness of Religion. . . . Such People should inform themselves better of the Tendency of religious Opinions that differ a little from their own, and of the natural Right of Mankind, and be no longer so weak and illiberal. A Man may soon be convinced that there are flourishing and happy Governments where the Subjects, though of every Denomination, yet live in Harmony." The Reverend Professor Samuel Henley soon became openly and repeatedly associated with opinions such as this. He was believed to be the author of a letter printed over the signature

"Hoadleianus," which gave offense by its vigorous attack on enforced religious conformity. Similar views were expounded in a sermon that Henley
preached before the House of Burgesses: *The Distinct Claims of Government
and Religion.* . . .[47]

Since Henley's stay in Virginia was brief, it is more valuable for a study of
the polarization of opinion within colonial society to focus attention on a
passionate statement made by one of his pupils, who was the scion of an established Virginia family. The *Oration in Commemoration of the Founders of
William and Mary College* (given in 1772 by James Madison, cousin of the later
president) expounded a Lockean contractual theory of government, intensified by bold assertions of the ideal of the autonomous individual. Madison
also made a fervent plea for a religious liberty that would accommodate the
challenging forces of dissent within a new moral order. The young student
professed to understand the predicament of his elders and articulated the uncertainty of the time: "I am well aware," he declared, "that even the Idea of a
free Toleration in Matters of Religion, has been a Source of endless Apprehensions," and that "to some, this Freedom of Mind . . . may seem the
ready Avenues to Corruption and Depravity. Human Life, thus unhinged, the
universal Fabric appears already dismembering." The anti-inquisitorial imagery that had been prominent in the episcopacy controversy was now passionately turned against those who sought to maintain the jurisdiction of civil
magistrates over matters of the spirit. Madison denounced them as "the open
Enemies to Truth . . . [who] hold the prepared Fetters, and declare their Resolution to enslave," and who may, "when assisted by particular Courts,
proper Officers, well-timed Severities, . . . [and] excrutiating Inquests, impose any Belief, however absurd." In place of such horror Madison offered his
audience a vision of a "generous and unconfined" establishment and gave
millenarian assurances concerning the future of mankind under a regime of
liberty. In his peroration he addressed himself to the rising generation: "Fellow Students, . . . We were born to be free," he declaimed. "It is not less
criminal to sleep upon the Watch, than to desert the Station. . . . Crouch
not to the Sons of Bigot-Rage." His warning was clearly directed not against
ministry and Parliament but against an internal enemy—the intolerance that
the young orator discerned in Virginia's own ruling gentry.[48]

The concurrent development of the debate over the American episcopate
and the struggles concerning toleration in Virginia during 1771 and 1772 re-

veal important aspects of the moral and social crisis that was developing alongside the imperial conflict. The implications of these disputes were not confined to contentious clerics and to a small number of newspaper readers, for the Church occupied a crucial place in traditional Virginia society, and yet clergy and laity continued to show themselves divided in the face of serious threats.

The call for a bishop was one attempt to meet the dangerous challenges of the time by formalizing Church structure and holding it up as a model for society. The strong reaction against the episcopacy proposal, however, revealed the predicament of the whig-patriot gentlemen in Virginia. Their rhetoric and imagery portrayed traditional forms of government as alien and hostile. Their polemics were especially directed against hierarchy, or symbolically legitimated inequality, in the highest levels of society. Yet at the same time the whig leadership was strongly attached to the threatened Church of England and to the parochial social order associated with it. A fundamental dilemma was thus created: if established authority was not to be strengthened by consolidation at the top, what alternatives were open to the ruling gentry as they confronted change and dissidence? The interlocking episcopacy and toleration debates reveal a sharp polarization in which contradictory answers were passionately propounded. For the moment (until the Revolution made their stand untenable) the hard line defenders of the status quo rejected bishops but upheld the Church of England. They predominated over those like Samuel Henley and his college following who were inspired by the secularizing humanitarian ideals of the age and who sought solutions in a new order in which a liberated populace would give free assent to enlightened leadership.

EPILOGUE

Liberty . . . must prove that Bethesda, whose salubrious Waters contain a Remedy for every Disease. . . . Thus, the Mind will be freed from servile Fear, a Gladness will be diffused through the Heart, inferior with superior be seen connected, and human with divine.[49]

This was the vision in which an ardent young Virginia radical found release from the tensions set up by changing alignments on the eve of the Revolution. It was ironically appropriate that when revolution had freed episcopacy from association with oppressive hierarchy and alien power and had formally replaced traditional authority by popular sovereignty and the social contract, the author of these lines, James Madison, became the first bishop of Virginia.

The newspaper war over church hierarchy and religious toleration gave rise to an affair that agitated the small but important town of Williamsburg. The parochial drama that developed as a sequel to the episcopacy controversy involved more of human personality and less of cultural archetype, yet it reveals much about the stresses to which the colonial cultural elite was subject in a time of changing values and challenged authority.

10

"TRANSACTIONS IN THE STEEPLE OF BRUTON"
A *Tableau of Cultural Provincialism*

The day is Saturday, June 12, 1773; the scene is a room, in the tower supporting the wooden steeple of Bruton Church; there twelve of Williamsburg's most worthy citizens are meeting. The occasion is a serious one. The Bruton Parish vestry is assembled not only to fill the vacant rectorship but to hear and assess testimony in support of charges brought against one of the candidates by a senior vestryman, the grave Robert Carter Nicholas, treasurer of the colony. Nicholas had alleged in opposition to the appointment of the Reverend Mr. Samuel Henley, the acting rector, both that he was an avowed enemy of the forms of the Church of England as by law established in Virginia, and that he maintained heterodox opinions derogating the divinity of the Savior.

It is doubtful that a crowd congregated outside the church—although supporters of the two contenders for the rectorship may have attended with the petitions that had been signed in favor of each. Certainly an unusual level of interest had been aroused in the little town by the methods used to canvass signatures and by the disputes that had arisen in consequence. Those who watched through the windows of nearby houses—perhaps peering through the wooden slats of lowered blinds—would have seen not only the assembling of the vestry but also the attendance of the great Peyton Randolph, Speaker of the House of Burgesses. "Some time after the vestry met," messengers were sent out to summon witnesses. The Reverend Mr. Henley, Colonel Richard

FIGURE 19.
The steeple of Bruton

Bland, Mrs. Anne Cary Nicholas, and her sister, Mrs. Molly Cary Ambler—all familiar figures in the parish—could be seen arriving at the great door under the church tower. Much later, after these witnesses had departed, three or four of the vestrymen withdrew, and the Reverend Mr. John Bracken, the successful candidate, was called. He was notified of his selection by those (mainly his supporters) who remained. Having heard the testimony and Samuel Henley's questioning of the witnesses, as well as his attempts at explanation, the vestry had decided not to retain Samuel Henley in the rectorship he had temporarily filled, but to give the parish to his rival, a minister newly arrived in the colony.[1]

The lines of conflict were already clearly established by the time these "transactions in the steeple of Bruton" took place, and the contest was to continue for a good while after that day of flurried activity in drowsy midsummer Williamsburg. From the tangle of charges and countercharges called forth by the rejection of Samuel Henley, the development of relationships between the opposed factions may be unraveled. The rewards include not just the fascination—great though that is—of small-town controversy spiced with heresy hunting but also an opportunity to observe the operation of some of the structures of this "patronage society." Also instructive are the revelations the episode affords of the cultural orientations of some members of provincial high society and the indications of conflicting responses to current metropolitan fashions of thought.

TOWN FATHERS AND REVEREND SCHOLARS

The stage for the drama of the disputed rectorship was shaped—socially and culturally as well as physically—by the axis between the college and Bruton Parish church. The seat of learning was a great, wide, three-story brick building, flanked by fine Georgian houses, situated at the western end of the town. The church stood near the center, on the edge of the green in front of the Governor's Palace. Built in 1715 to serve both the citizens and the dignitaries of colonial government as their official place of worship, it was of fine brick, with high rounded doorways and arches. In the chancel to the east of the great focal space where the transepts met the nave, were set the governor's canopied chair and the high pulpit that towered over it. The interior was proudly regarded as having been "adorned as the best churches in London." Further development of taste was marked in 1752 by the installation of a handsome organ and the appointment of a salaried organist. If the addition (in 1769) of a tower surmounted by a wooden octagon and spire was intended to bestow increased dignity, the effect was not universally acclaimed. Some two years before the vestry met there to weigh questions of orthodoxy, a correspondent had desired the printer of the *Virginia Gazette* to ask the inhabitants of Bruton Parish:

> Would ye not with more cheerfulness pay the assessment to have money raised upon you to mend the streets of Williamsburg . . . than to be taxed to pay for a STEEPLE which is much about as like one as the Emperour of Morocco's pigeon house, or the thing upon the Turkish mosques which they call a minaret where a fellow knocks upon a piece of wood with a mallet to call the mussulmen to prayers?[2]

Most of the records that tell directly of the relationship between the college and the nearby community concern the familiar story of town-and-gown riots and such matters as regulating the students' resort to the many taverns. Yet it was the great church where the scholars and inhabitants were gathered every Sunday that established the most intimate continuing relationship. The rectorship of the parish was customarily held by the president of the college, and the leaders of local society had long shown willingness to subscribe money to pay a reverend gentleman—usually a professor—to deliver a series of sermons, or "lectures," in addition to those incorporated in the regular divine service. The records of the lectureship are few and far between, but those that do survive provide valuable indications of intellectual taste and fashionable piety. A Williamsburg worthy noted of the Reverend Mr. Josiah Johnson, master of the grammar school at the college, not only that he had the character of "an excellent Scholar," but also that he performed "admirably well in church . . . and in his public capacity as a Clergyman he [was] learned, charitable and religious." For these reasons, the gentleman declared, "we shall get him for Lecturer." Erudition was a valued attribute in the clergy who were called upon to preach in the colonial capital, but they were expected to wear it with fashionable lightness. An example of what was needed to meet the demands of high society was contained in the Reverend Mr.

William Bland's request to a London correspondent, made in July 1772. Bland was a young clergyman who had just been nominated lecturer for the ensuing year. "I shall be obliged to you," he wrote, "if there are any short and pithy Sermons published lately would you send me a few by the first opportunity[,] Yorricks and Dodds excepted." Too many of his hearers would already be familiar with the fashionable collections that he excluded from his order.[3]

The Bruton controversy of 1773–1775 brought out still more about the ways in which contemporary clergymen in the first church of Virginia sought both to edify and to divert. The Reverend Mr. Henley believed in a style that was forthright and declamatory upon moral issues. He contemptuously referred to the fashionable source of the sermons of his more successful rival as "the delicious whipt Syllabubs of the jessamy Jacky Langhorne (preferable, no doubt, to *the Milk of the Word*)." He also deplored "the stronger Olios you since have regaled us with, compounded, like Harlequin's Snuff, by pilfering a Pinch out of every Body's Box." Mr. Bracken's reply is revealing of preferred styles and values. It was not the charge of plagiarism that rallied him but the imputation of undue vehemence. "What you mean by stronger Olios," he protested, "I know not, having never, I believe, advanced any Thing in the Pulpit that could be blamed by the most cool and rational Hearer."[4]

The demand for "delicious whipt Syllabubs" or "short and pithy sermons" was evidently considerable, yet some persons in polite society demonstrated more serious concerns. Reconstructing the evolution of intellectual refinement in Williamsburg is difficult, but there are signs that involvement in display of learning was becoming more intense and more open in the years around 1770. In 1769 an eager notice in the *Gazette* informed the public that the "ingenious Mr [James] Ferguson, so famous for his works in astronomy and the mathematicks, may be prevailed upon to accept the Professorship of those sciences in our College." In May 1773—as an organized expression of the intellectual awakening that was occurring—a "Philosophical Society" was formed "for the Advancement of Useful Knowledge."[5]

Without doubt a figure of crucial importance in hastening and encouraging this late flowering of high culture in colonial Williamsburg was Governor Norborne Berkeley, baron de Botetourt. He had made a profound impression, and after his death in 1770 his memory continued "to be held in the highest Estimation." The treasurer of the colony, Robert Carter Nicholas, busied

FIGURES 20–22.
*Cultural attraction. Governor Botetourt was celebrated for the
many public and social virtues that so eminently adorned his character*

DEEPLY IMPRESS'D WITH THE WARMEST SENSE
OF GRATITUDE FOR HIS EXCELLENCY THE
RIGHT HONBLE LORD BOTETOURT'S PRUDENT
AND WISE ADMINISTRATION, AND THAT THE
REMEMBRANCE OF THOSE MANY PUBLIC AND
SOCIAL VIRTUES, WHICH SO EMINENTLY
ADORN'D HIS ILLUSTRIOUS CHARACTER, MIGHT
BE TRANSMITTED TO LATEST POSTERITY,
THE GENERAL ASSEMBLY OF VIRGINIA
ON THE XX DAY OF IULY ANN: DOM: M.DCC.LXXI
RESOLVED WITH ONE UNITED VOICE, TO ERECT
THIS STATUE TO HIS LORDSHIP'S MEMORY.

LET WISDOM AND IUSTICE PRESIDE IN ANY COUNTRY;
THE PEOPLE WILL REIOICE AND MUST BE HAPPY.

AMERICA: BEHOLD YOUR FRIEND!
WHO, LEAVING HIS NATIVE COUNTRY,
DECLIN'D THOSE ADDITIONAL HONOURS, WHICH
WERE THERE IN STORE FOR HIM, THAT
HE MIGHT HEAL YOUR WOUNDS, AND RESTORE
TRANQUILLITY AND HAPPINESS TO THIS
EXTENSIVE CONTINENT: WITH WHAT ZEAL,
AND ANXIETY HE PURSUED THESE GLORIOUS
OBIECTS, VIRGINIA, THUS BEARS HER
GRATEFULL TESTIMONY.

himself on behalf of leading gentlemen who placed orders with him for the governor's "Picture in Miniature." In 1774 Nicholas chose to give the name of this gracious patron of learning and religion to his youngest son, who was baptized in that year. The noble governor's condescension had charmed Williamsburg and all Virginia with a sense of the benefits that might be secured for the distant province from closer cultural connections with the mother country. When Virginians came to erect a marble statue in his honor, the inscription drew particular attention to "those many public and Social Virtues which so eminently adorned his character." Lord Botetourt provided a shining example of genteel patronage of the liberal arts, having interested himself in the college 'and endowed two gold medals to encourage competition in public academic performance among the students.[6]

Into the little world of Williamsburg, where the prevailing fashion was for college and high society to draw closer together, came not James Ferguson, Fellow of the Royal Society, but two new and promising professors—the Reverend Samuel Henley and the Reverend Thomas Gwatkin. Mr. Henley had briefly been the minister to a dissenting congregation outside Cambridge, but on becoming the protégé of liberal churchmen at the university, had sought admission to Anglican orders. With the backing of the bishop of London he was soon appointed to the vacant chair of moral philosophy at The College of William and Mary. Mr. Gwatkin was a scion of a genteel English family and had attended Jesus College, Oxford. The arrival of these highly recommended young luminaries was keenly anticipated, and they were warmly welcomed by the town's leading citizens. Robert Carter Nicholas wrote reproachfully to Henley after they had become unrelenting opponents: "Upon your first coming over to this Country . . . I was pleased with your conversation. From the history of your Education, and the Early Pursuits of your Life, I almost congratulated our Church upon what I thought a valuable Acquisition. These Sentiments, it is well known, I frequently expressed." *

---

* Robert Carter Nicholas (1728–1780) was a grandson of Robert "King" Carter, though by a disapproved marriage between his daughter Elizabeth (widow of Nathaniel Burwell) and Dr. George Nicholas, an ambitious immigrant physician. Nevertheless, a close relation of Lt. Gov. William Gooch was a godparent at his christening. Orphaned at age six, the youngster was brought up by his uncle John Carter of Shirley Plantation, on the James River. Connections, ability, and a reputation for steady character enabled him to become a member of Williamsburg's Common Council by the time he was 21. In 1751 he sealed his acceptance into the close network

Mr. Treasurer Nicholas was not the only Williamsburg patron of learning who cultivated the acquaintance and commended the ability of the talented young professor. Evidently others were pleased to engage him in learned talk at the fashionable soirees—perhaps we should not call them salons—of the Williamsburg haut monde. John Page of Rosewell enjoyed a "long . . . intimacy and friendship" with the young scholar from Cambridge, whom he had "frequently" heard holding forth in serious discourse. The ladies might also gather round to listen. Colonel Richard Bland participated in discussions that might become quite technical, so that a bible or commentary would be brought and opened while texts were disputed upon "in the Company of ten or twelve Gentlemen." Once, when asked whether he intended to go on with the company to the theater, the colonel replied that he would "spend the Evening with Mr. Henley, with whom [he] had rather converse than see a Play."[8]

The fame of such activities and associations spread beyond Williamsburg. Colonel Bland recorded that on one occasion, "after my Return into the Country . . . [a] Gentleman told me he understood our present Minister intended to leave the Parish, and if he did, I should have an Opportunity of serving my Friend Mr. Henley, by endeavouring to get him into the Parish." Henley would later complain that when the rumor of his heresy spread about, "a poor man out of the Country came purposely to see the Creature not orthodox."[9]

The flattering attention, the invitations to enliven the company with his conversation, and the interest taken in his opinions, all were heady wine for the young Samuel Henley and seem to have overthrown what little caution

---

of leading families on the James-York peninsula by a marriage to the talented Anne Cary, daughter of Wilson Cary. (Two of her sisters made marriages into the family of Thomas, Lord Fairfax, the colony's only peer.) Soon after, in Oct. 1754, he became a vestryman of Bruton Parish, and in 1756 he was elected a burgess for York County, probably through the interest of John Norton, the London-Virginia merchant with whom he retained close connections. In 1766, when Speaker-Treasurer John Robinson died, and the scandal of his misappropriation of colony funds to assist his debt-burdened friends was revealed, Nicholas was appointed interim treasurer. After a bitter contest with the Randolph interest, he succeeded both in having the speakership and the treasurership separated and in retaining the latter for himself, while Peyton Randolph had to settle for the speakership alone—plus the succession to the attorney general's post for his brother, John.[7]

For particulars concerning Samuel Henley and Thomas Gwatkin, see p. 216, above.

existed in his makeup. Perhaps in the younger set and among those like Peyton Randolph of the older generation who liked to patronize liberal new
ideas, Henley found misleading assurance that he could speak freely without
creating alarm. John Page of Rosewell noted that he "always appeared to me
to be fond of publishing his doctrines" and to be ready to reveal his apparent
"disbelief" in the Trinity, even to comparative strangers. Strictness concerning doctrine, however, was not the tone in Williamsburg, and even pious
men like Richard Bland and John Page continued on amiable terms with
Henley despite their shocked reactions to his opinions. Nonetheless, a slight
movement may have begun in certain quarters of the little town to withdraw
the hem of the garment. Some persons began now to watch Henley's behavior in church closely, even when he was not conducting the service, and
noted that "our late worthy PRESIDENT BLAIR, in his last Illness" had sought
"the Assistance of a Clergyman" but refused to have Henley (who was then
the acting rector) and instead "desired that Mr Johnson might be sent for." [10]

DIVISIVE CONTROVERSIES

When the episcopacy debate began in 1771, the forthright, even scurrilous,
contributions of Henley and his colleague Gwatkin to the heated exchanges
provoked open censure of the flamboyant newcomers. A chorus of disapproval found outlet in the press. Henley's nonconformist past was now held
up against him and he was denounced as an "abandoned Villain . . . who
being bred up in violent dissenting Principles, comes over to the Church for
the Sake of the *Loaves* and the *Fishes*, and afterwards betrays her." His literary
pretensions and air of self-approbation drew satiric comment:

> Whilst ever and anon he calls the nine,
> Their tributes to bring to H——y's shrine;
> Bid each Gazette great H——y's name *encore*,
> And H——y, H——y, eccho ev'ry shore. [11]

It was the young newcomer's performances in the newspaper controversy
that caused Robert Carter Nicholas to alter his opinion of him. A coolness
developed between them. "Whence can have arisen this Change?" he later

asked Henley. "Review your Writings. . . . Must not every Man of Sense be convinced that your total Dislike to Church Government was the Ground of your Opposition [to the American episcopate]? . . . I was astonished to find that such Words could fall from the Pen of a Clergyman, as you made Use of in blackening the Character of . . . Archbishop Secker; a Prelate, who . . . appears to have been one of the greatest Ornaments of the Age." Nicholas reminded Henley that "it is very well known to many Gentlemen, that, in private Conversations, I had frequently blamed your Conduct respecting the Episcopate, and I had Reason to believe, from many Circumstances, that you knew this."[12]

The treasurer and others who had been watching the Reverend Mr. Henley closely by the end of 1771 had their worst expectations gratifyingly fulfilled by the sermon the embattled minister preached before the whole House of Burgesses on March 1, 1772. The newspaper contributions had shown how much Henley loved calling attention to himself—what pleasure he took in being outrageous in his opinions. We may imagine his exhilaration in mounting the great pulpit of Bruton Church while the principal representatives of authority in Virginia were seated beneath him.

The session that had just opened was at a critical juncture for the Burgesses: the Baptist itinerants were taking parts of the colony almost by storm while numbers of those in authority were hardening their resolution to maintain traditional authority by force if need be. Samuel Henley, giving freedom to the "native energy in the language of the heart," delivered a brief but powerful excoriation of bigotry and persecution, coupled with an encomium on toleration. He offered a pointed contrast between the policies of the Burgesses and his own heroic endeavors: "Though . . . the happiness of mankind is the end of all government, it is . . . a melancholy reflexion that this end hath never been persued by the most direct means. . . . When individuals of ability, rectitude and resolution arise to assert the rights of mankind, they must, always, expect opposition. Innovations will be inveighed against by the interested, and the proposers of them branded with infamy."[13] The argument itself was developed along familiar Lockean lines, emphasizing that "Society is founded upon motives purely human" and that "Obedience to human and divine laws arises from distinct motives." This must have been rather strong for many gentlemen accustomed to act as officers within the traditional framework of the parish community. Even more antagonizing was Henley's

intransigent tone implying that violent religious repression was imminent in
Virginia, if not already exercised by those who sat before him. "Is *every*
State," the outraged moralist asked, "infallible in the doctrines it imposes?"
"If not," he went on to exclaim, "how dreadful may be my condition who am
forced to receive" arbitrarily defined dogma. Having put himself at the center
of the imagined action, he cast his legislative audience as the persecutors,
intent on sacrificing him, "the victim of [their] superstition . . . at the shrine
of an infernal deity." The "votaries" of intolerance he declared to be more
"impious" than "the idolators of Moloch."[14]

Henley next sanctimoniously invited the legislators to look favorably upon
the shift in popular religious allegiance that so alarmed many of them:

> As Society cannot be injured but by actions which violate its property
> or peace, those who demean themselves honestly and orderly ought
> not to be molested, on account either of their sentiments, or worship.
> If these sentiments and this worship be the efflux of sincerity and devo-
> tion, absurd as they may be, God will approve them. The more such
> persons abound in every community, the better will that community
> become. . . . Would Legislators maintain the cause of Religion, let
> them shew its influence on their conduct.[15]

Robert Carter Nicholas, sitting solemnly among the burgesses in Bruton
Church, listened with horror as Henley delivered this scathing commentary
on the policies in defense of establishment maintained by the ruling authorities in Virginia. As the chairman of the Committee for Religion (the
first committee to be named this session), Nicholas felt himself directly attacked. He had been closely involved in the drafting of the toleration bill
that had received its first reading only three days before. The treasurer was
satisfied that under the proposed measure dissenters "will be allowed as complete a Toleration as they can desire." Together with the majority of the large
committee, he felt that the sects should not object to "Clauses . . . to guard
against the Corruption of our Slaves; to prescribe a Method for establishing
their [the dissenters'] Meeting Houses; and to confine the Teachers to certain
Places and Times of Worship." Aware that Henley and his associates had directed their most impassioned denunciations against his bill, Nicholas later
protested that "the whole World may judge, whether the Inhabitants of this
Country are, or whether I myself in particular, am actuated by that Spirit of
Persecution which you have more than once so daringly represented."[16]

Mr. Treasurer's patience was tried beyond the limit when, four days after Henley's sermon, Rind's *Gazette* printed a letter signed "Hoadleianus," which "was considered as an Address to the whole House" on the subject of toleration. Implicit in it was the same commentary on Virginia's religious scene that the sermon had conveyed. It disparaged the English Act of Toleration—the model for the Burgesses' bill—because "Revolutions of Opinions" had long since rendered that great statute obsolete. One sentence in the letter seemed both to prove to Robert Carter Nicholas that his suspicions concerning the intellectual tendencies represented by Henley were well grounded and to give him the opportunity to call a halt. "Hoadleianus" recommended: "Instead of demanding a Subscription to any of the Articles of the Church of England [as was required for the licensing of dissenting preachers] extend your Toleration to all who will subscribe to the Belief of a Supreme Being, his Government of the Universe and the Obligations of Morality. If this be not sufficient (tho' I be thoroughly persuaded that it is) add the Truth of the Christian Religion." [17]

Shortly after the letter appeared, in a debate on matters concerning the Church, the treasurer had occasion (as he recalled) to observe that "one Advantage . . . proposed by the American Episcopate was, that it would probably be of great Service to Religion to have such a respectable Person in Authority . . . [who could] superintend the Conduct of the Clergy, as well in Respect to their Lives and Conversations, as their Doctrines." A burgess who was present when this was said, "answer'd that there could be no Occasion for a Bishop to superintend the Conduct of the Clergy in Respect to their Doctrines, because Christianity had been preserved and inculcated in its greatest Purity, from our earliest Settlement." To this Nicholas retorted, "Tho' it might have been so hitherto, [he] did not know how long it might continue to be the Case when [he] saw such extraordinary Things publish'd in . . . Common News Papers." Referring to the "Hoadleianus" letter, he demonstrated that modern fashions in thought were corrupting the primitive Protestant purity on which his more rustic fellow burgess relied. "Doth he ["Hoadleianus"] not set the christian religion at naught?" asked the outraged upholder of orthodoxy. He went on to declare that the author (whom he believed to be Samuel Henley) was unfit to hold a parish in Virginia. By the time he was credibly informed that the writer was Thomas Gwatkin, Nicholas already knew that Henley had heard of this heated denunciation and had passionately avowed the letter to contain his own sentiments, and that the professor had expressed with "most violent Passion . . . Resentment that any one should presume to question and censure these Principles." It did not take long for reports of the antagonists' outbursts to be carried from one end of Williamsburg to the other, with nothing lost in the telling.[18]

The outrage produced by Henley's self-consciously reformist pronouncements was subsequently aggravated by his publication of the sermon on *The Distinct Claims of Government and Religion*. Because he had it printed in England, it could only be read as a severe censure of Virginia addressed to the wider world. Robert Carter Nicholas declared himself offended by the "pompous Dedication to your Friend" (Dr. John Jebb). The young preacher had ostentatiously linked himself in "the pursuit of truth" to that renowned Latitudinarian. Henley celebrated his patron for having entered in his prime upon endeavors that "LOCKE and NEWTON, towards the close of life, regretted they had not earlier begun." Where "LORD VERULAM" had attempted "to strike off the shackles from the human mind" through "the science of Nature," Jebb had "attempted it in the study of Revelation." In Henley's introduction the chairman of the Committee on Religion could not fail to see insulting references to himself and his colleagues as "some Gentlemen [who] have taken offence at the *subject*" of toleration. Nicholas believed that Henley had further blackened their characters with the melodramatic declaration that "however the doctrine, advanced in this Sermon, may be regarded by the intriguing, self-interested politician, or the gloomy narrow-hearted bigot, the Author avows it as the doctrine of Jesus; and hopes he should not want fortitude to maintain it at the stake." Who could Henley have envisaged as piling up the faggots and setting the torch, unless it was Robert Carter Nicholas?[19]

MR. HENLEY'S QUEST FOR PATRONAGE AND PREFERMENT

In July 1772 news reached Virginia that the Reverend the Honorable Mr. James Horrocks had died abroad, leaving vacant not only the positions of bishop's commissary in Virginia and the presidency of the college, but also the rectorship of Bruton. Samuel Henley was already officiating for Mr. Horrocks in his parish. Robert Carter Nicholas later reminded him that "upon a

Report of the Death of the late Commissary . . . , you applied to me, as a Vestryman, for my Vote to succeed him. I told you candidly, and with as much Freedom, as Civility would allow me, that our Sentiments in religious Matters seemed to differ so widely that I could not think myself justifiable to the Parish in complying with your Request. You answered that your Object was Truth, and in Reply, I told you that I hoped mine was so too."[20]

On July 30 the vestry announced the selection of "the Reverend Josiah Johnson, Master of the Grammar School in the College," to fill the vacant benefice. Henley evidently enjoyed some support, since the choice was declared to have been "by a Majority" only. Perhaps Henley had not improved his standing with some leading parishioners by preaching, on the announcement of Commissary Horrocks's death, a sermon in "Delineation of the clerical Character" in which he set out to "expose *Bigotry* under all its Forms." By disparaging "an Age which too generally substitutes *ritual Observances* for the *substantial Virtues of a good Life*," he was taken to have directly censured "a Majority of the Vestry." Nevertheless it appears that in the deliberations upon the choice of a new rector at this time, no one voiced doubts concerning Henley's fitness to be entrusted with the cure of souls.[21]

By the beginning of his third year in Virginia, Samuel Henley had become both a celebrity and a notoriety there. In addition to his performances in the press and in the pulpit he had been active as professor of moral philosophy at the college, where he had gathered a following and had exerted a significant influence on the thinking of some of his students. The rejuvenation of the college that had begun under Lord Botetourt's patronage must now have seemed to many at best a mixed blessing, since one of its most visible manifestations was the new freedom that young literati, encouraged by Henley's facetious and irreverent polemical style, assumed in the writing of newspaper satires. Robert Carter Nicholas declared that he was not alone in holding Henley responsible for the example set "when Gentlemen of your Order treat serious Subjects, and exalted Characters, with an unbecoming and indecent Freedom."[22]

For all his enjoyment of literary witticism, Samuel Henley was a passionate moralist. The influence of his reformist zeal upon the college became clearly apparent in August 1772. Founders' Day exercises had been given new life by Lord Botetourt's endowment of the two gold medals to be given as prizes for public orations. One of these ornamental addresses had been published to the world for the first time in 1771. It was delivered by the young William Leigh (soon to be ordained a clergyman), and it clearly bears the traces of "the Revolutions of Opinions" in which Henley and Gwatkin rejoiced. Much more striking in this respect, however, was the oration, already quoted in the preceding chapter, delivered the following year by the young James Madison (cousin of the later United States president). The orator took "Liberty" as his theme and celebrated the college's contribution to this cause. Echoing Samuel Henley, Madison concerned himself with the conduct of his tradition-bound elders in the matter of toleration—and proceeded to lay rationalist injunctions on them.[23]

Robert Carter Nicholas, as a member of the governing board of visitors of the college, was almost certainly present at these academic displays. He must have had difficulty in keeping his seat during the discourse when Madison projected a vision (again identifiable as Henley's) of the possibilities to be opened up by applying reason to Revelation. "The theoretical Knowledge of Mankind," the young disciple declaimed, "is susceptible of daily Improvement, of Refinements which not only sublimate Religion, but every Science that glows in the Poet, or shines in the Philosopher." If he did indeed sit through the performance, Nicholas had to endure a blistering denunciation of the firm upholders of the Church establishment as "the open Enemies to Truth . . . [who] hold the prepared Fetters, and declare their Resolution to enslave." As the oration developed, Madison even reiterated the offending proposal of "Hoadleianus" (Gwatkin) to omit formal professions of Christian faith: "There may be a Profession of Faith purely social, the Tenets of which, it is the Province of the Legislature to determine." Against a serene evocation of the "gladness [that] will be diffused through the Heart" by the liberation of the mind, the orator juxtaposed a martial exhortation to his fellow students that they "crouch not to the Sons of bigot-Rage."[24]

In March 1773 the conflict that had been slowly developing since the time of the episcopacy controversy, moved toward its climax when the Reverend Mr. Johnson fell ill. One evening in this spring season there was a face-to-face encounter between the two principal antagonists. Nicholas later reminded Henley (in order to discomfort him):

> When there was a Prospect of our Parish's becoming vacant a second
> Time . . . , contrary to my Expectation, you renewed your Applica-

tion to me, I own in the politest Terms, and it gave me Pain that I
could not comply. . . . But . . . my Objections were increased. I mentioned such only as your own Publications had furnished. . . . My Inclination was to give as little Offence as possible. . . . This Evening's
Conference produced from you a very genteel Letter. . . . You thanked
me for the very "candid and Manly Conversation," . . . and told me,
that, though you should be happy in having my Suffrage, yet, upon the
Principles, on which I acted, you could not pretend to blame me, if I
should not vote for you, but should esteem me, as if I had stood
amongst the foremost of your Friends.

The treasurer announced unctuously that he had been "exceedingly distressed
by this Letter" and had burned it, "that it might not fall into other Hands."
Henley retorted that the conversation had, in fact, turned upon a set of questions that Robert Carter Nicholas had raised about his printed sermon, and
that his letter had been sent as a reply to those queries.[25]

On April 4, 1773, the Reverend Mr. Johnson died, and the moves that
followed made it certain that the leading vestryman and the divine would
find future polite conversation between them impossible. Henley's supporters
in the Bruton vestry tried to rush him into the vacant rectorship. His antagonist soon informed the candidate and the world: "At our first Vestry, upon
your being proposed, and a Gentleman's expressing an earnest Desire that the
Matter should then be determined, I objected to you for the Reasons I had
given you in Private [i.e., the published sermon, considered an attack on
conformity in the Church], but confined myself to these alone." A while
later, "being summoned to a succeeding Vestry, I went from home, with a
Resolution indeed to vote against you, but determined . . . to rely on the
Vestry's remembering what I had before objected . . . without repeating it,
unless I was compelled to do so." Evidently Henley's supporters maintained
unmoved their preference for their talented but controversial candidate. The
treasurer, who "went prepared," carrying Henley's printed sermon in his
pocket, not only "made some few Animadversions" upon that work but was
stung by "something . . . which passed" (expressions in support of Henley's
radical tolerationism?) into informing the vestry "of some Heterodox Opinions, which I had been told by a Person of undoubted Credit, that [Henley]
had broached in Conversation." By this time Nicholas was promoting an al-

ternative candidate, the Reverend Mr. John Bracken, a cultured English clergyman about thirty years old and very recently arrived in the colony.[26]

Thwarted by this escalation of opposition to his ambition, Samuel Henley,
with the aid of admirers, set about mustering popular support in order to
bring pressure to bear on the vestry. It is inconceivable that even the au-
dacious young professor would have attempted such a strategy had he not enjoyed a measure of patronage, or at least were he not aware that he met with
sympathy in high places.

Mr. Bracken later revealed the high rank of Henley's most influential backers by his deferential declaration that "their favourable Opinion I shall always
wish to cultivate and deserve." Henley himself described them as "several of
the most respectable [i.e., eminent] Inhabitants" of the parish. The alarming
presumptuousness of the ambitious young cleric inhibited prudent dignitaries
from taking too public a stand on his behalf, but all the surviving tracks
lead to the door of Peyton Randolph, on Williamsburg's central green.* This
weighty figure was Speaker of the House of Burgesses as well as being the sitting member for Williamsburg and the grand master of its Lodge of Freemasons. Recent political controversies had given him no cause to love the
strictly orthodox treasurer, Robert Carter Nicholas.[28]

---

* Peyton Randolph (c. 1721–1775) was the leading member of Virginia's foremost family. He
was the son and heir of Sir John Randolph, who had briefly been attorney general (1727), and
then served concurrently as Speaker of the House of Burgesses and treasurer of the colony
(1734–1737). Peyton assumed his father's former offices in turn—save that the treasurership was
taken by Robert Carter Nicholas (see p. 217). In 1744 he became attorney general and was even
able to regain the post soon after Lt. Gov. Robert Dinwiddie dismissed him in 1754 when he left
the colony to act as agent for the Burgesses at Whitehall in their dispute with Dinwiddie over
the pistole fee. In May 1756, during the anxious period that followed the shattering of Brad-
dock's army in 1755, Peyton Randolph took the lead in a striking gesture of patriotism: "a great
Number of the principal Gentlemen" of Virginia "associated" themselves under his command to
equip themselves and the men in their pay and to march westward to defend the frontier. In 1766
Peyton Randolph became Speaker almost by right of succession, and his brother, John, stepped
into the attorney generalship he vacated. In 1774 he was further elevated in the service of his
country by being elected president of the First Continental Congress. His capacity to dominate
politics in the paternalist mode—learned in a long apprenticeship to Speaker Robinson—will be
illustrated in the following chapter. His membership in the Freemasons (the Grand Mastership
naturally followed) was significant, since the movement was strongly tinged at that time with
anti-dogmatic illuminism and tolerationism. Masonry, and its relationship to the ideals of the
American patriots, is a subject that cries out for careful study.[27]

Probably emboldened by awareness of this alignment, Henley drove on with his campaign through "Emissaries that were employed to collect Names" on his behalf. His antagonist denounced the proceedings as "a very extraordinary Canvass." Despite his dislike of all maneuvers to involve the populace in disputes among their betters and his firm belief that such practices had the least place in ecclesiastical affairs, the treasurer chose not to leave the field uncontested. It was not long before "a paper in opposition" to the unorthodox professor of moral philosophy circulated throughout Williamsburg.[29]

The course of the ensuing struggles illuminates the issues at stake and the powers of the leading gentlemen in this little society. Active on Mr. Henley's behalf were numbers of young gentlemen of the college—Mr. Samuel Shields and Mr. James Madison came to be named in the increasingly bitter polemics. The Reverend Mr. Gwatkin played his part, publishing a broadside in his friend's defense signed "A Clergyman of the Church of England." Also active as the "Chief Conductor" of moves to promote Henley's preferment was a "Mr. Russell," who can be tentatively identified as William Russell—soon to become secretary to the Williamsburg Lodge of Freemasons.[30]

On the other side, Robert Carter Nicholas enlisted one Joseph Kidd, whom he later described as "an inoffensive, honest Tradesman." He was "*employed* to procure the names of subscribers" who opposed the former acting rector. Kidd's blunt stratagem was to propagate a charge that Henley "did not believe the articles of the Church; and . . . was a Deist." Mr. Treasurer was soon to be reminded, however, that he stood not higher than number two in the hierarchy of Williamsburg citizens. Henley told the world that "a Magistrate of this City [Mr. Speaker Randolph, we must conclude from the sequel] . . . shocked at so black a contrivance, informed me of it. I, immediately, went to Kidd and expostulated with him: At first with much confusion he denied the fact. However, as the Gentleman had authorized me in the fullest manner to use his evidence and name, I told him my author. He then began to equivocate, at last confessed, [and] named . . . [Mr. Nicholas] as his authority for what he had said." Faced with the prospect of a slander suit, and with the name of the leading gentleman of the colony lined up against him, Kidd "not only expressed a *willingness* to acknowledge the injustice of the calumny, but, more than once, thanked me for my lenity to him." In due course a paid advertisement appeared in the *Gazettes* in which Joseph Kidd declared that, "whereas it is publickly reported that I accused the Reverend Mr Henley

Peyton Randolph

FIGURES 23 AND 24.
The Masonic symbol of the Universal Architect prominently displayed

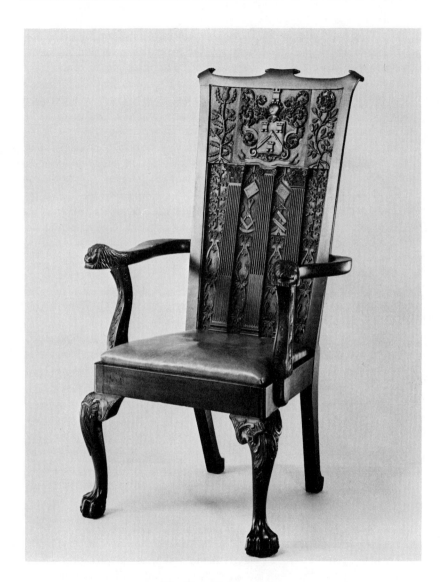

The Grand Master's chair

of *Deism*, and a disbelief in the *Thirty Nine Articles of our Church*, I do hereby, out of Justice to Mr *Henley*'s Character, declare that I never had Reason to believe that such were his Principles." Since Kidd had, almost unwittingly, contradicted statements made by Robert Carter Nicholas, then out of town, a newspaper wit cautioned him: "how soundly wilt thou be beaten on his return to thy city." Kidd's next letter to the press was much more assertive than his first and bears the marks of having been written for him by the treasurer.[31]

During the canvass for signatures in support of the rival candidates, some of the vestry majority that eventually opposed Henley wavered and promised him (or were taken by Henley to have promised) "their Votes, if a Majority of the Parishioners should be in [his] Favour." Henley meanwhile carried the war into the enemy's camp by inserting in the *Gazette* a letter to Robert Carter Nicholas commending his "Professions of Rectitude, Candour, and Religion" but warning that "if you . . . should unhappily transgress them, ingenuous Minds will behold you with Pain." Nicholas replied, setting forth the grounds of his conduct at great length. While the canvass continued in the town, a gigantic war of words began in the press. Before it was over, the wags who began to publish satires on it had dubbed the treasurer "Verbositas" and the quixotic Henley "Amadis de Gaul."[32]

The stern Robert Carter Nicholas would clearly have to strengthen his hand if he was not to be humiliated by defeat in a conflict with a flamboyant immigrant divine. During the course of this furious contest, therefore, he wrote a letter to Richard Bland, who had first alerted him concerning Henley's heterodox opinions. Nicholas asked Bland to give "from under [his] Hand, an Account of [his] Conversation with Mr Henley." After hesitation the colonel "gave him, in a Letter, the Substance of Mr. Henley's Explication of the Scripture Passage [Hebrews 1] . . . and left it to his [the treasurer's] Discretion to make Use of it or not."[33]

A HERESY HEARING AND ITS SEQUEL

On Thursday, June 10, 1773, Colonel Bland rode into town to see the great eye and ear healer, Dr. Graham, whose stay in Williamsburg was about to end. On arrival he visited his friend the treasurer, who "entreated" him to stay until Saturday, when the vestry was to meet, so that he might give evidence in person if called upon. Bland later recalled that

> I resolved to oblige the Treasurer, not only because he desired it, but also because soon after I arrived in Town, I was informed a mighty storm was gathering against me; that I was charged with betraying private Conversation at a Friend's House; that I had incurred his as well as Mr Henley's high resentment; and that a *young Gentleman*, and a *young* Lady, were to prove that no Conversation, like that . . . mentioned, passed at the Gentleman's House. . . . As I am not easily frightened, especially when I have Truth to support me, I determined to await the impending Storm. . . . But as it gave me Pain to have a Difference with the other Gentleman, upon Mr Henley's Account, I assured him, by a Letter, that I did not consider the Conversation as private . . . and that he was one of the last Men in the World I would have a difference with.

The offended gentleman whom Colonel Bland attempted to placate was none other than Mr. Speaker. Peyton Randolph's anger at the violation of the sanctity of his hospitality enables us to gain for a moment a more certain view of his posture in the cultural combat that had been joined. It appears that the Speaker insisted on attending the vestry meeting on June 12, 1773, in order to oversee the use made of evidence relating to events in his house. He was not then a vestryman, nor was he named even obliquely by Richard Bland as one of those invited to testify—yet he was certainly present at the meeting and actively commented on the testimony.[34]

It was "soon" after he got to town that Colonel Bland was told of the Speaker's displeasure. Williamsburg society was agog—attention fixed on the forthcoming vestry meeting. The fullest and most dependable account of the dramatic "Transactions in the Steeple of Bruton" that Saturday comes from Richard Bland. We may follow the proceedings, largely in his words, from the time that the witnesses who had been summoned (Mr. Henley, Mrs. Nicholas, Mrs. Ambler, and himself) were seated. First, Bland recalled, "Mr Treasurer . . . drew my letter from his Pocket, and gave it to Mr Henley who read it with an audible Voice." A painful exchange followed during which Henley took exception, not to Bland's comment that he was "*too fond of Egotisms*," but to Bland's intended "Compliment" that he was "*a Gentleman of good but not rigid morals*"! Bland then "gave a general Account of the Conversation" concerning the first chapter of the Epistle to the Hebrews and "appealed to the Gentleman [Peyton Randolph] at whose house it happened whether such Conversation did not pass." The Speaker "acknowledged it in general, but said he thought [Bland] misunderstood Mr. Henley." Mr. Randolph did confirm, however, that the colonel told "Mr Henley at the Time [that] he explained the Scriptures as a Socinian," but the Speaker added that he differed "in Opinion upon some of Mr. Henley's Expressions" and later "concluded with saying, he thought Mr Henley proved himself to be an able Divine." The atmosphere had grown tense. Colonel Bland noted: "To this I made no Answer, being unwilling to aggravate, but thought very differently, and that Mr Henley proved himself a mere Caviller and Perverter of the sacred Text, in one of the most important Doctrines of the established Church, which it was his Duty to defend." [35]

Samuel Henley also contended that Bland had misunderstood him, to which the colonel replied: "If I did mistake your Meaning I am sorry for it, but I am certain of the contrary; I am certain you explained the Chapter so as to deprive our Saviour of his Divinity." Mr. Henley then had leave to explain the chapter in question once more. Bland, who considered that he had a very distinct memory of the original conversation, asserted that Henley "varied very materially from his former Explication." The women were not meekly silent during this part of the hearing; Nicholas later reminded Henley that "when you were contradicting Colonel Bland in almost everything he asserted, Mrs Ambler told you that you need not deny what he charged you with, because she heard you preach a Sermon last Good Friday much to the *same Purpose*, in which you compared our SAVIOUR to *Moses*, and gave him but a *small Degree of Preference*." Mr. Henley then asked the colonel if he "knew any Thing further relative to his principles." Bland "desired him not to ask any more Questions." But Mr. Henley said, "Sir, my Character is at Stake, and I must insist upon an Answer." The colonel "was a little offended at his peremptory Manner, and replied, do you really insist upon it? He answered, I do." "Then," said the colonel, "I do know more . . . ; you hold the Doctrine of Annihilation, and that the Wicked, in the next Life, will, by means of their Punishments, be totally destroyed." Mr. Treasurer recalled that in the ensuing discussion, which dealt with the subject of Hell, "you [Mr.

Henley] ludicrously told us you did not know that the *Geography of it had ever been settled.*" Henley apparently admitted to belief in "annihilation."[36]

Colonel Bland also remembered that Mrs. Nicholas (who spoke "with great Clearness and Perspicuity of Expression") testified that she had once asked Mr. Henley how he could have sworn to conform to the doctrines of the Church. He had explained that "one of the Articles declares, that whatever is not contained in the Scriptures, or may [not] be proved from them, is not to be believed as an Article of Faith . . . so that he had a Right to exercise his private Judgement, and might with a safe Conscience, subscribe to the Articles."[17]

Richard Bland left the vestry before Mrs. Ambler was examined. Samuel Henley fought on determinedly, but an oppressive weight of righteous orthodoxy was steadily piled upon him, especially after "it was proved to the Vestry that our late worthy PRESIDENT BLAIR" had rejected the suspected heretic's ministrations when Blair was upon his deathbed a year and a half before. Henley must have known which way the decision would go, and most of his supporters had left before the Reverend Mr. Bracken was sent for.[38]

With this decision the matter should have ended, but Henley had stood in the great pulpit of Bruton; he wanted to stand there again. He had already come to see himself as a campaigner against bigotry, a son of the Enlightenment. He declared himself to have been deeply injured as a "Christian, a Clergyman . . . a Man of Honour." His frustrated ambition was fed in October 1773, when the governor, the earl of Dunmore, either from sympathy with his opinions, or, more probably, out of consideration for the Randolph interest, named him preacher to the General Court. Soon after that Henley yielded to the "*repeated* Applications" of certain gentlemen (later designated as "Several of the most respectable Inhabitants" of Bruton Parish) and allowed himself to be canvassed as a candidate for the Sunday lectureship. A substantial subscription was raised on his behalf, but the Reverend Mr. Bracken refused him the use of the church, pleading that he did not think he could properly admit to his pulpit a clergyman whose orthodoxy was in doubt. Another newspaper war developed, with Henley now attacking the new rector and being denounced in turn by him.[39]

The only perceptible results of Henley's renewed assault upon the orthodox "party" were further embroilments with provincial dignitaries, more amusement for the wits, and greater disgust felt by well-wishers of the Church. Robert Carter Nicholas was authorized by witnesses to print an extended summary of all the accumulated evidence showing Henley's heterodoxy. He added the testimony of the Honorable John Page of Rosewell to what the vestry had already heard. We can still, after two hundred years, hear the note of offended piety—of scandal savored—in Nicholas's triumphant disclosure that "this Gentleman [Mr. Page] will declare that he hath been frequently astonished at the strange Opinions you have maintained. . . . He hath heard you argue against the *Doctrine* of the ADORABLE TRINITY, and assert that by the *three Persons* was only meant the three *Characters* under which God had made himself known to Men, viz. as their *Creator, as the Means of their Redemption,* and *as inspiring them with good Thoughts;* for that the Word *Person* was borrowed from *Persona,* which signified an *Actor's Mask.*" [40]

Henley's replies, and the announcement that he was about to publish *A Candid Refutation* . . . in book form, only brought indignant and explicit rebuttal from Colonel Bland, "against Mr. Henley's bold Assertions in a Common Newspaper." John Page, newly sworn in as a member of the King's Council, soon followed Bland's example. The satiric wits were in their element, while angry protests were now heard against the scandal to the Established Church that this public feuding of clergymen was causing. One who signed himself "An Enemy to Captious Parsons" pointed out that "a general corruption of manners has diffused through . . . the lower parts of the country, whilst little else prevails in the upper counties . . . than an indissoluble aversion to, and an enthusiastic dissention from, the principles of our ecclesiastic establishment." The author admonished the contentious clergymen to direct their efforts to preserving their church from the desolation that seemed imminent. Attention was turned back to the anxiety-fraught issues of dissent and toleration that had provided the occasions for Henley's first clashes with leaders in the colony. [41]

The professor of moral philosophy had made himself impossible, even for those who might at first have sympathized. He had been treasurer of the Society for the Promotion of Useful Knowledge at its inauguration in 1773. He was not among its office-bearers announced in June 1774 at the commencement of its second year of existence. The bottom, however, had not yet been reached. In December 1774 Henley, made vindictive by his helpless antagonism to Robert Carter Nicholas, wrote under a pseudonym to accuse his enemy of hypocrisy. He charged the treasurer with breaking the patriotic non-importation agreement almost as soon as he had signed it. Newspaper exchanges resumed and were probably only stopped by Virginia's resort to arms during the spring of 1775. Henley and Gwatkin both took the side of His Majesty's Government and were compelled to seek refuge with the governor, Lord Dunmore, on a Royal Navy ship. The outbreak of Revolutionary hostilities had resulted, ironically, in the expulsion from Virginia of the two most prominent spokesmen for a free toleration of dissenters from the established Church of England.[42]

SMALL WORLD—GREAT ISSUES

In its bitter end as in much of its tragicomic course, the Bruton Parish affair seems to boil down to a demonstration of the smallness of the world of Williamsburg, and to a display of the poisonous intimacy of some of its hatreds. But there was more than that. The controversy also reveals important divergences of opinion in provincial high society, and with them something of the dilemmas of the colonial situation become more apparent.

In its inception, and even in the inflated pretensions of its principals, the dispute was a drama that involved conflict over some of the major intellectual trends of the day. This is not to say that personal factors can be set aside. The clash between the mercurial, witty, exhibitionist Samuel Henley and the solemn, ponderous Robert Carter Nicholas is certainly intelligible in terms of conflicting personalities, and yet our understanding is altogether incomplete if confined to that level of explanation. The clashing personalities were drawn to opposite poles in the high culture of their age.

What were the Reverend Samuel Henley's inspirational beliefs? The evidence is fragmentary—and further problems are created by Henley's efforts at deliberate obscurity when his orthodoxy was publicly questioned—but the outlines are discernible. Henley, influenced by certain Cambridge Latitudinarians with whom he had come in contact, had, while retaining an unquestioning faith in the sacred truth of Holy Writ, moved away from the Trinitarian doctrine of redemption that was central to traditional theology. Where difficulties arose for him in biblical interpretation, he readily invoked allegorical meanings. This in turn eased the way for the crucial step in the young dissenting minister's career. Having developed a soft line on the meaning of words and a deep conviction that dogmatic theology was irrelevant to the ethical systems of "reason" and "benevolence," which seemed most important to him, Henley persuaded himself that he could subscribe to the Thirty-nine Articles and find his vocation as a clergyman of the Church of England. He also came to feel that in the "persuit of Truth" according to his enlightened understanding he would be doing the work of that church more excellently than anyone who, being "bigotted to a formal 'Ritual,'" might be inclined, as he saw it, to set orthodoxy above good life.[43]

The lineaments of Henley's faith can be reconstructed from his writings and reported words. He continued to believe in a life after death and in a day of divine judgment, but his whole emphasis had shifted from eschatology to ethics. It is clear that when he called Christianity "a design most propitious to the happiness of man," he had primarily the life of this world in view. He was emphatic in putting the "*substantial Virtues of a good Life*" above "*ritual Observances.*" His outlook was grounded on a typical Enlightenment sense of universal benevolence toward all mankind—considered rather abstractly. Thus to Richard Bland he emphasized the superiority of Christ's teaching, not by means of the mystical doctrines of divine mediation and redemption, but by reference to His "*establishing an universal Religion.*" "I shall ever consider universal Love," Henley declared, "as the first Principle of Religion, that which infinitely supersedes all Knowledge and *Orthodoxy.* . . . If this be *Heresy,* I glory in it!" Underlying this declaration was a faith in a single rational order: "Whether we place the foundation of virtue in a conduct agreeable to nature or reason—the fitness of things—conformity to truth—the common good—or—the will of our Creator, the conclusion will . . . be the same: For since that which is most agreeable to nature and reason, will be best adapted to the fitness of things, intirely conformable to truth, and productive of the greatest good, it must necessarily be what God hath appointed." The conformity of Revelation to reason and the supremacy of supposedly rational ethical axioms were, of course, the dogmas of Henley's faith.[44]

It might be possible to outline Robert Carter Nicholas's beliefs in the same way—but it would be beside the point. The character of the vestryman's insistence on the importance of correct doctrine reveals that doctrine as such had a very different place in his world view, and that for him the meanings of the sacred formulas were implicit and lay in repetition itself. His was a conventional piety, covered—indeed defensively protected—by subscription to articles and creeds and by a reverent conformity in ritual. We need not doubt that Nicholas not only reverenced the liturgy but also found satisfaction in "so excellent a Form of Prayer prepared for us." He considered it "a signal Advantage to know what these prayers consist of" and therefore regularly set aside time to "meditate on them" in private.[45]

The essential contrast between the antagonists in this conflict lay not so much in their different beliefs as in their fundamentally different orientations toward the world. Henley and his associates felt they were preparing for a new era in the history of man through their effort "to strike off the shackles from the human mind" by applying reason "in the study of Revelation." Thus they conceived of their times as "these modern ages of free enquiry" and contemplated with exhilaration "Knowledge . . . susceptible of daily Improvement," which would render both "Religion . . . [and] Science" more sublime.[46]

To Robert Carter Nicholas this Enlightenment project smacked of gross presumption and aroused his strongest indignation. He resented the "ill digested Notions of *Modern Refinements*" that he believed had prompted the attacks of Henley and his disciples on Virginia institutions. The upholder of orthodoxy had warned the would-be rector: "Remember, Sir, that we have had Moses and the Prophets; above all we have already had the EVER BLESSED JESUS upon Earth, and that we have no Right or Reason to expect any future Miracles for our Instruction." The treasurer eventually perceived Samuel Henley with distaste, as one of those "devious, soaring Geniuses [who,] observing the good old Tract already beaten and possessed by others, find there is little left to gratify their Ambition; and then, *per Fas aut Nefas*, they attempt to strike out something new and extraordinary." All the initial provincial enthusiasm for the young professor from England, and the satisfaction with which Nicholas had "almost congratulated" the Virginia church for having made "a valuable Acquisition," turned into an antagonism expressed in mocking reproach. The treasurer taunted Henley for printing his sermon in Cambridge though he delivered it in Williamsburg, and ironically anticipated the publication of the "ETHICA HENLEYANA." The bitter colonial worthy suggested to the clever English professor that this work might "make a more conspicuous Figure" if its author were to "bind it up with [his] Life of PETRARCH, which the learned World hath so long waited for."[47]

Behind Nicholas's hostility to the younger man's avant-garde posture lay a whole set of values and beliefs. Challenged by the modernity of the upstart college divines, Nicholas was led to offer one of the fullest surviving articulations of the assumptions underlying the traditional role ascribed to the Established Church in the colonial Virginia of his youth.

The treasurer's conception ultimately rested on related beliefs concerning knowledge and social rank. For Nicholas, learning was a sacred, almost arcane, deposit. Through the church as the main vehicle, instruction should proceed from the upper ranks, in whom knowledge was vested for safekeeping, to the lower, who were to receive it deferentially:

> Suppose . . . every Man was allowed . . . *Freedom of Judgement* . . . let all Men, think and speak and preach as they will, or rather, as they *can*; instead of that Uniformity of Doctrine which our Church has formerly been blessed with, what a Babel of Religions should we have amongst us? . . . Look around the World, when you are thinking of the Rights of *private Judgement*, and consider who make up the far greater Part of its Inhabitants; are they capable of reasoning upon the many Parts of Religion? Would you have them hear and decide the Controversies of the Learned? . . . Must they not in a great Measure depend upon the Advice and Opinion of their Teachers? And whether, think you, might they rely with greater Safety upon the glorious Luminaries of our Church . . . or upon every private Preacher?

This view of relationships led Nicholas to declare that "the necessity of Rules and Articles must also be allowed; a Society without these is an Existence to me unintelligible." He considered ecclesiastical authority secure: "Our Church . . . formed the principal, leading Articles of her Faith from the Holy Scriptures . . . which [Articles] are approved and confirmed by the State; Provision is made for such as are qualified to become her Ministers; [and] that Uniformity . . . may be preserved, Subscription to her Articles is required."[48]

Proper decorum was, according to Nicholas's vision, an essential part of the instructional process. He therefore insisted on "Rules and Orders," and a strict regard for *bienséance*: "I own myself one of those, who should always expect to see a Clergyman on the orthodox Side of the Question." Nicholas gloried in "the numberless Beauties, with which our Liturgy abounds," and strongly preferred them to "every Thing extempore." These opinions were in turn supported by an idealization of the greatness of England's progress from Reformation to Revolution. "Need you be told, at this Time of Day," he asked, "that the best Defenders of Christianity and the ablest Expounders of the Sacred Writings are to be found in the Bosom of the Church of England? It is to their Wisdom . . . that we are indebted for our happy Establishment."[49]

To summarize: we may best understand the Bruton Parish conflict if we see it as a tiny microcosm of the tensions in the relationship—the love-hate relationship—between the maturing colony and the mother country. Virginians were eager to receive the latest fashions, to be in touch with the polite world, and to enjoy the benefits of a cultured high society in the provincial center. It was this craving that Lord Botetourt had answered so fully. The same need is seen in the warm reception, indeed the lionization, of the two talented young professors when they first came out to Virginia. But the affair involved another predictable response, since the colonial cultural province also manifested the tendency to discover a taint of corruption in the newest and most fashionable arrivals from the metropolis. The imports were measured against ideal images of the mother country and were found to be degenerate. Alarm at such discoveries led in turn to a defensive retreat toward an idealized self-image of the colony itself. This resort was epitomized by the unnamed burgess who questioned the necessity of Nicholas's call for supervision of the clergy's doctrine. Wounded provincial pride makes intelligible the recoil of those who rejected Henley's corrupting influence. They could only deplore the disturbance of "Christianity . . . preserved and inculcated in its greatest Purity from . . . the earliest Settlement" by an alarming thirst for novelty.[50]

As it has been analyzed within its immediate narrow time span, the little drama of Bruton Parish depicts the triumph of Robert Carter Nicholas and the discomfiture of Samuel Henley. If the time perspective is broadened and the dramatic focus is turned from the men to the issues, the outcome is strikingly reversed. Within two decades of this episode the "Church established by Law" of which the treasurer had declared, "I glory in professing myself one of her dutiful and grateful sons," lay in ruins. The surviving institutions—especially The College of William and Mary—were pervaded by modernist rational doctrines. Nicholas could not have foreseen these developments, and he died in 1780 before they were far advanced. Yet they must influence our understanding of the man and those who stood by him, for in his polemical writing one can discern a tragic sense of his entrapment between what seemed like the apostasy of cultural fashion in England and the anarchy of "ignorant and enthusiastick" popular evangelicalism in Virginia. This perception was behind his determined fight against the two reverend professors, who seemed bent on betraying the Established Church to both movements. Robert Carter Nicholas won this little skirmish, but the onslaughts of rationalist thought and popular revivalist religion could not thereby be defeated.

Nine years passed between the attempt of the Parliament at Westminster to raise an internal revenue by means of a stamp tax and its decision to reduce the colonies to submission by the "Coercive Acts" of 1774. In the aftermath of the destruction of a cargo of dutiable tea by the Boston patriots, the ministry sought to make an example of Massachusetts by closing the rebellious port and imposing an authoritarian regime on the colony. In Virginia the years of intermittent disputes concerning the form of control that the rulers of Great Britain might exercise over the colonies had impelled the local leaders to consider more closely their own provincial identity. The patriots searched themselves anxiously for signs of the corruption that they were convinced had taken hold in the parent country. They strengthened their resolve to act positively on the basis of the remaining pristine virtue that they could discover in their society. They would work its regeneration before all was lost. Meanwhile the lead in the evangelical movement, with its individual and collective exploration of guilt and longing for redemption, had momentarily passed from Baptists to Methodists.

11

POLITICAL ENTHUSIASM AND
CONTINUING REVIVALISM

Revolutions, like the social life whose symbolic reorganization they express, have no clear-cut beginnings and endings. Yet the start of an irreversible chain reaction can now be recognized in the actions of that momentous Wednesday, June 1, 1774, when "the Honourable the Speaker, and as many Members of the late Assembly as were in Town, with the citizens of Williamsburg, assembled at the Courthouse." From that venue they moved "in Procession to the Church, where an excellent Sermon, well adapted to the . . . unhappy Disputes between Great Britain and her Colonies was preached."[1]

A week before, the House of Burgesses had resolved to keep the first day of June (the date Parliament had set for the closing of the Boston port) as a day of "Fasting, Humiliation, and Prayer, devoutly to implore the Divine Interposition . . . that the Minds of his Majesty and his Parliament . . . may be inspired from above with Wisdom, Moderation, and Justice." The members were required to attend "in Order to proceed with the Speaker and the Mace to the Church," where the Reverend Mr. Price was appointed to read prayers, and the Reverend Mr. Gwatkin invited "to preach a Sermon suitable to the occasion." Mr. Gwatkin had returned an exquisitely Delphic answer to his invitation, informing the House that he could not comply—"on account of a disorder in his breast." But the governor, faced with such calculated dramatization of disapproval of His Majesty's Government, was more direct. He dissolved the Assembly immediately.[2]

On the day after the dissolution eighty-nine of the burgesses had met in an assembly room near the capitol to subscribe solemnly to an "Association" for common action in the crisis. This public signing revived a form of action that would become an important ceremonial means of mobilizing the populace, and at the same time, a means of giving them a heightened sense that the basis of society lay in the consent of its members. By the time the Speaker led the procession of burgesses down Duke of Gloucester Street to Bruton Church, many of the members had gone back to their counties. These added their dignity to the little replications of the Williamsburg enactment that took place in many of the parishes throughout the province. George Mason could not return to Fairfax County, but he sent instructions to his family there that reveal the striving of the gentry for dramaturgical effects. They were "to pay strict attention" to the fast, and his three eldest sons, with his two eldest daughters, were to "attend church in mourning."[3]

A brief but anxious period of suspense followed. In the ten years that had passed since the Stamp Act crisis had called forth an astonishing demonstration of Virginia's potential for patriot mobilization, the commitment of the leading gentry—as revealed in formally drafted resolves and remonstrances—had not been matched by the overall performance of either the gentry at large or the common folk. The non-importation movement of 1769 had quickly weakened, and after attempts to revive it had failed, it had simply been allowed to die. It was therefore uncertain in the summer of 1774 whether the Old Dominion would respond vigorously to the new situation. The crisis, after all, arose from events in the remote city of Boston and pertained to acts of Parliament directed at Massachusetts alone. Philip Fithian, the New Jersey tutor, noted in his journal for May 31: "The lower Class of People here [northern Virginia] are in a tumult on account of Reports from Boston, many of them expect to be press'd & compell'd to go and fight the Britains."[4]

It was imperative for the patriot gentry to communicate to the populace not only their fearful view of what awaited Virginians should they remain supine, but also the vision of the good life that inspired the struggle. At stake were "fortunes . . . liberties . . . and everything that is held most dear among men"—the heritage of "a brave, virtuous and free people." "Virtue," which was at the heart of patriot aspirations, was not just a moral quality or disposition; it was a program for the preservation and regeneration of society. The threatened British constitution was "the Gift of God . . . to relieve Virtue from every Restraint to its benificent Operation, and to restrain Vice. . . . It elevates the Soul, by giving Consequence to every Individual, and enabling him to support that Consequence." It was to this vision that the patriot leaders thrilled.[5]

MEDIA AND MESSAGES OF ANXIETY

Three principal channels existed for conveying views of the crisis and guiding responses: the printed word; word of mouth (including oratory); and dramatic statement through concerted community action.

The newspaper treatment of the Burgesses' responses to the closing of the port of Boston reveals the workings of communications in this period. A small-print notice in Purdie and Dixon's *Virginia Gazette*, coming after news from London, Boston, New York, and Philadelphia, presented only a simple outline of the steps taken by the Burgesses and the governor. We might be inclined to suppose from the lack of headline emphasis that contemporaries did not attach great importance to these actions. Yet abundant evidence demonstrates an immediate and widespread sense of their momentousness. The rapid spread of shock throughout Virginia in the absence of newspaper publicity gives an indication of the customary relationship of the press to the total information system of the time. Printed reports authenticated news of local importance that was expected to circulate in fuller versions by word of mouth. The newspapers, with their small type, their long reports from the courts of Europe, and their polemical exchanges in learned literary style, were not directed to the general populace. The printed word was of the greatest importance in mobilizing opinion, but humble persons were expected to receive the more important messages through the mediation of leaders in society. The contents of the fine print would reach the plain folk through reading aloud and through conversations at courthouses, ordinaries, and other places of assembly. This oral dissemination incorporated news into the common stock of knowledge, opinion, and feeling.[6]

It is difficult to form impressions of the spoken word from written texts. Little supports an attempt, since very few transcriptions, or even reports, of patriot speeches survive. It seems, indeed, from the character of the texts available that courthouse oratory was scarcely more effective than the newspaper as a medium for the communication of the gentry's sense of emergency to ordinary Virginians. (Patrick Henry's rhetoric was a conspicuous exception that will be discussed below.) The language and terms of Classical republicanism that underlay the literate gentry's conception of the struggle could not readily arouse a populace whose limited experience of higher culture was of the Bible rather than of the Classics. More effective than the imagery of Roman republicanism was the Anglo-Virginian sense of identity as a Protestant people.[7]

The specter of the popish menace, long a part of Anglo-American folk culture, was raised afresh by Parliament's recent steps in the 1770s to establish the Roman Catholic church in the conquered French province of Quebec. In the *Virginia Gazette* a swinging ballad to a shanty tune categorized the king's advisers as "Papist Knaves" and asked defiantly whether "free born men" would be "rul'd by Popish law, Because they freedom claim." The words of a gentleman in Henrico County show the intensity of feeling on this issue in his community, where "the Idea of loosing civil or [and?] religious Liberty at one Stroke has raised such an enthusiastick spirit of Love of both as cannot be extinguished but with Life itself." He then emphatically declared that "there is no widdow among us who would not put the sword into the Hand of her only Son to fight [for] the Cause of God and our Country." The "Thoughts" of a writer in the newspaper reveal repellent ethnic stereotypes that reinforced the identification of oppression with popery:

> Possessed of our inestimable Constitution, we may pour forth our
> Prayers and Thanksgivings to its Donor, with Peace, Purity, and Inno-
> cence. Let it be trifled away, and how shall we address him. . . . When
> legal redress of Injuries is denied, every Man becomes the Carver of his
> own Satisfaction. He infuses the Poison, he whets the Dagger; he does
> what the native Irish, the Portuguese, [and] the Neapolitans . . . have
> done before. . . . [Thus] our pure Religion must depart with our Lib-
> erty. It does not afford those Consolations the Horrours of our Con-
> science will require. We must involve ourselves in the Mazes of Super-

stition, and endeavour, by Penances, Absolutions, and a Thousand Mummeries, to quiet the Worm within, under a total Subversion of all the Principles of Reason and Understanding.[8]

Liberty, virtue, and pure Protestant religion were all inextricably intertwined. Here lay nagging sources of anxiety that gave deep meaning to the play of emotions within the patriot movement. What if America—if Virginia—was already deficient in virtue? Corruption and the sinister designs of the overmighty in Great Britain could be readily discerned and denounced, but were there not signs that the same disorder was spreading to the colonies? This secular anxiety had a popular religious counterpart in the abhorrence with which converts to the evangelical culture suddenly viewed the ways of their society. The code of conduct prescribed in the non-importation association imposed upon upholders of the patriotic cause a similar set of forbearances to those obligatory for the adherents to "vital religion." Article eight of the association, adopted by the Continental Congress on October 20, 1774, and enforced in Virginia, engaged signatories to "discountenance and discourage every species of extravagance and dissipation, especially all horse-racing, and all kinds of gaming, cock-fighting, . . . and other expensive diversions and entertainments." In parts of Virginia the patriot committees took dancing to be forbidden, although it had not been specifically listed in the terms of the association.[9]

The obligatory renunciation of important customary forms of social intercourse expressed a growing uneasiness at effete luxury among all ranks of free men. Concern over indebtedness not only vented itself in attacks on the Scots merchants but also highlighted misgivings about the way of life that the tobacco staple sustained in Virginia. Indebtedness, attributed in part to extravagant living, was seen to be more deeply responsible for the failure of craft industries to develop in Virginia. The absence of such industry—and of the frugality and virtue that it was believed to promote—was in turn ascribed to the importation of African servile labor in place of "freemen and useful manufacturers." A ban on the importation of slaves was imposed by the second article of the Virginia association adopted in convention on August 6, 1774. A fervent petition had been addressed to the king from the Virginia House of Burgesses as early as April 1772, pleading for royal consent to legislation ending the importation of slaves because "it greatly retards the Settlement of the

Colonies, with more useful Inhabitants." A patriotic writer suggested that the Privy Council's veto of this restrictive legislation arose from the conspiring ministry's determination that Virginians' love of liberty should continue to be undermined by their dependence on slaves. The author feared that the ministers "will therefore endeavour to increase amongst us the Number of those unhappy People." [10]

DRAMATIZED IDEOLOGY

Verbal pronouncements, whether in spoken or written addresses, did not emerge in Virginia in 1774 as the most effective means of alleviating widespread anxieties or seeking to realize aspirations. Rather, it was through participation in patterned forms of communal action that broad mobilization proceeded most effectively.

Since Parliament's measures for disciplining Massachusetts were the occasion of the crisis, dramatization of the plight of the Bostonians—and of Virginians' identification with them—played an important part in the activation of the patriot movement. Gentlemen like Landon Carter labored to fire sentiments of indignation and compassion in the hearts of the freeholders, developing ceremonies of concern that fixed attention on the victims of oppression. Subscription lists were opened, followed by the display of a solemn public promise by gentlemen who offered an example to the community, "subscribing" a generous donation to the cause. The celebration of this patriotic zeal was a powerful means of intensifying shared commitment.

The social process involved is clearly observable in a notice from Fredericksburg that "very liberal contributions have been made, in this place, for the relief of the poor in *Boston. Mr. Mann Page*, Junior, one of our Representatives, has taken uncommon pains to promote the subscriptions." An example of the community mobilization that the leaders were striving for is seen in the announcement late in July that "the county of Surry, from the highest to the lowest, are actuated with the warmest affection towards the suffering town of Boston . . . [and] that immediately after the meeting of freeholders and others, . . . upwards of 150 barrels of Indian corn and wheat were subscribed . . . for the benefit of those firm and intrepid sons of liberty, the Bostonians."[11]

When the county community was gathered at the courthouse, the quest was above all for unanimity. This was especially evident in what a hostile observer called "the grand meetings for signing the association." In Princess Anne County, to take a well-documented example, the striving for solidarity evidently began overtly in July 1774 with a "meeting of a respectable body of Freeholders of the County at the Court-House, . . . for the purpose of choosing Deputies . . . and of entering into resolutions expressive of the sentiments of the County, in support of their just rights and privileges." One Mr. John Saunders alone "obstinately refused [to sign the resolves], though particularly solicited by some of the principal gentlemen then present." Subsequent events were to reveal the awkwardness that the county leaders felt at this open breach of solidarity. Perhaps for this reason the official minutes passed it over in silence, noting that "the above resolutions being unanimously agreed to, and signed . . . they then repaired to a place prepared for the occasion," where the freeholders drank a series of toasts expressive of unifying patriotic sentiments. Three weeks later, at the courthouse again, "the Provincial Association . . . was read, and offered to the people that they might express their approbation by signing it." Once more Mr. Saunders dissented publicly. Eventually the county committee published an account of his recalcitrance and declared him an enemy to the American cause.[12]

The reports of these county meetings at the courthouse reveal the powerful communication made possible through the display of formal documents in a society where the written word was not yet commonplace. The first meeting ceremoniously adopted a set of resolutions embodied in a Latinate, literary draft that had been prepared in a gentleman's library. At the second meeting, three weeks later, the printed text of the provincial association, composed by some of the colony's most cosmopolitan gentlemen, was formally read aloud. This procedure was strongly calculated to reinforce the cultural dominance of the gentry. Later, when the copies of such papers were handed about, literary and dramaturgic modes of expression were spliced together as public signing in a communal context gave writing the character of emphatic gesture. Setting one's hand to a written bond was in itself an act of significance in this agrarian world.

The Princess Anne County committee's account of its tireless but unsuccessful efforts to persuade Mr. Saunders to adhere to the non-importation agreement suggests the depth of the patriot yearning for communal unanimity. The ultimate publication of Saunders's name as an enemy to American liberty was a boundary-marking ceremony. Ostracism formally restored consensus by putting the offender outside the community. The patriot movement initially conceived of itself as a defensive mobilization to preserve a threatened constitutional status quo. Rituals of detestation were of great importance in defining the danger and amplifying the community's alarm at it.[13]

More reassuring, however, were occasions when the denunciation of deviants was the preliminary, not to exclusion from the benefits of society, but to a public act of contrition on the part of the offender. The general fervor for the cause might, as in religious ritual, move the delinquents to purge their own guilt by confession. Thus "Silas Kirby, James Ingram . . . [and others] voluntarily appeared before [the Southampton County] committee, and acknowledged they had been guilty of violating the . . . association, by gaming . . . that it was an error they were unthinkingly led into, and are convinced of its evil tendency." The committee magnanimously declared that although these men had been guilty, "in consideration of their candid behaviour," they hoped that "the public will join . . . in considering the aforesaid persons as not inimical to American liberty."[14]

Elaborate acts of contrition might be demanded, as in the case of Andrew Leckie, who had been present at the courthouse for "colonel EDMUND PENDLETON's address to the people of Caroline [County]." After "the resolutions of the association were . . . read to a company of people convened for the purpose of acceding to the association, and of raising contributions for the town of Boston," Leckie "was so unguarded and imprudent as to address [himself] to a negro boy who was present in this indecent manner: 'Piss, Jack, turn about, my boy, and sign.'" For this indelicate expression of contempt he was made to read before the committee and "a great concourse of people" on Caroline court day, a full confession and a hearty avowal of friendship to the principles and measures of the patriots. His statement concluded with an open supplication "to regain the favour and good opinion of the public; an assurance of which would be the greatest consolation . . . under the insupportable weight of public censure and public hatred."[15]

The rituals of detestation and the striving to bring deviants into conformity were, in some sense, negative celebrations of harmonious community. As popular passions were stirred up, the movement also elaborated a set of rituals whose tendency was to affirm the "virtue" of challenged Virginia society. The most direct of these rituals of affirmation were enactments of frugality and industry. These were of particular importance because they served as palliatives to nagging doubts about the moral soundness of Virginia society—anxieties over indebtedness (supposed to arise from luxurious extravagance) and over slavery (supposed to be the source of a debilitating indolence that exacerbated the same extravagance). Public declarations of frugality by wearing homespun also provided the patriot gentry with a means of setting an example to their inferiors while simultaneously narrowing social distance as signaled by richness of apparel. In a letter to George Mason discussing the 1769 non-importation proposal, George Washington expressed the view that it would be possible to check purchases "if the Gentlemen in their several Counties wo'd be at some pains to explain matters to the people, & stimulate them to a cordial agreement." The more he considered the scheme, the more ardently he wished it success "because . . . there are private, as well as public advantages to result from it." By being "curtail'd in . . . living & enjoyments . . . the penurious Man . . . saves his money, & . . . saves his credit. . . . The extravagant & expensive man has the same good plea to retrench his Expenses. He is thereby furnished with a pretext to live within bounds. . . . And in respect to the poor & needy man, he is only left in the same situation he was found; better I might say, because as he judges from comparison, his condition is amended in Proportion as it approaches nearer to those above him." This statement, and its enactment in the wearing of homespun, epitomized the whig-republican ideal for society. Distinctions of rank based on material fortunes were to be subtly transformed into distinctions based on moral excellence.[16]

But true virtue in the traditional social order of Virginia could not be "private" or individualistic. Ultimately it must contribute to, and draw from, a communal harmony that could most surely be restored and sustained by readiness to sacrifice oneself to the general good. The rallying to support Boston, the associations, the purge of unsound members, and the displays of frugality all contributed to the demonstration of the presence of such virtue in Vir-

ginia, but the most reassuring exhibitions were made through adaptations of
that aspect of the constitution that was most dear to the patriots, namely
elections.

In order to understand the dramaturgical potential of elections we have to
divest ourselves of nearly all our current assumptions. Trials of strength between contending social classes and popular choice between rival programs
were precisely the lines upon which it was believed elections should not be
conducted. Polling, as we have seen, was a testing, face-to-face procedure in
old Virginia, dominated entirely by the gentry, with the candidates confronting the voters over the table as the latter publicly declared their preferences.
The true purpose was to enable the community to endow with authority those
members whose manly virtue showed most clearly in their persons. An exhortation that reveals the idealizations that gave election procedures their meaning appeared in a paper signed "No Party Man," addressed to the freeholders
of Accomack County in 1771. This broadside outlined the model that the
patriots would seek to depict in action at the county courthouses. The voters
should give their suffrages to gentlemen of "penetrating Judgment," who were
able "to scan each Proposal, to view it in every Light . . . and, piercing into
Futurity, behold even how remote Posterity may be thereby affected." The
ideal representative should be able "to strip every Measure of that Disguise
under Cover of which it may be artfully obtruded on his Mind, and penetrate
through all the sinister Designs and secret Machinations of the Enemies of
Freedom, the Slaves of Interest. . . . It is absolutely necessary that he be a
Man of Probity . . . One who regards *Measures*, not *Men*" and who will follow his country's interest regardless of the effect of his course upon either his
friends or his foes. To this end he must have "that Fortitude, or Strength of
Mind, which enables a Man, in a good Cause to bear up against all Opposition, and meet the Frowns of Power unmoved."[17]

Manly virtues were required not only of the representatives but also of the
voters who were to select them. To begin with, the electors must be imbued
with a strong sense of their exalted role: "It is your greatest Glory, . . . that
you give Being to your Legislature, that from you they receive their political
Existence. This renders an American Planter [i.e., farmer] superiour to the
first Minister of an arbitrary Monarch, whose glittering Robes serve but to
veil from vulgar Eyes the Chains of Slavery. Guard it then, as the most precious Pledge committed to you by the Deity. Let every Gentleman's true

Merit determine his Place in the Scale of your Interest." Altogether it was an inspiring vision, conjuring up a sturdy yeomanry who with dauntless honesty would by their virtuous trust elevate the wisest and sternest of the "Gentlemen" to give laws and "to meet the Frowns of Power unmoved."[18]

Actual representations of this scenario, dramatically affirming the virtue that inspired the patriot cause, were staged in a series of unanimous elections at the commencement of the final crisis in 1774. A single example will convey how the vision could be translated into action. Rind's *Virginia Gazette* of July 14, 1774, reported:

> On Wednesday . . . came on the election of burgesses to represent the county of Prince George in the ensuing general assembly, when the people, sensible that their late representatives had discharged their duty to their country, in opposing those baneful, ministerial measures, which have been lately taken to enslave this continent, and highly applauding those sentiments of union among the colonies which occasioned the dissolution of the last assembly, unanimously agreed to re-elect RICHARD BLAND and PETER POYTHRESS, esquires, who were returned without a poll being taken.

This simple courthouse enactment—the election by acclamation of the representatives and the explanation of the reasons for according this honor—was highly effective in dramatizing to freeholders the awful menace of British power and the noble solidarity of Americans. A glow of virtue was combined with the exhilarating sense of brave defiance gestured on a world stage.[19]

Virginia election customs provided another possibility for ideological statement. Demonstrations of the highest political virtues might be merged with the affirmation of frugality by the simple inversion of the time-honored custom of the candidates' treating the voters. On July 8, 1774, "a considerable number of the inhabitants of [Williamsburg] . . . met at the courthouse" to present an address to their representative, proposing that because they were

> greatly scandalized at the practice which has too much prevailed . . . of entertaining the electors (a practice which even its antiquity cannot sanctify) and being desirous of setting a worthy example . . . for abolishing every appearance of venality (that only poison which can infect our happy constitution) and to give the fullest proof that it

is to your singular merit alone you are indebted for the unbought suffrages of a free people . . . we earnestly request that you will not think
of incurring any expence . . . , but that you will do us the honour to
partake of an entertainment, which we shall direct to be provided for
the occasion.

Five days later the freeholders met their representative, "attended by many
respectable inhabitants, at the courthouse . . . to elect him again . . . ,
when he was immediately unanimously chosen." After the election the voters
"conducted him to the Raleigh, where almost every inhabitant had met, a
general invitation having been given by the generous electors, whose conduct . . . will be long remembered as a laudable . . . precedent, and highly
worthy of every county . . . to adopt. Notwithstanding the festivity, and the
pleasing, social intercourse, which here prevailed, harmony, decency, and
decorum, were strictly maintained." It must be supposed that those who "directed" the "entertainment . . . to be provided" at the tavern were not the
whole body of electors, but the men of substance among them. Treating thus
continued to prove the liberality of genteel patrons, but their role could now
be freed of "every appearance of venality." The prevailing "harmony, decency, and decorum" were signs of virtue diffused throughout the ranks of the
free community.[20]

The dramaturgical potential for celebrating the patriotism of local notables
was even more fully realized in the feting of the heroes of Virginia and America at large. In these ceremonies they and their cause could be glorified in
such a way that the heroes' own virtue and that of the people who identified
with them were simultaneously affirmed. The sense of immediate participation in drama on a grand scale (already noted in the acclamation of the
Prince George representatives) could thereby be intensified. The patriot leaders, of course, owed a great deal of their charisma to their own sense that they
were engaged in a momentous struggle that would determine the destiny of
mankind. Peyton Randolph, Williamsburg's representative, Speaker of the
House of Burgesses, and president of the Continental Congress, had certainly
transcended local and provincial forms of authority, yet his manners and outlook epitomized him as a "liberal" Virginia gentleman in the traditional
style—a clubman at ease with persons of all ranks. The persona ascribed to
Randolph can be seen clearly in the report of a ceremony that took place on
May 28, 1775:

Last Monday, about 10 o'clock, the WILLIAMSBURG TROOP OF HORSE left this city, well accoutred, in order to meet our good and worthy speaker on his return from the continental congress. Notwithstanding the inclemency of the weather, these hardy friends and supporters of American liberty pursued their journey with the utmost eagerness, whilst the most unfeigned joy diffused itself in every countenance.

For order, good discipline, and regularity, this company was greatly applauded. Ruffen's ferry was the place where they met the object of their wishes, whom, after giving three hearty cheers, they conducted until they arrived within two miles of the city, when they were joined by the COMPANY OF FOOT, who also gave three cheers, and shewed every other mark of decency and respect. The pleasing deportment of the speaker, on account of this peculiar honour done him, animated, in the highest degree, every person that attended; and on Tuesday, about 5 o'clock in the afternoon, the whole body arrived . . . surrounding the FATHER of his COUNTRY, whom they attended to his house, amidst repeated acclamations, and then respectfully retired.[21]

In the feeling conveyed by the postures adopted (or believed by contemporaries to have been adopted) toward Peyton Randolph, we catch a vivid glimpse of the way in which the patriot movement momentarily evoked (or was intended by its leaders to evoke) the spirit of the traditional deferential social order. But as we see also in this account, men in arms were on the march. The struggle was unleashing forces that would not find their fullest expression in marks of "decency and respect."

A PEOPLE ARMED

The preceding accounts suggest that *tableaux vivants*, communicating more than words could do, worked to create a collective consciousness of belonging to a virtuous community unanimously roused in support of its dearest rights. The Anglo-American ideal of civic virtue was not, however, confined to frugality and political incorruptibility, for it enshrined martial valor at its heart. Military rituals provided opportunities for the self-presentation of the warrior that was expected to exist in every free man. Such displays ultimately had the greatest potential for stirring this aggressive, contentious people. During the initial phase of uncertainty in the summer of 1774, when the association was being promoted as a peaceful measure involving only "some inconveniences," warlike notes were not much sounded. By December 1774, however, the governor reported to the home authorities that every county was now "arming a Company of Men, whom they call an independent Company." Impressions of this new development can be gained from the record of a gathering at the Fairfax County courthouse on September 21, 1774. The proceedings reflect the valiant effort to produce a moral regeneration of the old order by the gentry's ostentatious assumption of public burdens. The minutes show that the gentlemen and freeholders who attended were "hoping to excite others by . . . Example." They formed themselves into "the Fairfax independent Company of Voluntiers," who would meet at times appointed for "learning & practising the military Exercise & Discipline; dress'd in a regular Uniform of Blue, turn'd up with Buff; with plain yellow metal Buttons, Buff Waist Coat & Breeches, & white Stockings" and furnished with a complete set of arms and equipment. Further, they would keep by them considerable stock of powder, lead, and flints. On the principle of noblesse oblige, the gentlemen (who alone could afford this dress and equipment) were setting an example of valiant patriotism (see figures XVII and XVIII).[22]

By February 1775 a plan "for Embodying the People" was being circulated in Fairfax County, and a new conception of uniform marked the intrusion of the style of the backwoodsmen. The drive was now for a volunteer militia, "intended to consist of all the able-bodied Freemen from eighteen to fifty Years of Age." The enlistment of poorer men rendered the prescription of uniform impossible, but the proposal did call for those who could "procure Riphel Guns . . . to form a Company of Marksmen . . . distinguishing [their] Dress . . . by painted Hunting-Shirts and Indian Boots."[23]

The aggressive assertion of plain countryfolk, as well as the excitement engendered by mustering for war, became manifest during the next phase of Virginia patriot mobilization, following the governor's seizure of the colony's store of gunpowder from the magazine in Williamsburg on April 21, 1775. It was the morning of Monday, April 24, when news of Lord Dunmore's coup reached Fredericksburg. "This being a day of meeting of the Independent Company," the assembled volunteers angrily considered the state of affairs and came "to a unanimous resolution, that a submission to so arbitrary an exertion of Government, may not only prejudice the common cause, by introducing a suspicion of a defection of this Colony from the noble pursuit, but will encourage the tools of despotism to commit further acts of violence." They informed the commanders of the companies in nearby counties that "this Company could but determine that a number of publick spirited gentlemen should embrace this opportunity of showing their zeal in the grand cause, by marching to *Williamsburgh*." They declared that "to this end, they have determined to hold themselves in readiness to march from this place as Light-Horse, on *Saturday* morning; and, in the mean time, to submit the matter to . . . the neighbouring Counties."[24]

The letters from Fredericksburg elicited immediate responses. The company in neighboring Prince William County was "called together . . . , and had the vote put, whether they would march to *Williamsburgh* . . . which was carried unanimously." Companies began to gather at Fredericksburg for a massive display of patriotism in warlike dress. The excitement, and the new tone that was becoming dominant, is conveyed in the words of a young gentleman volunteer, Michael Brown Wallace of Falmouth, who described for his brother's benefit how the governor's action "Occasioned . . . upwards of 1,000 men to assemble together at Fredericksburge among which was 600 good Rifle men." He was sure that "if we had continued there one or two days longer we should have had upwards of 10,000 men [as] all the frontier Countys of Virginia were in motion." It seemed to Wallace that "Fredericksburge never was honour'd with so many brave hearty men since it was a Town[,] evry man Rich and poor with their hunting shirts Belts and Tomahawks fixed of[f] in the best manner." Disappointment plainly showed, however, in Wallace's concluding note that "thir was a Council of war held three days saturday sunday & monday[.] the third day in the evening we were all draw'd up in ranks and discharg'd on some promise of the governor's delivery of the Powder."[25]

Patrick Henry, at the head of a body of men assembled at Hanover courthouse, was not so easily dismissed. He marched toward Williamsburg until some £330 was exacted from His Majesty's receiver general as reprisal for the confiscated powder. Henry was uneasy for an instant at the possible consequences of his conduct, but addresses from courthouses throughout the province revealed that the patriot movement was ready to go decisively into military action. He and his volunteers were congratulated upon showing "resentment" like true Virginians. When Henry soon after rode off to the Second Continental Congress, a succession of armed escorts proudly accompanied him on his journey. Ostensibly these were to protect him from arrest or insult; in fact, they were a defiant celebration of patriotism in martial array.[26]

The new tone of the patriot movement—more popular and more belligerent—was sharply and dramatically signaled by the appearance of the men in hunting shirts. These "brave hearty men" had honored Fredericksburg with their presence in early May 1775. By June a Norfolk tory was writing home that Dunmore would only return to Williamsburg "provided the shirtmen are sent away." He explained that "these Shirt men, or Virginia uniform, are dressed with an Oznab[urg] Shirt over their Cloaths, a belt round them with a Tommyhawk or Scalping knife." The term had initially been applied by their enemies—"the damn'd shirtmen"—and was then adopted as a badge of pride. The revolution in cultural orientation that was taking place is most readily apparent in the contrast of the shirtmen's attire with the "Uniform of Blue, turn'd up with Buff . . . yellow metal Buttons, Buff Waist Coat and Breeches and white Stockings," appointed for the gentlemen of the Fairfax Independent Company. For all their intense provincial patriotism, the Virginia gentry had always boasted a strong church-and-king loyalty. Looking to the English metropolis for cultural values, they had tended to despise the "buckskin" of the backwoods. Now suddenly the riflemen from the west were the "heroes in huntingshirts," to whom even the most cosmopolitan gentlemen looked for protection. On July 19, 1775, a young Virginian recently returned from studies at Princeton wrote to a friend in Pennsylvania that "the strength of this Colony will lie chiefly in the rifle-men of the Upland Counties, of whom we shall have great numbers." That sentiment had become almost universal by this time. The intensity of the westward reorientation and a readiness among the gentry to identify with the woodsmen is indicated in a published recommendation to the burgesses that they attend the forthcoming Assembly in June 1775 wearing shirtmen's attire, "which best suits the times, as the cheapest, and the most martial." The advice was heeded, and "numbers of the Burgesses" did attend in the uniform of "Coarse linnen or Canvass over their Cloaths and a Tomahawk by their Sides" (see figure XVIII).[27]

Preparation for war was now the principal source of excitement for the patriot movement. The Classical Greco-Roman attitudes so characteristic of the early phases of resistance were being overlaid by more robust and popular styles. The two are blended in the correspondence of Colonel Adam Stephen, who had written in August 1774 that in the Virginia convention he "should expect to see the spirit of the Amphyctions shine, as . . . in their purest Times before Debauch'd with the Persian Gold." Later Stephen wrote that, having heard "that Lord North has declar'd that he has a Rod in piss for the Colony of Virginia," he wished he could see his lordship in America, for "in Spite of all the armies of Commissioners, Customs house officers and soldiers, I would make the meanest American I know piss upon him."[28]

This last puts us in touch with the scatological ribaldry of the military camp. Although this form of communication appears little in the written records, it signifies the rude vigor of the male warrior fraternity that was more decorously manifested in the stirring resolves of the spring and summer of 1775. The "buckskins" and "Shirtmen" found solidarity not in Classical rhetoric but in forms of bravado, such as that which translated the old English "roast-beef" patriotism to a Virginia context. "Our peach-brandy fellows can never be beat," ran the line of a song. In this ethos the country squirearchy, many of whose members were schooled in boxing and quarter racing, could certainly hold their own; but social distance was inevitably reduced, while special advantages derived from cosmopolitan education were diminished and distinctions of rank were rendered less sharp. With the reduction in social distance, the momentary sense of a revived deferential order had passed. Gone was the celebrated unanimity that in 1774 had induced the freeholders of many counties to affirm the virtue of their communities. The spring elections of 1776 included "many . . . warm contests," and even that leading patriot, Colonel George Mason, was only "with great difficulty returned for Fairfax."[29]

The shift from tableaus of constitutional loyalty and civic righteousness to the bustling scenes provided by the mustering of men in hunting shirts inevitably contributed to the increasing alienation of Virginians from the mother country. No account exists of popular ceremonies at the courthouses directed to the dramatic "killing" or dethroning of the king. Something of the persistence of old forms—and of the readiness to see them changed—is captured in a report of April 1776 from Gloucester County: "We hear . . . that as the sheriff was opening the court . . . he was going to conclude with *God save the King*, when, just as he was about pronouncing the words a *five's ball*, struck by a soldier of the 7th regiment [playing handball], entered the window, and knocked him in the mouth, which prevented him from being guilty of so much impiety." Perhaps the impropriety of regicide enactments before an alternative locus of sovereignty had been declared, inhibited more deliberate performances.[30]

In Williamsburg the official celebration of the formal decision of the Virginia convention for independence took place on May 15, 1776. In accordance with ancient Virginia custom, "some gentlemen made a handsome collection for the purpose of treating the soldiery." After a parade and salutes to *"The American independent states,"* to *"The Grand Congress of the United States,"* and to *"General Washington and victory to the American arms,"* refreshments were supplied "and the evening concluded with illuminations, and other demonstrations of joy." The newspaper account stated that everyone seemed "pleased that the domination of Great Britain was now at an end, so wickedly and tyrannically exercised for these twelve or thirteen years past." It had already declared that independence was "universally regarded as the only door which will lead to safety and prosperity." The complacent tone of the account suggests that whatever anguish Virginians had suffered over denying loyalties that they had once so strongly affirmed was short-lived.[31]

NEW EVANGELICAL STIRRING

While the patriot cause was gaining momentum in 1774–1775, the Baptists' rate of advance was slowed. But another religious movement was spreading rapidly. Emissaries of the Anglican reformer John Wesley were gathering a great following in Virginia. The distinctive social and cultural meanings implicit in the Methodist upsurge are difficult to determine. Continuing the Great Awakening tradition, the Methodists met the same needs to which the Baptists had responded. Their rituals—extempore preaching and praying—served in the same way to bring to crisis the feelings of many of the plain folk and to give ecstatic release from their sense of lost, guilty aloneness. "Class" meetings, watch nights, love feasts, and quarterly meetings likewise offered close, supportive fellowship and emotional sharing. On matters of conduct and style of life the same strict evangelical code of observances and forbearances was demanded and imposed by group discipline. Yet Methodism was much less intransigent on issues of authority, church, and society. It remained (until 1784) a movement for "vital religion" within the Church of England. While free use was made of enthusiastic lay preachers, and chapels were constructed for their meetings, the connection with the traditional establishment was formally maintained. Methodists continued to be dependent on clergymen ordained by an English bishop to conduct the communion services that were given great importance in the love feasts and quarterly meetings of the faithful. The ambivalence of Methodism—rejecting customary social morality but avoiding a break with established authority—was further complicated in Virginia between 1774 and 1784 by John Wesley's notoriety as a "tory" who had published a strong statement urging the colonials to submit to the rule of Parliament and the king's ministers. The Baptists had rallied their supporters to the patriot cause, sending preachers to the army camps, and in time raising bodies of fighting men from among their membership. The Methodists did none of these things, and some of their lay preachers even aroused the hostility of the newly constituted republican authorities by declaring themselves pacifists and refusing to be drafted into the American forces. Thus the rival new movement shared with the Baptists a rejection of traditional social values but was initially set apart from them by its refusal to break with the Established Church. Less radical in its organization of authority, Methodism, through its veiled pacifism, may nevertheless have served as a subconscious means of popular protest against gentry-led republicanism.[32]

Methodism appealed primarily to the humble. The emotional release of the meetings was in sharp contrast to the ordered decorum of the services in the parish churches where the squires ruled. When Wesley's missionary Thomas Rankin came to Virginia in June 1776, he witnessed the climax in a surge of revivalistic piety that had been building up for some years:

> *Sunday*, 30 . . . in the afternoon I preached again, from "I set before thee an open door, and none can shut it." I had gone through about two-thirds of my discourse, and was bringing the words home to the present—Now, when such power descended, that hundreds fell to the ground, and the house seemed to shake with the presence of God. The chapel was full of white and black, and many were without that could not get in. Look wherever we would, we saw nothing but . . . faces bathed in tears. . . . My voice was drowned amidst the groans and

prayers of the congregation. I then sat down in the pulpit; and both
Mr. Shadford and I were so filled with the divine presence, that we
could only say, This is none other than the house of God! This is the
gate of heaven! . . . Those who were happy in God themselves, were
for bringing all their friends to him in their arms. This mighty effusion
of the Spirit continued for above an hour; in which time many were
awakened.[33]

After such gatherings, "the multitudes that attended . . . returning home
all alive to God, [would] spread the flame through their respective neighbour-
hoods, which ran from family to family." The intensity of the movement, reported Devereux Jarratt, was such that "scarce any conversation was to be
heard . . . but concerning the things of God. . . . The unhappy disputes between England and her colonies, which just before had engrossed all our conversation, seemed now in most companies to be forgot, while things of far
greater importance lay so near the heart."[34]

The Methodist organization was centralized, with tiered structures of "classes,"
"societies," "circuits," and "conferences"; yet its hold on its members, and
its impact therefore on local communities, was very similar to that of the
Baptists. The close group of the "class" operated in much the same way as
the independent "church meeting." Characteristically, candidates would be
"awakened" to a sense of sin during a sermon, and then, while they attended
both "classes" and preaching they would be guided through the desolate quest
for a sense of total self-abnegation before God. The lonely experience of de-
spair—the bleak sense that God's mercy could never reach the vile self—
would be followed by a blissful release when "the Lord . . . spoke peace to
their souls . . . [which] he usually did in one moment . . . so that all their
griefs and anxieties vanished away, and they were filled with joy and peace in
believing." Thus came the precious moment of ecstatic conversion.[35]

Ample testimony exists as to the usual intensity of the sense of relief from
guilt. Yet the experience was not in itself sufficient to confirm the convert in
a radically new way of life, for it was almost invariably succeeded by doubt.
Had God really extended His pardon and given the "present salvation" that
came to true Christians? The "class" provided a social context in which this
final anguish could be alleviated by the collective validation of each individual conversion. The self-discipline henceforth expected of the convert was

reinforced through the shared commitment of the group. The stern evangelical code of forbearances was strictly maintained, asserting the distance intended to be set between the new way and customary laxity.

Aspects of the movement appear most clearly in Methodist preachers' journals and their published accounts of the working of the Holy Spirit. Preaching was the "ordinance" central to the movement and its cult of conversion. Under preaching, persons became awakened; by it, candidates were guided through the stages of conversion; and in its message the faith of the converts was periodically renewed. The text was always an introduction to the theme of rebirth, the need for "present" salvation. The preaching was undertaken without notes as the preachers sought a sense of inspiration in themselves and a response, or "liveliness," from the people. The phrases that recur again and again in the preachers' writings concerning their striving were pregnant in this time of political revolution—"had liberty," "had not as much liberty as at some other times." The evangelicals' search was for a collective, emancipating sense of divine power.[36]

Through extempore preaching in search of "liberty," the oral culture of the people was surfacing in a form of rebellion against the dominance of the literary culture of the gentry. In the eighteenth century the Bible was still generally conceived of as the highest arbiter of ultimate truth. Custody of this precious deposit was therefore required to be vested in those whose mastery of the ancient languages enabled them both to interpret Holy Writ soundly and to make informed judgments concerning the learned arguments that surrounded the many points of dispute. It has been seen how unlearned farmers' assumption of authority to expound the Scripture, if they felt moved by a "gift" of the Spirit, was interpreted by the gentry as an offense against the twin hierarchies of nature and society. The ironic term "New Light," by which the evangelicals were designated in common speech, suggests a general perception that what was at stake was the proper authority of ancient learning. The resurgence of oral culture in the calling of semiliterate men to preach extempore was a transitional ambiguous phase. At the same time that it engendered great outpourings of the spoken word, uncontrolled by scholastic conventions, it induced among preachers and hearers alike unprecedentedly intense reading, study, and searching of the Scriptures—often in private.[37]

As with the Baptists so with the Methodists, a complex relationship can be discerned between their observances and the disturbed world into which they erupted. On the one hand their strict code of conduct symbolized order, and the close groups for the sharing and confirmation of religious experience functioned as effective popular agencies for discipline. On the other hand the individual loss of control and the collective confusion of the crowded revival meetings were both accorded sacred significance. The study of Scripture was intermediate—the quiet of close individual reading was preparation for the inspired outpourings of extempore preaching and exhorting. The popular evangelicals had instituted an inversion of customary relationships between religion and daily life. Where traditional conventions tended to assign compartmentalized times and places to religion—Sundays (and then the service hour only) at the churches—the New Lights strove to suffuse all aspects of living with reminders of God's wrath and of His saving grace. Where the liturgical services of the establishment had been short intervals of authoritative decorum in a rambunctious social world, the worship of the evangelicals was a tumultuous release from a social life upon which they sought to impose intense orderliness. Against the customary conviviality of proud contest and self-assertion was set solemn brotherhood commenced in denial of the flesh, confirmed in shared self-abnegation, and consecrated in an ecstatic release into joy through tears.

PATRIOTS AND NEW LIGHTS

The spread of Methodism continued the expansion of evangelicalism at the same time that the crisis in the imperial disputes brought on the climax of patriot fervor. We should at least briefly review the similarities and differences between the contemporaneous movements. The gentry had long denounced the evangelical New Lights as a set of ignorant "enthusiasts," meaning fanatics. By 1775 the passionate involvement of gentlemen and their followers in the patriot movement had reached the pitch where it could aptly be designated by a critical participant as "political enthusiasm." Indeed the movements shared certain features. Most notable was the use of popular assemblies for arousing collective emotions and for intensifying the involvement of plain folk. Despite common characteristics, differences are also apparent.[38]

The meetings of the patriot movement (typically to elect genteel delegates or to adopt resolutions cast in literary prose) were less participatory than those of the "vital religionists." Furthermore, they were less inclusive, since freeholders not from the gentry elite had a rather limited role, the landless white inhabitants were on the fringe only, and the blacks had no role at all. In the evangelical movement even the slaves participated vocally. A similar divergence is apparent in the leadership of the two movements. Patriot leaders were exclusively genteel, whereas many of the foremost evangelical preachers were self-taught men of humble origin. The prevailing tone of the meetings was again very different. We may contrast the preachers' strivings to achieve "liberty"—a state of ecstatic release—with such celebrations of order and deference as the feting of Peyton Randolph on his return from Congress.

But the most important distinction between the two movements lay in the relationship of each to the old way of life. Where evangelicalism began as a rejection and inversion of customary practices, the patriot movement initially tended toward a revitalization of ancient forms of community. The mobilization to defy Parliament—the meetings at courthouses, the elections, the committees and their resolutions—coincided with, and for a short-lived moment reinforced, the traditional structures of local authority. The independent companies were a barely popularized form of the old militia, while the ceremonies of the toasts and the feting were but adaptations of customary conviviality. With aggressions for the moment turned outward, all of these forms featured and intensified the style and values of pride and self-assertion that evangelicalism so sternly condemned. The political enthusiasts experienced no equivalent of the isolated anguish of the awakened who were awaiting conversion.

Fundamental shifts in values and organization that occur outside and against existing structures are highly subversive of established authority. The spread of concern for vital religion challenged the hegemony of the gentry; the patriot leaders, on the contrary, vigorously reasserted the cultural dominance of the elite. A view of the diametrically opposed social tendencies of the two movements raises the question of whether the patriot ideology did not gain in appeal among the Virginia gentry partly because it served as a defensive response to the open rejection of deference that was increasingly manifested in the spread of evangelicalism.

The concurrent taxation and toleration crises of the 1760s and 1770s had confronted the cultural and political elite of Virginia's mobile and expanding society with a dilemma that was inherent in their dependent situation. The gentry, having an image of themselves drawn from English models, had found themselves trapped between the nether millstone of popular disaffection and the upper millstone of imperial determination to keep the colonial ruling groups in a subordinate position. Lacking the means to bargain effectively with the authorities at the center of the empire, the greater part of the elites in all Britain's long-standing continental American colonies felt impelled to unite themselves with popular forces in their own communities to defy Westminster. In Virginia, a society that had begun to be riven by bitter internal discord found itself for the moment tightly bound in an enthusiastically accepted whig-patriot consensus under its traditional leaders. Only a tiny number of individuals were drawn in the opposite direction, to unite themselves with king, ministry, and Parliament. These Virginia tories were so isolated as to be ineffectual.*

RESONANCES

A deep-lying connection between popular evangelicalism and patriot republicanism can be more certainly established if we consider certain shared orientations. Viewed as social forms and as cultural expressions, the contrast and opposition between the values of the evangelicals and the patriots is striking, but both seem to have met a general need for relief from collective anxiety and perceived disorder. The two ideologies struck common chords. Certainly both called for positive individual acts of affirmation as the basis for a new

---

*Here the proposed model of the patriot rebellion as a social process seeks to go beneath the programs and forms of communication detailed in this chapter, to discover possible sources of emotional appeal—reasons why the gentry were so susceptible to the passions aroused by the movement of resistance to Parliament. Such an interpretation of collective psychology is necessarily more speculative than the study of statements and public enactments and must here be referred not to particular texts but to large configurations such as the undermining of gentry hegemony implicit in the rise of popular evangelicalism that is the major theme of this book. The interpretation of the Virginia patriot movement offered here is aligned with others that stress the importance of the Great Awakening as a crisis of authority that prepared the way for the Revolution among both colonial elites and lower orders.[39]

moral order. The patriots attested their participation in revitalized community by signing self-denying "Associations." The evangelicals did so by bringing to meeting the humble testimony of hearts regenerated by God's grace.

The resonances between the two movements can be sensed in the popular appeal of the man most universally celebrated in the troubled Virginia of his day. What was the secret of Patrick Henry's success? Full treatment of this question would be inappropriate here, but an answer may be briefly suggested. As it happens, Patrick Henry's surviving writings are few and give no clue to his powers, for he was a master of the *spoken word*—the spoken word in a form that did not derive, as did the Latinate oratory of his nearest rival, Richard Henry Lee, from the language of writing. His genius lay instead in the exploitation of the possibilities of the oral culture of his society. For this reason Henry could scarcely have prepared drafts of his speeches. The departure of his performances from the conventions of literary culture made even note-taking by others inappropriate. What has been passed on to us in writing, however, are vivid accounts of the impressions created by his rhetoric.

It is clear that when, some two or three decades after the patriot mobilization, Edmund Randolph wrote the history of his own times, he felt as though he was still in the presence of Patrick Henry's oratory. The memoirist, trained in letters, could not retain the verbal content of even the greatest of the speeches, but the manner of delivery and the thematic traits of Henry's performances had been indelibly impressed upon the young listener's memory. Randolph's constant recurrence to the subject indicates his virtual obsession with the conflict between Henry's style and that of his colleagues in the leadership of Virginia. Henry annihilated the Classical rules of rhetoric to which, as a gentleman, he should have adhered. Despite "an irregularity in his language, a certain homespun pronunciation," Henry entered public life "regardless of that criticism which was profusely bestowed on his language, pronunciation, and gesture," for he soon discovered that "a pronunciation which might disgust in a drawing room may yet find access to the hearts of a popular assembly." [40]

In his memory Randolph followed the orator through a powerful performance: "In Henry's exordium there was a simplicity and even carelessness. . . . A formal division of his intended discourse he never made." The ardent young patriot would fix his eyes "upon the moderator of the assembly addressed without straying in quest of applause." In this way "he contrived to

be the focus to which every person present was directed, . . ." and so "trans-
fused into the breast[s] of others the earnestness depicted in his own features,
which ever forbade a doubt of sincerity." The memoir then drops the most
revealing clue concerning the effectiveness of Henry's mode of oratory: "His
was the only monotony which I ever heard reconcilable with true eloquence."
Here was a form of sermonic chant, intended primarily to arouse moral fervor. Most of the remaining traits fall into place around this core:

> [The] chief note was melodious, but the sameness was diversified by a
> mixture of sensations which a dramatic versatility of action and of
> countenance produced. His pauses, which for their length might some-
> times be feared to dispel the attention, riveted it the more by raising
> the expectation. . . . His style . . . was vehement, without transport-
> ing him beyond the power of self-command. . . . His figures of speech
> . . . were often borrowed from the Scriptures. The prototypes of others
> were the sublime scenes and objects of nature. . . . His lightning con-
> sisted in quick successive flashes, which rested only to alarm the
> more.[41]

Henry had brought into the politics of the gentry world an adaptation of
that popular oral form, the extempore sermon, that had been setting different
parts of Virginia ablaze ever since the coming of the New Side Presbyterians
in the 1740s. The success of this mode of oratory with the assemblies of country squires on whose reported impressions Henry's popularity must largely
have rested, is striking evidence of fundamental cultural continuities between
"gentle" and "simple" folk in the Virginia countryside. Living closely integrated in rural society, the squires could respond fervently to this style of oratory when it was introduced in the service of their own cause rather than in
direct condemnation of their life-style (see figure XV).

Throughout his career Patrick Henry remained firmly attached to the
world of the gentry. His mastery of the convivial style of that world is suggested by some of the earliest recollections of him as an excellent performer
on the "violin," whose "passion was music, dancing and pleasantry." Henry
never made the dramatic renunciations characteristic of evangelical converts, but his personal conduct developed with sensitivity to the popular
moral concerns of the time and achieved a harmony above the clashing dis-
cords of the old traditional culture and the new evangelical counterculture.

The great patriot always retained the easy affability of the gentleman, yet he adopted a sober manner of dress and became deeply preoccupied with fostering Christian virtue in his society. Supremely, what enabled Patrick Henry to tower above his generation—in its general estimation—was his ability to communicate in popular style the passion for a world reshaped in truly moral order that lay at the heart of both the religious revolution of the evangelicals and the political revolution of the patriots.[42]

The gentry-led patriot movement, mobilizing the hardhanded common farmers in Virginia, had generated new political symbols—and hence new expectations concerning authority—in society. Before the breach with the mother country the evangelical movement had already been effecting radical cultural changes within the lower ranks in society. The social implications of the two revolutionary processes and the transformations of community ethos that, in combination, they worked, become clear in a struggle that ensued over the terms of a religious settlement.

12

REVOLUTIONARY SETTLEMENT
Religion and the Forms of Community

It is a Saturday in June 1826. At Monticello Thomas Jefferson sits in the study that commands a view away north along the outlines of the Blue Ridge and out across the low rolling hills of the Piedmont. The words he was writing are reproduced on the following page. They convey characteristically precise instructions concerning his tombstone.

Alas for the last wishes of a man who was becoming even in his lifetime a symbol and a legend! Far from destroying his monument "for the value of the materials," later generations first chipped it away for souvenirs and then, considering the prescribed proportions too modest for so great a man, ordered it replaced by the double-sized one that is now to be seen in the family burying ground on the southwestern brow of the little mountain.

Jefferson's modesty in reducing the list of his achievements to three has often been admired. Yet he did proudly focus attention on his successes as a philosopher-statesman. In 1776 the author of the Declaration of Independence had turned away from the affairs of the emergent union of states in order to assist in recasting the laws of the newborn Commonwealth of Virginia. In matters of franchise, governmental constitution, and education he was thwarted in his reformist aspirations. Only in religion did a great institutional transformation take place, and there the revolutionary statute was Jefferson's—although his formulation was not adopted until five years after he had retired from Virginia politics distressed and defeated. It is appropriate to inquire what made possible the passage of the "Act for Establishing Freedom

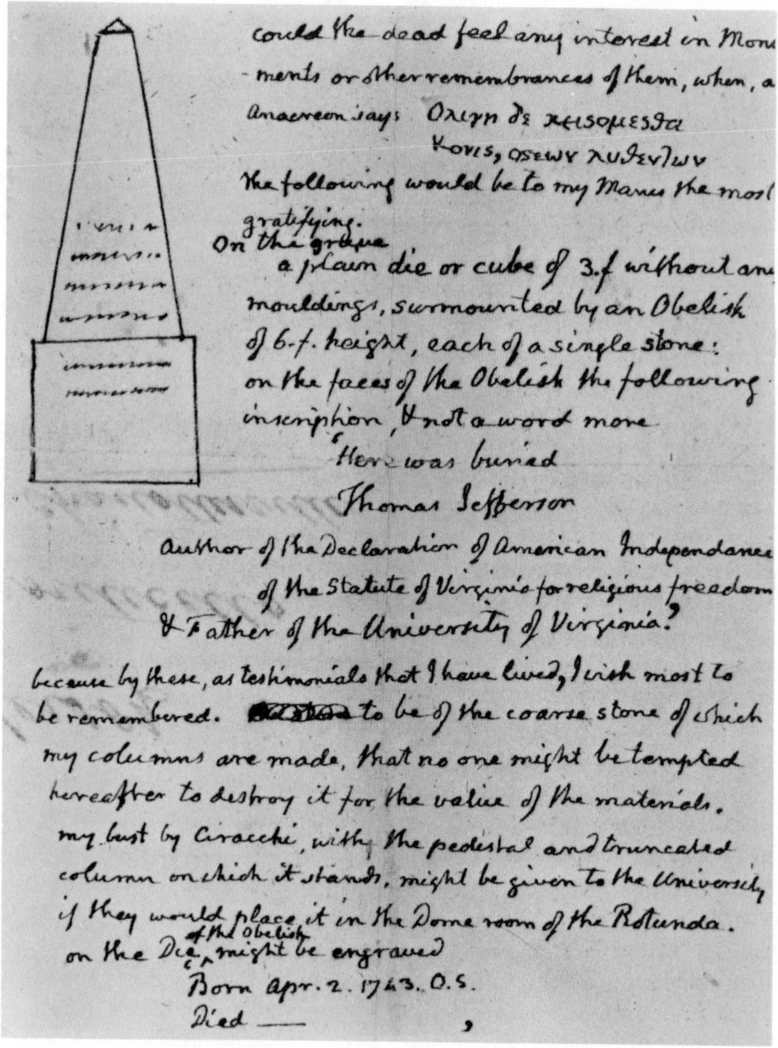

could the dead feel any interest in Monu
-ments or other remembrances of them, when, a
Anacreon says: Ολιγη δε κεισομεσθα
         κονις, οςεων λυθεν]ων
the following would be to my Manes the most
gratifying.
On the grave
     a plain die or cube of 3.f without any
mouldings, surmounted by an Obelisk
of 6.f. height, each of a single stone:
on the faces of the Obelisk the following
inscription, & not a word more
     Here was buried
      Thomas Jefferson
Author of the Declaration of American Independance
    of the Statute of Virginia for religious freedom
& Father of the University of Virginia.'
because by these, as testimonials that I have lived, I wish most to
be remembered. ~~could these~~ to be of the coarse stone of which
my columns are made, that no one might be tempted
hereafter to destroy it for the value of the materials.
my bust by Ciracchi, with the pedestal and truncated
column on which it stands, might be given to the University
if they would place it in the Dome room of the Rotunda.
    of the Obelisk
on the Die, might be engraved
      Born apr. 2. 1743. O.S.
      Died ___   ,

FIGURE 25.

and practiced in Hanover County, near the heart of Virginia's regions of settled population. Dr. Robert Honyman was an observer of rather than a participant in politics. As great events and the acts of the legislature impinged
on his little part of Virginia, he filled his journal with a mixture of news and
local opinion—reports of a distant war, comments on reactions at home. As
early as 1778 he noted an unwillingness among neighboring farmers to fill
draft quotas. Repeated rumors of peace were signs of a rather fainthearted
longing for it. On March 16, 1780, Honyman commented sorrowfully: "The
attention of the people of this state is very little taken up with the war at this
time, or indeed for a year or two past. . . . The greatest part of the people are
entirely taken up in schemes of interest of several kinds. Immense fortunes
have been made by trade, or speculation . . . & almost all ranks are engaged
in some sort of traffic or another." Soon he was to remark that although the
"people interest themselves in Elections at this time more than ever," yet
"they find fault with everything that has been done . . . [,] grumble exceedingly at the taxes . . . & choose those who make fair promises of altering
things for the better." Honyman felt that in these circumstances "many of
those chosen are men of mean abilities & no rank."[2]

In several entries Honyman described resistance to the draft. There was
threatened or actual mutiny among the Virginia conscripts. The disgrace of
the militia at the battle of Camden provoked the comment that "after they
run away they never stopped till they came home." He also recorded a wave
of anger against authorities who were no longer in command of the situation.
Governor Jefferson and his Council were universally condemned "for their
neglect & supineness" upon the occasion of Arnold's raid on Richmond in
January 1781: "It is chiefly ascribed to them that this country has been in-
sulted in such an extraordinary manner by a handful of men." The valor of
the Virginia militia at Guilford courthouse lightened the gloom, but that
sense of relief was soon overwhelmed in the confusion brought about by
Cornwallis's marches and countermarches. When the British forces came
right past Honyman's door, he was forced to witness the willing neutrality of
many of the neighboring farmers and the distressing number that went ea-
gerly to the invaders in order to be paroled and—as they hoped—thereby
rendered ineligible for military duty in the service of the commonwealth.
Some reassurance could be gained from the formation of volunteer horse
companies—"chiefly Gentlemen . . . exceedingly well mounted"—but even

in that case it could not be overlooked that some of them were badly armed, "& all under very little discipline and hard to govern."[3]

The humiliations inflicted by the freewheeling campaign of Cornwallis were transformed into an allied triumph by the conjunction of Washington's army with the French fleet to effect the surrender at Yorktown in October 1781. But the defeat of the invaders did not bring an end to Virginia's distress. The state's currency had become worthless, taxes could not be collected, and the legislature seemed incapable of taking action—either independently or in concert with the Continental Congress. In the midst of all the confusion, hardship, and public bankruptcy, ruthless individuals, often employed by the government, seemed only too capable of finding ways to secure immense profits. Wartime anxiety over the decline in public morality was intensified. Behind a general "torpitude and lethargy" numbers of commentators discerned a universal "sordid and selfish . . . love of gain." Letters in the newspapers dwelt, with more than usual gloom, on "the degeneracy of the times." The same sense of "ignominy and disgrace" also featured prominently in private correspondence.[4]

Of the leading patriot reformers who had come forward in the making of the Revolution, some like Richard Henry Lee and James Madison (the future president) had become deeply involved in Continental and foreign politics. Thomas Jefferson, who had determined to devote his principal efforts to the reshaping of Virginia, had retired from that work frustrated, embittered, and despairing. Patrick Henry and George Mason were the two great figures who remained most closely and persistently concerned with the condition of Virginia—the first as a participant, the second as an observer and exhorter. It is through the eyes of George Mason that we may see the dark scene that confronted the public-spirited on the morrow of Yorktown.

In the hour of victory, the squire of Gunston Hall was appalled by the rapacity of government requisitioning agents who ruthlessly took advantage of measures for the relief of their country's dire emergency. He denounced them as "licentious & infamous" men who "plundered & empoverished the People to enrich themselves." The legislators had allowed the sheriffs and other tax collectors to default on payments with impunity. Unchecked, revenue officers profited flagrantly from inflation. Thus "by encouraging Knavery, & legalizing Fraud, [the legislators] have corrupted & depraved the Morals of the People."[5]

By May 1783 Mason was convinced of the urgency of the situation, and of the need to apply a republican remedy—reform of electoral laws and practices. He wrote to a number of leaders in the forthcoming Assembly, exhorting them to reestablish just laws and "by a strict Adherence to the Distinctions between Right & Wrong for the future, to restore that Confidence and Reverence in the People for the Legislature, which has been so greatly impaired by a contrary Conduct." Mason had already declared himself in favor of compulsory voting as a means of securing the election of cultured and distinguished men "of Weight and Influence" in a whole county, against the too-prevalent type of "factious bawling Fellow, who will make a Noise [only] four or five miles around him"—but who, in times when elections were "so little attended," was able to "prevail upon his party to attend . . . [and so] carry an Election."[6]

There were many, however, who did not believe that adjustments in the secular republican apparatus would provide an effective remedy for the moral disorders that plagued Virginia. They attributed the problem rather to the disastrous decline of religion caused by the new commonwealth's shameful neglect of public worship. Patrick Henry took an active lead in the campaign to revive Christian virtue, and by November 11, 1784, had gained a majority of 47 to 32 in the House of Delegates in favor of renewing the state's commitment to organized religion. The state of affairs that faced these would-be reformers, and the attitude they adopted, can only be rendered intelligible by reviewing the course of legislation concerning the Church in the preceding years of war and revolution.[7]

COLLAPSE OF ESTABLISHMENT AND
ATTEMPTS AT RENEWAL

As the patriot mobilization against British dominion got under way, the establishment of the Church of England still seemed—even to its enemies—so far sacrosanct that no hint of a challenge to it was mooted in the political forum. Certainly the Separate Baptists had been outspoken in their denunciation of ecclesiastical authorities. As one offended churchman reported: "Worse could not be said of the Pagans & Idolators, who sacrificed their Children to Moloch, than has been said . . . concerning the church and its Members, the Ministers not excepted." Yet, although the Virginia General Assembly was repeatedly petitioned for greater freedom of assembly, the establishment was so entrenched before the Revolution that the Baptists never dared even hint at aspirations to be relieved from taxes for the support of the Church.[8]

The unassailable position of the Church—and with it the inhibitions of the dissenters—was soon undermined by the new political conditions created by mobilization for revolutionary war. In May 1776 a "Convention" assembled in Williamsburg to decide on the question of independence and to set up a complete new regime in place of the regal government that had been virtually suspended for two years. The convention felt impelled to commence its constructive work by a Declaration of Rights that would lay out the foundations upon which the republican constitution should be raised. The concluding item (article 16) in that declaration was the only one that dealt directly with religion. Perhaps it was no accident that the most contentious and divisive issue was left till last.

The genesis of article 16 is revealing of the leaders' caution. There seems to have been a deliberate obscuring of intentions as the delegates sought a formula for consensus at a time of all-out war with the former sovereign. George Mason, who was given the task of drafting the declaration, penned a cautious article that did no more than update the English Act of Toleration, which had been uncertainly applied in Virginia for decades. The extent of his proposal was that "all men should enjoy the fullest toleration in the exercise of religion." The future president James Madison, attending his first legislative assembly, urged an alternative version that decisively proclaimed an end to the old framework of church establishment. His amendments not only substituted "free exercise of religion" for "fullest toleration" but also declared "that no . . . class of men [i.e., the clergy] ought, on account of religion to be invested with peculiar emoluments." The version adopted by the convention retained Madison's uncompromising "free exercise" phrase but eliminated the rider clause that precluded a tax-supported establishment.[9]

During the debate on article 16 Patrick Henry, who spoke in favor of it, was asked point blank whether the more liberal wording "was designed as a prelude to an attack on the established church." To this question he gave an emphatic negative. From this reported exchange, and much else that followed, it is clear that to the majority in the convention the article was no more than a declaration of limited intent. Evangelists would no longer be arrested merely for preaching without a license. The prospect of preachers being arrested, however, was not eliminated altogether. In their initial drafts George Mason, James Madison, and even Thomas Jefferson had all included words designed to uphold action by the authorities against persons who "under colour of religion . . . disturb the peace, happiness, or safety of society." The potential of religious radicalism for social disruption in a world that held so many slaves could not be overlooked. We may be sure that the representatives who consented to omit such a stated exception did so from a sense of its redundancy rather than from any principled disapproval of its intent.[10]

The time when limited concessions might stabilize the status quo, however, had passed. Article 16 proved immediately to be a breach in the hitherto impregnable political defenses of the establishment. Dissenters took it as a decisive confirmation of their belief that the old establishment could have no place in the new order. Interpreted in this sense, the article became their banner during decades of struggle, first to overthrow the establishment and then to eradicate all vestiges of it. Rallying to this standard they were able to secure important early victories. When the convention reassembled in the fall of 1776 as Virginia's first House of Delegates, it found itself confronted by a "ten-thousand name" petition (circulated by the Baptists) in which the signatories declared that "their hopes have been raised and confirmed by the declarations . . . with regard to equal liberty . . . [and] that having long groaned under the burden of ecclesiastical establishment, they pray that this, as well as every other yoke, may be broken and that the oppressed may go free." Other petitions to the same effect were also presented to the House.[11]

With the war raging, the establishmentarian majority in the House had to recognize that substantial disestablishment was a fait accompli—a real though unintended consequence of republicanization. Their prudent response was to temporize and to adopt a series of six resolutions that provided relief for the dissenters. They nevertheless discreetly maintained the principle of establishment through the assertion that "proper provision should be made for continuing the succession of the clergy and superintending their conduct." (This was an oblique allusion to the dismembered state of the Anglican church, now cut off by the war and independence from the apostolic succession as transmitted through the English bishops.) The resolutions also reaffirmed the determination of the slave-owning, pro-establishment gentry to have the legal right to control, by force if need be, popular meetings within their communities. It was bluntly declared that "public assemblies of societies for divine worship ought to be regulated." [12]

The only positive legislation enacted during this session was a bill that exempted dissenters from being taxed to support the Established Church and suspended the payment of the statutory salaries of the clergy. The exemption was perpetual; the suspension was temporary—for one year in first instance. A highly significant clause appended to this act indicated that the legislature had explored the possibilities of a "general assessment"—a tax to support a non-exclusive, multi-denominational establishment. This addendum stipulated, however, that because agreement was for the moment unattainable, it was "thought most prudent to defer this matter to the discussion and final determination of a future assembly, when the opinions of the country in general may be better known." [13]

The preamble of the exemption statute asserted that "there are within this commonwealth great numbers of dissenters." Thomas Jefferson, preparing notes for a speech at the time, had realistically set the figure at fifty-five thousand. He probably counted only white adherents, which would make the proportion about one-seventh of the total free population. (Ten years later, in his *Notes on the State of Virginia*, Jefferson published the statement that "two-thirds of the people had become dissenters at the commencement of the present revolution," clearly revealing how rapidly the Established Church had *seemed* to lose ground in the new situation.) The political strength of the dissenters, however, was out of proportion to their numbers, since they were not evenly dispersed. In addition to the numerous converts that the Baptists had made in the southwestern region and in the central Piedmont, there were marked concentrations of Scotch-Irish Presbyterians in the west. From these areas came many of the "heroes in hunting shirts" upon whom Virginia relied for its defense during the war. [14]

For the majority in the House of Delegates, the exemption act of 1776 was an unavoidable concession somewhat grudgingly made to groups whose support could not be dispensed with. The success of an amendment to the original bill nevertheless shows that reformers inspired by the Enlightenment had taken an active part in framing the measure. Clauses based on Jefferson's drafts were added, repealing with a flourish a series of harsh, dogmatic English statutes that had long been dead letters. A less ostentatious, but probably more strategic, victory was achieved by opponents of the Established Church. The preamble to the act contained the assertion that "it is contrary to the principles of reason and justice that any should be compelled to con-tribute to . . . a church with which their consciences will not permit them to join, and from which they can therefore receive no benefit." Thus was lightly surrendered one of the primary defenses of the traditional establishment: that the support of public worship in a branch of Christ's Church was for the good of the whole of society, even if expediency made it appropriate to tolerate persons whose consciences forbade them to join in the forms of service main-tained by law. On the one hand the act, with its references to "dissenters" and "the church," formally maintained traditional distinctions; on the other hand opponents of establishment were allowed to include in it a formula that undermined the corporate conception of society that had legitimated the spe-cial status of the Church.[15]

For nearly three years the temporization of the legislature continued. The act suspending the established clergy's salaries was twice renewed for a year at a time. On June 4, 1779, however, the House was led to give consideration to a more definite settlement. Thomas Jefferson's "Bill for Establishing Religious Freedom" was brought forward from the report that he had completed on be-half of the Committee for the Revisal of the Laws, but was allowed to lapse. Its author or his associates, however, had it printed for general circulation. In this form it sparked off another round of public controversy, and when the House reassembled in the fall, it found that petitions in favor of the bill were outweighed by those expressly rejecting it and calling for a general assessment for the support of religion. A petition from Lunenburg County expressed forcefully the sentiments to be found in all the pro-establishment petitions. It contended that experience had already proved that voluntary support of re-ligion "will be very inadequate . . . [and that] Men of Genius and Learning will be discouraged from engaging in the ministerial office . . . and the State [thus] . . . deprived of one of the best Means of promoting its Virtue, Peace, and Prosperity." In this adverse climate the supporters of Jefferson's bill were discouraged from reviving it. A law of opposite tendency was proposed on

October 25, 1779. This "bill concerning religion" took the form of a general levy for the support of organized churches. It specified that each taxpayer designate the denomination that was to receive his payment. The measure attempted to adapt old custom to new circumstance by declaring that "the Christian Religion shall in all times coming be deemed the established Religion of this Commonwealth." All peaceable denominations were to be eligible for support under this arrangement, provided their ministers and those entrusted with the management of their affairs would subscribe to four very general articles affirming the existence of God; "a future State of Rewards & punishment"; the truth of the Scriptures; and the social duties of Christians. The ministers also had to endorse a solemn declaration concerning the pastoral function—a declaration that was pointedly directed at Baptist and Methodist "mechanic" preachers in its stress on the importance of sacred learning. This bill, in its turn, was shelved after a second reading on November 15, 1779.[16]

The House once again resorted to expedients. The members recognized that the old exclusive establishment was gone beyond recall, and they ordered a bill that would end the Church's state of suspended animation and encourage it to organize on a voluntary basis. While the bill, when enacted, explicitly confirmed legal title to ecclesiastical properties and endowments, it abolished forever the salaries of the parish rectors, along with all tax levies for the support of "the former established Church." This phrase obliquely avowed disestablishment. The structure of the Church, however, was still far from wholly dismantled. The vestries, although no longer authorized to levy taxes to support their parish churches, continued as public bodies entrusted with the care of the poor and needy, while their membership was still confined to churchmen. Episcopal clergymen—although greatly reduced in number through death, desertion, and exile—still enjoyed extensive advantages.[17]

Ecclesiastical law remained on this basis for the next five years, until the growing concern at lapsed public morality caused the question of renewed religious establishment upon a multi-denominational basis—the "general assessment"—to be taken up once again with Patrick Henry leading the advocates of the measure. He and his supporters were no doubt encouraged by a memorial, dated October 28, 1784, from the presbytery of Hanover. The

Presbyterians had been as bitterly opposed as the Baptists to the survival of any vestiges of the old establishment, but momentarily—moved by the rapid decline of "public worship of the deity"—they guardedly accepted the principle of "supporting religion in general by an assessment." On November 11, 1784, the House of Delegates, being petitioned again for such an assessment, resolved by a vote of 47 to 32: "That the people of this Commonwealth, according to their respective abilities, ought to pay a moderate tax or contribution annually for the support of the Christian religion." "A Bill for Establishing a Provision for the Teachers of the Christian Religion" was soon introduced in furtherance of this resolution. It passed the readings necessary to clear it through the House, but support for it diminished steadily. Committee discussion must have brought many supporters face to face with the practical difficulties of implementation. How could they, on returning to their counties, justify their legislative act to their neighbors—to hard-bitten tax resisters as well as to those groups that were known to have religious objections? By the third reading, the bill's majority had shrunk to two, with only 44 in favor and 42 against. It was subsequently determined (45 to 38) that the bill should be printed and referred to the public for further discussion.[18]

An avalanche of replies in the form of petitions and protestations came back to the House at its next session in the fall of the following year. Some eighty papers were directed against the proposed bill (including thirteen copies of James Madison's famous "Memorial and Remonstrance") and eleven in favor of it. (The "noes" secured about eleven thousand signatures; the "ayes" got only one thousand.) The assessment proposal had drawn forth an awesome counterblast, and the Christian teachers bill was never brought forward again. Jefferson's "Act for Establishing Freedom of Religion" supplanted it and was carried with overwhelming support.[19]

James Madison informed the author of the bill that its enactment had "in this Country extinguished for ever the ambitious hope of making laws for the human mind." More soberly the historian may ask what ideals and aspirations had been abandoned or frustrated in the convulsions that transformed a majority of fifteen in favor of establishment into a majority of fifty-four in support of a statute—utterly without precedent in the Atlantic world—declaring the unqualified separation of church from state. The campaign for a general assessment in support of churches had been introduced under the sponsorship of Patrick Henry, Virginia's most popular republican leader and moralist. It had evoked at least wistful expressions of support from George Washington and Richard Henry Lee. It is worthwhile to enquire into what had been at stake both for the campaign's partisans and for its opponents.[20]

CONFLICTING SYMBOLS OF
THE SOCIAL ORDER

Certainly the former establishment (incorporated in 1784 as the Protestant Episcopal church) would have gained most immediately from the general assessment in support of Christian teachers, since a large residue of habitual but inactive allegiance would have been compulsorily turned into cash payments. Such a law would, however, have brought substantial benefits to the other denominations, all of which experienced difficulties over the remuneration of their clergy. As already noted, the Presbyterian ruling body even gave momentary support to the proposal—support that was crucial to getting the bill launched in the legislature. The importance of calculations and interested motives in the controversy is difficult to assess, however, since the polemics did not dispute the proposals in such terms. Symbolic issues predominated in the debate and provide an important key to the responses of different groups in society.

The petitions are rich in revelations of the deep concerns of the partisans on either side of the great question. Their texts convey something of what the participants perceived when they surveyed the course of the momentous events of their times. Their visions of what the future might hold tended to be expressed in images drawn from worlds of past experience. The parson had been an important symbolic figure in the traditional community. (Persistent anticlericalism had only served to underscore his significance.) For the evangelicals the preacher was an even more awesome figure. He was a fearless witness to the ends to which all were born; often he was designated a "father in the Gospel." It is not surprising that contrasting icons of true ministers and false messengers were recurrent in the rhetoric of the conflict.

Two powerful stereotypes recur in the petitions of the gentry who supported establishment. A stark negative image was set against a glowing positive one. With the collapse of the old parish structure, the menace of the unlettered itinerant loomed even larger. Traditionalists were horrified at the increased likelihood that "any layman, or mechanic, [who] if he finds a motion within him from the spirit, may leap from the anvil or the plough, and in a few minutes go forth a preacher of the word of GOD." Neither the evident absurdity of the claim of such "Licentious and Itinerant Preachers" to "supernatural Communications" nor the disorderliness of their meetings prevented them from drawing a following. Experience proved to believers in the old order that "the poor are seduced from their Labor" and were liable to be "too often led astray by the wild, enthusiastic Doctrines of Men, whose peculiar Misfortune it is to be bewilder'd, and to delude others." Indeed, the popular movement seemed "to threaten a general Delusion." Among the most "dismal consequences of the Doctrines taught by these new Teachers" were the night meetings for the instruction of slaves. Such gatherings "could produce nothing but Deeds of darkness" and had "already produced their proper fruits of disobedience & insolence to Masters & glorying in what they [the slaves] are taught to believe to be persecution for Conscience's sake."[21]

Against this disquieting prospect, upholders of establishment set a reassuring counter-image of the minister "rightly qualified for that Office by Virtue, Learning & Study." He must be one of a body of "Men of real Merit. . . . Men of Family & Education." Such learned persons would stand in the high pulpits—"proper Places for the . . . Exercise of their sacred Function"—to give "Public Instruction" and "in a rational, solemn, and reverend Manner," lead in "public & stated Expressions of . . . Veneration." Only gentlemen of independent standing could properly exercise ministerial authority. To that end establishmentarians urged that the clergy should be supported in "a liberal and plentiful Manner" and should not have to wait subserviently "to be compensated . . . by the capricious Will of a Multitude."[22]

The same pair of opposed icons appear in evangelical anti-establishment rhetoric—but with the objects of approval and detestation reversed. The learned ministers endowed with the independence of gentlemen were deplored as "hirelings whose Chief Motive and Design would be Temporal Interest." The wild mechanic preachers were respected as "usefull and Faithfull Men" whom "Divine Grace hath called to that Work." On the question of their means of support, the dissenters held that, as they were "the Voluntary

Servants of the Church, So every Church . . . should be left to reward them
. . . as they shall think their services deserve." They explicitly rejected the
notion "that Christian Knowledge and liberal Arts and Sciences [i.e., genteel
learning] are . . . essentially connected together." The advocates of establishment were reminded that "neither were *they* learned Teachers (according to
the common acceptation of the words) who were chosen at first . . . to diffuse
Christian Knowledge through the World." Separate Baptist insurgents, themselves inured to persecution, identified preachers with the apostles of the
primitive Christian Church, not only for their simplicity but also for their
ability to advance the gospel "against all the Powers of the Earth." Genteel
independence and polite learning were part of the insignia of those worldly
powers that had always stood opposed to the way of salvation.[23]

Behind the paired positive and negative images—genteel parsons and ignorant enthusiasts, as opposed to inspired messengers and ambitious hirelings—lay sharply contrasting backgrounds of social and religious experiences. The very different kinds of experiences in turn arose from opposite
orientations to community.[24]

The general assessment proposal was part of a quest for the restoration of
an ethos that was passing—if it had not already vanished. The parson "of real
merit . . . Family & Education" belonged to a distinctive social setting—the
high pulpit, the squires seated in the foremost great pews, and the measured
decorum of the Prayer Book service. Such arrangements encapsulated fundamental definitions not only of the nature of true religion but of its relationship to society, and hence a delineation of how the world should be ordered.

The supporters of the general assessment sought public commitment to a
learned clergy through the establishment of conditions that would make it
worthwhile for young men to prepare themselves adequately. Genteel ministers as guardians of the authority of high culture would be symbols of the traditional social order. "We believe," declared a petition from Surry County
presented in November 1785, "that the reputation of Religion will considerably depend on the literary as well as moral & religious Qualifications of its
Teachers." The insistence that the learned be accorded precedence went with
a strong sense of the intellectual dependence of the majority of society. The
common folk were the "ignorant and unwary," the "vulgar" upon whose
"credulity" the enthusiastic itinerants readily imposed. "From their circum-

FIGURE 26.
High pulpit, squire's pew, and prayer book decorum

FIGURE 27.
"Neither were they learned preachers." A blacksmith expounds the Word

stances," the Christian teachers bill explained, laboring people "cannot attain Knowledge" for themselves and so stand in need of a properly instructed
ministry.[25]

The issue of establishment and the elevation of the pulpit assumed crucial
importance because at this time the symbolism of learning communicated
most directly the principle of due subordination within the society of free persons. Learning was one aspect of a hierarchical social structure that could
readily be republicanized. Knowledge of books was manifestly not an inher-
ited characteristic; claims to deference for those who had acquired education
were incontestably legitimate within the framework of a commonwealth. Indeed, learning could be represented graphically in the familiar icons of "The
Choice of Hercules," the path of Virtue, and the toilsome ascent of Parnassus
(see figure 28). The wisdom stored in texts was a mountain to be scaled by all

SOC. AMER: WHIG: al AMICITIAM, LITERAS. MORES que colendas Inst? AD MDCCLXIX.

FIGURE 28.
*"The Progress of Reason." Learning stored in texts was
a mountain to be scaled by republicans who had the Spartan
fortitude to persevere*

who had the Spartan fortitude to persevere in the arduous endeavor. The
claim to a command of higher understanding was the most convincing legitimation that remained to a republican gentry as a rationale for its traditional
domination over communities of semiliterate husbandmen.[26]

The popular evangelical petitioners had a completely different vision.
They did not regret the lost corporate, deferential community for which
many of the gentry still hankered. In the view of humble dissenters the appro-

priate context for the man of God was not an elegant Classical church where
the pulpit and furnishings symbolized hierarchy. Their valued religious experience was associated with plain barnlike structures with congested seating
and at most a rough platform or reading desk. The full members of the congregations that met in such settings considered themselves "called out of the
world . . . to live together, and execute gospel discipline among them." They
emphasized the segregation of their tight circles from society at large by the
strict code of forbearances enforced on members (see figures XII and XIII).

Assertion of the separateness of true religion from the world and the
world's concerns, powers, and dignities was the constantly repeated fundamental rationale for the evangelicals' rejection of establishment and for their
support of Jefferson's bill for religious freedom. The full implications of this
atittude were made explicit in one of the last anti-assessment petitions to be
presented to the Assembly: "Civil Government & Religion are, and ought to
be, Independent of Each other. The one has for its object a proper Regulation
of the *External* conduct of men . . . ; [the other] our *internal* or *spiritual* welfare & is beyond the reach of human Laws." [27]

Uncompromising evangelical separation of religious from secular authority
tended to leave civil society a spiritual desert without its own life-giving well-
springs of true morality. The state, in this view, was an aggregate of individuals lacking the capacity to provide for their ultimate fulfillment. The best that
individuals could do was to contract with one another to respect the search
for salvation of each in his or her own way. In this manner a social order
based on voluntary contract would facilitate the proliferation of gathered
churches. These were themselves voluntary contractual associations—
though of a different kind, since it was chiefly through them that God provided for the saved. Gospel fellowships were the only organs of divine authority in a society at large that was irredeemably secular. [28]

Contractualism was implicit in the evangelicals' view of the world. It became very explicit in their formulation of the case against an establishment
in any form. The patriot leaders had exploited the dramaturgic possibilities of
the signing of contracts in the mobilization rituals that included the circulation of "associations." The new Virginia constitution was prefaced by a
lengthy articulation of the reasons why the contract between the people of
Virginia and King George was no longer valid. The principle was also pro-

claimed in a Declaration of Rights—the foundation for the new contract that brought the commonwealth into being. The point was not lost on dissenters; the republican framework of legitimacy provided a firm basis from which to demand the eradication of the old establishment. A Baptist petition of 1776 had sought to end church establishment using the words of a contract proposal: "These things being granted, we will gladly unite with our Brethren of other denominations, and to the utmost of our ability promote the common cause of *Freedom*." [29]

Almost every petition against establishment appealed to the Virginia Declaration—usually styled the "Bill"—of Rights. This tablet of fundamental law served as the legitimation for demands directed from the spiritual domain of the evangelical churches into the secular realm of the legislature. The extent of the dissenters' commitment to secular contractualism was made starkly clear in the longer version of the petition circulated by the Baptists—the petition that attracted by far the greatest number of signatures in the campaign of 1785. The text declared that the assessment proposal and the foundation agreement by which the society had been contractually reconstituted were incompatible. The question was bluntly asked whether those "who are not Professors of the Christian religion who were in this State at the Passing of this Bill [of Rights]" would not, "when they shall be obliged to support the Christian Religion, think that such Obligation is a departure from the true . . . meaning" of the declared fundamental rights. Evangelicals readily assumed that society was a neutral ground for contractual relationships. They took for granted what was anathema to the traditional establishmentarians—namely, that the great majority in Virginia (or anywhere) was composed of non-Christians (that is, persons who had not, and might never have, a saving experience of God's grace). [30]

The case for separation of the state from concern with religion was also made from a rationalist republican point of view. James Madison's famous "Memorial and Remonstrance" is even more explicitly contractual than the full-length Baptist petitions. Madison referred to human society as an "Association" in which individuals' rights and obligations would be regulated by the terms on which they entered the founding compact. In the torrent of signatures that ultimately swept away the Christian teachers bill, a significant group of supporters of Enlightenment secularism stood side by side with a much greater number of evangelical separationists. For the moment the two groups were united against the traditional conception of community as a hierarchy of head and members whose corporateness was symbolically expressed in an obligation to provide for public worship.[31]

JEFFERSON'S BILL: ASSEMBLY'S ACT

The abandonment of the general assessment proposal and the overwhelming support accorded Jefferson's Bill for Establishing Religious Freedom can be seen on the one hand as an exercise in political prudence, and on the other as a manifestation of complex cultural realignments. The switch that transformed a working majority in support of multi-denominational establishment into a landslide for radical separation of church and state must be understood in part as a timely step to eliminate from politics the one issue—religious sectarianism—that could have brought about a successful electoral challenge to the leading families in the counties of Virginia. Yet the shift must also be seen as part of a pattern of changes all tending to legitimate the autonomy of the individual against the moral claims of the community. The extent of the triumph of individualism is evident not just in the rejection of the parochial squirearchy's aspirations but also in the frustration of the larger purposes of the author of the successful bill.

Jefferson's bill was a forceful anticlerical condemnation of dogmatism and religious coercion. It was also a lofty assertion of the sovereignty of reason, recognizing both the capacities and the limitations of the human mind. As enacted, however, the law was more limited and primarily negative in purpose—a means to set aside the general assessment forever. The narrowing of vision becomes readily apparent if the measure is reviewed in the context from which legislators in search of expedients had wrenched it.

The Bill for Establishing Religious Freedom did not stand alone in the Report of the Committee of Revisors, compiled by Jefferson. It came as the fourth and culminating item in a tight cluster of measures designed not simply to terminate the old religious establishment but to replace it with a positive alternative. The three draft laws (numbered 79, 80, and 81) that preceded the famous one that alone became law were bills "for the More General Diffusion of Knowledge"; "for Amending the Constitution [and totally reorganizing the curriculum] of the College of William and Mary"; and "for Establishing a Public Library." Studies of Jefferson have stressed the innovative republican and philanthropic character of these measures, but a twentieth-century habit of taking secular education for granted as an institutionalized element of state activity has tended to obscure important continuities between long-standing Virginia traditions and these proposals for the revisal of the laws.[32]

The supporters of the general assessment directed their efforts toward securing the public maintenance of "Christian *teachers*." This wording was not simply an expedient formula to render a controversial measure more acceptable. The ministers of the establishment had long been seen, from the point of view of those who held themselves responsible for the moral welfare of the community, in an instructional rather than a sacerdotal role. Conservatives like Robert Carter Nicholas and liberals like Samuel Henley (among whom Jefferson may certainly be numbered) had quarreled less over the function of the clergy than over the content of their instruction—whether it should be dogmatic orthodoxy or rational enlightenment. Given the preponderance in society of unlettered and laborious tillers of the soil, the teaching function of the clergy was seen as an obvious necessity. The public pulpits were so many points distributed as evenly as possible through the countryside from which the light of learning could relieve the gloom of ignorance. What Jefferson proposed to do in the "Bill for the More General Diffusion of Knowledge" was to replace the old ecclesiastical community of the parish by a new one (with an old name revived), the "Hundred," and to replace the pulpits with publicly supported teachers' desks. Since instruction would no longer be combined with religious duty, it would have to be directed at the young and would be steeped in secular republican morality. The Bible had until this time been the reading primer employed in Virginia. Jefferson's plan would change that. "At every of these schools," declared the bill, "the books which shall be used . . . for instructing the children to read shall be such as will at the same time make them acquainted with Graecian, Roman, English, and American history."[33]

A new Virginia republican "establishment" would replace the old Anglican Christian one. Community involvement in the moral formation of its members would be reaffirmed. Hierarchy was given both symbolic and functional form in this arrangement of things. Over regional groupings of the local "hundred" schools, where poor children could get three years of free instruction toward basic literacy, were set grammar schools for the sons of the gentry, and for one poor boy (the most promising) per year from each of the elementary schools. Half of these scholarship boys were to be sent home after one year; all bar one were to be dismissed at the end of the second year. From among those who survived this drastic pruning, one in the whole of Virginia was to be chosen annually "to proceed to William and Mary College," there to be "educated, boarded, and clothed, three years." No text could more eloquently convey the instinctive insistence of a Virginia gentleman on the empyrean exclusiveness of the higher culture. Jefferson's scholarships may be seen as an institutional embodiment of the arduous mountain way to which Athena directed the young aspirant in the icon.[34]

When Jefferson's proposals for a secular republican establishment were brought forward, they were frustrated as effectively as had been his gentry opponents' design for a Christian one. With the enactment of the bill for religious freedom, religion was declared to be a matter for the individual alone; with the rejection of the alternative of republican instruction, morality also was de facto left to be a private concern. Tax resistance—undoubtedly a contributory factor in the defeat of religious establishment proposals—was the major consideration in setting aside the Bill for the More General Diffusion of Knowledge.[35]

At the conclusion of the war dismayed patriots had cried out for measures that would restrain the self-seeking individualism they saw rampant around them. In 1781 the future president James Madison had even contemplated the revival of the patriotic county committees that had been such direct expressions of the corporate moral force of the community in 1774. In the event, it was communitarianism, in secular as well as in sacred form, that was defeated. Religious privatism was overtly legitimated. Voluntary contractualism was reinforced as property escaped being subjected to forms of taxation that would have signified corporate responsibility for spiritual well-being.

III

AFTERVIEW

13

CHANGED LIVES—CHANGED LANDSCAPES

Water and trees, trees and water—the physical terrain occupied by Virginians, both black and white, continued in 1790 to be dominated by rivers and forests. A much higher proportion of the 750,000 inhabitants now lived beyond the Tidewater and indeed over the hills and along the fast-flowing streams that ran down toward the Ohio, the Tennessee, and the Mississippi. Land usage, however, had scarcely changed; villages and towns, though larger and more numerous, contained only a tiny percentage of the total population at the end of the eighteenth century. Yet changed outlooks entailed changed worlds—changed landscapes as experienced in life. New landmarks appeared; old landmarks and familiar patterns assumed new meanings. Some of the transformations that had taken place can be glimpsed in the scenes and perspectives that follow.

THE WORLD THE NEW LIGHTS MADE

Evangelicals now saw Virginia to be a place chosen for God's work. The minutes that recorded the founding of the Albemarle Separate Baptist Church in 1773 declared that it "hath pleased the Lord of his Gre[at] mercy to alarm and awaken out of the learthygy of Sin the inhabitants of Virginia by Sundry of

his servants as embassaders Both from the south and north parts of america."
The resistance that God's messengers encountered elevated their work to an
epic of endurance, an epic the Baptists have grimly commemorated ever since.
In 1810 Robert Baylor Semple published *The History of the Rise and Progress of
the Baptists in Virginia*, a work that the leaders of the movement had been
promoting since 1788. This book incorporated, and so strengthened, a growing
legend of heroic struggle. Enshrined in the Baptists' legend is a Virginia very
different from that proclaimed in the myth of the cavaliers or the cult of George
Washington so familiar to American historians. The Virginia of Semple and
his successors in Baptist historiography was a dark place of persecution, enlightened only by the divinely inspired witness of evangelists and martyrs.[1]

The adherents of the new faith also found their immediate localities transformed. Involvement with "vital religion" gave the awakened person a new
sense of his or her nature and destiny. Commitment was expected to extend
profoundly into daily life. Even the fields, where most of the population endured long hours of drudgery, might be suffused with religious significance.
The Virginia-born apostle of Methodism Jesse Lee relates that in the great
revival of 1787,

> it was known that the people . . . would quit work and pray together
> in the fields, and their neighbours hearing them would run and join
> them; and the Lord blessed and converted souls in the fields. One man
> said his people were at work in three separate companies; and he went
> out to see them at their work, he found the first company . . . in
> prayer . . . [and] the next . . . [and] the third . . . so he went back to
> the house and let them pray.[2]

The Baptists also found religious revival overflowing into places of work at
this time. The Baptist preacher John Leland wrote in 1790 that "in the last
great ingathering, in some places, singing was more blessed among the people
than the preaching was." He had "travelled through neighborhoods and
counties at times of refreshing" by the Holy Spirit. He rejoiced that the "spiritual songs in the fields, in the shops and houses, have made the heavens ring
with melody." In such song—especially when it was combined with rhythmic
movement—evangelical religion released forms of expression appropriate to
African celebrations of the sacred. The combination of spirituals and laborious work in the fields filled the countryside with a new set of shared, or

apparently shared, meanings—hallowed meanings very different from those that traditionally infused workaday activities.[3]

While the fields became scenes for collective redemption, the woodland wilderness became the proper setting for individual spiritual quests. Jesse Lee's father, "one day when his conviction [of his lost state] was deep, and his distress very great, . . . went out into the woods, and continued travelling about, and mourning for his sins." His sons, in their turn, took themselves off into the wilderness. Indeed such solitary wandering seems to have been an expected preparation for conversion. John Taylor sought out "a lonesome mountain, where nobody lived," and James Ireland constantly sought "solitude and retirement, in the woods" (even when he was living as the lone inhabitant of a remote schoolhouse). For these men the wild forest had become the appropriate haunt of the isolated individual and a symbol of his quest. (Similar identifications appeared in non-evangelical contexts, for example, William Wirt's portrayal of the young Patrick Henry as a lone wanderer in the woods.)[4]

For the vast majority of whites a field cleared from the woods was the usual home site. Traditionally, the house of such a freeholder had special importance. The social standing of the head of the household was demonstrated in various rituals of hospitality. In the celebration of christenings, marriages, funerals—the great rites of passage for members of his lineage—his role as host-provider was supremely fulfilled. But the evangelical code forbade the conviviality customary at such celebrations. The style appropriate to the patriarchal role, and with it the function of the house itself as a symbol of social position, were altogether changed. A view of this transformation is afforded in Leland's description of an encounter in the winter of 1787–1788:

> As I was returning from Fredericksburg, in the lower part of Orange, a young man had married and brought his bride to his father's, where there was music and dancing. I stopped in the road, and the groom came out and wished me to drink sling with him. I asked him what noise it was that I heard in the house? He answered it was a fiddle. As he was going to the house, I requested him to bring the fiddle to me. But as this was not done, I lighted off my horse and went into the house. By the time I got in, the fiddle was hidden, and all was still. I told them, if fiddling and dancing was serving God, to proceed on, and

if I could gain conviction of it, I would join them. As they did not proceed, I told them I would attempt to serve God in my way. I then prayed among them and took my leave. The next week I was sent for to come and preach at the same house. The power of the Lord was present to heal. In the course of a few weeks, numbers were converted and turned to the Lord, whom I baptized in a stream of water near the house.[5]

The stern witness of evangelicalism was present and its reproach felt—in consciousness if not in direct confrontation—wherever there was "music and dancing." The hiding of the fiddle showed that the people, though engaged in traditional forms of celebration, anticipated and responded to the preacher's disapproval. The awakening within members of this household radically altered the social orientation of their home; it would no longer be a center for convivial hospitality.

DOMESTICITY AND PRIVATE SPACE

Dramatic evangelical successes such as the one described above were exaggerations of quieter trends that were taking place quite apart from the New Light movement. In the last quarter of the eighteenth century the Anglo-Virginians, whether evangelized or not, were gradually altering their social customs. Whereas travelers had once found themselves actively sought out by would-be hosts for the company they could offer, such hospitality was less frequent by the 1780s. Virginians admitted that "their doors were oftentimes closed to strangers; and . . . their much-praised hospitality is by no means unrestricted but is confined to acquaintances, and those who are recommended." John Bernard, the English actor and humorist who visited toward the end of the century, found that the members of polished society already mocked the open-house customs of twenty years earlier. He was told facetious stories of the avidity with which the country gentleman had once schemed "to draw guests to his convivial roof." Much was made of the contrast with the present, when the householder who once might have sought to ensnare travelers and force them at gunpoint to accept his hospitality, was now more likely to use threats to be rid of a stranger. New ways had superseded that "generous custom" whereby the patriarch of the great house used "to send the negroes round at nightfall to the nearest inns . . . with a note to any lady or gentleman who might be putting up there, stating that . . . Mr.—— would be happy to see them at his house close by, to which a black with a lantern would conduct them." At mid-century an English traveler had felt that "an universal Hospitality" prevailed in Chesapeake society, characterized by "full Tables and Open Doors, the kind Salute, the generous Detention." It recalled for him a legendary past in England—"the roast-Beef Ages of our Fore-Fathers." This era, it seems, had also become a legend in Virginia by 1800.[6]

Commenting on the marked change of manners among the gentry, Bernard perceptively attributed it to the increasing refinement that accompanied the more prominent role that ladies assumed in household entertainment. Refinement, like the domesticity with which it was associated, expressed an increasingly felt need to shield individuals from close interaction with an enveloping social world, a world that was now held to be impure and vulgar. A long perspective over time is needed to clarify the gradual changes that had been taking place. Social occasions even among the gentry in the seventeenth century had involved a degree of merged communality—close, comparatively unrestrained crowding of body against body that is altogether shocking to modern sensitivities. A Frenchman who attended a seventeenth-century gentry wedding in Gloucester County described the avidity with which the guests proceeded to "drink, smoke, sing & dance." He was startled to find that when the hour grew late, "they do not provide beds for the men" so that some were "already lying on the floor." Others "caroused all night long" and by morning not one "could stand straight." The extent to which social interaction had become more constrained among the gentry during the ensuing century is suggested by an English traveler's stress on the refinement displayed at a wedding he attended in 1785. He was impressed by the "elegant" provision that the master of the house had made, and by the "elegant . . . manners" with which the guests honored the host in return. This characterization referred to the social ceremonies that had come to control behavior. Individual space was enlarged and protected, and physical contact more restricted. All of the physical functions—defecation, urination, bathing, sexual relations, even eating—came under new codes of behavior that emphasized privacy or, in the case of eating, refinement.[7]

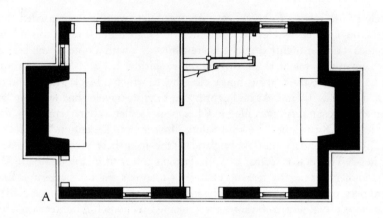

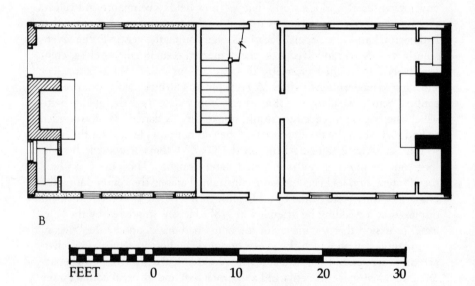

FIGURE 29.
Houses once "open" became "closed"

The restructuring of space within houses is itself revealing of changing social attitudes. Architecture is guided by the planner's awareness of the forms
of action a building is meant to contain or segregate; the organization of space
in a building will, in turn, help mold social conduct. The increasing consciousness of individual separateness, already evident in the spatial divisions
in the gentry houses of 1740, was slowly becoming more general. In time
it would be apparent not only in modified social custom (as in the closing of
doors once hospitably open to strangers) but also in the altered internal arrangement of common planters' houses.[8]

During the eighteenth century a new basic conception of how a house
should be organized came to have wider and wider currency. In the earliest
structures (see figure 29a) there was little segregation of persons, and particular rooms were not specifically set aside for such activities as cooking, eating,
and bedding down. The communal area, usually called "the hall," lay immediately open to anyone who crossed the threshold. The new plan (see figure
29b) introduced a "passage" between the outside door and the now specialized rooms for sleeping, taking of meals, and sitting at ease.[9]

"Privatization" is an ugly neologism, but it fits the overall trends observable in Anglo-Virginian living environments. Change was slow in coming to
the dwellings of poor planters, who continued to live crowded in one-room or
two-room houses until well into the nineteenth century. The basic equipment that such persons needed for daily living was, however, in the process of
being transformed. An elaboration and specialization of items of daily use had
taken place in the half century before the Revolution. Well before plain
men's houses came to be divided into more distinctly private spaces, congested seating on benches, on chests, and on the floor even, gave way to seating on chairs. In many houses below the gentry level, matched individual
place settings of china and cutlery began to replace the small stock of communal vessels and utensils that formerly had to do duty for everyone.[10]

THE QUARTER: COMMUNITY INTENSIFIED

Architecture and furnishings were inscribing private domesticity, in both
great and minuscule characters, upon the landscape of Anglo-Virginians, and
so widening the cultural rift that separated the whites from the blacks. Slave

dwellings often stood physically close to, but apart from, the houses of the masters. Culturally, this pattern of closeness offset by segregation was being intensified. The developments of half a century had narrowed the distance between slaves and masters in certain obvious respects. In 1740 approximately half the inhabitants of the quarter had been born in the Old World and so had been forced later in life to acquire painfully the English vocabulary that provided the medium of verbal communication in their new environment. By 1790 the number of slaves who had been raised within a fully developed African culture was reduced to a small proportion of the whole. For the Virginia-born the "creole" speech of the quarter was their native tongue. Furthermore, an increasing number of blacks were coming to employ Judaeo-Christian symbols to formulate their conceptions of their own origins and destiny. Yet by the end of the century, despite superficial anglicization, the shape of the slaves' homeplaces clearly indicated the consolidation of a communal pattern from which the masters' increasingly individualized way of life was diverging.[11]

Alone in their field and woodland settings, Anglo-Virginian houses were more than ever closed places for the private withdrawal of the families that occupied them. At the same time, the society at the quarter was maturing and developing in the opposite direction. The rise of an overwhelmingly native-born black population brought about for the first time a balance of the sexes, which in turn improved opportunities for stable marriage and residence of married couples on the same plantation. The percentage of slave children growing up in the presence of both parents advanced from perhaps a third toward a half. Nevertheless, these developments among the blacks cannot be interpreted as an extension of the same domesticity we have observed arising in the Anglo-Virginian house. The size of the average quarter with its closely grouped cabins had grown considerably, especially in the longest-settled parts. Carefully collected figures suggest that whereas in 1740 about one-half of the slaves lived in settlements of less than ten persons, by 1790 less than one-third were in such small groupings. Within the same time the proportion who lived in settlements of more than twenty persons had risen from about 15 percent to more than 40 percent. (The size of white households averaged less than six.) The communal ethos that set the quarter apart from the freeholder's isolated residence was thus enhanced.[12]

This different ethos pervaded not only daily life but also the night time and

Sunday gatherings for dance and song—occasions that had much more in common with seventeenth-century Anglo-Virginian celebrations than with the prescribed, and physically inhibiting, refinements characteristic of polite Virginia society by 1790. The contrast in the cultures appears in the distinctive character that black culture gave to evangelical Christianity. Preoccupations with sin and control of the body in a war of the spirit against the flesh were not central features of the Afro-American value system. Hence, the crying out, falling down, and ecstatic release that appeared both in slave worship and in white evangelical meetings had different connotations for participants drawn from the different cultures.

Little is known about early evangelicalism among the slaves, but some outlines of their religious life can be reconstructed from the indirect evidence that survives. John Leland reported in 1790 that "the poor slaves . . . discover as great inclination for religion as the free-born do"; that "it is nothing strange for them to walk twenty miles on Sunday morning to meeting, and back again at night"; that "they are remarkable for learning a tune soon"; and that in time of a revival, "they are remarkably fond of meeting together, to sing, pray, and exhort, and sometimes preach, and seem to be unwearied in the exercises." He also noted that "they seem, in general, to put more confidence in their own color, than they do in the whites." [13]

Making allowances for Leland's evident condescension toward the slaves—he is surprised they can learn a tune—we nevertheless get a glimpse of the emerging black Christianity that is often regarded as being the core of Afro-American culture. Like most commentators after him, Leland could not appreciate the distinctiveness of the emerging religion that he unwittingly described. He was misled by all the observable elements—the idioms of belief and behavior—that were shared with whites. Recent scholars have cogently argued that the configuration into which the slaves worked these elements was overwhelmingly African. The fundamental differences between the religion of the slaves and that of the whites, even when they worshiped together, derived mainly from the absence in Afro-American life of a sharp line between the religious and the secular—certainly blacks did not draw such a line in the same way that Anglo-Saxons had long drawn it. In time, the inclusion of communal dancing in black religious expression highlighted the differences that were less openly evident in the preaching and the singing. White evangelical prohibition of dancing arose out of a need (not shared by the slaves) to create powerful symbols of sinful worldliness, and so to find signs of redemption in abstinence, bodily inhibition, and withdrawal from the world.[14]

It seems that the slaves, unlike their masters, inhabited a world pervaded by sacred meaning and a sense of the potential for collective redemption. This state of consciousness cannot be documented from the few shreds of evidence surviving from the eighteenth century. Its intensity, revealed in the actions and utterances assiduously collected by nineteenth-century folklorists, provides strong grounds for reading it back into the earlier period and for concluding that a basically African cultural matrix had been in the process of acquiring evangelical content at the time of Leland's observations.[15] *

SLAVERY BECOMES A PROBLEM

Ever since they had been established as a separate group at the quarter, the slaves had been evolving a way of life quite different from that of their masters. The rate of divergence was accelerated by the advance of private domesticity within Anglo-American culture, an advance that had been expressed in the individualistic emphasis of both the evangelical and republican movements. The institution of slavery came under censure partly because the direction in which the masters' culture developed undermined the ultimate legitimacy of the slaves' status and of the relationships arising from it. Formerly Anglo-Virginians had felt a general complacency about the system—a complacency of the kind that had enabled William Byrd to pen the idyll of his way of life surrounded by his "Bond-men" and "Bond-women." His traditional English world view had not only incorporated distinctions of status and kind but was also rooted in a scarcely conscious assumption that the cosmos,

---

* The study of slavery has too much been conducted as though the slaves could be understood in isolation from the whole society of which they were a part, and as though there was no evolution in slave culture or transformation in the ways blacks interacted with whites. By default it has been tacitly assumed that the development of the black social and cultural system has been uniformly directed toward assimilation of whites' ways. The consequent conclusion has been either that the basic institutions of the masters' society, such as "the family," have provided the organizational principles of the slaves' world, or else that the "weak" development of these institutions within black culture constituted a form of social "pathology."[16]

with which the social order must be in harmony, consisted of a vast, continuous hierarchy of parts, each in its degree on the scale. Slavery did not pose a problem within such a system. Differences in kinds of social being and the state of total subjection itself were part of the nature of things. Over the plantation was raised, not only its own proper patriarch, but also the imagery of a whole series of ruling fathers extending beyond the king to the Creator.

American republicanism had broken this chain of governance. Sovereign authority under the new regime was based on the mutual contract of the individuals who composed society. Within this system, both the slave's status and the relationships that resulted from it were anomalous. Provisions were made to accommodate slavery, but Virginians could no longer complacently take it for granted within the new framework. The Virginia Declaration of Rights had formally disposed of the problem by limiting its protection to "men . . . when they enter into a state of society." Slaves, like women, were not parties to the contract—they were the captives of the free white men who had formed the association.[17]

Legalistic formulas might have proved adequate to forestall individual crises of conscience had there been no alterations in the traditional patriarchal household system that encompassed slavery. While the basic organization of plantations remained the same, the fine texture of domestic life in the great houses was changing under the subtle but pervasive influences of cosmopolitan culture. Privatization of space and refinement of manners had proceeded furthest in the great houses, and romantic novels (a mid-eighteenth century "invention" and boom product) were avidly read. Familial relationships were tending to be controlled less by formal rules and increasingly by concern for individual feelings. Personalities were thus being radically altered. In the age of "sensibility" patriarchy was being sentimentalized into paternalism. In a social system that was less rigidly organized according to status categories and more attuned to the play of personal emotions, slavery became problematic.[18]

In the realm of moral philosophy this change registered itself as "humanitarianism." There was a growing revulsion against orthodox Christian acceptance of suffering as the consequence of Adam's sin, and an increasing determination to work out the claims that human beings could rightfully make upon the benevolence of their fellows. Slavery could not go unchallenged in a world in which values were becoming focused on individuals and their quest for fulfillment. The protests against slavery came predictably from two sides—the adherents of enlightened (that is, humanitarian) philosophy, and the zealots of evangelical religion. Theologically at opposite poles, these two movements had at least one thing in common: they both voiced heightened concern for the definition of the moral claims of individuals against the traditional world. (In one case that world was seen as darkened by barbarous custom; in the other, by sinful pride.)[19]

For a few of the masters the sense of strain between their domestic sensibilities and the relationships that tied the quarter to the great house became so great that the tension could only be eased by setting their slaves free. This did not happen on a scale sufficient to transform prevailing social patterns, but the incidence was great enough (together with the act of Assembly in 1782 that legalized manumission) to show that the traditional conception of authority had been fundamentally disturbed.[20]

A NEW METAPHOR OF SOCIAL ORDER

It was on August 11, 1774, that the freeholders of Caroline County had gathered at the courthouse to record their defiance of Parliament. An "Association" had been passed around with the expectation that all heads of households would subscribe it. It was intended to be a foundation for community solidarity as events strained old allegiances and undermined customary forms of higher authority. The signing explicitly depicted the metaphor that larger society was a voluntary association founded on mutual "compact." The earlier non-importation associations had been secular precursors of this enactment on a lesser scale; a sanctified variant of the idea had been communicated in the covenanting of fellowship each time a Baptist church was created.[21]

Setting one's name to the paper obviously signified entry into contractual association, but this act encapsulated another even more powerful cultural metaphor. The idea of patriarchy was ceasing to be the overarching concept for the organization and understanding of authority in society at large. Contractual entry into association made prominent the image of an autonomous individual giving free assent. That image was part of an emergent cultural pattern already glimpsed in the preachers' isolated searches for salvation among the forests; in the individual guilt and heightened responsibility for one's own conduct that evangelical morality imposed; in the closing of houses to the larger world; and in the creation of more segregated individual space within the house itself. Our twentieth-century outlook induces us to see unquestioningly the individual as the primary social reality whose self-fulfillment supplies the ultimate meaning and purpose in life. Yet "the individual" is no less a great metaphor applied to the interpretation of social realities than hierarchies of ruling fathers have been. The principle of individual autonomy, only just establishing an ascendancy destined to last until the present, was reorganizing late eighteenth-century Anglo-Virginians' perceptions of their world and the expectations they had of it.[22]

WESTWARD MOVEMENT: THE INDIVIDUAL IN PURSUIT OF GAIN

Aspects of the reorganization of social action and social expectation can be discerned in the great movements of population that were taking place in the wake of the Revolution. A radical redirection of cultural outlook was already apparent in the celebration of the shirtmen of '75. After the opening of the Kentucky land office in 1779 the westward orientation—"the prevailing and favorite scheme . . . of purchasing back lands on the river Ohio and its branches"—grew more intense, and the steady flow of settlers over the mountains swelled to a prodigious flood. The region between the Chesapeake and the Blue Ridge had changed its relative position. From being on the transatlantic margin of the British maritime empire, it became part of the eastern seaboard of an expanding continental nation-state.[23]

An English prisoner of war was maliciously pleased at the weakening of old Virginia that he saw resulting from the massive exodus. He noted that those who took part in these "amazing emigrations" faced a journey of "near a thousand miles," yet they "appear cheerful and happy" in spite of leaving behind "comfortable houses and plantations, which have been the labor their whole lives to clear and bring to perfection." In the magnitude of the movement, and in the scale of the speculative transactions on which it was based, can be seen an epitome of the new ethos. A hundred miles—several days' traveling —had seemed a wrenching journey into the west for the young Devereux Jarratt in 1750; the thousand-mile, two-month journeys in which heads of

households were now involving their families entailed a far more final sever-
ance. As old connections were broken and distant new settlements formed, a
pattern of voluntary association (and dissociation) was transforming the
scene. Land dealing on a vastly expanded scale contributed to an accelerated
mobility. The ideal of the free man engaged in "the pursuit of happiness" was
more and more closely linked with the acceptance of the self-seeking individual in pursuit of gain. The controversy over public support for religion had
revealed the anxieties that customary leaders felt over the values that seemed
to predominate in the young republic. The same concern appears in the journal of the country doctor whose record of wartime morale has been outlined
in the previous chapter. He deplored "the immense fortunes . . . made by
trade, or speculation as it is called," and expressed alarm at the way such successes "raised a wonderful passion in almost all to aggrandise their fortunes."
The diarist's concern was with the example set by successful large-scale opera-
tors, but common planters also contributed to this ethos when they emigrated
to the west, even though their objective was usually a highly traditional one.
(One man, for instance, explained to a traveler that he would move "over the
mountains to Kentucky where he could buy as much land as would give each
of his children a sufficient portion.") [24]

Western movement and speculation in land were among the activities that
had worked most persistently to mold Virginia society from its beginnings.
What was altered during the Revolution and its aftermath was not just the
geographic scale but the human context that supplied cultural meaning. In
migration and in speculative dealing, the metaphor of money—powerful
since colonization, although opposed to the metaphor of patriarchy—gained
new potency in combination with the greatly enhanced metaphor of the self-
sustaining individual. The obligations underpinning the ancient forms of
community were further weakened.

COMMUNITY DIMINISHED

The turn inward of the once open Anglo-Virginian house meant that shared
festivities at a neighborhood level were restricted. Meanwhile the evangelical
and republican revolutions together had partially dismantled the larger community framework that had formerly encompassed all households.

The parish church was gone. Only wreckage remained as a painful reminder to those who had struggled to salvage something of what it had symbolized. The disrepair of Virginia churches was a shocking sight to Europeans whose upbringing conditioned them to expect church buildings to be monumental expressions of corporate worship. In 1796 an English traveler, Isaac Weld, commented that he "scarcely observed one [church] that was not in a ruinous condition, with the windows broken, and doors dropping off the hinges, and lying open to the pigs and cattle wandering about the woods." Even where small numbers continued to attend, attempting to maintain the liturgical forms of the Book of Common Prayer, the morale of the congregation was sometimes "so low . . . and so few [were] disposed to respond, that . . . [the minister] used to read only such parts as needed no response, and not all of them." [25]

In 1799 the Baptists' relentless petitioning campaign bore fruit in an act of the General Assembly that stripped the Protestant Episcopal church of the property it had accumulated as the official establishment. An act of 1801 provided for the sale of this property by the overseers of the poor—minor elected office-bearers who had succeeded the self-recruiting vestries of gentlemen. Glebe lands, and in some cases church plate, came under the auctioneer's hammer. Moneys thus raised were not applied to the creation of new monuments (such as schools) for reoriented community; they eased poor relief and road taxes for a year or so and were gone.

Neglect of the churches turned into spoliation. "About the year 1810" the Bay Church in Isle of Wight County, which had been built in the mid-eighteenth century, "was pulled down and a kitchen built of the bricks; the sides and backs of the pews were used to make stalls for a stable . . . , [while] the bell of the church was exchanged in Richmond for a brandy-still." Another church, in Lunenburg County, "being deserted of worshippers . . . was filled with fodder." It was reported to have "taken fire while some negroes were playing cards in it by night." At Pope's Creek, near George Washington's ancestral home, the old church was burned down deliberately "in order to prevent injury, from the falling of the roof, to the cattle which were accustomed to shelter there" (see figure XIX). [26]

The broken down, neglected churches—not to mention those pillaged for momentary gains—imprinted unmistakably on the landscape the collapse and abandonment of an ideal of society as a network of coercive but inclusive communities. The official ascendancy in the old regime of mutuality over individual gain had been formally declared with the legal requirement that ministers, churchwardens, and vestrymen should levy community support for the maintenance of worship and the care of the poor. Yet the collective constraints had never been very strong in the fluid conditions of colonial society and had effectively been superseded by the triumph of republicanism in 1776. In Virginia the nominally inclusive Christian community of the parish had at no stage conditioned pervasive social values to the extent that it controlled behavior generally. Nevertheless, when the republican/evangelical settlement of 1776–1786 put an end to the traditional forms and replaced them with an ideology in which "the individual" was the legitimating metaphor, a significant cultural reorientation took place. The old order had induced a sense of obligation to public service among those whose family and fortune had set them over their neighbors in parish and county. Within the new framework of contractual association the local units seemed to be less like patriarchal protectorates and more like outlets for the electoral ambitions of individuals. An acute sense of lost public spirit resulted. [27]

In some parishes old churches were abandoned or reduced to shells for shriveled kernels of liturgical performances; in others the downfall of the system to which they were shattered monuments was even more completely signified as the buildings were occupied by the once-despised dissenters. The triumph of popular evangelicalism was then most clearly written upon the old setting.

In defiance of the vestry of Bristol Parish, Prince George County, the Methodists persisted in using one of the old churches of the establishment. Richard Garrettson preached there "to a crowded congregation" that overfilled the building. He preached but could not conclude, for "in the application . . . five hundred at once broke out in loud praises, whilst sinners were struck with a divine power." The tumult of collective emotion was such that "in the height of this stir eleven rafters of the house [of God] broke down at once." The cracking beams made a "dreadful noise" and yet "not one person seemed to hear it; so mighty was the power of God among the people!" [28]

The new sense of social and religious relationships, so evident during revivals, was commonly given visible shape in the reorganization of the interiors of churches that were taken over. The opposing images of the popular preacher and the establishment parson that were implicit in the rhetoric of the assessment debate were made explicit in the rearrangement of church furnishings. At the "lower chapel" of Christ Church Parish, Middlesex County, the New Lights made concerted efforts "to destroy every vestige of Episcopal taste and usage." It was reported that "the high pulpit and sounding-board have been removed, and the reading-desk placed within the chancel." Accounts of a number of remodelings disclose the setting up of a kind of rough "stage," suitable to the persona of the evangelical preacher—a "platform made by laying a few planks across the backs of two pews." Such arrangements were made even when "the old-fashioned pulpit" was available for use. In one case, "after the Episcopal Church had ceased to have services . . . and other denominations had taken possession, on the occasion of some protracted and very exciting meeting, when the old pews seemed to be in the way of promoting a revival, it was proposed . . . that they be taken away and benches put in place of them." The close fellowship—the merging of individuals in a mass—that was sought in times of revival was felt to be better served by huddled, knee-to-knee seating on benches "made of the outside slabs from the sawmill, with legs as rude thrust through them, and of course no backs." [29]

The evangelical meetinghouses inscribed on the landscape their own distinctive messages about the individual and the community. The buildings that housed the first New Light evangelical gatherings in Virginia had been tobacco houses; the Baptists' and the Methodists' chapels remained rude and unadorned. In these plain structures, scattered irregularly throughout the countryside, occurred some of the forms of religious exercise practiced by those who had brought liturgical worship low. There was the weekly fulfillment of the covenant "to meet together Every Lords Day . . . to celebrate the worship of god" in extempore prayer, preaching, singing, and Scripture reading, while church members endeavored "to keep the day holy and to watch over [their] . . . families . . . that they doe the same." And then there was the yet more sober, even chillingly repressive, monthly meeting for the fulfillment of the covenant obligation "to watch over one another . . . and to admonish . . . and to Reprove if need be." Grim-faced, perhaps—were it not that releases of emotion might break through any of these proceedings, resonating the fundamental shared experiences of awakening and conversion that were the basis for the fellowship of the church members. Indeed, the tension between disciplined control and ritualized unloosing was resolved during times of revival in a literal overflowing from the enclosed space of the meetinghouses into the outdoors. [30]

The religious behavior associated with the tightly disciplined Baptist churches and Methodist classes manifested a pattern of alternation between strict control of the body and valued forms of loss of control. In this respect the popular evangelicalism of the humbler tobacco growers invites comparison both with black religion and with the decorum of assemblies of the gentry. Among the slaves, individual self-punishment through bodily austerity was little apparent, while the communal inducing of states of ecstasy through dance and song was highly developed. The increasing "refinement" of the gentry elite necessarily involved a high level of internalized self-discipline—a level that admitted of no sanctioned public total release. The world of the humbler whites can perhaps be best understood in terms of its intermediate position. The characteristic forms of expression alternated between the opposite poles of strict self-containment and shared communal outpouring. The privatization of houses with increasingly individualized furnishings, and the repressive discipline of the new evangelical mores, indicate an impulsion toward tighter controls. The emotional releases associated with revivalism manifested a continuing need for unconstrained bodily communication. The semiliteracy of yeomen and tenant farmers endowed them with a mix of the sensitivities of oral and typographic cultures. In the same way their changing material conditions of life left them torn in two directions between the individualizing trends of contemporary Anglo-American culture and the appeal of the surviving communalism of their own traditions. On the one hand, a segregation of the physical self; on the other hand, a free acceptance of close bodily contact. The proximity of a black society that was highly communal in its religion and way of life could only reinforce the latter tendencies in white popular evangelical forms of worship.[31]

In September 1804 there was a huge gathering at Suffolk, south of the lower James River. A zealot in the work of revival reported that it had been "a camp-meeting" and had begun "on Friday and continued day and night without intermission till Monday evening." During that time there had been "upwards of four hundred souls, including the blacks . . . powerfully converted to God." A mounting excitement had communicated itself bodily through the close-packed crowds of people—many of whom were accustomed to living in small, isolated households. Participants on such occasions felt that "the Lord was in the midst of the assembly [as] . . . many fell to the ground and cried for mercy," while the "Christians" were seen to be most "fervent and interested for mourners; [as] their prayers and supplications were without intermission throughout the whole day and night." The preachers stood with their hands "constantly held up by the prayers of thousands." There was a prodigious sound as "the strong-lunged men exerted themselves until the whole forrest echoed, and all the trees of the woods clapped their hands." At the climax, when it was felt that God came near, "sinners fell in abundance, Christians rejoiced and shouted, and a glorious sacrifice of praise ascended to God." The name "camp-meeting" was new to Virginia in 1804, yet it only served to give ultimate institutionalization and bolder form to modes of religious behavior that had for half a century been establishing themselves as a prominent part of the culture.[32]

THE COURTHOUSE

Court day, unlike obligatory divine service at the parish church, remained as a generally shared time of public assembly. It had to carry a larger share of such sense of inclusive community as survived. The occasion continued to provide the venue for a monthly country fair, but many of the associated convivial customs now marked a sharp division in society between those who adhered to ancient ways and puritans who condemned them. The common folk must still be pictured in the surrounds of a courthouse "of Brick and handsome appearance," engaged in fighting and gouging, or "Collected there to see quarter Races." It might be that "Grog as usual had Great effect" so that "the Noisyed Crew" would be "¾'s of them in a state of intoxication." The aggressive roisterers that Fithian had noted with repugnance were certainly present at the end of the century and beyond. The contest pastimes, noted by Hugh Jones in 1724, still drew common planters from home "to the courthouse, or to a horse-race." But itinerant evangelists now frequently used the county seat as a place for preaching, exhortation, and prayer. As with the convivial celebration of the hospitality of the home, so with carousing at the court day fair, the stern witnesses of the new faith were necessarily present in consciousness, if not in person. Now the riotous drinking on the green served to sustain the preachers' lurid metaphors concerning the depravity of fallen man. Some of the brawlers would certainly in time be brought to a stricken renunciation of their ways. No such metaphors had polarized the consciousness of the Reverend Mr. Jones or of the men of the 1720s whose ways he commented on; no such awakening and conversion experience had been imminent for them.[33]

Inside the courthouse the persistence of old forms is amply indicated by the records, as justices, juries, and witnesses were sworn to try endless series of actions in debt, detinue, trespass, and petitions in chancery. Yet the transformations in the representation of authority and in the dominant metaphors of the culture had made for significant changes in the meanings implicit in transactions at the courthouse. Most obvious, the great patriarchal symbol of authority was gone. Proceedings were no longer in the king's name. Crimes were declared to have been committed, not "against the peace of our sovereign lord the King," but "against the peace and dignity of this commonwealth." The studied retention of most of the customary form of words did not prevent an altogether different statement from being made. The commonwealth was no father figure but the fictive, impersonal product of a "compact" between its members. Its government was considered to be strictly limited, and its constitution explicitly denied to the governor any of the arcane powers designated in English tradition as the "royal prerogative."[34]

The exercise of public authority in the community now derived, not from a patriarch-king presiding over a Parliament and dignitaries in accordance with the practices of the ancestors "time out of mind," but from a written document embodying a contract in "visible form." The implications of this transformation were far-reaching, though slowly felt. The constitution provided an archetype for all law as *written* law—and so a balance that had for centuries been tilting from law as custom to law as code was tipped decisively. The common law—"the ancient immemorial, unwritten law of England"— came to be suspect, not simply because it was English, but precisely because it was a body of custom for which the repository was the wisdom of learned judges. In January 1800 both houses of the General Assembly of Virginia declared the ancient common law to be "obsolete and unknown," since it arbitrarily "subjects the citizens to . . . the judiciary will, when he is left in ignorance of what this law enjoins as a duty, or prohibits as a crime." With tradition condemned and sound law envisaged as written compendium, the role of judges was subtly reduced. More especially was this true of the county justices who, at a time when the concept of common law was unchallenged, had sat as elders in their courthouses, presiding authoritatively over the dispensation of law according to community custom. Complaints of the ineffectualness of local government came to be legion.[35]

The processes at work weakening the gentry's consensual domination of county society can be discovered in connection with another important means of transmitting authority. The election at the courthouse had traditionally projected a corporate, rank-ordered mode of community. The body of freeholders chose the most informed, judicious gentlemen to think and act for their counties, as the head does for the other members of the body. During the Revolution the demands of wartime, and the turbulence of rebellion (perhaps combined with the requirement of annual elections) had caused a great many of the county society's traditional leaders to withdraw from contests at the polls. The ensuing period witnessed rapid turnover of representatives and alarm at the decline in public spirit and the lowered tone of legislative politics.

Overt ideological divisions developed in the 1780s and grew sharper in the 1790s. Although "parties" were ineradicable, they were felt to be illegitimate and subversive of community forms of political authority. An election in 1800, following the turmoil of 1798–1799 over the Virginia Resolves, shows how party feuding, when no longer contained by an ideal of searching out the most informed and judicious of the gentry, might develop into a different kind of contest. A brief narrative of the events reveals how symbolic issues, dividing Federalists from Republicans, had now come to the fore: "At the election at Hanover court-house, in the fall of 1800, Col. Mayo expressed his disapprobation of the policy of the last Virginia Legislatures. Col. Mayo . . . heard Mr. Penn call him a d——d rascal, and say he was not worthy to black the shoes of some of the members. Penn denied the 'd——d' but acknowledged the other, and a duel, next day . . . took place, Col. Mayo being slightly wounded." Neither the duel nor the political "party" had been permitted a place in the parochial order of the ancien régime. With the increased scale of the social and political system, cosmopolitan fashions and ideological disputes were penetrating the courthouse community and causing it to identify its own conflicts with definitions derived from a supra-local, national forum.[36]

Paradoxically the revolution that had severed the counties from the metropolis three thousand miles away had subtly provincialized them. The community decisions made in 1774 and 1775 had placed the Virginia courthouses on the stage of a great historical drama, but the subsequent developments that led to the creation of the Federal Union had the effect of dwarfing local centers in comparison with the new national governmental structures that now loomed over them.

Under the old regime the county courts had meshed closely with a House of Burgesses that was, in accordance with ancient traditions of authority, a county court writ large. Under the new form of government, with its carefully written separation of powers, such a continuum of authority could not persist even though the elected representatives continued to be drawn largely from among the justices of the county benches. After 1789 the functions of the Virginia Assembly were subsumed in part by the powers of the superior government of the United States. Federal elections, taking place at the court-houses, inevitably provincialized the innumerable local elections. [37]

Authority based on individual contract; government empowered by a printed constitution; the ascendancy of statute law over ancient custom; and an increase of scale that effectively provincialized local government—all can be seen as components of "modernization." In these changes can be traced the intensified impact of a print-oriented cosmopolitanism upon an already weakened localistic oral culture. The forms of community that centered on the courthouses were accordingly diminished. [38]

CHANGE AND CONTINUITY

Much remained the same—especially in fields and houses. Patriarchy, and its adaptation, paternalism, continued to be a powerful principle in a thoroughly agrarian society where households small and great were still the social units of production. Yet the reordering of cultural metaphors necessarily worked transformations in the landscapes of experience.

In 1740 an integrated official set of symbols had served to shape the awareness of those Virginians who could be drawn or coerced into entering the consensus that was expressed in land boundaries, tobacco warehouses, court-houses, and churches. The Africans and Afro-Virginians, with their own ways of comprehending the world, remained largely outside this system of persuasion, and the gentry orchestrators of the otherwise inclusive, compulsory community were clearly content that it should be so. We can scarcely tell to what extent the hardhanded common planters internalized their roles as supporting cast in the staging of parish and county performances. They had no positive, organized alternative until the appearance of New Light churches at mid-century. After that time the rapid growth of the Baptist and Methodist following among the lower ranks showed how readily weak attachment turned into active disaffection.

By the 1790s affairs were greatly changed: diverse cultural and countercultural possibilities had manifestly appeared to fracture shared definitions and ways of seeing things. Evangelicalism continued to gain converts and transform consciousness. Republicanism had meanwhile been turned around. Launched at first by the gentry as a means of regenerating traditional authority, it had become a vehicle of popular assertion. The "shirtmen" and their kind, mobilized from within an already mobile population, had given the new ideology a more radical twist and so made it the ready means, not for renewing coercive, rank-ordered community as found in the parish churches, but for dismantling such institutions and for resisting attempts to revive a system that legitimated forms of deference.

The unchallengeable republican ideology that emerged from the decades of turmoil lacked the capacity to encompass all that the metaphors of the traditional establishment of 1740 had been able to bind together. Republicanism could be, and was, used as a basis for reincorporating the loose networks of Virginia's agrarian society within a new empire called the United States of America, but with the king's commissions gone, the principles of patriarchal household order and higher authority were less integrated. Republicanism was symbolically less inclusive than monarchy had been. Organized religion was explicitly excluded from the support and surveillance of a regime that now derived its legitimacy from an idealization of individual autonomy.

Socially, republicanism worked to formalize a deep division by excluding the slaves to whom its membership and its promises did not extend. The cult of self-sufficiency enshrined in republicanism affirmed the trends already being expressed in the continuing process by which whites' living spaces were being privatized—the trends away from the communal set of values that had established itself as an enduring cultural tradition at the slave quarter. Meanwhile, among Anglo-Virginians themselves sharp differences in outlook had become institutionalized. A fundamental incompatibility existed between the humbling, soul-searching culture of the New Lights and the proud, assertive culture of the gentry and their adherents. Accommodations could, and did, take place as many evangelicals became more genteel, and many of the gentlefolk became more evangelical, but complete assimilation was impossible. The vivid culture of the gentry, with their love of magnificent display, had now to coexist with the austere culture of the evangelicals, with their burden of guilt. A polarized world had emerged in which *both* the dramatic ritualizations of self-abasement in the falling down seizures of camp meetings, *and* the dramatic ritualizations of pride in the now-prevalent practice of duelling, could be highly significant forms of action. Virginia entered the nineteenth century still a wholly agrarian society, yet with a complex of cultures that was fractured by a widening ethnic rift and an enduring legacy of conflicting value systems.

A DISCOURSE ON THE METHOD
Action, Structure, and Meaning

Ethnography—the branch of anthropology directed to the interpretation of particular cultures—has become a major source of guidance for social historians who believe that the reconstruction of the distinctive mentalities of past peoples is an important part of their task. Two main approaches present themselves to those who engage in this interdisciplinary enterprise. The first, encouraged by anthropologists' preoccupation with comparison, seeks supposedly relevant models out of the vast array of ethnographic reports from around the world. It is hoped that a living example of a kinship support-group or of a patriarch-dominated extended household will illuminate the uncertain patterns of a vanished past. The second approach attends less to ethnographers' specific findings and more to the methods and concepts they have developed to assist them in understanding and explaining unfamiliar societies and systems of meaning.

Powerful reasons make the second approach preferable. The orientation of most historians is very different from that of mainstream comparative anthropologists. The discipline of history has long since turned away from the task of scanning the total record of the past and classifying its configurations in a search for comprehensive patterns that might be the key to a science of human nature. The notorious obsession of historians with the seemingly intractable particularities of nonrecurrent, unique events has stood as a barrier to interchanges with aggressively generalizing, nomothetic social sciences. But it is becoming clear that, like historians, ethnographers dealing with particular cultural systems also have subjects of enquiry that are unique and nonrecurrent in their complex configurations. Thus both anthropological and historical ethnographers need a stock of general concepts by which the particular patterns of the societies that they study may be analyzed and made intelligible to the observer. This book will therefore conclude with a discourse on method in which I shall attempt to lay out systematically, beginning with fundamentals, the principal concepts that have informed the methods of research and presentation used throughout the work. The first and most important of these fundamentals is obvious but little regarded: society is not primarily a material entity. It is rather to be understood as a dynamic product of the activities of its members—a product profoundly shaped by the images the participants have of their own and others' performances.[1]

The direct observation and interrogation methods of anthropology cannot be applied to social worlds long vanished, but there is an approach by which the historian can approximate, albeit fragmentarily, the notebook of the field ethnographer. A large proportion of such research data consists of accounts of the doings of particular people in particular circumstances. Often the actions may have been recorded as having a patterned recurrence. Not infrequently the entries relate to doings with peculiar features of a nonrecurrent kind. Both varieties of record are important to the ethnographer. Now, in the documents surviving from the past, the social historian can everywhere find traces—occasionally vivid glimpses—of *people doing things*. The searching out of the meanings that such actions contained and conveyed for the participants lies at the heart of the enterprise of ethnographic history.[2] Actions must be viewed as statements.

It is true particular difficulties stand in the way of ethnographic historians. They see no actions for themselves, but depend on the recorded impressions of others, who wrote down only what they chose to report and were not engaged in answering the historian's questions. These informants cannot be examined directly; they must be screened in absentia. Who were they? What understanding did they have of the encounters they documented? The "sources," with the purposes and meanings of their authors, always stand between historical ethnographers and the worlds they seek to know. Yet with patient attention to the processes of reporting it is possible to collect action-statements and to set about interpreting them.

"Translation" is the fundamental task of ethnographers, and in its inherent perplexities lies their greatest challenge. A culture may be thought of as a related set of languages, or as a multichannelled system of communication.

Consisting of more than just words, it also comprises gesture, demeanor, dress, architecture, and all the codes by which those who share in the culture convey meanings and significance to each other. Sentences in a given language cannot be translated unless, as we say, we "know" the language. If we ask how we get to "know" a language, we see that it can only be accomplished by repeated exercise in the handling of particular words and sentences, until we have learned and internalized both their individual meanings and the syntax by which they are strung together into intelligible statement. Much the same is true for the process of mastering the paralinguistic forms of expression—deportment, costume, buildings, etc.—that make up the total communications repertoire of a society. Ethnographers cannot understand and translate action-statements unless they have some comprehension of the culture; but such grasp can only be effectively acquired by close attention to particular action-statements. This inescapable circularity is all the more characteristic of the process by which, in the course of empirical research, existing understanding is refined into ever more discriminating appreciation of the subtle nuances of cultural forms. Through a process of elucidating contexts, structures, and meanings, we can learn to reconstruct something of the participants' worlds as they experienced them. The importance of the distinction between observers' categories (that is, our own as twentieth-century social scientists) and participants' categories (that is, those of the past peoples we study) should be borne in mind throughout the reading of this methodological discourse.[3]

"Homo sum. . . ." The search for understanding of others—be it persons of different time and place, or merely of different identity from oneself—lies at the heart of the whole humanistic enterprise, and it is not a pursuit in which anthropology serves as the only guide. The concepts—and the artistry—of all who have found ways to enter powerfully into alien worlds of experience, whether as novelists, dramatists, painters, literary critics, or social scientists, must be employed wherever they promise to be serviceable in the quest. Yet it must be remembered that, while there can be no historical understanding or interpretive statements without explanatory models in the shape of verbal formulations, diagrams, or statistical tables, these models are not to be confused with the ineffably complex worlds to which they are applied. A case is made in this book, and in this essay on method, for the insights that may be gained from reviewing the interaction of past people as though the episodes considered were displayed in a theater. Yet it is not to be supposed that the writer mistakes the world for a stage. Limited aspects of life may be illuminated, but the whole (no matter what the pushers of systems may affirm) can never be summed up in any interpretive scheme.

CONCERTED RITUAL*

A start may be made with a set piece that encapsulated a very explicit statement about social relationships in an elaborate formal pattern of actions. The time is October 1770, the place is Williamsburg. The newspaper report has the quality of a *tableau vivant*, with the very evident intention of idealizing the meanings expressed in the disposition of persons depicted:

Scenario 1

This being the day appointed for interring the remains of our late beloved Governor, at one o'clock the Church, College, and Capitol bells, began tolling; and the company repaired to the Palace, according to invitation, precisely at two. At three, the corpse being placed on the hearse, the procession began to move, in the following order, to the church, both sides of Palace street being lined with the city militia, and those of York and James city counties.

The HEARSE,
Preceded by two mutes, and three on each side the hearse,
    Outward of whom walked the pall bearers,
    Composed of six of his Majesty's Council,
And the Hon. the Speaker, and Richard Bland, Esq;
    of the House of Burgesses.
His Excellency's servants, in deep mourning,
    The Gentlemen of the Clergy, and
    Professors of the College.

---

* The primary resources for the method expounded here are records of human encounters. For clarity and ease of reference the depictions of action that are collected as materials for close analysis will be labeled and numbered: *Scenario 1*, *Scenario 2*, etc. These will be subdivided (a), (b), (c), etc., for every significant shift in the time or place of action.

Clerk of the church, and Organist,
Immediately followed the hearse, the Chief Mourners.
Gentlemen of the Faculty
Mayor, Recorder, Aldermen, and
Common Council of the city,
With the mace before them.
Gentlemen of the Law, and Clerk of the General Court,
Ushers, Students and Scholars of William and
Mary college,
All having white hatbands and gloves.
And then the company, which was very numerous,
Two and two.

At the western gate the corpse was removed from the hearse, and, carried by eight bearers, the Gentlemen appointed supporting the pall, placed in the centre of the church, on a carpet of black. The altar, pulpit, and his Excellency's seat were likewise hung with black. Then the service began and an anthem, accompanied by the organ, was sung, conducted by Mr. Woolls. The Rev. the Hon. the Commissary then delivered a discourse, from Psalm xlii part of the 7th verse, *Put thy trust in God*; which, joined to the deep affliction felt by the whole audience for the loss of such an excellent man, and so good a Governor, drew tears from many. Sermon being ended, the corpse was again placed on the hearse, and the company moved in the same order to the College, entering at the front gate, and so proceeding through the College to the Chapel, where the corpse was deposited in a vault, the militia firing three vollies at the interment. The coffin was of lead, with a cover of crimson velvet, adorned with silver handles, and a large silver plate, on which was this Inscription:

NORBORNE, Baron de BOTETOURT
Ob xv Oct. MDCCLXX
Aetat. LIII.[4]

A full explication and interpretation of the statements condensed within this elaborately staged event would require a book-length exploration of Anglo-Saxon culture and its Judaeo-Christian and Latin infusions up to the time of the event. But more briefly we can discern an encompassing hierarchical order of dignities which provided the essential structure of the enactment, an order that was adapted, however, to fit the ceremonial requirements of the particular solemn event. The councillors had precedence in their own right. The association of these members of the Upper House with the Speaker and the senior burgess (Richard Bland, Esq.) meant that the governor was escorted on his last earthly journey by representatives of the General Assembly, itself the corporate personification of the province over which his lordship had presided. The immediate proximity of the servants "in deepest mourning" referred to the patriarchal role of the unmarried proconsul as ruler of a house of his own. The professors were the masters of the house (the college) that was to receive his body. The clergy and "the Faculty" (of physicians) had, in addition to the precedence accorded their liberal professions, a particular association with a ritual that marked the death of the body and the passage of the soul. The fathers of the city were accorded due place, followed by the worthy "gentlemen of the law," and (their own internal rankings observed) the young gentlemen of the house of higher learning.

Both sacred and secular ritual readily assume the tableau format observable in the governor's funeral cortege. Such action-cosmology presents formal statements about the nature of the social universe. If the complex configurations are to be intelligible, however, they must incorporate elements belonging to everyday life as it is interpreted in the particular culture. Elaborately orchestrated rituals offer social and cultural historians clear declarations of how the nature of things was intended to be understood at the time of the ritual. More mundane social dramas present recalcitrant complexities that are not so easily unraveled, since we typically find in them competing and conflicting definitions of what the actual situation was. Yet it is to these structures of everyday life that we now must turn.

DRAMATIC INTERACTION AND STRUCTURES OF EVERYDAY LIFE

The step-by-step exposition of concepts that makes up the greater part of this discourse will begin with illustrations drawn from a complicated episode involving a gentleman plantation owner and his slaves. The record of encounters analyzed here is an unmatched source of insights into the intercon-

nections of blacks with one another on an eighteenth-century Virginia plantation. It also offers valuable glimpses of slaves' relations with their master,
his family, and his neighbors. The documented episode is further suited to
present purposes because it contains within itself most of the information
available for its interpretation and for the elucidation of the relationships
that it brings into view. (In a few places I have parenthetically supplied vital
information drawn from other parts of the record.) The view of the actions
that we first receive is, of course, depicted from a perspective dictated by the
diarist's sense of himself as master of house, fields, and slaves. The gentleman
planter's expectations of his people, which arose from assumptions about
their proper roles, are the prime determinants of what he recorded and the
way he presented it. Nevertheless when he was surprised by something that
happened—a frequent occurrence—he would enter a fuller description, enabling the social historian to infer the meaning that the actions held for the
slaves themselves.

The long passage that follows contains a multitude of scenarios. Some of
these will later be extracted and closely scrutinized. The time of this extended
dramatic sequence was the cold, wet spring of 1766; the place was Sabine
Hall, the seat of Colonel Landon Carter, situated in Richmond County on
the northern shore of the Rappahannock River. Action extended also to the
colonel's outlying Mangorike quarter and its fields.

> March 4th being tuesday The serch Warrant I obtained from Wmson
> Ball[,] a Justice [,] being yesterday executed at the House of Robt.
> Smith Junr., and there being found there 80-1/2 [lbs.] of wool, Washed
> and unwashed; also a Cart Rope that had been stolen. That warrant
> was . . . returned and enquired into before the Justice Who ordered a
> Called Court on that day week.

> *12. Wednesday*
> This day all the Evidences attended the called Court, but no Court
> held. At night found that my ox carter, Simon, was run away and ex-
> amined Billy the foreman who said he [Simon] complained of the belly
> ake and went away, The Overseer being an [evi]dence at Court.
>
> Extremely wet all through the month, but very few drye days; but no
> Snow to speak of. [April too was cold and wet with occasional hard
> frosts.] . . .

April

23. Wednesday

Began yesterday to cart out my cow yard dung which I fear will be a long and troublesome job. . . . Oxen brake but badly—out of 8 taken up to break to the draft. 1 broke its neck, 2 more so sullen that nothing can do with them therefore turned out again. The fellow to the broken neck oxen also turned out as much hurted by his fellow. Two only work [tolerably?]. The other still very sullen.

24. Thursday

Simon [the oxcarter], one of the Outlaws, came home. He run away the 12th of March and by being out and doing mischief was outlawed in all the Churches 2 several Sundays [;] and on the 10th of this month having a great suspicion that he was entertained at my home quarter where his Aunt and Sisterinlaw lives, Mr[s.] Carter's favourite maid, I had him R[illegible] watched by Talbot and Tom with Guns loaded with small shot; and Toney withdrew. Just at dark according to my suspicion they came along my lane; [and] over the lucern field talking loudly, as if secure they should be concealed When Talbot commanding them to stand, upon their running, shot Simon in the right leg[,] foot[,] and ham. He got away and Simon has stayed out ever since then, so that he has been now shot to this day 14 days. . . .

It seems that Simon the runaway was shot at only about 11 days agoe. And he did not come in himself; for Mangorike Will [alias Billy the foreman?], seeing a smoke yesterday amongst Some Cedars by the side of the corn field when he was working; at night went to see what it was, and was long hunting for it as smoke is but rarely seen in the night. At last he got to some burnt Coals and saw no one there, but creeping through the Cedars he came to a fire burning and Simon lying by it; Who instantly started up to run away, but Billy was too swift and after a small struggle made him surrender and brought him in to Tom and Nassau who concealed this from me, in order to make as if the fellow came in himself. Willy says he was not lame last night, although he has now strummed it on account of his leg being shot. I shall punish him accordingly. . . .

25. Friday . . .
My man Bart came in this day, he has been gone ever since New year's day. His reason is only that I had ordered him a whipping for saying he then brought in two load of wood when he was coming with his first load only. This he still insists on was truth Although the whole plantation asserts the contrary, and the boy with him. He is the most incorrigeable villain I believe alive, and has deserved hanging; which I will get done if his mate in roguery can be tempted to turn evidence against him.

Bart broke open the house in which he was tyed and locked up; he got out before 2 o'clock but not discovered till night. Talbot is a rogue. He was put in charge of him. I do imagine the gardiner's boy Sam, a rogue I have suspected to have maintained Bart and Simon all the while they have been out. . . . I sent this boy with a letter to the Island ferry at breakfast, but he never returned although he was seen coming back about 12, and was seen at night by Hart [Fork?] George at night pretending to be looking for his Cattle. I kept this fellow up two nights about these fellows before And have given Rit the Miller a light whipping as having fed them by the hands of Gardiner Sam. . . .

27. Sunday
Yesterday my son [who constantly finds fault with my management] brought a story from Lansdown old Tom, that Johnny my gardiner had harboured Bart and Simon all the while they were out, sometimes in his inner room and sometimes in my kitchen vault. Tom had this from Adam, his wife's grandson: That they were placed in the Vault in particular the day my Militia were hunting for them.

This Simon owned, and the boy Adam repeated it to me; but Tom of Lansdown said that George belonging to Capn. Beale saw them in my quarter when he came from setting my Weir. It seemed to me so plausible that I sent Johnny [to] Goal and locked his son in Law Postilion Tom up. Note: every body denied they had ever seen them, and, in particular Mrs Carter's wench Betty, wife to Sawney, brother of Simon, denied that she had ever seen them; as she did to me with great impudence some days agoe. However Capn. Beale's George this day came to me and before Mrs. Carter, [in whom I see all the ill treatment my son gives and has given me] told the story, and in Simon's hearing, that, coming from the Weir he went into Frank's room and then into Sawney's room, when Simon came in to them. So that favourites and all are liars and villains.

These rogues could not have been so entertained without some advantage to those who harboured them; from whence I may conclude the making away of my wool, wheat etc., and the death of my horses. I never rightly saw into the assertion that negroes are honest only from a religious Principle. Johnny is the most constant churchgoer I have; but he is a drunkard, a thief and a rogue. They are only [honest] through Sobriety, and but few of them.[5]

Seen as a whole this affair of the runaways has the appearance of a series of dramatic events meshed together like the figured knots in a lacework ribbon. Human lives generally have this texture—significant encounters strung together by continuing relationships. Interaction episodes initiate, reshape, or more often, repeat and confirm patterns of association. This depiction of ongoing social life as knots of dramatic encounter suspended in nets of continuing relationships is one to be kept in mind as a visual model for the apprehension of social process. In the ensuing reconstruction of a portion of the fabric of a single eighteenth-century plantation society, we must attempt (by close study of some nodal events) to reach an understanding of how the meshes of continuing threads spread out, and (by attention to patterns of the converging strands) to interpret more surely the intermeshing that occurred in the knots of drama.

STRUCTURE IN ACTION

The capture of Simon was clearly the key episode in the tangled ribbon of events and disclosures recorded in the long diary excerpt.

Scenario 2

Mangorike Will [alias Willy, alias Billy] seeing a smoke . . . amongst Some Cedars by the side of the corn field when he was working; at night went to see what it was, and was long hunting for it. . . . At last he got to some burnt Coals and saw no one there, but creeping

> through the Cedars he came to a fire burning and Simon lying by it;
> Who instantly started up to run away, but Billy was too swift and after
> a small struggle made him surrender and brought him in to Tom and
> Nassau.

The taking of a captive by a captor constitutes a hostile act. It establishes a relationship that may be treated as the central *structure** of this dramatic action, although we do not as yet have sufficient knowledge to determine whether this relationship was newly created by the encounter or whether existing strands in the lacework ribbon were being multiplied. Mangorike Will had evidently gone beyond the minimal course of duty and had run considerable risks of injury in order to return Simon to servitude. This first *action-structure*, then, may be expressed in the formulaic mode:

Mangorike Willy (M.W.) v. Simon the Oxcarter (S.)

In the conclusion to this continuous sequence Tom and Nassau were enlisted as associates in Will's undertaking, indicating a more complex structure of apparent alliance against Simon. Perhaps the captor's transfer of his captive to these slaves followed the lines of hierarchical relationships on the plantation. Tom and Nassau were the master's personal attendants. More probably the delivery of the prisoner had to do with residence patterns—another potential source of structured relationships. It was doubtless late at night when Will came to the Hall. The master was most likely inaccessible, and Will, away from his own home quarter, had no choice but to enlist the help of the household slaves. At this stage the structures of alliance and adversary relationships appeared as:

M.W. + Tom (T.) + Nassau (N.) v. S.

In the sequel we can see a realignment of some of the structures:

Scenario 3

> Tom and Nassau . . . concealed this [Simon's capture] from me, in
> order to make as if the fellow came in himself. . . . He has now
> strummed it [i.e., played the part of being lame and in pain] on
> account of his leg being shot.

---

* The terminology that epitomizes the basic concepts that this discourse is designed to expound will be distinguished in the text by italics.

Tom and Nassau, co-opted as Will's agents in delivering Simon to the master, had formed a conspiracy with Simon and cut Will out. The lineup was now:

$$T. + N. + S. \text{ v. Landon Carter (L.C.)} + M.W.$$

The next encounter further complicated the structures that connected the actors, and also reinforced and made more explicit some of the antagonistic relationships already expressed in the previous two interactions.

Scenario 4

[Willy has come to me and tells] that Simon the runaway was shot at only about 11 days agoe [not 14, as first reported]. And he did not come in himself. . . . Willy [further] says he [Simon] was not lame last night. . . . I shall punish him accordingly.

Mangorike Willy had now not only engaged in hostile acts toward Simon, he had entered into a league with the master, intensified the hostility between himself and his captive (who would be punished "accordingly"), and engaged in antagonistic action against Tom and Nassau, whose deception he had uncovered.

Crucial parts of this last scenario (shown in square brackets) are deduced by inference of a kind that the historian concerned with reconstructing interaction sequences for ethnographic observation will frequently have to employ. The logic of the situation, indicated by the diarist's changed information, requires us to postulate an interview between Landon Carter and Mangorike Will. The unquestioning tone of the colonel's initial entry of misinformation suggests that he did not go out making inquiries, but that the inferred interaction took place on Willy's initiative. This is a deduction which has important implications for the picture of structured relationships that we see emerging from this close study. A system is revealed in which an alliance was offered on the one hand while a conspiracy was exposed on the other.

$$M.W. + L.C. \text{ v. S. } + T. + N.$$

This method of scenario analysis may be applied to all the encounters of which the extended sequence contains traces. The action-structures may be identified in each incident, and the relationships between interactants may be plotted. A pattern of relationships surrounding each participant can thus be established. Taking the runaway oxcarter as an example, the pattern may be rendered verbally or diagrammatically. Simon had a trio of known kin-

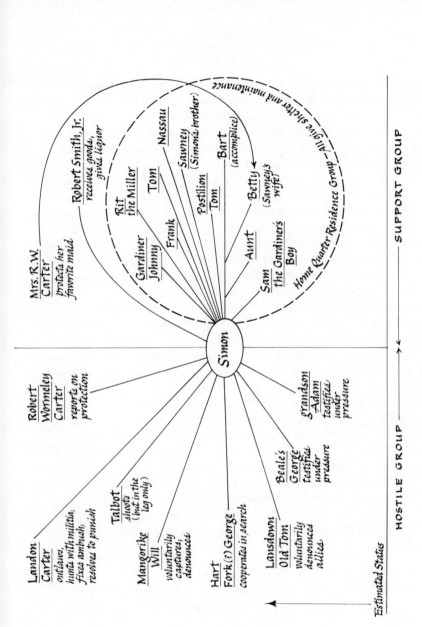

FIGURE 30.

Simon the oxcarter: enemies and allies

folk—a brother, a sister-in-law, and an aunt—who lived at Carter's home quarter. Betty, his sister-in-law, was a favorite of the colonel's detested daughter-in-law. The kin group showed marked solidarity and worked together under pressure with the master's slave assistants and other residents at the "home quarter." Talbot, who shot Simon in an ambush, was evidently not as deeply involved in protecting the runaway as the others, although the shot was directed very low, and he was later suspected of giving help to Simon's accomplice, Bart.   Robert Smith, Jr., a neighboring small planter, must be included in the supportive configuration. If Landon Carter's suspicions were well founded, Smith was the channel through which were supplied the payments (in the form of liquor) that helped cement the alliance. All this may also be represented graphically, with supportiveness measured to the right and hostility to the left of a horizontal zero axis, and estimated social status plotted on the vertical scale (see figure 30).

The complexity of this diagram derives from the conjunction of many elementary action-structures such as were analyzed in scenarios 2-4. Because of this juxtaposition of incidents, larger patterns become visible that otherwise would not be apparent. Two kinds of Anglo-Virginian involvement on the side of an Afro-Virginia conspiracy show up in the diagram: the receiver of plundered goods who supplied liquor in payment, and the lady who protected her favorite maid—perhaps an indication that female alliance against the dominating males might at times transcend the lines of rank and race. The most notable pattern, however, is that Simon's supporters all seem to have belonged to the "home quarter" residence group, while the antagonistic witnesses are all identified as belonging to settlements at other quarters. From Mangorike, the Fork, and Lansdown came the three who took action or volunteered information against members of the home quarter confederacy. Beale's George, who had spread accounts of the goings-on and confirmed such accounts to the outraged Landon Carter, was from another plantation altogether.

DRAMATIC INTERACTION AND THE
DYNAMICS OF EVERYDAY LIFE

Diagrams of the kind just considered have a great weakness in relation to the approach expounded in this discourse. They collapse onto the flatness of a page the time dimension that is such a vital part of the fullness of human interactions and continuing relationships. We need to look for concepts that fix our attention directly on the dynamic character of so-called social structures.

EXCHANGE

Consider once again scenario 4, in which Willy comes to the master to tell his story. To make the interaction fully available for ethnographic interpretation we must clearly go beyond anatomizing skeletal structures. We must run it through the talking-picture projector of the mind. We then become concerned not just with noting that Willy's approach constituted an offer of cooperative alliance against Simon, Tom, and Nassau, not even just with the main content of what he had to tell—his account of the capture on the night of April 23. We need to locate Willy's narration of his actions in the context of the developing drama. We can picture Willy's approach to communicate his version of the capture. In the diarist's resumé of what he had been told, we can sense Willy's manner of speaking, if not his actual words. We can see Willy telling emphatically how carefully he noted the location of the smoke as he kept to his labors in the cornfield; how thoroughly he searched the dark woods, without a telltale column of smoke visible to reveal the place he sought. He boasts that he continued his search even after he had found a cold fire. We must imagine him coming to the climax of his narration as he relates how stealthily he crept through the cedars; how swiftly he sprang on the escaping Simon, and how "small" a struggle the runaway (who was not really lame) was able to maintain against this determined attack.

As captor, Willy incurred or intensified the ill will of Simon and his faction. As informer, he extended the direct impact of his antagonism by exposing the conspiracy to deceive. Willy's actions have to be understood as part of a proposed *exchange*. He was offering information and collaboration to the master in expectation of goodwill. He calculated that the benevolence of the master would offset the malevolence of those whom he had offended. Although this example is obvious enough, it serves to draw our attention to a constant *accounting process*—most of it far more subtle and elusive than this—that runs through nearly all significant interaction. The gratifications exchanged in social transactions are not, of course, exclusively or even primarily material. Respect, approval, thanks, kindness, and companionship are some of the most valuable considerations sought; while scorn, deferential self-effacement, malice, and hostility are among the prices dearly paid.[6]

THE SIGNIFICANT OTHER

Mangorike Willy was engaged in *social trading* with Landon Carter on decidedly uneven terms. But the imbalance is not to be understood simply as an anomaly arising from the extreme character of master-slave relationships. Although exchange of gratifications is a vital part of social intercourse—and hence of social structure in its dynamic aspect—it does not usually take the form of equal bargains. Even within peer groups there are almost always leaders for whose approval and favors the rest must compete, with obvious consequences in terms of the nature and extent of the gratifications exchanged.

The term *significant other*, drawn from social psychology, will be introduced here to designate those whose responses in the interaction process are of particular importance to the persons whose behavior is under observation. "Feedback" from the significant others—whether they be acknowledged superiors, equals, or inferiors—typically plays a vital role in the maintenance of the identity of every social person. The most important exchanges and the most valued gratifications are likely to arise from social transactions with the significant others. For this reason the most painstaking performances are certain to be addressed to those who stand in this relationship to the actor. Mangorike Willy's emphatic narrative of his forceful capture of Simon was clearly an elaborate presentation made to a figure who loomed large in his social scene.[7]

SOCIAL POWER AND AUTHORITY

One who stands in the relationship of significant other to considerable numbers of persons is thereby endowed with *social power* and enters into transactions upon markedly advantageous terms. Typically the inequalities of interactional exchanges in such cases are formalized into modes of *deference* on one side and *condescension* on the other. Where inequalities are extreme, explicit self-abasement may be a ritualized part of the behavior of the "inferior" party and marks of disdain characteristic of the "superior." Such ritualization of postures makes them readily available for at least partial internalization by the interactants as inherent to the order of things.* Where this is the case the social power of the dominant significant other becomes formalized as *social authority*.

The relationship of master to slaves entailed extremes of inequality, but even in this case it is evident that for authority to be effective as social *power*—or *control*—meaningful reciprocal exchanges had to be constantly performed. The master's disposition of material and social resources, extending even to the domicile of the slaves, inevitably rendered him an extremely potent figure in the slaves' world. Nevertheless in order to convert that power into authority he had not only to provide subsistence and protection, but also to dispense appropriate acknowledgments of services rendered by his subordinates. Only if he could induce in them respectful demeanor and cooperation could he gain any satisfying, identity-confirming sense of masterfulness. Landon Carter's ineptitude in managing such exchanges is clearly revealed in the extended extract. His use of his diary as an outlet for his frustration and overflowing passion supplies us with this particular set of records for ethnographic analysis.[8]

ACTION-MEANING

Action in the social world is patterned by culture. Generalized concepts of relationships and abstract theories concerning the exchange of favors can serve to identify basic social and dramatic structures. But such concepts and theories are inadequate if they do not draw us on to seek an understanding of the specific forms of response to hostility and of the ways normative expectations shape the support given by allies in a particular society. The valuations of benefits exchanged are not fixed according to some universal scale of just

* It should be clear from this whole interpretation of the runaway episode that it is not intended to suggest "deference" as a concept with wide explanatory power derived from an assumption that social "inferiors" naturally act out the roles assigned to them by "superiors." It is implied, however, that unchallengeable status relationships restrict the range of possible definitions of the situation in encounters between persons of different ranks, and thus circumscribe strategies in the struggles for advantage that constantly take place. It is a reasonable, though unwelcome, assumption that the constant accommodation of adopted strategies to such constraints in the course of social life must have a strong formative influence on each participant's sense of identity.

prices, but are determined by the culturally relative meanings with which participants imbue both actions and objects. The main interest humanists have in exploring the activity of mankind ultimately lies in discovering those meanings and so entering into the imaginative universes of other persons. Because meaning is so specific to context, purely formal analysis of basic action-structures cannot usefully be incorporated in completed historical reports of findings. Such analyses must be subsumed in descriptive narrative or incorporated in commentary on specific cultural features—or both. The storyteller's art, informed by ethnographic perspectives, must be developed as a vital part of social history.[9]

PARTICIPANTS' PERCEPTIONS

How did the actors themselves perceive these dramas, which thus far have been analyzed only from the perspective of a social science observer? They certainly would not have interpreted their own and others' actions and intentions in terms of such elemental structures as the "hostility" between Mangorike Willy and Simon, or the "exchange" offered in Willy's approach to Landon Carter.

We must ask, What did Willy think he was engaged in, down among the cedars on the night of April 23? The entire record conveys strong impressions of an ethos of close neighborhood, in which the maneuvers of every person were known to a great many others—or could be guessed. It is probable, then, that Willy had at least a shrewd idea that it was the smoke of a runaway's fire that he saw. Would he have gone alone had he expected both the marauders to be there? Had he word then that there would only be one—and that it would be Simon? Willy may have been the same person as Billy the foreman and may thus have had a grudge arising from (or intensified by) the circumstances of Simon's departure. He may have suffered for having been deceived and taken advantage of by the oxcarter, who "complained of the belly ake and went away."[10]

Beyond personal motivation, however, a more telling question for the ethnographer is how Willy's actions vis-à-vis Simon appeared to fellow members of their social world. The master's matter-of-fact acceptance of the slave foreman's conduct appears upon the diary page. The resentment of Simon and his supporters has been assumed in the analysis so far, but that assumption alone does not tell us the meaning the victims assigned to the action. Did they see it as treason by one of their own kind? Although we, as twentieth-century persons, may find this view compelling, the evidence suggests that Willy's contemporaries did not perceive the situation that way. Four years later Simon himself was selected by the master to lie in wait and catch another runaway who was being given shelter by a sibling. The residence pattern perhaps supplies a key. Informers and victims were consistently from different quarters, and it may be that membership in different settlements was the basis of accepted factional divisions—with life perceived as a struggle in which the master's power was a legitimate weapon in the hands of whichever side could use it to gain advantage. All this is reasoning to the limit from a scattering of clues, but if we are to get anywhere in our quest to understand the worlds of obscure men like Simon and Willy, we must assume the searching keenness of Sherlock Holmes rather than the stolidity of Dr. Watson.

Continuing the enquiry, we may ask what Simon the oxcarter was doing on his own, making a fire within sight of the field in the daytime. Was he preparing to make contact? to negotiate a return-to-work settlement? We do know that the time would have been right for a deal, since Landon Carter was on that very day taking note of how "troublesome" the task of carting out the dung was likely to be, given the poor condition of the draft oxen. If the runaway ox handler (and trainer?) may be assumed to have been attached to the beasts that his patient skill had transformed into working teams, then it can be supposed that he was doubly concerned to seize this moment to be reinstated by the master, so that he could return to lead his creatures before any more injuries occurred. By such reasoning we may have gained insight simultaneously into the meaning of Simon's movements on April 23 and into one of his self-defining identifications. By such surmises we can, perhaps, catch a fleeting glimpse of Simon's world of meanings and even know something of him that is not entirely from an angry master's point of view.

METAPHOR AND DEFINITION OF THE SITUATION

We can see a little more surely into the meanings the participants found in their situations and expressed in their actions by examining a different sequence of encounters, one that occurred a day and a half after Simon's capture:

Scenario 5

[a]

25. Friday . . . My man Bart came in this day, he has been gone ever since New year's day. His reason is only that I had ordered him a whipping for saying he then brought in two load of wood. . . . This he still insists on was truth Although the whole plantation asserts the contrary, and the boy with him. He is the most incorrigeable villain I believe alive, and has deserved hanging; which I will get done if his mate in roguery can be tempted to turn evidence against him.

[b]

Bart broke open the house in which he was tyed and locked up; he got out before 2 o'clock but not discovered till night. Talbot is a rogue. He was put in charge of him. I do imagine the gardiner's boy Sam, a rogue I have suspected to have maintained Bart and Simon all the while they have been out.

The structure of the encounter centers on a proffered exchange that was at first accepted as a basis for negotiations but was then rejected so as to renew intense conflict. Bart's initial "gift" (or *prestation*) lay in his artfully assigning to his master the estimable role of fair judge in appeal. We can readily see how the primary form and meaning of the encounter were shaped by this opening move. The delinquent slave evidently "came in" of his own accord, went directly before the master, and initiated a rehearing of charges made against him nearly five months before. He insisted that the defense he then offered "was truth." Bart's opening, by casting Landon Carter as judge and himself as appellant against wrongful conviction and unjust sentence, suggested a context for their dealings analogous to that of the courtroom. The master could have instantly disallowed the judicial *metaphor* by ordering the runaway seized and whipped. Indeed, had he done so he would only have been insisting that his own earlier orders be carried out. Landon Carter's immediate response, however, further filled out the proposed metaphor by calling witnesses (or by recalling their former testimony). A retrial appeared to be granted at this point. Clearly Bart hoped to have his innocence formally established, the sentence against him quashed, and his four-and-a-half-month withdrawal of labor and obedience accordingly pardoned.[11]

Although the master's initial response implied acceptance of Bart's metaphor as a point of departure for the proceedings, things did not turn out as the returned runaway had designed. Such is the nature of dramatic, as opposed to routine, interaction. Bart was apparently isolated by the lineup of witnesses who testified against him—whether under duress or not we cannot tell. Furthermore, the master was judge in his own cause—such is the nature of slavery—and so the encounter was terminated when Landon Carter, angered at the slave's refusal to yield to his overbearing insistence, gave Bart as prisoner into Talbot's charge, to be "tyed and locked up," himself turning to enter a vengeful judgment in his diary-cum-court record.

The master's anger is ethnographically instructive in a number of ways. We may see in it the manner in which power and meaning, structure and statement jangle together in the clashes of dramatic interaction. Bart's *definition of the situation* constituted a power play, creating the forms of action that have been noted. He might, indeed, have opened with a feigned or real confession, with contrition and a plea for mercy. Yet even under pressure the slave refused to switch to such a grovelling line, though the master evidently urged it upon him by the way he confronted him with the testimony of the witnesses. In his course of action Bart was not only adhering to his own initial definition (in a court trial a man may persist in asserting his innocence), but he was also laying claim to independent social personality—itself a form of power. It was this last that particularly evoked Colonel Carter's wrath—in turn revealing clearly how the master had come to redefine the situation.[12]

The sequel to Bart's incarceration shows that Carter was right to feel threatened. His will in the matter and his animosity toward the prisoner were clear to all, yet when Bart "broke open the house in which he was tyed and locked up," many hours passed before the escape, known "before 2 o'clock," was reported to the master. We must assume that Bart's escape was connived at, if not actively assisted, by those who knew when it occurred. Landon Carter had overbid his hand in this power play. The runaway had come in freely and proffered his master a worthy role as judge, with the opportunity to make a dignified retreat. In return Bart received an attempted demonstration of his social isolation, rough treatment, and dark threats of worse to come. Yet Bart was indeed a "person"—not isolated, but rather endowed with evident social power. He had no need to submit to the crushing of his social personality; he could not so easily be held a prisoner in the close little world of Sabine Hall when it became clear that Carter would not accept his offer of terms. Bart was once more able to step outside the metaphoric framework of "plantation law," which he himself had evoked, and resume the life of an outlaw, freebooting in the woods. In Bart's powers as a person (including his ability to open granaries and stores to supply extras to a needy people) lay the roots of Landon Carter's humiliation. The gossip that reached Sabine Hall from the slave Lansdown old Tom, telling how the outlaws had been concealed in the colonel's kitchen vault while his militia (that is, poorer neighbors called from their crops) were out hunting for them, must have been for Bart's faction an epic of the master's shaming, and so of the hero's triumph.

JUDGES AND FATHERS

The master's imprudent anger is significant in another way. Taken in conjunction with the great deal we know about the self-defeating rages to which Landon Carter was prone—with his close kin, as well as with his slaves—it suggests that the meaning of the encounter with Bart is not adequately rendered if it is taken simply as a retrial upon appeal, followed by judicial confirmation of sentence, imprisonment, and escape. The strong emotion evident in the master's diary entry was incompatible with the role of stern judge that was implicit in the definition of the situation as he first accepted it. Tracing the course of the encounter, we see how rapidly Landon Carter was moved to redefine the action. In place of the courthouse metaphor with which Bart had opened, the master began passionately to act out another— that of the outraged "father" whose will must prevail in the settlement of disputes within his household. (His outrage against Simon, in scenario 4, seemed likewise to be directed less at the six-week "strike" than at the employment of deceptions—pretended voluntary return, and shammed lameness—to evade an abject submission.)

One of the dominant metaphors of the culture from which Landon Carter derived his entire social identity, and Bart an important part of his, was patriarchalism—the image of stern fatherhood. The metaphor found some of its most powerful expressions in the context of the plantation community—

often referred to as "my family" by the patriarchs—but it was a pervasive mode of construing social authority in the North as well as in the South, on the eastern as well as the western side of the Atlantic. Before leaving the context of Sabine Hall, therefore, let us have a close look at a further enactment that featured prominently the two-sided metaphor of stern judge-father/ father-judge. This figure had it in his power to punish or pardon and typically was less concerned with consistent performances than with the readiness of his dependents to adopt the submissive posture considered appropriate to a child confronted by a parent:

.Scenario 6

[a]

[Nassau was Landon Carter's surgeon. He had been sent to attend to an overseer who feared he was dying. Nassau was also a chronic alcoholic. He had previously, at church, arranged with a slave from another plantation to supply him with liquor.] Yet Nassau went to this man [his supplier], whose name he says he does not know, and there took such a dose that Just held him to get to the overseer; and what he did then God only knows; but I do hope he [God] was graciously Pleased to prevent the drun[k]ard's doing wrong and [to] bless my endeavours in this humane way with Success. But what should I not do to Mr. Nassau? Nobody could find him; at last Tom Parker on horseback found him at sunset a Sleep on the ground dead drunk; as soon as he was got home I offered to give him a box on the ear and he fairly forced himself against me. However I tumbled him into the Sellar and there had him tied Neck and heels all night and

[b]

this morning had him stripped and tied up to a limb and, with a Number of switches Presented to his eyes and a fellow with an uplifted arm, He encreased his crying Petitions to be forgiven but this once, and desired the man to bear witness that he called upon God to record his solemn Vow that he never more would touch liquor. I expostulated with him on his and his father's blasphemy of denying the wholy [holy] word of God in bolding [boldly] asserting that there was neither a hell nor a devil, and asked him if he did not dread to hear how he had set the word of God at nought who promised everlasting happiness to those who loved him and obeyed his words[,] and eternal torments [to those] who set his goodness at nought and dispised his holy word. After all I forgave this creature out of humanity, religion, and every virtuous duty with hopes though I hardly dare mention it that I shall by it save one soul more Alive.[13]

On this occasion for Landon Carter, the image of a merciful father, though initially eclipsed by that of a wrathful one, finally shone forth radiant. Thus he was left with the prayerful hope that his clement example might lead the soul of his servant into dependent gratitude toward his God. The resistance of the recurrently repentant but incurably alcoholic slave to the doctrine of hellfire—and perhaps his ambivalence toward an alternately harsh and merciful God—is finely caught in the master's stinging accusation, even as the victim offered expiatory oaths, that he—and his father—had blasphemously set the word of God (including its promises of forgiveness) at nought.

The reference to Nassau's father reminds us forcibly of the constrictive closeness of this little world of ongoing generational face-to-face interaction. Therein we see clearly the social context of the comprehensive metaphor of fatherhood, encompassing as it did all order and rebellion, crime and punishment, suffering and relief. The close intimacy of extended household relationships was projected onto the cosmic order by the metaphor of the Father-Creator.

A meaningful social history of Anglo-America might be written in terms of the rise of impersonal contexts of interaction (including "the media") on one hand, and the declining relevance and pervasiveness of the patriarchal metaphor for authority on the other.[14]

CULTURAL FRAMEWORKS

Most of the steps that have been spelled out so far have been concerned with the ethnography of a single episode—a close look at some of the knots of interaction and the strands of continuing relationships that were twisted into the extended lacework of social life on one plantation. No apology is offered for this narrow focus. Clearly, empirical ethnography must begin with tracing the strands through closely observed nodal actions. Historians are unable, in the manner of field anthropologists, to generate their own documents by looking around themselves, notebook in hand. They are restricted to the "notebook" entries that past record systems and the hazards of survival have left them, and so must make a virtue of their necessity through a very close reading of those "notes" that do survive.

In real life the encounters that are the units of study in action-oriented ethnography do not occur—as they may on a page—isolated from context. The participants must operate within particular frames of reference that enable them to orient themselves to one another in order to share, exchange, or even contest meanings. It is necessary to consider now some systematic approaches to the generally available, public symbols and shared meanings through which actors relate to, and communicate with, one another. The action approach must explicitly take into account some of the ways in which culture is composed of interlocking sets of paradigms, or metaphors, that shape participants' perceptions by locating diverse forms of action on more or less coherent maps of experience.

INTERCHANGEABLE METAPHORS

The course of the interaction in scenario 5 started out from Bart's definition of the situation as a "courtroom" appeal to a "judge" and was changed by Carter's redefinition. In the end Carter, a righteous father and angry patriarch, was chastising a rebellious dependent. Similarly, the ordeal for Nassau (scenario 6b) owed its development to Landon Carter's transformation of himself from stern "judge" to forgiving "father." The identification of these pairs of alternatives in each case need not pose a dilemma in the interpretation of the scenes, nor does it suggest a confusion that renders analysis in terms of metaphoric definitions of the situations inappropriate. On the contrary, these two cases serve as homely examples of important cultural processes that link encounters to each other to form patterns that are intelligible in the first instance to the participants—and, after careful "reading," to the ethnographer.

The sequences of metaphoric definition and redefinition noted above did not disturb the coherence of the encounters because the two *metaphors* of authority—the judge and the patriarch—were in marked degree *interchangeable*. They stood as two sides of the same coin: either can be presented upper-

most—the other is known to be simultaneously present. This reading of the
situation can be reinforced, first, by taking note of the colonel's angrily stated
program for vengeance upon the recalcitrant Bart, and second, by an extract
from a court record.

When Landon Carter blustered to his diary that he would get Bart hanged
"if his mate in roguery can be tempted to turn evidence against him," he
made it clear that the forms of judicial action were present in his own consciousness—present not merely as metaphor but as institutionalized social
constraint. The law placed limits on the kinds of reprisals that could be taken
against the slave without a form of court process that involved the testimony
of witnesses. Landon Carter, himself the presiding judge in his county, had
deeply internalized the judicial role and its legal constraints.

In the following extract, drawn from an earlier period, another example
may be seen of the metaphor of the patriarch confronting a "family" member
from whom he expected a child's submission. In this case, however, the actual context was the courthouse. That real judges assumed the paternal role
indicates the extent to which the stern fatherhood metaphor pervaded society beyond the slave plantation:

Scenario 7

Att a Court Contd. and held for Richmond County [Va.] the Ninth
day of March 1715—

Present

John Tarpley	}	Edward Barrow	}	
William Robinson		William Fantleroy		Gent Justices

The Court takeing into Consideration the Order passed on Wednesday
last against William Leach, upon the sd. William Leach's appearing in
Court and with humble Submission on his Knees acknowledging his
offence and begging the Court's pardon, have Ordered that the Fine of
Fifty Shillings Currant Money imposed on him by the sd. Order be
remitted.[15]

The complementary relationship between the judicial and the patriarchal
metaphors appears even more clearly when the above is considered in the
setting from which it was drawn. Earlier chapters in this book have stressed
how continuously the court rituals—supported by seating arrangements and

insignia—proclaimed that the justices sat as commissioned agents of a father-king. The figurative presence of this being, and of a father-god above him, makes it evident that the image of patriarchy provided an *encompassing metaphor* of social relationships and that the judicial mode was one expression of the attributes of fatherhood in their fullest extension.

THE CONTENT OF METAPHORS

The task of the ethnographer begins rather than ends with identifying and labeling the metaphors that inform encounters and link them together in a patterned system of socially established meanings, or *typifications*.[16] Neither fatherhood nor the judicial role are universals that carry the same meaning at all times and in all places. In the present day, for example, both have connotations vastly different from those discernible in the foregoing encounters. Metaphors, then, may be likened to containers that must be handled in each case according to their actual content. The contents of metaphors of the kind we have considered here are closely related to forms of action. The actual behavior of fathers and judges in a given society will influence the particular meanings of the paternal and judicial metaphors in that culture. Conversely, metaphoric meanings enter into and shape actions. The reciprocal relationship between metaphor and action is such that each is simultaneously producer and product, cause and effect. In the terminology of social theory such a system of reciprocal relationship is called a *dialectic*.[17]

SOURCES OF METAPHORS

The metaphors considered in this review of method had arisen in the Anglo-American world from the association of images of one familiar social role with another. Institutionalized forms of action are not, however, the only sources of cultural metaphors. The human body, for example, is a ready source of the most pervasive ways of understanding society. Constant usage dulls our awareness that phrases such as "head" of a household and "member" of society are figures of speech that have the body as referent. The content and operation of these metaphors depends, of course, on the ways in which the body itself is understood and experienced. Landon Carter's diary makes it clear that he—along with his contemporaries—had a sense of the body's functioning quite different from our own (see above, chapter 3). For progress to be made in historical ethnography we shall have to break down the artificial walls that preserve in separate compartments such important modes of perception as those usually considered only under the heading "medical history" and seek to discover the ways in which anatomical and physiological metaphors entered into past people's understanding of their own world.[18]

THE COMMUNICATION OF POWER AND AUTHORITY: A THEATER MODEL

Concepts for the analysis of encounters are the appropriate first steps in a methodology for the ethnographic history of the everyday world, but parts must not be mistaken for the whole. We must ask how the encompassing social system may be viewed in an action perspective.

The intent of social interaction is typically both *expressive* and *instrumental*. The successful externalization of one's inner states in order to orient others to oneself and make them "understand," contains inherent satisfactions, as has already been implied under the heading "exchange." But interaction frequently embodies purposes beyond the immediate gratifications that arise from successful communication. To the degree that this is so, the actions may be defined as instrumental. The social power of a person is commensurate with the capacity to make others' actions subservient to his or her own ends. Historians have traditionally been preoccupied with such instrumental relationships. In reaction, much recent social history, concerned with culture and communication, has been devoted to the study of rituals and expressive forms of action. This trend should not go to extremes, however, and ethnographic historians concerned with reconstructing the life of the past as participants experienced it must be very attentive to forms of power and the social means by which the actions of some were made instrumental to the purposes of others.[19]

The whole congeries of social-dramatic devices through which interaction communication—expression, direction, and ultimately coercion—may be accomplished is conveniently designated by the term *dramaturgy*. It will readily be seen that each culture and subculture has its own distinctive drama-

turgical kit, consisting of "settings," "props," "costumes," "roles," "script formulas," and, as elusive as they are important, "styles" of action and gesture.
The word "role" has become so much a commonplace not only of sociological
but of everyday discourse that its origin as a metaphor drawn from the theater
has been obscured. Its vitality and usefulness will be greatly enhanced if we
constantly remind ourselves of its original reference and employ it explicitly
in the context of dramaturgical analysis.

The theater model serves to emphasize the formalities that govern so much
of social life. The shared meanings with which settings, costumes, roles, and
styles are invested serve at once as limiting constraints on the actors and as
channels through which effective—indeed powerful and coercive—communications can be directed. If we relate this model to the earlier discussion
of definitions of the situation and encompassing metaphors it can be seen that
tacitly agreed upon definitions of the situation resemble actor-initiated stage
directions for particular scenes. Great metaphors of the culture enter into the
creation and interpretation of settings; they are a major source of available
roles; and they also govern the actors' styles of self-presentation. Above all it
is the great metaphors that control the very perception of what constitutes
significant action, or drama.

SETTINGS

The application of ethnographic method to the particular dramaturgical
"kit" belonging to a past regional culture can best begin with one of the most
concrete and determinative of the items involved: physical setting.

Willy's capture of Simon in the woods has been observed (scenario 2);
Bart's appeal to Landon Carter for justice has been analyzed (scenario 5). It is
true that Simon's campfire among the cedars effectively defined—especially
at night—a social space in that wild surround, and that, as Willy burst in to
overpower Simon, this setting contributed to the shaping of the action. Yet
so tenuous a demarcation hardly lends itself to formal analysis. The contrary
is true of Bart's calculated play for reinstatement. Whether it took place in
the courtyard, or at one of the grand portals, or as is most probable, in the
hallway of the great house, this enactment was contained within a highly formal setting.

Architecture provides a potent medium for elaborately coded nonverbal

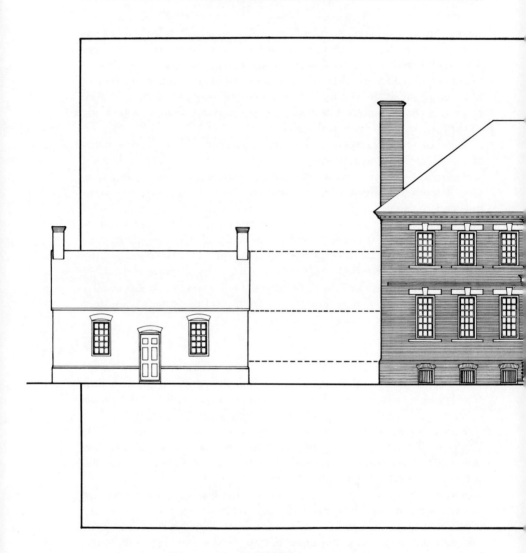

FIGURE 31.
*Sabine Hall: "An edifice . . . [with] every part . . . in its due place
and fit situation, neither above nor below its dignity"*

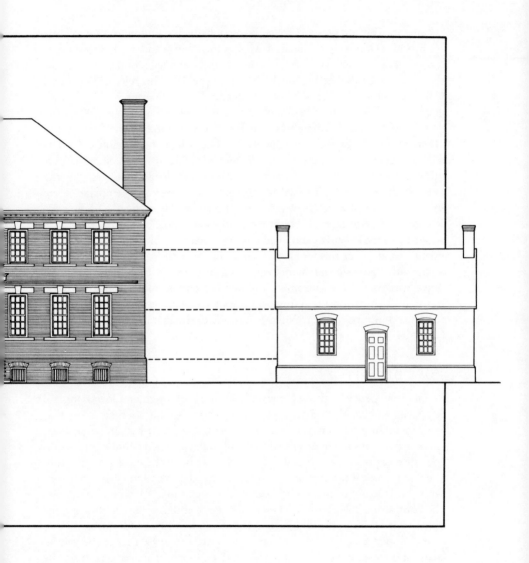

statement. The comprehensive messages embodied in buildings were in close reciprocal relationship to much of Anglo-American—and even Afro-American—significant action. A brief review of the statements of dignity and authority made by the setting in which Bart's appeal and his rejection occurred will illustrate the importance of architectural interpretation for the ethnographic historian. Sabine Hall was a gentleman's seat, built about 1740 on the pattern of extended symmetries that had become standard in Virginia and other parts of the English-speaking world. The design of the whole—with its dignified centerpiece and subordinate dependencies, its elevated grand portal, and its stately reception rooms—not only provided a fine stage for the master's displays of high social worth, but also served as a template of the social hierarchy of which he was the patriarchal head (see pp. 30–42, above). In a close, face-to-face society in which the gentry had extensive control of access to scarce resources and filled most of the significant symbolic roles, one might bargain over the terms of domination as Bart did, but one could not argue with the basic statements embodied in the great buildings. The great house was essential in sustaining the master's part in social drama. It stood in a dialectic relationship to him, for it took its meaning from his social existence, and in turn, it contributed powerfully to the shaping of his patterns of behavior.

ROLE DEFINITION

Polarities—such as those between light and dark, high and low, right and left, male and female—enter profoundly into the socialization processes that both maintain and transmit culture. As with all else in human perception, these oppositions are internalized with culturally assigned content and meaning.[20] An oppositional structure of sex roles is one of the most basic items in the dramaturgical kit of every culture, but the identification of this item—as with the labeling of metaphors—is only a beginning. Each culture endows the contrasting roles with a different degree of intensity and with a specific content drawn from the whole complex of action forms and meanings.

In colonial Virginia the most prestigious male role was that of the gentleman, and as we have seen, this role derived much of its content from the encompassing metaphor of patriarchy. At church services those who made the proud entry into the church "when the service was beginning" were those who played the patriarchal part in the churchyard, before and after, when they issued invitations to dine (see p. 60, above). A man could not be a gentleman in the fullest sense of the word in this society unless he was the independent head of his own household, having slaves certainly, and a wife and children ideally, to reflect, in their degrees, the greatness of the master. The way in which sex-role oppositions underpinned the maintenance of the gentleman's social personality is subtly reinforced by the contrast recorded in the New Jersey diarist's note on the ladies' riding-out attire. In contrast to the bold-faced gentlemen, these females used kerchiefs to protect delicate complexions from a climate considered ferocious.

MILIEUS

The distinction between gentry and others also established a dichotomy in the culture between "high" and "low" status. Reviewing the illustrations of dance forms at different levels in society, a clear distinction emerges between vulgar modes of performance and the elevated style that conveyed courtly representations of polite social intercourse between males and females (see pp. 80–87, above). The cultural provincialism of Virginia and other parts of America at the time meant that the knowledge that these dance forms were derived from the fashionable circles of the English metropolis contributed strongly to their appreciation as high style.

With the opposition of "high" to "low" styles, and provincial to metropolitan fashions, we confront a familiar phenomenon—diverse cultural systems that are contained within the larger framework of a single society. The authors of the classic anthropological ethnographies did not face this problem in acute form. These pioneer students of "savage" societies certainly had to contend with a radical division into male and female subcultures; but, in contrast to urbanized, class-divided Western society, "tribal" societies seemed "simple," and were designated as such. By and large they could be treated as the repositories of single, rather than multiple, cultural systems. It seems, however, that the use of writing in a society both indicates a fairly high degree of specialized division of labor and reinforces such divisions by the uneven development of literacy skills. Thus historians working from written records invariably face actual or incipient cultural plurality as a fact of the social worlds they study.

By extending the application of the theater model, it may be seen that every social system has congeries of action-settings with overlapping casts, styles, and conventions. Such clusters, based on shared "stagecraft," may be designated *milieus*. In this context the term must operate as the counterpart in dramaturgical terminology of the concept "subculture"—itself a term that in the ethnographic perspective subsumes the phenomenon that is commonly designated by the word "class." The meanings conveyed by the word milieus should render it particularly useful as an aid in the analysis of such small-community social systems as made up nearly all of early America. The term suggests habitual associations, specialized styles of communication, and mutual understandings, without having the connotations of self-contained exclusiveness that are strong for such terms as *subculture* and *class*—connotations that are inappropriate to the face-to-face intimacy of interaction extending from top to bottom in premodern agrarian societies.

The observed diversity of dance forms in Virginia society provides us with a little paradigm of distinct but intercommunicating milieus. A range of performance styles made significant social statements. The "high" and "low" ends of the range met, indeed, making a circle, as can be inferred both from the inclusion of "Negro" measures in gentry dancing (p. 84) and from the imitation of the masters' ways in slave celebrations. (A black Virginian who lived on into the time when makers of written records took notice of these things told how "Us slaves watched white folks' parties where the guests danced a minuet and then paraded in a grand march. . . . Then we'd do it too, *but we used to mock 'em*, every step."[21]) Such interlocked systems are not only found in the potent action statements of the dance, they are common in speech, where the words "accent" or "tone" are applied, and in writing, where they are comprehended under the heading "style"—which in turn supplies our "model" for all coded ways of performing a given action.

CONCLUSION

Relationships developed during interaction supply the threads of which social fabric is woven. The quality and patterning of such threads in a society, or in a milieu, will largely determine the texture of its members' lives. Both in the chapters of this book and in this discourse I have attempted to develop a method for the closer comprehension of the spinning and weaving of the fabric of one past society. Since our main concern has been with forms of action, the structural model of threads and lacework has had to be complemented by another more dynamic one—the theater—to which processes of communication are central. I have attempted to systematize an ethnographic history that reaches out to understand life as it was experienced by "actors" on past "stages," each playing his or her own part, and responding to the roles of others in ways that expressed their particular conceptions of the nature of the "play." (The quotation marks appear here as a reminder, should one be needed, that it is not true that "all the world's a stage." Models are the inevitable basis of any understanding, but they belong to the discourse of knowledge, not to the ineffably complex world that they radically simplify by rendering it into words or other signs.)[22]

The step-by-step approach adopted in this discourse has intentionally stressed the need for systematic analysis rather than intuition. The objective of the ethnographic historian's enterprise—understanding and depicting life itself—is, however, very close to the aims of the artist. It should not be surprising, therefore, that devices developed in forms of art, and concepts arising in discourse concerning art, such as *metaphor, dramaturgy,* and *milieu,* have been found serviceable for incorporation in the models proposed for use in ethnographic analysis.

Systematic method is essential in science, for it demands that investigators review and test their assumptions, evidence, and processes of inference. The method delineated above will have served its purpose if it helps the reader (as the setting out has the writer) to sharpen awareness of procedures and to heighten sensitivity to modes of social communication in their proper contexts of time and place. If, however, ethnographic history is not just to be information stored in an investigator's head (or on note cards), it must itself aim at effective *performance.* The final presentation of one's research should not be primarily a record of the researcher's labors, but a *persuasive reconstruction of the experiences of past actors.* Let it be through the traditional skills of the storyteller or through newer forms developed by scenario writers—but art that conceals art must make its contribution to the presentations in which ethnographic historians evoke ways of life in vanished worlds.

ACKNOWLEDGMENTS

The sense of need to return gratitude will mount in any ten-year project, but it must mount higher still—and be more important to stress—when one works, as I have done, by developing thoughts as I talked with others who would talk with me—learning from them. Very often passages subsequently written were continuations of these arguments and discussions. Those involved already know who they are, and how very much I owe them, but I must thank in particular Paul Bourke (who set me going), Allan Kulikoff, and Donna Merwick. Gordon Wood and Jack Greene first welcomed me to the field of early American history and have given me critical encouragement ever since. Jack has tirelessly organized ways and means for the advancement of my work. Richard Beeman met me as a fellow Virginia historian, and we have become brothers in the enterprise, to our mutual enrichment.

I have benefited enormously from the sharing of interests in social history with colleagues I found when I came to La Trobe University. Allan Martin gave me confidence when I most needed it. Greg Dening gave me a sense of the possibilities opened up by the ethnographic approach and with few but well-chosen comments has prevented me ever after from complacency about being on the right road. Inga Clendinnen was drawn to the same light at the same time, and since that time she has read in early draft (and partly rewritten) nearly everything that appears in this book, contributing bold critical insights and her astonishing flair. Philip Greven, Ken Lockridge, and Thad Tate read the first draft of the whole book and gave invaluable help. Cary Carson generously made his expertise available in the preparation of the drawings and the illustrations. The finished version has benefited immensely from June Philipp's understanding both of social theory and of how to wield a logical razor. Norman Fiering as editor has contributed superbly, as have Cynthia Carter Ayres and Doris M. Leisch. If it is still not enough, that is not their fault.

I was fortunate enough to owe more than I can express to certain of my formal teachers (whom I shall name in the order in which I came to them): Griff Mullins, Arthur Jayes, Rodney Davenport, Leonard Thompson, Christopher Hill, Richard Southern, and Peter Brown. In addition, since historians must be conscious of their relation to the past, I feel I have a special debt to Charles Sydnor, David Mays, and Douglass Adair—three Virginia historians whom I never had the opportunity to meet in person, but whose work gave me a first sense of a vivid world worth trying to understand.

Inevitably I have imposed on many typists for many drafts. Irma Chelsworth, Shirley Gordon, Louise Bennie, Shirley-Ann Jones, and Merelyn Dowling of the La Trobe University history department have all cheerfully turned untidy pencil scrawls into ordered typescript. To them, and to Olive Clark, who did the same in Williamsburg, I express admiring appreciation.

Last but not least I must thank the librarians and collection keepers at La Trobe University, at the Virginia State Library, and at the Research Department of the Colonial Williamsburg Foundation. Without their patient help I could not have got through with this. The same is true of the staff at the Institute of Early American History and Culture in Williamsburg. Since I have, in general, enjoyed the work so much, I am especially grateful to the Newberry Library, Chicago (where my real initiation began), to La Trobe University, to the Australian Research Grants Committee, and to the American Council of Learned Societies, all of whose grants have made research possible for me during the last ten years.

NOTES

CHAPTER 1

1. The most searching estimate of population size and proportions at the end of the 17th century is in Edmund S. Morgan, *American Slavery, American Freedom: The Ordeal of Colonial Virginia* (New York, 1975), 404, 422–423. Thereafter I have followed (making round figures) the United States Bureau of the Census, *Historical Statistics of the United States: Colonial Times to 1970, Bicentennial Edition*, Part 2 (Washington, D.C., 1975), Series Z-14. For an estimate on density (here assumed generalizable), see Carville V. Earle, *The Evolution of a Tidewater Settlement System: All Hallow's Parish, Maryland, 1650–1783*, University of Chicago, Department of Geography, Research Paper no. 170 (Chicago, 1975), 59. Precision about sizes is very difficult when boundaries have shifted so much. If Gloucester County (where the lines have been stable since the mid-17th century) is taken as a guide, then parishes of 15 miles by 8 miles would be usual, with two or three of these in a good-sized, well-settled county. The extent of parishes and counties was much greater in more recently settled areas to the west, but they were then divided and redivided as population became more dense. See Charles Francis Cocke, *Parish Lines: Diocese of Virginia* (Richmond, Va., 1967); George MacLaren Brydon, *Virginia's Mother Church and the Political Conditions under Which It Grew* (Richmond, Va., and Philadelphia, 1947–1952), I, 363; Morgan P. Robinson, "Virginia Counties: Those Resulting from Virginia Legislation," Virginia State Library, *Bulletin*, IX (1916), 90–99; and John Henry, *A New and Accurate Map of Virginia Wherein Most of the Counties Are Laid Down from Actual Surveys . . .* (London, 1770), photostat in the library of the

Research Department of The Colonial Williamsburg Foundation, Inc., Williamsburg, Virginia.

2. Robert Beverley, *The History and Present State of Virginia*, ed. Louis B. Wright (Chapel Hill, N.C., 1947), 296, 314, 298. See also pp. 128, 297.

3. On the evolution of the Classical tradition relating to Arcadia, see Erwin Panofsky, *Meaning in the Visual Arts: Papers in and on Art History* (Garden City, N.Y., 1955), 295–320.

4. Beverley, *History of Virginia*, ed. Wright, 140, 316, 308, 233, 156, 225 (emphasis added). The allusion to the Garden of Eden is made explicit in a statement that the Indians "seem'd to have escaped . . . the first Curse, *Of getting their Bread by the Sweat of their Brows*" (p. 17).

5. *Ibid.*, 232, 319, 233, 296, 57, 58, 295. The aspiration to create townscapes in Virginia was strong so long as English emigrants remained a high and influential proportion of the population. The legislature made repeated attempts by statute to accomplish this purpose. See John C. Rainbolt, *From Prescription to Persuasion: Manipulation of the Eighteenth [Seventeenth] Century Virginia Economy* (Port Washington, N.Y., 1974), 113, 116–117, 132–135, 152–154, 157–158.

6. Hugh Jones, *The Present State of Virginia, from Whence Is Inferred a Short View of Maryland and North Carolina*, ed. Richard L. Morton (Chapel Hill, N.C., 1956), 101; see also pp. 81, 93, and *passim*, for acceptance of the need to adapt to the ways of the country.

7. See Rhys Isaac, Letter to the Editor, *William and Mary Quarterly*, 3d Ser., XXXI (1974), 530.

8. Jones, *Present State of Virginia*, ed. Morton, 72, 73, 74, 75. On the consignment system, see Arthur Pierce Middleton, *Tobacco Coast: A Maritime History of Chesapeake Bay in the Colonial Era* (Newport News, Va., 1953), 104–110.

9. Jones, *Present State of Virginia*, ed. Morton, 97, 83.

CHAPTER 2

1. Beverley, *History of Virginia*, ed. Wright, 278, 225. For an excellent, illuminating account of the law and custom of processioning, see William H. Seiler, "Land Processioning in Colonial Virginia," *WMQ*, 3d Ser., VI (1949), 416–436.

2. Christ Church Parish, Lancaster County, Processioners' Returns, 1711–1783 (1785), [39], Virginia State Library, Richmond.

3. Richmond County, Deed Book 9 (1734–1741), Apr. 7, 1740, Va. State Lib.

4. George Webb, *The Office and Authority of a Justice of the Peace . . .*

(Williamsburg, Va., 1736), 346. On headrights, see Wesley Frank Craven, *White, Red, and Black: The Seventeenth-Century Virginian* (Charlottesville, Va., 1971), 9–10. On metaphor, see pp. 341–351, below, and the references given there. On patriarchy, see Peter Laslett, *The World We Have Lost* (New York, 1965), 1–21; and Lawrence Stone, *The Family, Sex and Marriage in England, 1500–1800* (New York, 1977), *passim*. Professor Stone focuses on Puritan rather than "traditional" patriarchy. "Paternalism" rather than "patriarchy" is discussed (without attention to the distinction) in Eugene D. Genovese, *Roll, Jordan, Roll: The World the Slaves Made* (New York, 1974), 3–7, and *passim*. On the family-communal aspect of landownership in early American society (New England and the Middle Colonies), see James A. Henretta, "Families and Farms: *Mentalité* in Pre-Industrial America," *WMQ*, 3d Ser., XXXV (1978), 3–32.

5. Robert E. and Katherine B. Brown, *Virginia 1705–1786: Democracy or Aristocracy?* (East Lansing, Mich., 1964), 13, 75.

6. Money as a culture principle in the New World is given fascinating treatment in Richard Slotkin, *Regeneration through Violence: The Mythology of the American Frontier, 1600–1860* (Middletown, Conn., 1973), 43–45. On the sale of headrights, see Edmund S. Morgan, "Headrights and Head Counts: A Review Article," *Virginia Magazine of History and Biography*, LXXX (1972), 361–371. On the lack of restraints in the early rush to get rich, see Morgan, *American Slavery*, 108–130.

7. On entails, see C. Ray Keim, "Primogeniture and Entail in Colonial Virginia," *WMQ*, 3d Ser., XXV (1968), 545–586. On money, see James H. Soltow, *The Economic Role of Williamsburg* (Williamsburg, Va., 1965), 107–176; and Joseph Albert Ernst, *Money and Politics in America, 1755–1775: A Study in the Currency Act of 1764 and the Political Economy of Revolution* (Chapel Hill, N.C., 1973), xv–xix, 12–17.

8. Harry J. Carman, ed., *American Husbandry*, Columbia University Studies in the History of Agriculture (New York, 1939), 165. (This work was originally published anonymously, in London in 1775.)

9. Jones, *Present State of Virginia*, ed. Morton, 77. See also William Tatham, *An Historical and Practical Essay on the Culture and Commerce of Tobacco* (London, 1800), 5–17. Tatham makes interesting observations on the "rustic mirth" that characterized the bonfires associated with field clearing (p. 12), as well as on the pooling of resources between neighbors (pp. 53, 56). On the slash-and-burn cycle of land use and the necessary balance between cleared fields and woodland, see Earle, *Tidewater Settlement System*, 24–34.

10. Jack P. Greene, ed., *The Diary of Colonel Landon Carter of Sabine Hall, 1752–1778* (Charlottesville, Va., 1965), I, 317–318, 314. The quotations that

follow are all drawn from the diary for the year 1766. They are not footnoted individually, since they can be most readily located from the dates that are given in the text.

11. For the quotations describing the preparing of the beds and the character of the soil, see *ibid.*, 140, 157. The details concerning the method of planting come from *The Journal of Nicholas Cresswell, 1774–1777* (New York, 1924), 18, hereafter cited as *Cresswell Journal.*

12. Jones, *Present State of Virginia*, ed. Morton, 77. The part of Carter's diary recording the actual crop made in 1766 has not survived. It is interesting to note how much he preserved a customary sense of the primacy of his tobacco crop, although market conditions in the late 1750s and 1760s made his wheat crop more valuable in some years. I am indebted for this point—and for the illumination of a great many others—to Paul G. E. Clemens, who has generously made available to me portions of his manuscript, since published as *The Atlantic Economy and Colonial Maryland's Eastern Shore: From Tobacco to Grain* (Ithaca, N.Y., 1980).

13. On the processing and handling of the tobacco crop, see Middleton, *Tobacco Coast*, 101–104. On the increasing role of the Scots in the transactions, see Jacob M. Price, "The Rise of Glasgow in the Chesapeake Tobacco Trade, 1707–1775," *WMQ*, 3d Ser., XI (1954), 179–199. On the connection with Continental markets, see Jacob M. Price, *France and the Chesapeake: A History of the French Tobacco Monopoly, 1674–1791, and of Its Relationship to the British and American Trades* (Ann Arbor, Mich., 1973).

14. Jones, *Present State of Virginia*, ed. Morton, 75; [Edward Kimber], "Observations in Several Voyages and Travels in America," *WMQ*, 1st Ser., XV (1906–1907), 148 (originally published in the *London Magazine*, July 1746). Note: In the original edition of vol. XV of the 1st Series of the *Quarterly*, the pagination is irregular.

15. The reference to a "Barreck" is from John Norton to Bataille Muse, Nov. 4, 1782; the diary entry is R. W. Carter's, dated Feb. 2, 1768. Both are cited in Philip David Morgan, "The Development of Slave Culture in Eighteenth Century Plantation America" (Ph.D. diss., University College, London, 1977), 52. I am extremely grateful to Dr. Morgan for making his valuable thesis available to me, and for generous sharing in the course of discussions.

On the sole married-pair household, see Laslett, *World We Have Lost*, 90. For a discussion of persistent African preferences in housing, see James Deetz, *In Small Things Forgotten: The Archaeology of Early American Life* (Garden City, N.Y., 1977), 148–152. On the increasing social isolation of the family dwelling in England at this time, see Stone, *Family, Sex and Marriage*, 123–150. For indications that masters in the Chesapeake were segregating their servants already by the mid-17th century, see Cary Carson, "Doing History with Material Culture," in Ian M. G. Quimby, ed., *Material Culture and the Study of American Life* (New York, 1978), 52–54. On the size of slave residence groups, see Allan Kulikoff, "The Origins of Afro-American Society in Tidewater Maryland and Virginia, 1700–1790," *WMQ*, 3d Ser., XXXV (1978), 241–242, 246–249. On percentages of two-parent and one-parent households, see Kulikoff, "The Beginnings of the Afro-American Family in Maryland," in Aubrey C. Land, Lois Green Carr, and Edward C. Papenfuse, eds., *Law, Society, and Politics in Early Maryland* (Baltimore, 1977), 179–180. Husband-and-wife separate residence remained general for the 19th-century marriages studied in Herbert G. Gutman, *The Black Family in Slavery and Freedom, 1750–1925* (New York, 1976), 131.

16. Hunter Dickinson Farish, ed., *Journal and Letters of Philip Vickers Fithian, 1773–1774: A Plantation Tutor of the Old Dominion* (Williamsburg, Va., 1957), 202–203. The explanation in square brackets is from the diary entry for Apr. 10, 1774, p. 96.

17. J. F. D. Smyth, *A Tour in the United States of America . . .* (London, 1784; facsimile reprint, New York, 1968), 46. For detail on African and Afro-American dance and song in this period, see Dena J. Epstein, *Sinful Tunes and Spirituals: Black Folk Music to the Civil War* (Urbana, Ill., 1977), 38–46, 73–76.

18. Cary Carson, "The 'Virginia House' in Maryland," *Maryland Historical Magazine*, LXIX (1974), 192–193; Jones, *Present State of Virginia*, ed. Morton, 74; and Smyth, *A Tour*, 49.

19. Henry Glassie, *Folk Housing in Middle Virginia: A Structural Analysis of Historic Artifacts* (Knoxville, Tenn., 1975), 122–136. Glassie's dating of the specimens he studied so closely is now questioned (personal communication from Cary Carson). For illuminating observations on a switch from a mentality of transience to a culture based on a sense of at-homeness, as reflected in transformations in house construction around 1700, see Cary Carson, Norman Barka, William Kelso, Garry Stone, and Dell Upton, "Impermanent Architecture in the Southern American Colonies," *Winterthur Portfolio*, XVI (1981), 135–196.

20. Gregory A. Stiverson and Patrick H. Butler III, eds., "Virginia in 1732: The Travel Journal of William Hugh Grove," *VMHB*, LXXXV (1977), 35; Beverley, *History of Virginia*, ed. Wright, 314; Smyth, *A Tour*, 69. On slovenliness in agriculture, see Beverley, *History of Virginia*, ed. Wright, 291, 292; Stiverson and Butler, eds., "Virginia in 1732," *VMHB*, LXXXV (1977), 33–35; Jones, *Present State of Virginia*, ed. Morton, 77, 84; *Cresswell Journal*, 25.

21. [Thomas Anburey], *Travels through the Interior Parts of America in a Series of Letters by an Officer* (London, 1789; facsimile reprint, New York, 1969), II, 324.

Virginians themselves were struck by the contrast between their landscape and that made by Pennsylvania farmers. See "A Friend to Virginia," *Virginia Gazette* (Rind), June 14, 1770.

22. Stiverson and Butler, eds., "Virginia in 1732," *VMHB*, LXXXV (1977), 26–28.

23. *Ibid.*, 28. See also Beverley, *History of Virginia*, ed. Wright, 289; and Jones, *Present State of Virginia*, ed. Morton, 71.

24. Gilbert Chinard, ed., *A Huguenot Exile in Virginia, or Voyages of a Frenchman Exiled for His Religion with a Description of Virginia and Maryland* (New York, 1934), 142; Stiverson and Butler, eds., "Virginia in 1732," *VMHB*, LXXXV (1977), 26; Howard C. Rice, trans., *Travels in North America in the Years 1780, 1781 and 1782 by the Marquis de Chastellux* (Chapel Hill, N.C., 1963), II, 431. A convenient summary of the conventional form of the "Georgian" house can be found in Deetz, *In Small Things Forgotten*, 111–112. On the evolution of country-house forms in relation to the very highest styles of English gentry life, see Mark Girouard, *Life in the English Country House: A Social and Architectural History* (New Haven, Conn., 1978), *passim.*

25. On the design and construction of the Governor's Palace at Williamsburg, see Thomas Tileston Waterman, *The Mansions of Virginia, 1706–1776* (Chapel Hill, N.C., 1946), 31–44. It has been argued that the disposition of actual elements in the Virginia great houses built after the palace owed most to English design books, which then became current (see Marcus Whiffen, *The Public Buildings of Williamsburg, Colonial Capital of Virginia: An Architectural History* [Williamsburg, Va., 1958], 65–66). It is nevertheless reasonable to assume that architectural Classicism and the ordering of dependencies in a symmetrical design received inspiration from the palace.

26. William Byrd II to Charles, Earl of Orrery, July 5, 1726, in "Virginia Council Journals, 1726–1753," *VMHB*, XXXII (1924), 27 (the Scripture reference is to Mic. 4:4); Greene, ed., *Diary of Landon Carter*, I, 59. For a more extended commentary on the metaphor embodied in the house, see the essay on method, pp. 351–354, below.

27. Bernard Bailyn, "Politics and Social Structure in Virginia," in James Morton Smith, ed., *Seventeenth-Century America: Essays in Colonial History* (Chapel Hill, N.C., 1959), 90–115.

28. The lateness of the design featured in the picture is shown by decorative detail and the manner in which the lateral dependencies have been drawn into the central structure.

29. Byrd to Orrery, July 5, 1726, in "Virginia Council Journals," *VMHB*, XXXII (1924), 27. The size and nature of the residence group idyllically presented by Byrd is an essential context for the disposition and distribution of emotional commitment that has been discerned in Byrd's diary (see Michael Zuckerman,

"William Byrd's Family," *Perspectives in American History*, XII [1979], 253–311). We are looking here at thoroughgoing *patriarchalism*, before it had been domesticated into *paternalism*. For further comment on this important distinction, see below, pp. 308–310.

CHAPTER 3

1. Devereux Jarratt, *The Life of the Reverend Devereux Jarratt, Rector of Bath Parish, Dinwiddie County, Virginia, Written by Himself, in a Series of Letters Addressed to the Rev. John Coleman . . .* (Baltimore, 1806; facsimile reprint, New York, 1969), 14; [Kimber], "Observations," *WMQ*, 1st Ser., XV (1906–1907), 216. See also Beverley, *History of Virginia*, ed. Wright, 295. The first part of Jarratt's reminiscences was published with a valuable introduction and scholarly notes in Douglass Adair, ed., "The Autobiography of the Reverend Devereux Jarratt, 1732–1763," *WMQ*, 3d Ser., IX (1952), 346–393.
2. Stiverson and Butler, eds., "Virginia in 1732," *VMHB*, LXXXV (1977), 29; [Kimber], "Observations," *WMQ*, 1st Ser., XV (1906–1907), 158 (see chap. 2, n. 14).
3. Stiverson and Butler, eds., "Virginia in 1732," *VMHB*, LXXXV (1977), 32; Jarratt, *Life*, 14, 26.
4. Stiverson and Butler, eds., "Virginia in 1732," *VMHB*, LXXXV (1977), 29–30; [Kimber], "Observations," *WMQ*, 1st Ser., XV (1906–1907), 146; Beverley, *History of Virginia*, ed. Wright, 292.
5. Farish, ed., *Journal of Fithian*, 129, 38, 31; Smyth, *A Tour*, 44–45.
6. Jarratt, *Life*, 13–14.
7. Lois Green Carr and Lorena S. Walsh, "Changing Life Styles in Colonial St. Mary's County," Working Papers from the Regional Economic History Research Center, I, no. 3 (1978), 73–118; Barbara Carson and Cary Carson, "Styles and Standards of Living in Southern Maryland, 1670–1752" (unpublished paper delivered at the Southern Historical Association meeting, Atlanta, Georgia, Nov. 1976), table 2. I am grateful for permission to use these papers as well as for all the helpful discussions and criticism I have had from their authors. For a briefer outline of the remarkable findings of the St. Mary's City researchers, see Lois Green Carr and Lorena S. Walsh, "Inventories and the Analysis of Wealth and Consumption Patterns in St. Mary's County, Maryland, 1658–1777," *Historical Methods*, XIII (1980), 81–104.
8. Charles Singer and E. Ashworth Underwood, *A Short History of Medicine*, 2d ed. (Oxford, 1962), 46. Environmental determinism was a simple truism of 18th-century "social science." For a brief account of medical theory and a great

deal of valuable information on Virginia practice, see Harold B. Gill, Jr., *The Apothecary in Colonial Virginia* (Williamsburg, Va., 1972); and the materials collected in Wyndham B. Blanton, *Medicine in Virginia in the Eighteenth Century* (Richmond, Va., 1931). For an illuminating study of the persistence of ancient cosmological beliefs, see Herbert Leventhal, *In the Shadow of the Enlightenment: Occultism and Renaissance Science in Eighteenth-Century America* (New York, 1976).

9. Beverley, *History of Virginia*, ed. Wright, 296; Jones, *Present State of Virginia*, ed. Morton, 84–85; Beverley, *History of Virginia*, ed. Wright, 306.

10. Jarratt, *Life*, 29.

11. Greene, ed., *Diary of Landon Carter*, II, 797, 1111. For a slave asking for bloodletting, see *ibid.*, I, 206. The slaves had remedies of their own that embodied a different world view. Whites not infrequently had recourse to this alternative. The implications of slave lore in this area are discussed in Lawrence W. Levine, *Black Culture and Black Consciousness: Afro-American Folk Thought from Slavery to Freedom* (New York, 1977), 55–80.

12. Greene, ed., *Diary of Landon Carter*, I, 321.

13. *Ibid.*, 356. On the system of knowledge and classification that preceded the 19th-century development of the organic/inorganic dichotomy, see Michel Foucault, *The Order of Things: An Archaeology of the Human Sciences* (New York, 1970 [orig. publ. Paris, 1966]), 144–145, and *passim*. See also Garry Wills, *Inventing America: Jefferson's Declaration of Independence* (New York, 1978), 95–97. On the correspondence of the body politic with human physiology as then understood, see Gordón S. Wood, *The Creation of the American Republic, 1776–1787* (Chapel Hill, N.C., 1969), 29, and the pronouncement by "Virginius" (*Va. Gaz.* [Pinkney], June 29, 1775) cited there, and "Final Draft of the Virginia Declaration of Rights," in Robert A. Rutland, ed., *The Papers of George Mason, 1725–1792* (Chapel Hill, N.C., 1970), I, 289. See also the *Oxford English Dictionary*, s.v. "constitution" and "corruption."

14. Greene, ed., *Diary of Landon Carter*, I, 372, 344, 391. Colonel Carter also believed concerning the configuration of the moon that "the more she leans on her back the weather is generally the wetter" (p. 285, and *passim*). For a study of American astrological beliefs regulating agricultural operations, see Leventhal, *Shadow of the Enlightenment*, 39–47.

15. Greene, ed., *Diary of Landon Carter*, I, 513.

16. On the persistence of the humoral physiology well into the 19th century, see Charles E. Rosenberg, "The Therapeutic Revolution: Medicine, Meaning, and Social Change in Nineteenth-Century America," *Perspectives in Biology and Medicine*, XX (1976–1977), 485–506.

17. Levine, *Black Culture*, 102–135. On opening of cornhouses and the social

power of those who could, see pp. 343–344, below, and Greene, ed., *Diary of Landon Carter*, I, 301, 309. On stock killing, see Kulikoff, "Origins of Afro-American Society," *WMQ*, 3d Ser., XXXV (1978), 250.

18. For a suggestive—though controversial—account of the nature and form of slave speech, see J. L. Dillard, *Black English: Its History and Usage in the United States* (New York, 1972), 84–86, and *passim*. For alternative interpretations, see Deborah Sears Harrison and Tom Trabasso, eds., *Black English: A Seminar* (Hillsdale, N.J., 1976).

19. On the polite exchange of greetings between gentry and common planters, see "Notes of Judge St. George Tucker," in "William Wirt's Life of Patrick Henry," *WMQ*, 1st Ser., XXII (1913–1914), 252.

20. Farish, ed., *Journal of Fithian*, 29. The assertion concerning white females' avoidance of stores and ordinaries is based on oral communication from Allan Kulikoff concerning analyses he has made of daybooks.

C H A P T E R 4

1. [Kimber], "Observations," *WMQ*, 1st Ser., XV (1906–1907), 158; Farish, ed., *Journal of Fithian*, 167. I have found no description of how—if at all frequently—common planters' wives and daughters came to church.

2. Thomas Mutter to Sir Peyton Skipwith, Mar. 20, 1775, Skipwith Papers, Box 1, p. 17, Earl Gregg Swem Library, The College of William and Mary, Williamsburg, Va.; Farish, ed., *Journal of Fithian*, 93.

3. Farish, ed., *Journal of Fithian*, 29.

4. The quotation is from Bishop William Beveridge, *A Sermon concerning the Excellency and Usefulness of the Common Prayer, etc.* (London, 1682). It is cited in Horton Davies, *Worship and Theology in England: From Watts and Wesley to Maurice, 1690–1850* (Princeton, N.J., 1961), 26–27. For an exploration of the origins of the particular form of Christ Church, Lancaster, see Alan Gowans, *King Carter's Church* [Victoria, B.C., 1969], 7–32. Gowans attributes the design to Christopher Wren but omits discussion of the perfect conformity of this building to Wren's sense of the requirements of churches as "auditories." See G. W. O. Addleshaw and Frederick Etchells, *The Architectural Setting of Anglican Worship: An Inquiry into the Arrangements for Public Worship in the Church of England from the Reformation to the Present Day* (London, 1948).

5. For a brief commentary on the tone of the liturgy, see Church of England, *The Book of Common Prayer, 1559: The Elizabethan Prayer Book*, ed. John E. Booty (Charlottesville, Va., 1976), 379–382.

6. On the functioning of the vestries, see William H. Seiler, "The Anglican Parish in Virginia," in Smith, ed., *Seventeenth-Century America*, 120–142.
7. Farish, ed., *Journal of Fithian*, 42; Jarratt, *Life*, 16; Byrd to Orrery, July 5, 1726, in "Virginia Council Journals," *VMHB*, XXXII (1924), 27.
8. Farish, ed., *Journal of Fithian*, 137. See also p. 145.
9. For a persuasive interpretation, strongly inferring the vital survival of African forms and modes of expression, see Levine, *Black Culture*, 3–30.
10. Jones, *Present State of Virginia*, ed. Morton, 97.
11. *Ibid.*, 97 (emphasis added), 100.
12. Levine, *Black Culture*, 25–30.
13. Jones, *Present State of Virginia*, ed. Morton, 97; Farish, ed., *Journal of Fithian*, 43; Beverley, *History of Virginia*, ed. Wright, 312–313. See also a description of Maryland that identifies traits common to both Chesapeake societies ([Kimber], "Observations," *WMQ*, 1st Ser., XV [1906–1907], 146; and Jones, *Present State of Virginia*, ed. Morton, 84). The "openness" of a great house to visitors and the importance of the role of host to the sense of identity and persona of a gentleman have been very sensitively discussed in Zuckerman, "Byrd's Family," *Perspectives in American History*, XII (1979), 253–311. For a discussion of later changes in this emotional economy, see pp. 309–310, below.
14. Carson, "'Virginia House' in Maryland," *Md. Hist. Mag.*, LXIX (1974), 192–193. For discussion of the significance of this type of house plan, see Glassie, *Folk Housing*, 120–121; and Deetz, *In Small Things Forgotten*, 115–117. There is a general review of the increase in private space in English houses at different social levels in Stone, *Family, Sex and Marriage*, 253–256.
15. Carson and Carson, "Styles and Standards of Living," table 2A, 34. See also Aubrey C. Land, "Economic Base and Social Structure: The Northern Chesapeake in the Eighteenth Century," *Journal of Economic History*, XXV (1965), 639–654.
16. Carson and Carson, "Styles and Standards of Living," 18; Carr and Walsh, "Changing Life Styles," 9–10.
17. Carr and Walsh, "Changing Life Styles," 23.
18. Carson and Carson, "Styles and Standards of Living," tables 1 and 2. For assertions on continuities in housing that contradict the interpretations proposed by Professor Glassie, I have relied on personal communications from Cary Carson and from Dell Upton. I am particularly grateful to Dr. Upton for giving up time when he was very busy to lessen my ignorance concerning such matters, and for sharing some of the impressive results of his years of intensive research, both on surviving structures and on documentary sources.
19. The journal dates from 1773–1774. It reveals a refinement of genteel style that

would be hard, if not impossible, to match in the second quarter of the 18th century. There also appears, with the man of "sensibility" in this later period, the beginnings of an ethos of domesticity in the Carter family that would not have been found earlier. See Jan Ellen Lewis Grimmelmann, "This World and the Next: Religion, Death, Success, and Love in Jefferson's Virginia" (Ph.D. diss., University of Michigan, 1977), 259–299. See also Daniel Blake Smith, *Inside the Great House: Planter Family Life in Eighteenth-Century Chesapeake Society* (Ithaca, N.Y., 1980).

20. Farish, ed., *Journal of Fithian*, 80.
21. *Ibid.*, 80, 129, 51, 133.
22. *Ibid.*, 80, and *passim*.
23. *Ibid.*, 158. See also pp. 93, 110, 129, 185. On social relations as calculated exchange, see Peter M. Blau, *Exchange and Power in Social Life* (New York, 1964).
24. Farish, ed., *Journal of Fithian*, 121, 67, 42, 40, 141, 117, 71, 56.
25. For examples of giving toasts, see *ibid.*, 47, 62, 64, 75, 77, 83, 84, 87, 95, 141, 191, 196, 198. The extended quotations are on pp. 34, 125.
26. *Ibid.*, 138, 142.
27. *Ibid.*, 56–57.
28. *Ibid.*, 147, 150, 156, 172, 177, 183.
29. Jarratt, *Life*, 44.
30. The original of the painting is in the Abby Aldrich Rockefeller Folk Art Center, Williamsburg, Virginia. The picture was found in South Carolina and is thought to show a plantation in that region, but it could as well be Virginia. The words quoted were applied to black dance and song in *Cresswell Journal*, 19.
31. Farish, ed., *Journal of Fithian*, 177.
32. *Ibid.*, 33, 34; Burnaby, *Travels*, 26; *Cresswell Journal*, 53. On the college's attention to dancing lessons, see President James Blair's remark in 1705 on the hall as "the most useful place in the College for here we sometimes preach and pray [the chapel was not yet built], and sometimes we fiddle and dance; the one to edify, and the other to divert us." Quoted in Jones, *Present State of Virginia*, ed. Morton, 11. See also Stiverson and Butler, eds., "Virginia in 1732," *VMHB*, LXXXV (1977), 26.
33. Farish, ed., *Journal of Fithian*, 61, 62. For an instance of slave parodying of the masters' dance movements, see Levine, *Black Culture*, 17.
34. *Cresswell Journal*, 18–19. See also Levine, *Black Culture*, 6–19, 25–30; and Epstein, *Sinful Tunes*, 63–76.
35. *Cresswell Journal*, 26, 30; *Va. Gaz.* (Purdie & Dixon), June 24, Sept. 9, 1773.
36. Louis B. Wright and Marion Tinling, eds., *Quebec to Carolina in 1785–1786:*

Being the Travel Diary and Observations of Robert Hunter, Jr., a Young Merchant of London (San Marino, Calif., 1943), 231.

37. James Ireland, *The Life of the Rev. James Ireland . . .* (Winchester, Va., 1819), 49–50.

CHAPTER 5

1. Louis B. Wright, ed., *The Prose Works of William Byrd of Westover: Narratives of a Colonial Virginian* (Cambridge, Mass., 1966), 373–374.

2. *Va. Gaz.* (Rind), Aug. 4, 1768. The best account of the work of the court, and of the character of assemblies at the courthouse, remains Charles S. Sydnor, *Gentlemen Freeholders: Political Practices in Washington's Virginia* (Chapel Hill, N.C., 1952), reissued as *American Revolutionaries in the Making* (New York, 1965). On the design of courthouses, see John F. Millar, *The Architects of the American Colonies; or Vitruvius Americanus* (Barre, Mass., 1968), 54–56.

3. Webb, *Justice of the Peace*, 202. For a full dramaturgic analysis of courthouse procedures, see A. G. Roeber, "Authority, Law, and Custom: The Rituals of Court Day in Tidewater Virginia, 1720–1750," *WMQ*, 3d Ser., XXXVII (1980), 29–52.

4. Court proceedings still follow this form in our age of universal literacy, but with the significant addition of stenographic (and latterly, electronic) recording of the spoken word.

5. On communication and knowledge in cultures with a powerful oral component, see chap. 6, below; see also Rhys Isaac, "Dramatizing the Ideology of Revolution: Popular Mobilization in Virginia, 1774 to 1776," *WMQ*, 3d Ser., XXXIII (1976), 358–362, and the references cited there. On juries for felony trials, see Hugh F. Rankin, *Criminal Trial Proceedings in the General Court of Colonial Virginia* (Williamsburg, Va., 1965), 91. The intention of harnessing oral tradition to legal procedures is very clear in the documents cited in Seiler, "Land Processioning," *WMQ*, 3d Ser., VI (1949), 419–420.

6. Rankin, *Criminal Trial Proceedings*, 46; Webb, *Justice of the Peace*, 82–83; *Va. Gaz.* (Dixon and Hunter), Jan. 6, 1776.

7. On the routine work of the court, see Sydnor, *Gentlemen Freeholders*, 86–91. On the cornering of tobacco inspection patronage by the courts, see William Waller Hening, ed., *The Statutes at Large; Being a Collection of All the Laws of Virginia . . .* (Richmond, Va., 1809–1823), IV, 127, 326. For an example of delay granted as a favor, see Greene, ed., *Diary of Landon Carter*, I, 432.

8. For a searching discussion of the 18th century as a "moment" in the history of

the relationship of law and society in the English tradition, see E. P. Thompson, *Whigs and Hunters: The Origin of the Black Act* (New York, 1975), 258–269. On the supreme importance of independence and its basis in property, see Jack P. Greene, *All Men Are Created Equal: Some Reflections on the Character of the American Revolution: An Inaugural Address* (Oxford, 1976).

9. "Journal of a French Traveller in the Colonies, 1765, I," *American Historical Review*, XXVI (1920–1921), 743.

10. *Ibid.*, 747; Morgan Edwards, "Materials toward a History of the Baptists in the Province of Virginia, 1772," MS, 86–87, Furman University Library, Greenville, S.C. (microfilm kindly supplied by the Historical Commission, Southern Baptist Convention, Nashville, Tenn.). For an instance of sparring between gentlemen who were neighbors, see Greene, ed., *Diary of Landon Carter*, II, 937. Particulars from a variety of sources that touch on ordinaries have been ably drawn together in Patricia Ann Gibbs, "Taverns in Tidewater Virginia, 1700–1774" (M.A. thesis, College of William and Mary, 1968). Instances of sword wearing are: 1722, "Narrative of George Fisher. Commencing with a Voyage from London, May, 1750, for Yorktown in Virginia and Ending in August, 1755 . . . ," *WMQ*, 1st Ser., XVII (1908–1909), 122–123; 1771, in Greene, ed., *Diary of Landon Carter*, II, 938. In a famous episode in 1766, Colonel Chiswell appears to have left his sword in a house near the ordinary. See Carl Bridenbaugh, "Violence and Virtue in Virginia, 1766: or, The Importance of the Trivial," Massachusetts Historical Society, *Proceedings*, LXXVI (1964), 4.

11. Farish, ed., *Journal of Fithian*, 183; [Anburey], *Travels through America*, II, 349; Winslow C. Watson, ed., *Men and Times of the Revolution; or Memoirs of Elkanah Watson . . .* (New York, 1856), 60. Among the gentry in mid-18th-century Virginia, inhibitions on physical contact had not yet found ritualization in the duel with pistols. Boxing and wrestling were still contemplated—if not frequently undertaken. See Courtland Canby, ed., "Robert Munford's *The Patriots*," *WMQ*, 3d Ser., VI (1949), 475; and Jane Carson, *Colonial Virginians at Play* (Williamsburg, Va., 1965), 167–168.

12. On the violence of the first decades of English settlement and the consolidation of order on the basis of slavery, see Morgan, *American Slavery*, 71–130, 292–387. On violence as a part of life in England, see J. H. Plumb, *Men and Places* (London, 1963), 9–10. A very suggestive discussion concerning the inherently contestful nature of oral cultural systems is offered in Walter J. Ong, *The Presence of the Word: Some Prolegomena for Cultural and Religious History* (New Haven, Conn., 1967), 192–222.

13. John Bernard, *Retrospections of America, 1797–1811*, ed. Mrs. Bayle Bernard (New York, 1887; facsimile reprint, New York, 1969), 155. On quarter racing

generally, see J. Carson, *Virginians at Play*, 108–112. T. H. Breen, "Horses and Gentlemen: The Cultural Significance of Gambling among the Gentry of Virginia," *WMQ*, 3d Ser., XXXIV (1977), 239–257, offers an admirably full account of these activities in the period around 1700. A case for the social functionality of gambling is vigorously argued.

14. Jones, *Present State of Virginia*, ed. Morton, 84; Farish, ed., *Journal of Fithian*, 177; C. G. Chamberlayne, ed., *The Vestry Book and Register of St. Peter's Parish, New Kent and James City Counties, Virginia, 1684–1786* (Richmond, Va., 1937), 478. I am indebted to Thomas E. Buckley for this last reference.

15. Cited in Ernst, *Money and Politics*, 46 (the punctuation has been silently altered to make the reported speech intelligible); and H. R. McIlwaine and John Pendleton Kennedy, eds., *Journals of the House of Burgesses of Virginia* (Richmond, Va., 1905–1915), *1752–1755, 1756–1758*, 100 (hereafter cited as *Journals of Burgesses*). The "pistol[e]" was a Portuguese American coin much in use in Virginia.

16. Farish, ed., *Journal of Fithian*, 24–25. On the evolution of forms of horse racing, see J. Carson, *Virginians at Play*, 105–132.

17. Edward Miles Riley, ed., *The Journal of John Harrower: An Indentured Servant in the Colony of Virginia, 1773–1776* (Williamsburg, Va., 1963), 65.

18. J. Carson, *Virginians at Play*, 152, 153; Robert Wormeley Carter, Diary, May 2–7, 1768, typescript in Colonial Williamsburg Research Library, Williamsburg, Va.

19. Watson, ed., *Men and Times*, 261–262; Evelyn M. Acomb, trans. and ed., *The Revolutionary Journal of Baron Ludwig von Closen, 1780–1783* (Chapel Hill, N.C., 1958), 177; Rice, trans., *Travels by Chastellux*, II, 386–387.

20. Farish, ed., *Journal of Fithian*, 91, 96; J. Carson, *Virginians at Play*, 155–157.

21. *Va. Gaz.*, Nov. 19, 1736. The notice of a repeat of this occasion the following year (Sept. 30, 1737) stressed the determination of the organizers to maintain "Decency and Sobriety," suggesting that the presence of an unruly element had given alarm previously. Nevertheless the meeting was still said to be for the benefit of the "Gentlemen, Merchants, and creditable Planters" of Hanover County. Once again the *opposed* juxtaposition of the terms "gentlemen" and "planters" shows that they were not then synonymous (see Isaac, Letter to the Editor, *WMQ*, 3d Ser., XXXI [1974], 530). The "creditable Planters" referred to in the *Gazette* notice were presumably yeomen who, in the presence of the gentry, showed their deference by "Decency and Sobriety."

22. On the workings of English rank-structured, patronage society, see Harold Perkin, *The Origins of Modern English Society, 1780–1880* (London, 1969), 17–62; Laslett, *World We Have Lost*, 22–52; and E. P. Thompson, "Eighteenth-

Century English Society: Class Struggle without Class?" *Social History*, III (1978), 133–165. For fuller discussion of rank-structured society, see chap. 6, below. The clear signs of increasing refinement and segregation, and the emergence of the lineaments of a "class" society more familiar to us, are noted in the Afterview, below.

23. Hening, ed., *Statutes at Large*, VII, 93.
24. *Ibid.*, 93–95, 98–99.
25. *Ibid.*, 93 (emphasis added).
26. *Ibid.*, 95, 104–105.
27. *Ibid.*, IV, 202.
28. [Kimber], "Observations," *WMQ*, 1st Ser., XV (1906–1907), 147–148. The lines are an adaptation of "Cymon and Iphiginia" (1700). See John Dryden, *Poems*, ed. James Kinsley (Oxford, 1958), IV, p. 1751.
29. *Journals of Burgesses, 1752–1755, 1756–1758*, 360.
30. Louis B. Wright and Marion Tinling, eds., *The Secret Diary of William Byrd of Westover, 1709–1712* (Richmond, Va., 1941), 234, 233 (entries for Sept. 21 and 22, 1710).
31. *Ibid.*, 414–415 (Oct. 2, 1711).
32. *Ibid.*, 415. Once again we see the readiness of gentlemen to engage physically, man-to-man, with their inferiors in this rank-structured, "pre-class" system. Wrestling and cudgel play were open-challenge contests included in the Hanover County sports advertised in 1736 and 1737. *Va. Gaz.*, Nov. 19, 1736, Sept. 30, 1737; see n. 21, above.
33. Wright and Tinling, eds., *Diary of William Byrd*, 410, 411, 403.
34. [Kimber], "Observations," *WMQ*, 1st Ser., XV (1906–1907), 147. The journal of the anonymous French traveler of 1765 noted of Colonel Johnson that he was "Colonel in the Militia, and likes well to be called so" ("French Traveller's Journal," *AHR*, XXVI [1920–1921], 747). My observations on the sense of self reinforced in William Byrd by his role in the militia complement Michael Zuckerman's analysis of the household (but not "familial," as 20th-century Westerners understand that word) values of the master of Westover. See Zuckerman, "Byrd's Family," *Perspectives in American History*, XII (1979), 253–311.
35. Paraphrased in J. G. A. Pocock, "Machiavelli, Harrington, and English Political Ideologies in the Eighteenth Century," *WMQ*, 3d Ser., XXII (1965), 549–583. The quotation is from p. 582.
36. William Gooch to Board of Trade, Mar. 26, 1729, C.O. 5/1321, Public Record Office (typescript in Colonial Williamsburg Research Library).
37. Gooch to Board of Trade, Sept. 14, 1730, C.O. 5/1322, 158–159.
38. Quoted by Sydnor, *Gentlemen Freeholders*, 21–22. Late and idealized as the ex-

ample is, it conveys admirably the ethos of intense yet decorous contest that must frequently have prevailed at the courthouse polling tables.

39. *Journals of Burgesses, 1727–1734, 1736–1740*, 370, entry for Dec. 9, 1738. Colonel Scarburgh was seated by the House against the recommendation of the investigating committee.

40. *Ibid.*, *1758–1761*, 83. For Madison's own account of his rejection in 1777 by voters he had declined to treat (on virtuous republican grounds), see Ralph Ketcham, *James Madison: A Biography* (New York, 1971), 77.

41. See Perkin, *Origins of Modern English Society*, 17–62.

CHAPTER 6

1. Jarratt, *Life*, 25, 29, 42.

2. Diaries suggest that active, plantation-managing gentry, especially if they had a taste for gambling as well, almost lived in the saddle. For an example of such incessant movement by a master and his "people," see Louis Morton, ed., "The Daybook of Robert Wormeley Carter of Sabine Hall, 1766," *VMHB*, LXVIII (1960), 301–316; and the unabridged typescripts of the diaries of R. W. Carter in the Colonial Williamsburg Research collection. The movement of slaves into the Piedmont is noted in Kulikoff, "Origins of Afro-American Society," *WMQ*, 3d Ser., XXXV (1978), 252–253.

3. Richard Beale Davis, ed., "The Colonial Virginia Satirist: Mid-Eighteenth-Century Commentaries on Politics, Religion, and Society," American Philosophical Society, *Transactions*, N.S., LVII, Pt. 1 (1967), 48.

4. Minton Thrift, *Memoir of the Rev. Jesse Lee, with Extracts from His Journals* (New York, 1823; facsimile reprint, New York, 1969), 5. See also Jarratt, *Life*, 30, where striving to "excel" in "*merriment, banter, buffoonery* and such like" is described. On being "where the action is," see Erving Goffman, *Interaction Ritual: Essays in Face-to-Face Behavior* (Chicago, 1967), 149.

5. For discussion of Bentham's concept, and the now classic application of it to analysis of charged interaction situations, see Clifford Geertz, *The Interpretation of Cultures: Selected Essays* (New York, 1973), 432–442. See also Greene, ed., *Diary of Landon Carter*, II, 830, and Greene's discussion of the subject, *ibid.*, I, 52–53. On pleasure taken in the anguish of others, see Keith Thomas, "The Place of Laughter in Tudor and Stuart England," *Times Literary Supplement*, Jan. 21, 1977, 77–81, esp. 80.

6. Jarratt, *Life*, 102; Ireland, *Life*, 51, 59. For a summing up on the highly secular character of Virginians, see Burnaby, *Travels in North-America*, 23–24. For a very suggestive discussion of social systems characterized by close boundaries and

clearly defined statuses, contrasted with open, extended societies in which individual success is relentlessly pursued, see Mary Douglas, *Natural Symbols: Explorations in Cosmology*, 2d rev. ed. (New York, 1973), 136–172. Mid-18th-century Virginia would have to be viewed in this perspective as a system where the two tendencies were simultaneously present, in tension with each other.

7. Jones, *Present State of Virginia*, ed. Morton, 117–118.

8. On oral culture in a historical context, see Ong, *Presence of the Word*, 1–9, 17–87. For a fine interpretation of the implications of media study for early American history, see Harry S. Stout, "Religion, Communications, and the Ideological Origins of the American Revolution," *WMQ*, 3d Ser., XXXIV (1977), 519–541. See also Jack Goody and I. P. Watts, "The Consequences of Literacy," in Jack Goody, ed., *Literacy in Traditional Societies* (Cambridge, 1968), 27–68; and Jack Goody, *The Domestication of the Savage Mind* (Cambridge, 1977).

9. The most recent, critically appraised figures are to be found in Kenneth A. Lockridge, *Literacy in Colonial New England: An Enquiry into the Social Context of Literacy in the Early Modern West* (New York, 1974), 73–87. The modest title of this book belies the importance of its wide-ranging comparative data and broad interpretation. For a lively commentary on the place of "talk" in the lives of the gentry, and indeed for what are probably the best few pages on old Virginia to be found anywhere, see Douglass Adair's review of Robert Douthat Meade's biography of Patrick Henry, *WMQ*, 3d Ser., XVI (1959), 589–593.

10. Representations of the process of the learned overawing the vulgar abound in literature. A famous example is that of the schoolmaster and the parson in Oliver Goldsmith's verses on "The Deserted Village" (lines 210–220). Since most of the applications of contemporary medicine were more apt to kill than to cure, it may be suggested that much of whatever therapeutic value there was came from the reassurance the patients found in the book-learned utterances of the physicians. For a parody of such performances, see Henry Fielding's adaptation of Molière in his play *The Mock Doctor*.

11. Jarratt, *Life*, 19, 16, 17, 18.

12. *Ibid.*, 15, 16, 19, 20.

13. *Ibid.*, 24, 25, 26, 27.

14. *Ibid.*, 28.

15. *Ibid.*, 30.

16. *Ibid.*, 31–32.

17. *Ibid.*, 31, 32, 33, 34. Douglass Adair identifies the author named, as John Flavel (1630?–1691), a Presbyterian divine whose many religious writings were noted for a "fine play of fancy and dramatic imagery." Adair, ed., "Autobiography of Jarratt," *WMQ*, 3d Ser., IX (1952), 370.

18. Jarratt, *Life*, 34.
19. *Ibid.*, 38, 39, 40, 41. The authors named were William Russel (d. 1702), a Baptist minister, and William Burkitt (1650–1703). The prized volume was *Expository Notes, with Practical Observations, on the New Testament*, 1st ed. (London, 1724). Adair, ed., "Autobiography of Jarratt," *WMQ*, 3d Ser., IX (1952), 373, 374.
20. Jarratt, *Life*, 44, 45.
21. The quotation is from an address "To the Honourable William Gooch . . . [from] the Council," Feb. 1745, C.O. 5/1326/182, Public Records Office (microfilm at Colonial Williamsburg Research Library). For an outline of the founding of the college and the expectations leading Virginians had of it, see Richard L. Morton, *Colonial Virginia* (Chapel Hill, N.C., 1960), I: *The Tidewater Period, 1607–1710*, 337–338, 345–347, 357–359. On the troubled history of the college in the 1750s, 60s, and 70s, see *ibid.*, II: *Westward Expansion and Prelude to Revolution, 1710–1763*, 765–783; and Robert Polk Thomson, "The Reform of the College of William and Mary, 1763–1780," Am. Phil. Soc., *Proceedings*, CXV (1971), 187–213. Contentious publications and speeches by members of the college are treated extensively in chaps. 9 and 10, below.
22. On independence as a supreme value, see Greene, *All Men Are Created Equal*, 23–33. On the English tradition, see Pocock, "Machiavelli, Harrington, and the Eighteenth Century," *WMQ*, 3d Ser., XXII (1965), 553–583.
23. For a dated but still valuable discussion (with references) of gentility, see Louis B. Wright, *The First Gentlemen of Virginia: Intellectual Qualities of the Early Colonial Ruling Class* (San Marino, Calif., 1940), esp. 1–37. A profoundly insightful exploration of the basis of genteel sensibility in nurture and social context is presented in Philip Greven, *The Protestant Temperament: Patterns of Child-Rearing, Religious Experience, and the Self in Early America* (New York, 1977), 265–331. The heuristic model set up in this work is very valuable, although a social, as opposed to psychological, approach would have to assign most of Greven's "moderates," and even some "evangelicals," to the ranks of the gentry. The expected avocations of the English gentleman are succinctly summed up in Perkin, *Origins of Modern English Society*, 56.
24. For a study spotlighting a clear case of merchants' inclusion in the gentry, see Emory G. Evans, *Thomas Nelson of Yorktown: Revolutionary Virginian*, Williamsburg in America Series, X (Williamsburg, Va., 1975), 5–14.
25. On the place of debts owed by poor neighbors in the assets of wealthy gentlemen, see Land, "Economic Base and Social Structure," *Jour. Econ. Hist.*, XXV (1965), 640, 646, 650. On the nature and distribution of political power in Virginia, see Sydnor, *Gentlemen Freeholders, passim*; and Jack P. Greene, "Foun-

dations of Political Power in the Virginia House of Burgesses, 1720–1776," *WMQ*, 3d Ser., XVI (1959), 485–506. The important subject of the correlations between influence on the King's Council and land-grant patronage did not fall within the scope of Professor Greene's study. It is a matter much in need of systematic investigation.

26. Davis, ed., "Colonial Virginia Satirist," Am. Phil. Soc., *Trans.*, N.S., LVII, Pt. 1 (1967), 52.

27. Beverley, *History of Virginia*, 255; Greene, ed., *Diary of Landon Carter*, I, 75, 93. See also *ibid.*, 124. The political aspect of the county court is treated in Sydnor, *Gentlemen Freeholders*, 78–93, and *passim*.

28. The session analyzed is that of the spring of 1752—the only one for which a full diary record survives. See Greene, ed., *Diary of Landon Carter*, I, 65–107; and *Journals of Burgesses, 1752–1755, 1756–1758*, 3–100.

29. There is a valuable discussion of archaic understandings of the nature of law and authority, sovereignty and power in colonial America in Wood, *Creation of the American Republic*, 263–264. See also Samuel Johnson, *A Dictionary of the English Language . . .* , 3d ed. (London, 1765), where the relevant explication of "law" is "a rule of justice," and the explication of "justice" is "the virtue by which we give to every man his due." For an account that emphasizes colonial politics as the disposition of resources, see Bernard Bailyn, *The Origins of American Politics* (New York, 1968), 98–101. Professor Bailyn notes, however (p. 102), that this was the de facto situation, and that it did not fit comfortably with conventional cultural stereotypes of legislative authority. If this point is stressed, an additional source of the disquiet with which colonial politics were fraught becomes apparent.

CHAPTER 7

1. William Kay to the bishop of London, June 14, 1752, in William Stevens Perry, ed., *Historical Collections Relating to the American Colonial Church*, I: *Virginia* (Hartford, Conn., 1870), 389. There was, however, another side to this affair that does not appear anywhere in the clerical correspondence. "William Kay, Clerk," had twice been called into Richmond County court to answer complaints that he subjected his wife to ill-usage—even making her "afraid of her Life." Both times he was bound over to keep the peace. Richmond County, Criminal Trials, [1710]–1754, Aug. 4, 1746, July 4, 1748, Virginia State Library, Richmond.

2. Perry, ed., *Historical Collections*, I, 389–390. On the court decision, see Fulham

Papers, 14, 53, Lambeth Palace Library, London (Virginia Colonial Records Project microfilm, Colonial Williamsburg Research Library), hereafter cited as Fulham Papers. On Carter's appeal, see Greene, ed., *Diary of Landon Carter*, I, 106. On Kay's settlement, see Perry, ed., *Historical Collections*, I, 409–410; and Fulham Papers, 14, 6, 30, 15, 139.

3. "Narrative of George Fisher," *WMQ*, 1st Ser., XVII (1908–1909), 123.

4. Richard Bland, *A Letter to the Clergy of Virginia* . . . (Williamsburg, Va., 1760), 10; Hening, ed., *Statutes at Large*, VI, 90. On Apr. 24, 1749, Landon Carter had petitioned the House of Burgesses for a clarification of the relevant laws! *Journals of Burgesses, 1742–1747, 1748–1749*, 375–376.

5. Both narrative and argument in this chapter have been condensed from Rhys Isaac, "Religion and Authority: Problems of the Anglican Establishment in Virginia in the Era of the Great Awakening and the Parsons' Cause," *WMQ*, 3d Ser., XXX (1973), 3–36. Considerations of space forbid the repetition of the attempt made there to do justice to the tone of righteousness that characterizes disputes within a genteel church or college. For detailed information on clergymen and their activities, see Joan Rezner Gundersen, "The Anglican Ministry in Virginia, 1723–1776: A Study of Social Class" (Ph.D. diss., University of Notre Dame, 1972).

6. Mar. 11, 1754, in Perry, ed., *Historical Collections*, I, 410; W. Robinson to the bishop of London, [1763], *ibid.*, 486 (emphasis added). The commissary and the bishop had been discussing schemes to curb the power of the vestries over the appointment of parsons; see also letter of July 23, 1753, *ibid.*, 406.

7. Motion in General Court, May 2, 1747, reprinted in William Henry Foote, *Sketches of Virginia, Historical and Biographical*, 1st Ser. (Philadelphia, 1850), 161; Samuel Davies, *The State of Religion among the Protestant Dissenters in Virginia* . . . (Boston, 1751), 10–11. Luther's "Comment upon the Galatians," his "Table Discourses," and "Sundry Pieces of honest Bunyan's" were named by Davies as the tracts first used. Later, a text of Whitefield's, "Sermons preached in Glasgow, and taken from his Mouth in ShortHand," came into use (*ibid.*, 9–10). On denunciation of the clergy, see Rev. Patrick Henry, Sr., to Rev. William Dawson, Feb. 13, 1744/5, *WMQ*, 2d Ser., I (1921), 263. See also George William Pilcher, *Samuel Davies, Apostle of Dissent in Colonial Virginia* (Knoxville, Tenn., 1971), 27–34.

8. Davies, *The State of Religion*, 11.

9. Henry to W. Dawson, Feb. 13, 1744/5, *WMQ*, 2d Ser., I (1921), 263; Waller to W. Dawson, Jan. 30, 1744/5, Dawson Papers, 18–20, Library of Congress.

10. The official records are printed in Foote, *Sketches of Virginia*, 1st Ser., 135, 137,

141, 142, 161, 162, 168; and Wilmer L. Hall, ed., *Executive Journals of the Council of Colonial Virginia*, V (Richmond, Va., 1945), 228.

11. "Nicholas Nameless," *Va. Gaz.*, Oct. 31, 1745; Samuel Davies, *The Impartial Trial, Impartially Tried, and Convicted of Partiality* . . . (Williamsburg, Va., 1748), 27–38. The occasion for this anonymous outburst was the recent visit of George Whitefield to Virginia. The year 1752 is the only one in the period for which more than an occasional issue of the *Virginia Gazette* survives. The 1752 file contains two heartless satires on the New Lights. See issues of Apr. 17 and May 22, 1752.

12. Henry to W. Dawson, June 8, 1747, *WMQ*, 2d Ser., I (1921), 273; petition of five clergymen (D. Mossom, Patrick Henry, John Brunskill, John Robertson, and Robert Barrett), enclosed in William Dawson's letter to the bishop of London, Aug. 16, 1751, in Perry, ed., *Historical Collections*, I, 381; Governor Gooch to the grand jury, Apr. 18, 1745, in Foote, *Sketches of Virginia*, 1st Ser., 135–136; Henry to W. Dawson, Feb. 13, 1744/5, *WMQ*, 2d Ser., I (1921), 265–266.

13. Lee to Commissioners for Trade and Plantations, Nov. 6, 1750, in Brydon, *Virginia's Mother Church*, II, 134. For Gooch's assurances, see *ibid.*, 74. For appeals by settled dissenters, see *ibid.*, 91. A similar attitude is described in Henry's letter of Feb. 13, 1774/5, to William Dawson, recounting his conversations with the Rev. John Thomson, an Old Side Presbyterian. *WMQ*, 2d Ser., I (1921), 261.

14. Davies, *The State of Religion*, 19, 32. On the license issue, see Foote, *Sketches of Virginia*, 1st Ser., 169–170.

15. May 11, 1750, C.O. 5/1327/181; extract of letter from the Board of Trade to Colonel Thomas Lee, president of the King's Council in Virginia, sent by William Dawson to the bishop of London, Aug. 16, 1752, in Perry, ed., *Historical Collections*, I, 380; Peyton Randolph to Lee, n.d., Virginia Miscellaneous, Box I, 1606[?]–1772, Lib. of Cong., hereafter cited as Va. Misc. The document may be dated 1750 with tolerable certainty (see extract of letter from the bishop of London to Philip Doddridge and Samuel Davies, Dec. 25, 1750, in Foote, *Sketches of Virginia*, 1st Ser., 177). In his diary Davies later described Peyton Randolph as "my old adversary." George William Pilcher, ed., *The Reverend Samuel Davies Abroad: The Diary of a Journey to England and Scotland, 1753–55* (Urbana, Ill., 1967), 79.

16. Randolph to Thomas Lee, n.d., Va. Misc.

17. Foote, *Sketches of Virginia*, 1st Ser., 210–213, 297; Hening, ed., *Statutes at Large*, III, 170–171.

18. The problems arising from an assumed but undefined replication of English forms by institutions in the colonies are given illuminating treatment in Bailyn, *Origins of American Politics*, 59–96. See also chap. 9, below.

19. Greene, ed., *Diary of Landon Carter*, I, 90; *Journals of Burgesses, 1752–1758*, 62; William Stith, *The Nature and Extent of Christ's Redemption . . .* (Williamsburg, Va., 1753), 30.

20. For the legend, see Henry R. McIlwaine, *The Struggle of Protestant Dissenters for Religious Toleration in Virginia*, Johns Hopkins University Studies in Historical and Political Science, IV (Baltimore, 1894), 64; Wesley M. Gewehr, *The Great Awakening in Virginia, 1740–1790* (Durham, N.C., 1930), 97–99. On the crisis of morale, see Peter Fontaine to his brothers, Mar. 2, 1756, Maury Letterbook, American Philosophical Society, Philadelphia; Richard Bland's verse letter to Landon Carter, June 20, 1758, Miscellaneous Manuscripts, Morristown National Historical Park, Morristown, N.J.; and Governor Dinwiddie, "A Proclamation, for a Fast," *Va. Gaz.*, Sept. 12, 1755. On Davies's denunciations, see Samuel Davies, *The Crisis; or, the Uncertain Doom of Kingdoms at Particular Times . . .* (London, 1757). The "Spirit of Security, Sloth, and Cowardice . . . in these Southern Colonies" is denounced and an unfavorable comparison is made with "the New England Provinces [where] a brave Spirit seems to prevail" (pp. 18, 12). See also the following by Davies: *Religion and Patriotism the Constituents of a Good Soldier . . .* (Philadelphia, 1755); *Virginia's Danger and Remedy . . .* (Williamsburg, Va., 1756); and *The Curse of Cowardice . . .* (London, 1758). On Randolph's volunteers, mentioned in the course of a lament on "this . . . Country, formerly the Seat of Peace and Unity, now of Schism & war," see Thomas Dawson's draft letter, [1756?], Dawson Papers, 151. See also *Maryland Gazette*, May 20, June 17, 1756.

21. The sermon is noted in *Va. Gaz.* (Rind), Oct. 27, 1768. The beginnings of the rehabilitation of the Presbyterians in the face of more radical dissenters appear in a letter from the Rev. James Craig, a Church of England minister, to Thomas Dawson, Sept. 8, 1759, Dawson Papers, 217. Referring to the difficulties of the Church and of the Presbyterians in the southwestern counties, Craig deplored the way "the ignorant & en[thusiastic anti]paedo-baptists, subvert all *rational* and man[ly Religion again]st us both."

22. For examples of dissenter denunciation, see Davies, *Impartial Trial*, 6, 24, 26–27, 30–31. For the clerical petition, see *Journals of Burgesses, 1752–1758*, 257; and Greene, ed., *Diary of Landon Carter*, I, 122–123. For the quoted comments of establishment clergy, see communications to the bishop of London, Nov. 29, 1755, July 9, 1757, in Perry, ed., *Historical Collections*, I, 435, 454; Craig to T. Dawson, Sept. 8, 1759, Dawson Papers, 217.

23. Waller to W. Dawson, Jan. 30, 1744/5, Dawson Papers, 20; letter to bishop of London, Feb. 1, 1754, in Perry, ed., *Historical Collections*, I, 408.

24. Landon Carter, *A Letter to the Right Reverend Father in God, the Lord B——p of L——n* . . . (London, 1760), 15, 17. Colonel Carter's pamphlet had been first published in Williamsburg in 1759. The pagination in the two editions is different.

25. The characterization of clergymen, with its revealing order, is James Maury's (see his letter to Rev. William Douglas, Nov. 20, 1759). Greene, ed., *Diary of Landon Carter*, I, 122; Carter, *Letter to the Bishop of London*, 16, 36–37.

CHAPTER 8

1. Ireland, *Life*, 72, 83–85.

2. John Williams, Journal, MS, May 10, 1771, Virginia Baptist Historical Society, University of Richmond. The author is deeply grateful to the Society for making this and other records used in this study freely available to him. A parallel account of the episode occurs in Morgan Edwards, "Materials toward a History of the Baptists in the Province of Virginia, 1772," MS, 75–76, Furman University Library, Greenville, S.C. (microfilm at the Historical Commission, Southern Baptist Convention, Nashville, Tenn.). Edwards's narrative establishes that the men were mounted, and he mentions who the principals were.

3. Williams, Journal, May 10, 1771.

4. For examples of persecutors turned converts, see Edwards, "Materials," 34, 54, 55, 73.

5. On the movement of the Separatist Shubal Stearns out of Connecticut, see Gewehr, *Great Awakening in Virginia*, 108. On the relationship of the success of the intrusive new movement to the immature state of social organization in regions near the frontier, see Richard R. Beeman and Rhys Isaac, "Cultural Conflict and Social Change in the Revolutionary South: Lunenburg County, Virginia," *Journal of Southern History*, XLVI (1980), 525–550. For a profoundly insightful analysis of the cultural, psychological oppositions between "evangelicalism" and "gentility," and of the typical familial social systems associated with each, see Greven, *Protestant Temperament*, 265–331, and *passim*.

6. David Thomas, *The Virginian Baptist or a View and Defence of the Christian Religion as It Is Professed by Baptists of Virginia* . . . (Baltimore, 1774), 59; Robert B. Semple, *A History of the Rise and Progress of the Baptists in Virginia*, ed. G. W. Beale (Richmond, Va., 1894), 30; Upper King and Queen Baptist Church, King and Queen County, Records, 1774–1816, Sept. 16, 1780. The con-

demnation cited covered the wearing of gold by either sex, and of "high crown'd caps, Rolls, Necklaces, Ruffles Stays & Stomagers" by women. (Microfilm of this and subsequently cited Baptist church books kindly provided by the Virginia Baptist Historical Society, Richmond.) On the gentleman's finery, see Farish, ed., *Journal of Fithian*, 69.

7. John Leland, *The Virginia Chronicle: With Judicious and Critical Remarks under XXIV Heads* (Norfolk, Va., 1790), 27. See also Thomas, *Virginian Baptist*, 24–25; Chestnut Grove Baptist Church, Albemarle County, Records, 1773–1779, 1792–1811, or Albemarle-Buck Mountain Baptist Church, Minute Book (hereafter cited as Albemarle Baptist Church Book), Aug. 1776. James Ireland tells how, when he had given the company of travelers to the Sandy Creek Association of 1769 an account of "what the Lord had done for my soul . . . they were very much affected . . . so much so that one of the ministers embraced me in his arms" (*Life*, 141). The Baptists, it was sneered, were "always sighing, groaning, weeping." To which David Thomas replied, "It is true lively Christians are apt to weep much, but that is often with joy instead of sorrow." *Virginian Baptist*, 59.

8. Edwards, "Materials," 25.

9. Thomas, *Virginian Baptist*, 54. See also Semple, *History of the Baptists in Virginia*, ed. Beale, 29, 43–44, 59–60; and Leland, *Virginia Chronicle*, 23. Professor Richard R. Beeman has prepared correlations of wealth and religious allegiance for a sample county. The Baptists *who can be identified* on the Lunenburg County tax lists of the 1760s had land and slaveholdings averaging only four-fifths and two-thirds of the county averages. Even these more substantial Baptists who showed up on tax lists were to a large extent transients in the region. See Beeman and Isaac, "Cultural Conflict in the Revolutionary South," *Jour. So. Hist.*, XLVI (1980), 525–550.

10. Farish, ed., *Journal of Fithian*, 157; Thomas, *Virginian Baptist*, 34.

11. Quoted from Morgan Edwards, "Notes," in Lewis Peyton Little, *Imprisoned Preachers and Religious Liberty in Virginia* (Lynchburg, Va., 1938), 243. See also Leland, *Virginia Chronicle*, 36: "At times appointed for baptism the people generally go singing to the water in grand procession: I have heard many souls declare they first were convicted or first found pardon going to, at, or coming from the water." On the rarity of congregational singing in the parish churches, see Farish, ed., *Journal of Fithian*, 195.

12. Thomas, *Virginian Baptist*, 35–36. See also Albemarle Baptist Church Book, June 18, 1774.

13. John Taylor, *A History of Ten Baptist Churches . . .* (Frankfort, Ky., 1823), 296.

14. Edwards, "Materials," 56; Albemarle Baptist Church Book, Nov. 17, 1775, Aug. 1776; Semple, *History of the Baptists in Virginia,* ed. Beale, 81.

15. Taylor, *History of Ten Baptist Churches,* 7, 16. See also Ireland, *Life,* 191; Semple, *History of the Baptists in Virginia,* ed. Beale, 63; Garnett Ryland, *The Baptists of Virginia, 1699–1926* (Richmond, Va., 1955), 53–54. John Williams estimated that "4 or 5000" came to hear the preaching at the association meeting at Blue Run Church, Orange County, in May 1771 (see Journal, May 12, 1771). For a vivid contemporary account of the noisy manifestations associated with the large meetings, see Little, *Imprisoned Preachers,* 243.

16. Ireland, *Life,* 185. Laboring day and night, "preaching three times a day very often, as well as once at night," Ireland must have kept himself in an *exalté,* near trancelike condition. His instruction to those who came to him impressed with "their helpless condition" is also illuminating. "I would immediately direct them where their help was to be had, and that it was their duty to be as much engaged for the salvation of their souls, as if they thought they could be saved by their own works; but not to rest upon such engagedness." An evangelist's working compromise between predestination and free grace! *Ibid.,* 186.

17. The quotation is from Farish, ed., *Journal of Fithian,* 72. On the general sense of disorder, see introduction to Greene, ed., *Diary of Landon Carter,* I, 1, 14, 17–19, 21, 25, 33, 39, 44, 47, 52–53; Gordon S. Wood, "Rhetoric and Reality in the American Revolution," *WMQ,* 3d Ser., XXIII (1966), 27–31; and Jack P. Greene, "Search for Identity: An Interpretation of the Meaning of Selected Patterns of Social Response in Eighteenth-Century America," *Journal of Social History,* III (1969–1970), 195–205.

18. Edwards, "Materials," 25, 69, 89; Semple, *History of the Baptists in Virginia,* ed. Beale, 19–20, 27, 32–33, 227. I have closely read the following Baptist church records for the period up to 1790: Albemarle Baptist Church Book; Broad Run Baptist Church, Fauquier County, Records, 1762–1873; Chesterfield Baptist Church, Chesterfield County, Records, 1773–1788; Hartwood-Potomac Baptist Church, Stafford County, Minute Book, 1771–1859; Mill Swamp Baptist Church, Isle of Wight County, Records (1774), 1777–1790; Morattico Baptist Church, Lancaster County, Records (1764), 1778–1844; Smith's Creek Baptist Church, Shenandoah and Rockingham counties, Records, 1779–1809 (1805); Upper King and Queen Baptist Church, Recs.

19. Edwards, "Materials," 72–76, quotation on p. 73.

20. Albemarle Baptist Church Book, Dec. 1776; Morattico Baptist Church, Recs., Feb. 17, 1783.

21. Mill Swamp Baptist Church, Recs., Mar. 13, June 19, 1778; Hartwood-Potomac

Baptist Church, Minute Book, 1776, 9–10. The scope of the "queries" (the standard form for raising an issue for consideration in the monthly meetings of the church members) is a clear indication of the extent to which the Baptists were engaged in a radical reappraisal of traditional mores. In 1778 the Mill Swamp Baptist Church, Isle of Wight County, even discussed the question, "Is it agreable to the Spirit of Christiannity to buy and sell principally with a view of getting gain[?]" (Not surprisingly, they decided: "yes if no unlawfull means be taken." Recs., Mar. 13, 1778.)

22. Ireland, *Life*, 44; Thomas, *Virginian Baptist*, 34–35.

23. Thomas, *Virginian Baptist*, 57–58, 24, 31. On the use of bodily "purity" as a symbolic system for the control of social boundaries, see Douglas, *Natural Symbols*, 12, and *passim*.

24. Mill Swamp Baptist Church, Recs., Apr. 4, 1778. See also W. Harrison Daniel, "Virginia Baptists and the Negro in the Early Republic," *VMHB*, LXXX (1972), 60–69.

25. Semple, *History of the Baptists in Virginia*, ed. Beale, 291–292. I am indebted to Philip Morgan for discussion of this aspect of the movement, and to Donald G. Mathews, *Religion in the Old South* (Chicago, 1977), 185–250, where extremely valuable formulations are given concerning the meaning of conversion for the slaves.

26. Thomas, *Virginian Baptist*, 57; John Blair to the king's attorney in Spotsylvania County, July 16, 1768, in Little, *Imprisoned Preachers*, 100–101.

27. On the rate of growth, see Gewehr, *Great Awakening in Virginia*, 117.

28. Little, *Imprisoned Preachers*, 36; Thomas, *Virginian Baptist*, 54; Leland, *Virginia Chronicle*, 23; *Va. Gaz.* (Purdie and Dixon), Oct. 31, 1771. See also Semple, *History of the Baptists in Virginia*, ed. Beale, 29, 43–44, 59–60.

29. Edwards, "Materials," 86–88.

30. John Waller to an unknown fellow Baptist, Aug. 12, 1771, in Little, *Imprisoned Preachers*, 276; Thomas, *Virginian Baptist*, 33–36.

31. *Va. Gaz.* (Purdie and Dixon), Oct. 4, 1770. Thomas stated that there was no evil that "has not been reported of us" (*Virginian Baptist*, 6). James Madison referred in a letter to the "religion . . . of some enthusiasts, . . . of such a nature as to fan the amorous fire" (Madison to William Bradford, Apr. 1, 1774, in William T. Hutchinson *et al.*, eds., *The Papers of James Madison* [Chicago, 1962–], I, 112). See also Richard J. Hooker, ed., *The Carolina Backcountry on the Eve of the Revolution: The Journal and Other Writings of Charles Woodmason, Anglican Itinerant* (Chapel Hill, N.C., 1953), 98, 100–104, 113–117, for more unrestrained fantasies concerning the emergent southern Baptists.

32. Ireland, *Life*, 129–134.

33. Edwards, "Materials," 88. Although Samuel Harris, renouncing the world, gave up his newly built countryseat to be a meetinghouse for his church, the role of patron died hard. He would occasionally slaughter cattle for the love feasts that were held at the meetinghouse. *Ibid.*, 57.

34. The tension was manifested in bitter but inconclusive debates on adjustments to the religious institutions of the society. These debates (the subject of the next two chapters in this book) took place not only in newspapers and pamphlets but also in the exalted House of Burgesses.

CHAPTER 9

1. Thomas Gwatkin, *A Letter to the Clergy of New York and New Jersey . . .* (Williamsburg, Va., 1772), 4; *Va. Gaz.* (Purdie & Dixon), May 9, 1771, hereafter cited as *Va. Gaz.* (P & D).

2. For a brief account of anticlericalism—scarcely adequate in view of the subject's importance to its author's study—see Peter Gay, *The Enlightenment: An Interpretation,* I: *The Rise of Modern Paganism* (New York, 1966), 371–380.

3. On the dark and fearful view, see Bernard Bailyn, *The Ideological Origins of the American Revolution* (Cambridge, Mass., 1967), 55–93. On "Gothick" liberty, see Pocock, "Machiavelli, Harrington, and the Eighteenth Century," *WMQ,* 3d Ser., XXII (1965), 561–583.

4. Gwatkin, *Letter to the Clergy,* 4–5. This is clearly a partisan account. However, it corresponds to impressions generally received concerning what had happened. See also Richard Bland's reference to "Jangle and Disputation" in his letter to Thomas Adams, Aug. 1, 1771, in *WMQ,* 1st Ser., V (1896–1897), 153.

5. *Va. Gaz.* (P & D), June 6, 1771; *Va. Gaz.* (Rind), June 6, 1771, hereafter cited as *Va. Gaz.* (R). Hewitt and Bland's protest is not extant save for a portion quoted in [Thomas Bradbury Chandler], *An Address from the Clergy of New-York and New-Jersey, to the Episcopalians in Virginia . . .* (New York, 1771), 38–39.

6. Perry, ed., *Historical Collections,* I, 471. For biographical profiles, see Edward Lewis Goodwin, *The Colonial Church in Virginia* (Milwaukee, Wis., 1927), 258, 278. On Camm's contentious role in the Parsons' Cause affair, see Isaac, "Religion and Authority," *WMQ,* 3d Ser., XXX (1973), 10, 12, 13, 15–16, 20–21. On Henley and Gwatkin, see E. Alfred Jones, "Two Professors of William and Mary College," *ibid.,* 1st Ser., XXVI (1917–1918), 221–231; Ray Hiner, Jr., "Samuel Henley and Thomas Gwatkin; Partners in Protest," *Historical Magazine of the Protestant Episcopal Church,* XXXVII (1968), 39–50; and especially Fraser Neiman, "The Letters of William Gilpin to Samuel Henley," *Huntington Library*

Quarterly, XXXV (1971–1972), 159–162. Professor Neiman has corrected a number of prevailing errors concerning Henley; I am grateful to him for sharing his scholarship and his interest with me.

7. Bland to Adams, Aug. 1, 1771, *WMQ*, 1st Ser., V (1896–1897), 153; it appears that there were some 32 contributions to the debate in the two newspapers (not all extant). Of these, 16 can be identified on either side. There were 8 protagonists of episcopacy (of whom John Camm and William Willie signed their papers; the others wrote under pseudonyms). The corresponding figure for the opposition was 9 antagonists, of whom 2 (Henley and Gwatkin) wrote under their own names.

8. *Va. Gaz.* (P & D), June 20, 1771; Bland to Adams, Aug. 1, 1771, *WMQ*, 1st Ser., V (1896–1897), 154.

9. *Journals of Burgesses, 1770–1772*, 122.

10. See Carl Bridenbaugh, *Mitre and Sceptre: Transatlantic Faiths, Ideas, Personalities, and Politics, 1689–1775* (New York, 1962), *passim*. A brief account, largely concerned with intercolonial connections, is included in Arthur Lyon Cross, *The Anglican Episcopate and the American Colonies* (New York, 1902; reprinted Hamden, Conn., 1964). The imperial conflict aspect of the debate is stressed in George W. Pilcher, "Virginia Newspapers and the Dispute over the Proposed Colonial Episcopate, 1771–1772," *Historian*, XXIII (1960–1961), 98–113. See also Brydon, *Virginia's Mother Church*, II, 341–364.

11. "Country Clergyman" quoted by "Country Gentleman," *Va. Gaz.* (P & D), June 27, 1771; "Protest of the Revd. Messrs. Hewitt and Bland," cited in [Chandler], *An Address*, 38–39.

12. "A Real Layman," *Va. Gaz.* (P & D), June 20, 1771; "A Country Clergyman," *ibid.* (R), July 18, 1771.

13. "The Collector," *ibid.* (P & D) and (R), May 16, 1771; "Criticus," *ibid.* (P & D), Jan. 23, 1772; Samuel Henley, *ibid.*, Oct. 17, 1771.

14. I have used the edition printed by Samuel Keimer (Philadelphia, 1723). For Trenchard and Gordon's part in the formation of American political world views, see Bailyn, *Ideological Origins*, 35–54. That issues of Church and State were not the dominant ones in the American Revolution has naturally resulted in a deemphasis of one of the leading preoccupations of the publicists who established much of the framework of American Revolutionary political thought. It is clear from abundant repetitions that—like Voltaire—Trenchard and Gordon saw in clericalism the principal enemy. They were obsessed with the power of the priesthood to mold the minds of the credulous majority into shapes of deference and submission altogether incompatible with their own ideals of secular, limited, and strictly controlled government.

15. William Nelson to Edward Hunt, May 11, 1771, *WMQ*, 1st Ser., V (1896–1897), 149; Bland to Adams, Aug. 1, 1771, *ibid.*, 154.

16. *Va. Gaz.* (P & D), June 13, 1771; *ibid.* (R), Aug. 1, 1771; *ibid.* (P & D), Oct. 10, 1771. See also "Country Gentleman," *ibid.*, July 4, 1771; and "Country Farmer," *ibid.*, Dec. 19, 1771.

17. Richard Burn, *Ecclesiastical Law* (London, 1763), I, 485–486. The question of deprivation became more complex when the parish church was considered a "donative." *Ibid.*, 534–535.

18. The origin of the Virginia debate has generally been assumed to be pressure from Church of England clergy in the Middle Colonies (Cross, *Anglican Episcopate*, 231; Bridenbaugh, *Mitre and Sceptre*, 317–318). Such pressure was exerted, and reference is made to it in letters from Dr. Chandler ("Country Gentleman," *Va. Gaz.* [P & D], May 30, 1771) in the first extant polemic. However, the Chandler group had been seeking support from the South since 1766 (Bridenbaugh, *Mitre and Sceptre*, 317), and therefore a reason must be sought as to why a response to their exhortation came at this particular time.

19. William Nelson to Lord Hillsborough, Apr. 17, 1771, in John C. Van Horne, ed., *The Correspondence of William Nelson as Acting Governor of Virginia, 1770–1771* (Charlottesville, Va., 1975), 137.

20. Brydon, *Virginia's Mother Church*, II, 324–331; Fulham Papers, 15, 127.

21. Thomas Jefferson, *Reports of Cases Determined in the General Court of Virginia, from 1730–1740; and from 1768–1772* (Charlottesville, Va., 1903; orig. publ. 1829), 52–53; Brydon, *Virginia's Mother Church*, II, 327, 331. George Wythe rested his case simply on the wording of the statute establishing the court, which gave it "cognisance of . . . all causes relating to . . . any person or persons ecclesiastical or civil." Richard Bland, a veteran defender of the rights of vestries, expressed the opinion that the Virginia church was sui generis on account of the circumstances under which it was established; that the vestries were the founders and patrons; and that they accordingly held the right of visitation, empowering them to deprive their own incumbents if they saw fit. Thomas Jefferson maintained an opposed position: that parishes were established not by the vestry but by statute, and that therefore patronage and visitation belonged to the crown, to be exercised in Chancery (or its Virginia substitute, the General Court). Jefferson, *Reports of Cases*, 52–53.

22. *Journals of Burgesses, 1770–1772*, 275, entry for Mar. 27, 1772. Wise heads must have counseled the managers of the House that such an invasion of royal prerogative would never be permitted, since no more came of this proposal.

23. From the start of the polemical exchange allusions were made to clerical immorality in general and to this pending case: "Country Gentleman," *Va. Gaz.*

(P & D), May 30, June 20, 27, 1771; John Camm, *ibid.*, June 13, 1771; "A Churchman," *ibid.* (R), Sept. 26, 1771. For the argument that clerical delinquency made a bishop indispensable, see "Country Gentleman," *ibid.* (P & D), June 20, 1771.

24. "The Country Gentleman's Answer to the Real Layman," *ibid.*, July 4, 1771; "A Country Farmer," *ibid.*, Dec. 19, 1771.

25. Williams, Journal, May 12, 14, 1771.

26. Little, *Imprisoned Preachers*, 44–49, 229, 249, 275–276, 312, and *passim*; Edwards, "Materials," 74, 76. At least a further 10 bonds to keep the peace had been demanded, though the records do not reveal whether imprisonment resulted.

27. William Green to Nathaniel Saunders, Feb. 7, 1767, in Little, *Imprisoned Preachers*, 78. The writer also protested: "Worse could not be said of the Pagans & Idolators, who sacrificed their Children to Moloch, than has been said by some of your Society, concerning the Church and its Members; the Ministers not excepted" (*ibid.*, 80–81); "An Address to the Anabaptists," *Va. Gaz.* (P & D), Feb. 20, 1772. Morgan Edwards, "Materials," is suffused with evidence of the intensity with which the Baptists had taken on the identity of a people persecuted for righteousness' sake and committed to spiritual combat against the existing order.

28. The Baptists were constantly so designated by their opponents. For an obvious attempt to associate the Virginia movement with the "excesses" of the Munster "Anabaptists," see *Va. Gaz.* (P & D), Oct. 4, 1770.

29. "A Country Farmer," *ibid.*, Dec. 19, 1771; "A Country Gentleman," *ibid.*, May 30, 1771; and "A Country Man," *ibid.* (R), Sept. 5, 1771. See also "A Country Gentleman," *ibid.* (P & D), July 4, 1771; "Church of England Man," *ibid.*, Oct. 10, 1771; and "An American," *ibid.*, Nov. 21, 1771.

30. "Church of England Man's Ammanuensis, J. H.," *ibid.*, Jan. 9, 1772; Gwatkin, *Letter to the Clergy*, 15; *Va. Gaz.* (P & D), Nov. 21, 1771.

31. "Church of England Man," *Va. Gaz.* (P & D), Oct. 10, 1771; "An American," *ibid.*, Nov. 21, 1771; "Country Farmer," *ibid.*, Dec. 19, 1771. For an extremely illuminating treatment of the role of idealized images of England, see Greene, "Search for Identity," *Jour. Soc. Hist.*, III (1969–1970), 205–218.

32. "Country Clergyman," quoted by "Country Gentleman," *Va. Gaz.* (P & D), June 27, 1771; "Churchman," *ibid.* (R), Sept. 26, 1771; Bland to Adams, Aug. 1, 1771, *WMQ*, 1st Ser., V (1896–1897), 154. See also Samuel Henley, *Va. Gaz.* (P & D), June 20, 1771: "the *gorgeous Trappings of Hierarchical Pomp.*"

33. Samuel Henley, *Va. Gaz.* (R), Aug. 8, 1771; "A Real Layman," *ibid.* (P & D), June 20, 1771; James Madison, *An Oration, in Commemoration of the Founders of*

William and Mary College . . . (Williamsburg, Va., 1772), 8–9. Emphasis added to the last quotation.

34. "A Churchman," *Va. Gaz.* (R), Sept. 26, 1771; Richard Henry Lee to William Lee, June 19, 1771, James Curtis Ballagh, ed., *The Letters of Richard Henry Lee* (New York, 1911–1914), I, 59; same to same, May 21, 1772, *ibid.*, 66.

35. Gwatkin, quoted in Camm, *Va. Gaz.* (P & D), Aug. 15, 1771; *ibid.*, Mar. 5, 1772.

36. For questioning of the courts, see "Philo Virginiae," *ibid.*, Oct. 24, 1771; "Philo Patriae," *ibid.*, Dec. 12, 1771. See also "A Traveller," *ibid.* (R), Feb. 18, 1773; and "Country Justice," *ibid.*, Dec. 30, 1773. On the college, see "Philanthropos Americanus," *ibid.* (P & D), Feb. 20, 1772; and "Academicus," *ibid.* (R), May 19, 26, 1774. On the militia, see *ibid.*, May 12, 1774.

37. Hening, ed., *Statutes at Large*, II, 46, III, 361. See also *ibid.*, IV, 244, and V, 225–226, where it quite clearly appears that the purpose of the 1705 Virginia legislation was the maintenance of Christian morality, and that the problem of allowing for Protestant dissent was largely ignored.

38. See p. 151, above. The greater stringency of the Virginia application of the law appears clearly in a letter from Philip Doddridge to Samuel Davies, 1751, in Foote, *Sketches of Virginia*, 1st Ser., 174–176. It must be supposed that the belief that the Act of Toleration applied to Virginia, although it could only be validated by reference to the Virginia statute 4 Anne c. xxx, was not based on that act but rested rather on the assumption that the Toleration Act was an essential part of the British constitution. For the power of assumed analogy between the constitution of Britain and those of the colonies, see Bailyn, *Origins of American Politics*, 59–65.

39. MS in Virginia Baptist Historical Society, University of Richmond, quoted in Gewehr, *Great Awakening in Virginia*, 94n; President John Blair to king's attorney in Spotsylvania County, July 16, 1768, in Little, *Imprisoned Preachers*, 100–101. The Orange County bench, making a similar committal three weeks later, however, added a denunciation of the religious character of the offenses. The preachers were charged not only as "Vagrant and Itinerant Persons" but also "for Assembling themselves unlawfully . . . Under the Denomination of Anabaptists and for Teaching . . . Schismatick Doctrines." The absence of reference to the actual laws violated suggests that strong feelings served as a substitute for rigorous legality among the magistrates. *Ibid.*, 135–136.

40. Fauquier County, Order Book, 1768–1772, pp. 163–164, entry for Feb. 26, 1770; Caroline County, Order Book, 1770–1772, p. 211, entry for June 13, 1771, both printed in Little, *Imprisoned Preachers*, 193, 236 (see also *ibid.*, 141, 246, 249, 269, 280, 312); James Ireland, *Life*, 179. In the case of Phillip Spiller (one

of the dissenters tried) the magistrates displayed further confusion, ruling: (1) that the Baptist church itself could authorize preachers; and (2) that unlicensed preachers might legally preach at licensed meetinghouses. Little, *Imprisoned Preachers*, 70–71.

41. "An Address to the Anabaptists," *Va. Gaz.* (P & D), Feb. 20, 1772.

42. *Ibid.*, Aug. 22, 1771.

43. "An Address to the Anabaptists," *ibid.*, Feb. 20, 1772.

44. *Journals of Burgesses, 1770–1772*, 185–186. For other petitions, see *ibid.*, 160, 182–183, 186. The bill was printed in *Va. Gaz.* (R), Mar. 26, 1772. For a firsthand account of its passage through the committees, see Robert Carter Nicholas, *ibid.*, June 10, 1773.

45. *Journals of Burgesses, 1770–1772*, 249.

46. James Madison to William Bradford, Jan. 24, Apr. 1, 1774, in Hutchinson *et al.*, eds., *Madison Papers*, I, 106, 112.

47. "Timoleon," *Va. Gaz.* (P & D), Aug. 22, 1771. The "Hoadleianus" letter is only partly extant. Some of its contents and the indignation it aroused can be reconstructed from the protests of Robert Carter Nicholas printed *ibid.* (R), June 10, 1773. See also Samuel Henley, *The Distinct Claims of Government and Religion Considered in a Sermon Preached before the Honourable House of Burgesses, at Williamsburg, in Virginia, March 1, 1772* (Cambridge, Mass., 1772).

48. Madison, *An Oration*, 9–14.

49. *Ibid.*, 13.

CHAPTER 10

1. The evidence upon which this reconstruction is based is scattered in the following sources: Samuel Henley to John Bracken, *Va. Gaz.* (P & D), Feb. 3, 17, 1774; Richard Bland to Purdie and Dixon, *ibid.*, Mar. 10, 1774; Robert Carter Nicholas to Samuel Henley, *ibid.*, Feb. 24, 1774; Nicholas to "Clergyman of the Church of England," *ibid.*, June 3, 1773; John Bracken to Samuel Henley, *ibid.*, Dec. 23, 1773, supp., Mar. 3, 1774. Henley still had possession of the "Church Plate and the Poor's Money," which he was obliged to deliver to Bracken after his election. Bracken to Henley, *ibid.*, Mar. 3, 1774.

2. Jones, *Present State of Virginia*, ed. Morton, 70; *Va. Gaz.* (P & D), Feb. 15, 1770. On the architecture of Bruton, see Whiffen, *Public Buildings of Williamsburg*, 77–84, 146, 150–152.

3. For early references to the lectureship, see Jones, *Present State of Virginia*, ed. Morton, 70; and James Blair to the bishop of London, July 15, 1724, in Perry,

ed., *Historical Collections*, I, 299. For the worthy's comments on the Reverend Mr. Johnson, see William Nelson to John Norton, Dec. 13, 1766, Norton Papers, Research Department Library, Colonial Williamsburg Foundation, Inc., Williamsburg, Va. See also obituary of Johnson, *Va. Gaz.* (R) and (P & D), Apr. 8, 1773. For the indication of tastes in divinity, see Bland to John Norton, July 1772, in Frances Norton Mason, ed., *John Norton & Sons, Merchants of London and Virginia: Being the Papers from Their Counting House for the Years 1750–1795* (Richmond, Va., 1937), 259. The sermons of Yorrick (Laurence Sterne) and William Dodd evidently corresponded so well to current taste that they were in stock at the printing office in Williamsburg and thus were too well known to serve. See *Va. Gaz.* (P & D), June 10, 1773.

4. Henley to Bracken, *Va. Gaz.* (P & D), Feb. 17, 1774 (my emphasis); Bracken to Henley, *ibid.*, Mar. 3, 1774. The *Oxford English Dictionary* entry under "jessamy" is in itself an eloquent commentary upon the taste and style of an age! John Langhorne (1735–1779) was an English clergyman, poet, and fashionable man of letters. His collected *Sermons on Practical Subjects* . . . were published in 1773 in London. Perhaps the Reverend Mr. Bracken brought the two volumes out with him in his luggage (see *Dictionary of National Biography*, 2d ed., s.v. "Langhorne, John"). For a witty verse satire upon a contemporary sermon borrower, see *Va. Gaz.* (R), Mar. 11, 1773.

5. *Va. Gaz.* (P & D), Aug. 24, 1769, May 13, 1773. For the career of James Ferguson, Fellow of the Royal Society (1710–1776), see *DNB*, 2d ed.

6. Nicholas to John Norton, Apr. 24, 1773, in Mason, ed., *John Norton & Sons*, 314; *History of William and Mary College* (Baltimore, 1870), 36.

7. The information concerning Nicholas's career has been ably drawn together in Victor Dennis Golladay, "The Nicholas Family of Virginia, 1722–1820" (Ph.D. diss., University of Virginia, 1973). See also David John Mays, *Edmund Pendleton, 1721–1803: A Biography* (Cambridge, Mass., 1952), I, 188; and Ernst, *Money and Politics*, 180–184, 187–192.

8. Nicholas to Henley, *Va. Gaz.* (P & D), May 20, 1772; John Page of Rosewell to Mrs. Rind, *ibid.* (R), May 19, 1774; Bland to Purdie and Dixon, *ibid.* (P & D), Mar. 10, 1774. See also Nicholas to Henley, *ibid.*, Feb. 24, 1774.

9. Bland to Purdie and Dixon, *Va. Gaz.* (P & D), Mar. 10, 1774; Henley to Nicholas, *ibid.*, June 3, 1773.

10. *Ibid.* (R), May 19, 1774; Bland to Purdie and Dixon, *ibid.* (P & D), Mar. 10, Feb. 24, 1774.

11. "Church of England Man's Amannuensis: J. H.," *ibid.*, Jan. 9, 1772; "Ruricola," *ibid.* (R), Feb. 6, 1772.

12. *Ibid.* (P & D), May 20, 1773, supp., Feb. 24, 1774.

13. Henley, *Distinct Claims*, [vi], 1–2; Nicholas to "Hoadleianus," *Va. Gaz.* (R), June 10, 1773. The "Dedication" and "Advertisement" in the printed sermon are not paginated.
14. Henley, *Distinct Claims*, 4, 8, 14.
15. *Ibid.*, 16.
16. Nicholas to "Hoadleianus," *Va. Gaz.* (R), June 10, 1773. The bill was approved by the whole House on Mar. 12, 1772, but "some Gentlemen . . . express'd their Apprehensions that *these* [restrictions] might give Uneasiness to some of the Dissenters" and requested that after the bill was engrossed it might be printed and referred to the public for discussion (*ibid.*). See also *Journals of Burgesses, 1770–1772,* 249.
17. Only part of the "Hoadleianus" letter is extant (*Va. Gaz.* [R], Mar. 5, 1772). The remainder has had to be reconstructed from Nicholas's extensive commentaries. The passages above are quoted from Nicholas to "Hoadleianus," *ibid.*, June 10, 1773.
18. For Nicholas's exchange with his fellow burgesses, his denunciation of "Hoadleianus," and the latter's reply, see *ibid.* (R), June 10, 1773, and "Hoadleianus" to Nicholas, *ibid.*, June 3, 1773. Nicholas's reply elicited the virtual admission that "Hoadleianus" was Henley's associate (Gwatkin, *ibid.*, June 10, 17, 1773). "Hoadleianus" made the statement that Nicholas's denunciation took place during "a late debate concerning an American Episcopate." Since no record exists of a debate on this topic in the House of Burgesses after Mar. 5, 1772, we may conclude that the proceedings were those that gave rise to the order on Mar. 27, that a bill be prepared "to establish a Jurisdiction for superintending the Conduct of the Clergy" (*Journals of Burgesses, 1770–1772,* 275–277). The issue of clerical discipline was, of course, inextricably intertwined with that of episcopacy. On Henley's outburst, see *Va. Gaz.* (P & D), May 20, 1773, supp.
19. *Va. Gaz.* (R), June 10, 1773; Henley, *Distinct Claims*, [iii–iv, vi, viii].
20. *Va. Gaz.* (P & D), May 20, 1773.
21. *Ibid.*, July 30, 1772, May 20, 1773, supp.; Henley to Nicholas, *ibid.*, June 3, 1773.
22. *Ibid.*, 1772–1774, *passim.* Especially see "Criticus," *ibid.* (P & D), Jan. 23, Feb. 6, 13, 1772; also "Adante Brioso," *ibid.* (R), Mar. 4, 1773, and replies, Mar. 18, 1773; and *ibid.* (P & D), Mar. 18, 1773. For Nicholas's censure, see *ibid.*, May 20, 1773.
23. William Leigh, *An Oration, in Commemoration of the Founders of William and Mary* . . . (Williamsburg, Va., 1771); Madison, *An Oration,* 9.
24. Madison, *An Oration,* 10, 11, 13.

25. Nicholas to Henley, *Va. Gaz.* (P & D), May 20, 1773, supp.; Henley to Nicholas, *ibid.*, June 3, 1773.

26. *Ibid.* (R), Apr. 8, 1773; Nicholas to Henley, *ibid.* (P & D), May 20, 1773, supp. John Bracken was a young clergyman about whose antecedents and coming to Virginia little is known (see Rutherfoord Goodwin, "The Reverend John Bracken [1745–1818]: Rector of Bruton Parish and President of William and Mary College in Virginia," *Historical Magazine of the Protestant Episcopal Church*, X [1941], 354–389). He went along with the patriot movement, became master of the grammar school at The College of William and Mary, served briefly as president, and in 1812 was bishop-elect of Virginia but resigned before consecration. He married "well"—into the Burwell family (related to Robert Carter Nicholas) in 1776—thereby cementing his relationship with some of the chief families of the Old Dominion.

27. See Thomas Jefferson, "Biographical Sketches of Distinguished Men," in Andrew A. Lipscomb and Albert Ellery Bergh, eds., *The Writings of Thomas Jefferson* (Washington, D.C., 1903–1904), XVIII, 135–140; *Dictionary of American Biography*, s.v. "Randolph, Peyton." On the march of the volunteers, see *Maryland Gazette*, May 20, 1756. The fullest compilation of information and scholarly reasoning on questions of chronology involved is to be found in the Colonial Williamsburg Research Department file on the Peyton Randolph House. I am deeply grateful for the assistance I have received through access to this and other research findings prepared by the Colonial Williamsburg Foundation.

28. For the exchanges that give clues concerning Henley's backers, see Bracken to Henley, *Va. Gaz.* (P & D), Dec. 16, 1773, supp.; Henley to Bracken, *ibid.*, Jan. 20, 1774; Henley to Nicholas, *ibid.*, June 3, 1773; "Hoadleianus" to Nicholas, *ibid.* (R), June 3, 14, 1773; see also Nicholas to Henley, *ibid.*, June 10, 1773; *Journals of Burgesses, 1773–1776*, 26. On Randolph's Masonic connection, see George E. Kidd, *Early Freemasonry in Williamsburg, Virginia* (Richmond, Va., 1957), 10, and *passim*. For an explicit reference to the feud between the Randolphs and Robert Carter Nicholas, see the memoir of the Speaker's nephew Edmund Randolph, cited in Moncure Daniel Conway, *Omitted Chapters of History Disclosed in the Life and Papers of Edmund Randolph . . .* (New York, 1888), 37.

29. Bracken to Henley, *Va. Gaz.* (P & D), Feb. 17, 1774; Nicholas to "A Clergyman of the Church of England," *ibid.*, June 3, 1773; Henley to "The Real Associator," *ibid.* (Dixon and Hunter), Mar. 4, 1775, hereafter cited as *Va. Gaz.* (D & H).

30. Henley, *ibid.* (P & D), Mar. 10, 1774. The broadside is not extant but its con-

tents can be partly reconstructed from Henley to Nicholas, *ibid.*, June 3, 1773; and Nicholas to Henley, *ibid.*, June 10, 1773. For Russell's role, see Henley, *ibid.*, Jan. 20, 1774; see also Kidd, *Early Freemasonry in Williamsburg*, 23, 29. Samuel Shields, like James Madison, was a William and Mary student who became a republican clergyman in the post-Revolution Protestant Episcopal church (see Edward Lewis Goodwin, *The Colonial Church in Virginia* [Milwaukee and London, 1927], 290, 307).

31. Nicholas to Henley, *Va. Gaz.* (P & D), Feb. 24, 1774; Henley to "Real Associator," *ibid.* (D & H), Mar. 4, 1775; Joseph Kidd, *ibid.* (P & D), May 20, 1773; Joseph Kidd, *ibid.* (Pinkney), Mar. 16, 30, 1775; "Lectum viri, vel legendum esse," *ibid.*, Mar. 23, 1775. The fun that the wits made of the tradesman who "commenced author" (*ibid.*) is a revealing comment on the social status of literacy in that age. Obsession with, and apology for, style appear everywhere. For a striking instance, see Page to Rind, *ibid.* (R), May 19, 1774.

32. Henley, *ibid.* (P & D), Mar. 10, 1774, May 13, 1773; Nicholas, *ibid.*, May 20, supp., June 3, 1773 (from which the "Clergyman's" broadside is partly known); "Hoadleianus," *ibid.* (R), June 3, 1773. The satiric names were bestowed by "Rigdumfunnidos," *ibid.* (Pinkney), Mar. 16, 1775.

33. Bland to Purdie and Dixon, *ibid.* (P & D), Mar. 10, 1774.

34. *Ibid.* For the identity of the angered gentleman, see Nicholas to Henley, *ibid.* (P & D), Feb. 24, 1774.

35. Bland, *ibid.* (P & D), Mar. 10, 1774. See also Nicholas to Henley, *ibid.*, Feb. 24, 1774, where it appears the proceedings began with the treasurer proposing that the witnesses be sworn, but Henley "was polite enough to desire that this Ceremony might be waved [sic]."

36. Bland to Purdie and Dixon, *ibid.*, Mar. 10, 1774; Nicholas to Henley, *ibid.*, Feb. 24, 1774; Henley to Bracken, *ibid.*, Feb. 17, 1774.

37. Bland to Purdie and Dixon, *ibid.*, Mar. 10, 1774.

38. Nicholas to Henley, *ibid.*, Feb. 24, 1774; Bracken to Henley, *ibid.*, Dec. 23, 1773.

39. Quotations from Henley to Nicholas, *ibid.*, June 3, 1773; and Samuel Henley to the Rev. Mr. Bracken, *ibid.*, Dec. 9, 1773, Jan. 20, 1774. On the lectureship squabble, see also Henley to Bracken, *ibid.*, Feb. 17, 1774; "A Parishioner of Bruton" to Bracken, *ibid.*, Dec. 16, 1773; Bracken to Henley, *ibid.*, Dec. 23, 1773, supp., Mar. 3, 1774; "An Inhabitant of Bruton" to Bracken, *ibid.*, Dec. 30, 1773.

40. Nicholas to Henley, *ibid.*, Feb. 24, 1774.

41. Bland to Purdie and Dixon, *ibid.*, Mar. 10, 1774; Page to Rind, *ibid.* (R), May 19, 1774; *ibid.* (P & D), Feb. 2, 1774; "An Enemy to Captious Parsons," *ibid.* (R), Apr. 21, 1774.

42. "An Associator," *ibid.* (P & D), Dec. 8, 1774; "A Real Associator," *ibid.*, Dec. 15, 29, 1775; Henley, *ibid.*, Dec. 22, 1775; *ibid.* (D & H), Mar. 4, 25, 1775. Joseph Kidd, *ibid.* (Pinkney), Mar. 16, 30, 1775; "Inimicus Mendaci," *ibid.*, Feb. 23, 1775. For the professors' departure, see Jones, "Two Professors," *WMQ*, 1st Ser., XXVI (1917–1918), 222, 225.

43. Henley, *Distinct Claims*, [iii]; Nicholas to Henley (quoting Henley), *Va. Gaz.* (P & D), May 20, 1773, supp.

44. Henley's writings, *passim*; Henley, *Distinct Claims*, 2, 11, 12; Henley to Nicholas, *Va. Gaz.* (P & D), June 3, 1773; Bland to Purdie and Dixon, *ibid.*, Mar. 10, 1774.

45. Nicholas to Henley, *Va. Gaz.* (P & D), May 20, 1773, supp.

46. Henley, *Distinct Claims*, [iii]; "Hoadleianus" to Nicholas, *Va. Gaz.* (R), June 3, 1773; Madison, *An Oration*, 10.

47. Nicholas to "Hoadleianus," *Va. Gaz.* (P & D), June 10, 1773; Nicholas to "A Clergyman of the Church of England," *ibid.*, June 3, 1773; Nicholas to Henley, *ibid.*, May 12, Feb. 24, 1774.

48. *Ibid.*, June 3, 1773.

49. *Ibid.*, May 20, 1773, supp.; Nicholas to "A Clergyman," *ibid.*, June 3, 1773.

50. *Va. Gaz.* (R), June 10, 1773.

CHAPTER 11

1. *Va. Gaz.* (P & D), June 2, 1774.

2. *Ibid.*, May 26, 1774.

3. *Va. Gaz.* (D & H), May 26, 1774; George Mason to Martin Cockburn, May 26, 1774, in Rutland, ed., *Mason Papers*, I, 191.

4. Farish, ed., *Journal of Fithian*, 111; for the decline of the non-importation association, see William Nelson to Lord Hillsborough, Dec. 1, 1770, in William J. Van Schreeven, comp., and Robert L. Scribner, ed., *Revolutionary Virginia: The Road to Independence*, I: *Forming Thunderclouds and the First Convention, 1763–1774: A Documentary Record* (Charlottesville, Va., 1973), 85.

5. "W.H.O.," *Va. Gaz.* (R), June 30, 1774; "D.C.," *ibid.* (P & D), Dec. 22, 1774. On the operations of virtue to support due regard for rank, see J.G.A. Pocock, "Virtue and Commerce in the Eighteenth Century," *Journal of Interdisciplinary History*, III (1972–1973), 125.

6. For reports of the spread of concern, see Farish, ed., *Journal of Fithian*, 111–113, 116, 117; Greene, ed., *Diary of Landon Carter*, II, 817–818.

7. For a fuller discussion of courthouse speeches and the relationships of oral and typographic culture in the context of the patriot movement, see Isaac, "Drama-

tizing the Ideology," *WMQ*, 3d Ser., XXXIII (1976), 357–371, and the references given there.

8. *Va. Gaz.* (R), Jan. 12, 1775; Thomas Adams to Thomas Hill, Nov. 1774, in *VMHB*, XXIII (1915), 178; "D.C." in *Va. Gaz.* (P & D), Dec. 22, 1774.

9. Peter Force, comp., *American Archives . . .* , 4th Ser. (Washington, D.C., 1837–1853), I, 915, col. 1. For analysis of this aspect of the Revolution, see Wood, *Creation of the American Republic*, 107–124, and Edmund S. Morgan, "The Puritan Ethic and the American Revolution," *WMQ*, 3d Ser., XXIV (1967), 3–43.

10. Van Schreeven, comp., and Scribner, ed., *Revolutionary Virginia*, I, 87, 23; "Associator Humanus," *Va. Gaz.* (P & D), July 18, 1771.

11. Force, comp., *American Archives*, 4th Ser., I, 787, col. 1; *Va. Gaz.* (R), July 28, 1774.

12. Force, comp., *American Archives*, 4th Ser., II, 76–77; Van Schreeven, comp., and Scribner, ed., *Revolutionary Virginia*, I, 155.

13. For an example of the burning of politically objectionable literature, see the report from Orange County in the *Va. Gaz.* (D & H), Apr. 15, 1775. Irving Brant in *James Madison, I: The Virginia Revolutionist* (Indianapolis, Ind., 1941), 163, suggests that Madison was the author of the account published in the newspaper. There was a hanging and burning of Lord North's effigy at Richmond County courthouse, and a report of a tarring and feathering in Isle of Wight County (*Va. Gaz.* [Pinkney], Aug. 24, 1775). In Nov. 1774 a pole with a bucket of tar and a bag of feathers was said to have been set up in Williamsburg. "Letters from Virginia," *Magazine of History*, III (Jan. 1906), 156.

14. *Va. Gaz.* (D & H), May 6, 1775.

15. *Ibid.* (R), Nov. 4, 1774.

16. Washington to Mason, Apr. 5, 1769, in Rutland, ed., *Mason Papers*, I, 97–98. See also *Va. Gaz.* (R), Dec. 14, 1769; *ibid.* (P & D), Dec. 29, 1774; and *ibid.* (D & H), Jan. 28, 1775. Evidence concerning Virginians' anxieties at signs of moral decline is collected in Wood, "Rhetoric and Reality," *WMQ*, 3d Ser., XXIII (1966), 27–30.

17. *Va. Gaz.* (P & D), Apr. 11, 1771.

18. *Ibid.*

19. For other reported instances of unanimous elections, see *ibid.* (D & H), May 20, 1775; *ibid.* (Purdie), May 26, 1775; *ibid.* (Pinkney), Mar. 9, 1775; and Force, comp., *American Archives*, 4th Ser., I, 1203.

20. *Va. Gaz.* (R), July 7, 1774 (the newspaper was released with additional material after the date was printed in the colophon), July 14, 1774. The practice of reversing the charges of treating went back at least to 1769. See *ibid.*, June 1,

1769, and *ibid.* (P & D), Sept. 14, 1769. For other reported examples in 1774, see *ibid.* (R), July 21, 28, 1774.

21. *Ibid.* (Pinkney), June 1, 1775.

22. "W.H.O.," *ibid.* (R), June 30, 1774; Rutland, ed., *Mason Papers*, I, 211.

23. Rutland, ed., *Mason Papers*, I, 215–216.

24. Hugh Mercer [*et al.*] to Capt. William Grayson, Apr. 24, 1775, in Force, comp., *American Archives*, 4th Ser., II, 395. A detailed chronological account of events can be found in Ivor Noël Hume, *1775: Another Part of the Field* (New York, 1966).

25. Capts. Grayson and Lee to Col. [George] Washington, Apr. 26, 1775, in Force, comp., *American Archives*, 4th Ser., II, 395; Michael Brown Wallace to Gustavus Brown Wallace, May 14, 1775, Wallace Family Papers, 1750–1781, Alderman Library, University of Virginia, Charlottesville. I am indebted to Emory Evans for this reference.

26. Force, comp., *American Archives*, 4th Ser., II, 516; Patrick Henry to Francis Lightfoot Lee, May 8, 1775, in Paul P. Hoffman, ed., The Lee Family Papers, 1742–1795 (microfilm publication, Charlottesville, Va., 1966); Committee for Orange County, in *Va. Gaz.* (Purdie), May 19, 1775, supp.

27. James Parker to Charles Steuart, June 12, 1775, "Letters from Virginia," *Mag. of Hist.*, II (Jan. 1906), 159; William Byrd to Ralph Wormeley, Oct. 4, 1775, photocopy in Virginia Historical Society, Richmond; James Madison (later president of the United States) to William Bradford, June 19, 1775, in Hutchinson *et al.*, eds., *Madison Papers*, I, 153; "An American," *Va. Gaz.* (Purdie), May 19, 1775; Lord Dunmore to earl of Dartmouth, June 25, 1775, C.O. 5/1353, ff. 160–172, Public Record Office (typescript at the Colonial Williamsburg Foundation). On Mar. 25, 1775, the Virginia convention, following trends already at work, had instructed the upland counties to concentrate on mobilizing riflemen in hunting shirts. Force, comp., *American Archives*, 4th Ser., II, 169.

28. Adam Stephen to Richard Henry Lee, Aug. 24, 1774, Feb. 1, 1775, Letters to Richard Henry Lee, American Philosophical Society, Philadelphia (microfilm, Colonial Williamsburg Foundation).

29. For the chauvinistic song, see Canby, ed., "Munford's *Patriots*," *WMQ*, 3d Ser., VI (1949), 466. On the close-called election, see Robert Brent to Richard Henry Lee, Apr. 28, 1776, in Kate Mason Rowland, *The Life of George Mason: 1725–1792* (New York, 1892), I, 222. For examples of stirring resolves expressive of armed posture, see Force, comp., *American Archives*, 4th Ser., II, 539, 547, 578, 710–711, 872, 938; *Va. Gaz.* (Pinkney), May 25, 1775; and *ibid.* (D & H), June 17, 1775.

30. *Va. Gaz.* (Purdie), Apr. 19, 1776.

31. *Ibid.*, May 17, 1776.

32. On the sudden rise of the Methodist movement in Virginia, see Gewehr, *Great Awakening in Virginia*, chap. 6; and William Warren Sweet, *Virginia Methodism: A History* (Richmond, Va., 1955), 49–117.

33. Thomas Rankin to John Wesley, June 24, 1776, in Elmer T. Clark *et al.*, eds., *The Journal and Letters of Francis Asbury* (London and Nashville, Tenn., 1958), I, 221.

34. Devereux Jarratt to Thomas Rankin, Sept. 10, 1776, *ibid.*, 211.

35. *Ibid.*, 217.

36. *Ibid.*, 351, 354, and *passim*. Baptist preachers had the same aspirations. See Williams, Journal, *passim*.

37. This aspect of evangelicalism is treated with great insight in Stout, "Religion, Communications, and the American Revolution," *WMQ*, 3d Ser., XXXIV (1977), 519–541.

38. Canby, ed., "Munford's *Patriots*," *ibid.*, VI (1949), 497.

39. See Stout, "Religion, Communications, and the American Revolution," *ibid.*, XXXIV (1977), 519–541. For a seminal discussion of the social sources of the emotional appeal of ideology, see Wood, "Rhetoric and Reality," *ibid.*, XXIII (1966), 24–32.

40. Arthur H. Shaffer, ed., *Edmund Randolph: History of Virginia* (Charlottesville, Va., 1970), 179.

41. *Ibid.*, 179–181. William Wirt Henry, *Patrick Henry: Life, Correspondence and Speeches* (New York, 1891), I, 13–16, stressed the influence of the Rev. Samuel Davies upon Henry's oratorical style. Henry's use of allusion to the Book of Jeremiah is finely demonstrated in an essay that rehabilitates the oral traditions concerning the thematic structures of the oratory. See Charles L. Cohen, "Give Me Liberty, Death, and Jeremiah: A Note on Religion and Revolutionary Rhetoric" (unpublished paper delivered to the 22d annual meeting of the Kroeber Anthropological Society, Berkeley, Calif., May 6, 1978).

42. Henry, *Patrick Henry*, I, 9, 18. Henry's gentry attachments as well as his preoccupation with *Christian* virtue are admirably described in Richard R. Beeman, *Patrick Henry: A Biography* (New York, 1974), 53, 57, 60, 67, 89, 92, 103, 110–116.

CHAPTER 12

1. On the history of Jefferson's bill and its passage, see Julian P. Boyd *et al.*, eds., *The Papers of Thomas Jefferson* (Princeton, N.J., 1950–   ), II, 545–553;

Hutchinson *et al.*, eds., *Madison Papers*, VIII, 295–298. For a close factual account of the assessment struggle, see H. J. Eckenrode, *Separation of Church and State in Virginia: A Study in the Development of the Revolution*, Special Report of the Department of Archives and History, Virginia State Library (Richmond, Va., 1910). The drawn-out conflict is more comprehensively treated in relation to the divisive issues of the period in Thomas E. Buckley, *Church and State in Revolutionary Virginia, 1776–1787* (Charlottesville, Va., 1977). Valuable documents and discussion are also to be found in Miryam Neulander Kay, "Separation of Church and State in Jeffersonian Virginia" (Ph.D. diss., University of Kentucky, 1967); and Mary Elizabeth Quinlivan, "Ideological Controversy over Religious Establishment in Revolutionary Virginia" (Ph.D. diss., University of Wisconsin, 1971).

2. Robert Honyman, Journal, MS, Library of Congress, Mar. 16, Apr. 15, 1780. Honyman was the son of a Scots Presbyterian minister, born in Kineff, Kincardineshire in 1747. He received an M.A. from Marischal College, Aberdeen, in 1765 and served for a time as a surgeon in the Royal Navy. In 1772 he emigrated to America and settled in Hanover County, Virginia. He was a moderate, avoiding the extremes in the polarized politics of his day, but as he had thrown in his lot with America he rejoiced in victories of the Continental forces, and he volunteered for active service with the Hanover militia in 1779. Biographical information has been conveniently collected in Philip Padelford, ed., *Colonial Panorama, 1775: Dr. Robert Honyman's Journal for March and April* (San Marino, Calif., 1939), vii–xiii.

3. Honyman, Journal, MS, Sept. 8, 1780, Jan. 28, June 23, 1781.

4. *Virginia Gazette, or Weekly Advertiser* (Richmond), Mar. 23, 1782. See also *Virginia Gazette, or, the American Advertiser* (Richmond), Sept. 7, 1782.

5. [George Mason], "A Petition and Remonstrance from the Freeholders of Prince William County [Dec. 10, 1781]," in Rutland, ed., *Mason Papers*, II, 705, 709.

6. George Mason to Patrick Henry, May 6, 1783, *ibid.*, 770; George Mason, "Remarks on the Proposed Bill for Regulating the Elections . . ." (c. June 1, 1780), *ibid.*, 630.

7. Eckenrode, *Separation of Church and State*, 86.

8. Little, *Imprisoned Preachers*, 80–81; Eckenrode, *Separation of Church and State*, 38–39, 42.

9. Rutland, ed., *Mason Papers*, I, 284, 289–291; Brant, *James Madison*, I, 243–250.

10. Boyd *et al.*, eds., *Jefferson Papers*, I, 344.

11. "To the Honourable Speaker and House of Delegates, the petition of the Dissenters from the ecclesiastical Establishment in the Commonwealth of Vir-

ginia . . ." (The Ten-Thousand Name Petition), Oct. 16, 1776, in Religious
Petitions, 1774–1802, Presented to the General Assembly of Virginia (microfilm
in Virginia State Library, Richmond), hereafter cited as Va. Religious Petitions.
Unless otherwise stated, dates for these petitions are those endorsed upon them
indicating when they were received by the Assembly. The other petitions received are listed and summarized in Eckenrode, *Separation of Church and State*,
46–48.

12. *Journal of the House of Delegates of the Commonwealth of Virginia*, 2d ed. (Rich-
mond, Va., 1828), 8, 48, 63, 76, 80, 83, 89, 90, hereafter cited as *Journal of
Delegates*; Hening, ed., *Statutes at Large*, IX, 164–167; Eckenrode, *Separation of
Church and State*, 49–50; Rutland, ed., *Mason Papers*, I, 318–319; Boyd et al.,
eds., *Jefferson Papers*, I, 525–558. See also Buckley, *Church and State*, chap. 1.
Of course there was the usual lively, partly scurrilous, newspaper controversy.
Va. Gaz. (D & H), Oct. 11, 18, 1776; *ibid.* (Purdie), Nov. 1, 8, Dec. 6, 13,
1776.

13. Hening, ed., *Statutes at Large*, IX, 165.

14. *Ibid.*, 164; Boyd et al., eds., *Jefferson Papers*, I, 539; Thomas Jefferson, *Notes on
the State of Virginia*, ed. William Peden (Chapel Hill, N.C., 1955), 158. Jefferson repeated this exaggeration in his autobiography, where a dramatic account
of the struggle in the fall session of 1776 is given. Adrienne Koch and William
Peden, eds., *The Life and Selected Writings of Thomas Jefferson* (New York, 1944),
41.

15. Hening, ed., *Statutes at Large*, X, 197–198; Rutland, ed., *Mason Papers*, I,
553–554; Boyd et al., eds., *Jefferson Papers*, I, 532–535, 539–544.

16. Lunenburg County, petition received Nov. 3, 1779, Va. Religious Petitions.
Eckenrode, *Separation of Church and State*, 55–64, gives an account of the sessions of 1779 and prints some of the bills that were debated. See also Boyd et
al., eds., *Jefferson Papers*, II, 545–547; Buckley, *Church and State*, 46–61, and
Appendix 1, 185–188.

17. Eckenrode, *Separation of Church and State*, 61–62.

18. "The Presbytery of Hanover, to the Assembly, in October 1784," in Foote,
Sketches of Virginia, 1st Ser., 337; resolutions of the House of Delegates, in
Eckenrode, *Separation of Church and State*, 86, 99–103. The Christian teachers
bill is reproduced in Kay, "Separation of Church and State in Jeffersonian Virginia," 353–355.

19. Hutchinson et al., eds., *Madison Papers*, VIII, 298. A tally of signatures in favor
of assessment gives a figure of 1,020 on the 11 petitions.

20. Madison to Jefferson, Jan. 22, 1786, *ibid.*, 474. For the opinions of George
Washington and Richard Henry Lee, see Washington to George Mason, in Rut-

land, ed., *Mason Papers*, II, 832; and Ballagh, ed., *Letters of Richard Henry Lee*, II, 304–305. Figures for the numbers of votes in the legislature are in Eckenrode, *Separation of Church and State*, 113.

21. *Va. Gaz.* (D & H), Dec. 13, 1776; Essex County, Oct. 22, 1779, Surry County, Nov. 14, 1785, King William County, Nov. 21, 1778, Cumberland County, Nov. 6, 1778, Va. Religious Petitions. See also petitions from Cumberland County, May 21, 1777, in *Journal of Delegates*.

22. Powhatan County, June 4, 1784, King William County, Nov. 21, 1778, Powhatan County, June 4, 1784, Surry County, Nov. 14, 1785, Powhatan County, June 4, 1784, King William County, Nov. 21, 1778, Va. Religious Petitions. For other strong assertions that ministers must have "Decent and Respectable Rank," be "men of Genius and learning," see Essex County, Nov. 2, 1785, Caroline County, Dec. 5, 1777, Lunenburg County, Nov. 8, 1783, and Amelia County, Nov. 8, 1784, *ibid.*

23. Brunswick County, Nov. 9, 1785, "Committee of the Several Baptist Associations in Virginia" (Powhatan County), Nov. 3, 1785, Accomack County, Oct. 28, 1785, Va. Religious Petitions. A petition from Rockbridge County, Dec. 1, 1784, abhorred the prospect of clerical salaries rendering Virginia once more "swarming with Fools, Sots and Gamblers." The words in the Brunswick petition follow a formula on which some 24 other petitions were based. See Kay, "Separation of Church and State in Jeffersonian Virginia," 361–363.

24. For a fuller discussion of the social forces arrayed against each other in this campaign, see Beeman and Isaac, "Cultural Conflict and Social Change," *Jour. So. Hist.*, XLVI (1980), 525–550.

25. Surry County, Nov. 14, 1785, Va. Religious Petitions; Cumberland County, May 21, 1777, in *Journal of Delegates*;. Mecklenburg County, May 29, 1777, Va. Religious Petitions; *In the House of Delegates, Friday the 24th of December 1784* . . . (Richmond, Va., 1784), 1. On the exalted meaning of the word "literary" at this time, see James McLachlan, "The *Choice of Hercules*: American Student Societies in the Early 19th Century," in Lawrence Stone, ed., *The University in Society*, II: *Europe, Scotland, and the United States from the 16th to the 20th Century* (Princeton, N.J., 1974), 486–488.

26. McLachlan, " The *Choice of Hercules*," in Stone, ed., *University in Society*, II, 449–458, 481–483, 489–492. For interest in this iconographic symbol—and an admired representation of it—during the Revolution, see L. H. Butterfield, ed., *Adams Family Correspondence*, II (Cambridge, Mass., 1963), 96–97, 102–103.

27. Botetourt County, Nov. 29, 1785, Va. Religious Petitions (emphasis added).

28. A sense of the separateness of spiritual authority was in no way a novelty. By

the late 18th century, it had accrued a very long history in the Mediterranean and Atlantic worlds. The policy of declaring the state to be altogether secular and proclaiming its withdrawal from any concern with religion was, however, startlingly new. The contrary opinion, that the state must underpin public religious observance—if only because of the unquestioned link between religion and morality—was frequently asserted. For examples, see petitions from the following counties: Warwick, May 15, Powhatan, June 4, Amelia, Nov. 8, 1784, Va. Religious Petitions.

29. Petitions from "a Baptist Church at Occaqon, Pr. William Coun[ty]," May 19, 1776 (received June 20, 1776), Va. Religious Petitions. For an establishmentarian rejection of such bargaining, see the petition from Mecklenburg County, May 29, 1777, *ibid.*

30. Brunswick County, Nov. 9, 1785, *ibid.* This was a formula petition. See n. 23 above. The strides that the Baptists took in escalating their demands, as the impregnable traditional order of establishment gave way to the contractual framework of the commonwealth, can be traced in the petitions. As late as May 1774 the petitioners were assuring the Assembly "that they wish for no indulgences which may disturb the Peace of Government." Even when in Aug. 1775 the Association had passed a resolution condemning the tax in support of the Church, they resolved to take no collective action. The petition from the Occoquan church of May 1776 (see n. 29, above) is the *only* extant appeal by dissenters to the legislature to remove this burden that was presented before the reorganization of the basis of government; see *Journals of Burgesses, 1773–1776*, 92; and *Va. Gaz.* (Pinkney), Aug. 31, 1775.

31. Hutchinson *et al.*, eds., *Madison Papers*, VIII, 298–304. For discussion of the alliance of evangelicals and Enlightenment rationalists, see Sidney Earl Mead, *The Lively Experiment: The Shaping of Christianity in America* (New York, 1963), 55–71. For an excellent review of the extent of the assault on tradition that was blandly subsumed in the axioms of Jefferson's views on religion, see David Little, "Origins of Perplexity: Civil Religion and Moral Belief in the Thought of Thomas Jefferson," in Russell E. Richey and Donald G. Jones, eds., *American Civil Religion* (New York, 1974), 185–210.

32. Boyd *et al.*, eds., *Jefferson Papers*, II, 526–553.

33. *Ibid.*, 528. For evidence of Jefferson's close relationship to Samuel Henley (although Jefferson never appeared in support of his friend when attacks on the establishment were still bad form), see Jefferson to Henley, June 9, 1778, *ibid.*, 198–199, and Mar. 3, 1785, *ibid.*, VIII, 11–12. On the educational system and the reading program to be adopted, see *ibid.*, II, 526–533. For a summary, making reference to the customary use of the Bible, see Jefferson, *Notes on Virginia*, ed. Peden, 146–147.

34. Boyd *et al.*, eds., *Jefferson Papers*, II, 528.
35. Financial opposition to the "Bill for the more general diffusion of knowledge" is mentioned in James Madison to Thomas Jefferson, Dec. 4, 1786, *ibid.*, X, 576, and confirmed in Madison to Jefferson, Feb. 15, 1787, *ibid.*, XI, 152. Jefferson himself told how tax resistance nullified the final adoption of the measure in 1796. See "Autobiography," in Koch and Peden, eds., *Life and Writings of Jefferson*, 50.

CHAPTER 13

1. Albemarle Baptist Church Book, Jan. 9, 1773; Semple, *History of the Baptists in Virginia*, ed. Beale, 29–50, 103. For examples of the determined commemoration of Virginia as the scene of Baptist martyrdom, see Little, *Imprisoned Preachers, passim*; Ryland, *Baptists of Virginia*, 172–173.
2. Jesse Lee, *A Short Account of the Life and Death of the Rev. John Lee, A Methodist Minister in the United States of America* (Baltimore, 1805), 15.
3. L. F. Greene, ed., *Writings of the Late Elder John Leland . . .* (New York, 1845; facsimile reprint, 1969), 115. That the Anglo- and Afro-Virginian modes were sufficiently compatible to be jointly enacted does not necessarily mean that they expressed or communicated the same meanings to participants of diverse cultural backgrounds. For a brief discussion of this issue, see pp. 307–308, below.
4. Thrift, *Memoir of Jesse Lee*, 6, 7, 8; Taylor, *Ten Baptist Churches*, 292; Ireland, *Life*, 77, 103; William Wirt, *Sketches of the Life and Character of Patrick Henry*, 2d ed. (Philadelphia, 1818), 4–6.
5. L. F. Greene, ed., *Writings of Leland*, 28.
6. Johann David Schoepf, *Travels in the Confederation [1783–1784]*, trans. and ed. Alfred J. Morrison (New York, 1968 [orig. publ. Philadelphia, 1911]), II, 93; Bernard, *Retrospections*, ed. Bernard, 151–153; [Kimber], "Observations," *WMQ*, 1st Ser., XV (1906–1907), 146.
7. For an important systematic review of the significance of refinement—the control and minimization of bodily manifestations—in the evolution of European culture, see Norbert Elias, *The Civilizing Process: The Development of Manners*, trans. Edmund Jephcott (Oxford, 1978), xi–xviii, 51–217. The evolution was far from complete by 1790, even among the gentry, as can be seen from the continued acceptance of bed sharing at taverns. The quotations are from Chinard, ed., *Huguenot Exile,* 138–139, and Wright and Tinling, eds., *Quebec to Carolina*, 206–208.
8. For an excellent discussion of early examples of newly introduced privacy partitions in 17th-century English farmhouses, see Cary Carson, "Segregation in Ver-

nacular Buildings," *Vernacular Architecture*, VII (1976), 24–29. The implications of the compartmentalization of the "Georgian" house arrangements are usefully summed up in Deetz, *In Small Things Forgotten*, 115–117.

9. Glassie, *Folk Housing*, 120–121. The dates set on the buildings analyzed by Professor Glassie seem to have been too early. Accordingly the rate at which the changes described entered into the house plans of poor planters appears to have been slower than he assumed (personal communication with Cary Carson).

10. For a powerful presentation of the revolution in the realm of artifacts, see Carson and Carson, "Styles and Standards of Living." The possible connection between trends in the artifact world and the formulation of the Declaration of Independence are discussed suggestively in Deetz, *In Small Things Forgotten*, 158–159. See also *ibid.*, 117, 121, 122–126. The theory that evangelicalism may have been a highly visible manifestation of deep underlying cultural trends is finely developed in Stout, "Religion, Communications, and the American Revolution," *WMQ*, 3d Ser., XXXIV (1977), 519–541. For a Chesapeake documentation of the change in foodways discussed by Deetz, see Henry Miller, "The Planters' Victuals: A Study of Changing Subsistence Patterns on the Colonial Chesapeake" (paper delivered at the Society for Historical Archaeology meeting, Nashville, Tenn., Jan. 1979).

11. Morgan, "Development of Slave Culture," 301–302; see also Kulikoff, "Origins of Afro-American Society," *WMQ*, 3d Ser., XXXV (1978), 226–259; Allan Kulikoff, "A 'Prolifick' People: Black Population Growth in the Chesapeake Colonies, 1700–1790," *Southern Studies*, XVI (1977), 391–428. On the incorporation of Christian symbolism in Afro-American life, see Levine, *Black Culture*, 3–80; Genovese, *Roll, Jordan, Roll*, 159–284; and especially Mathews, *Religion in the Old South*, 185–250.

12. Gutman, *Black Family*, 131, indicates a high continuing level of marriages between slaves living on different plantations in Virginia. Such a pattern must have heightened the communal, as opposed to domestic, ethos uniting the occupants of the quarter. On estimated size of settlements, see Kulikoff, "Origins of Afro-American Society," *WMQ*, 3d Ser., XXXV (1978), 241; also Morgan, "Development of Slave Culture," 5, 8.

13. L. F. Greene, ed., *Writings of Leland*, 98.

14. Levine, *Black Culture*, 32, 37–38, and *passim*. Professor Levine's analysis of the forms of black culture—as well as of the specific content of black religion and mythology—achieves the most comprehensive and persuasive interpretation I have seen. See also Sidney W. Mintz and Richard Price, *An Anthropological Approach to the Afro-American Past: A Caribbean Perspective*, Institute for the Study of Human Issues, Occasional Papers in Social Change, no. 2 (Philadelphia, 1976) for a theoretical formulation of a framework for interpreting Af-

rican cultural transference to the New World. Levine seems to have arrived at a similar approach in his vivid study of the North American case, without the baffling abstraction inevitable in a purely theoretical statement. Mathews, *Religion in the Old South*, 185–197, offers profound insights concerning the relationship of black religion to white evangelicalism.

15. Levine, *Black Culture*, 38.

16. It is invidious to cite examples. Among recent scholars, Eugene Genovese in *Roll, Jordan, Roll* explores subtly the interrelationships of the worlds of slaves and of masters, but by drawing his examples at will from across centuries of time and thousands of square miles of space, he ignores the evolution of both systems and their geographical variations. Herbert Gutman's *Black Family* rejects the pathology interpretation and provides fine analyses of living circumstances and the self-identifications involved in naming patterns, but he does not consider the implications of changing concepts of what "family" meant among both whites and blacks at different times and in different places. Gerald W. Mullin, in *Flight and Rebellion: Slave Resistance in Eighteenth-Century Virginia* (New York, 1972), is admirably sensitive to cultural contexts that are specific to region and period. He effectively traces trends toward occupational assimilation among blacks. In my view, however, he unduly neglects larger living patterns and so finds cultural convergence, where I consider cultural divergence to have been the main trend.

17. Rutland, ed., *Mason Papers*, I, 287–289. On patriarchal aspirations, see Mullin, *Flight and Rebellion*, 3–17. Our preoccupation with slavery as the anomalous institution that it had become before it was extinguished in the Atlantic world has led to an unbalanced concentration on the peculiarities that distinguished slavery from other legal and customary relationships. Our understanding of the transition from general acceptance to widespread denunciation of the institution cannot be further advanced until the changing deep patterns of life and perception in Atlantic culture are considered. A start has been made in Winthrop D. Jordan, *White over Black: American Attitudes toward the Negro, 1550–1812* (Chapel Hill, N.C., 1968), 48–56, and 217–228, where the hierarchy of nature, but not of society, is discussed. For a very valuable treatment of assumptions in this area see Greene, *All Men Are Created Equal, passim*. The views of some of the English gentry on laborers in their own society are treated in Morgan, *American Slavery*, 321–326. For a clear statement of the extent to which the English social-cultural system was still sustained in the mid-18th century by a sense of hierarchical social connections, see Perkin, *Origins of Modern English Society*, 44–51. I am much indebted to Professor Gordon Wood for discussion of the way slavery was not, but later became, an offensive anomaly.

18. The subject is too complex for adequate treatment here. The passage from rule-

bound formality to personality-oriented sentimentality can be traced (although these are not the categories that organize the analysis) in a fine dissertation on observable trends in Virginia gentry family letters from 1740 to 1830 (Grimmelmann, "This World and the Next"). Aspects of the end product, but scarcely the nature of the change, are analyzed in Smith, *Inside the Great House, passim*. On "paternalism" (without definition in relation to "patriarchy"), see Genovese, *Roll, Jordan, Roll*, 3–7, and *passim*. For a study of the master and his relationships in a configuration predating the intensification of familial domesticity alluded to in this brief discussion, see Zuckerman, "Byrd's Family," *Perspectives in American History*, XII (1979), 253–311.

19. On "humanitarianism," see Norman S. Fiering, "Irresistible Compassion: An Aspect of Eighteenth-Century Sympathy and Humanitarianism," *Journal of the History of Ideas*, XXXVII (1976), 195–218.

20. On the problems of reconciling slavery and republicanism, see Charles Grier Sellers, Jr., "The Travail of Slavery," in Sellers, ed., *The Southerner as American* (Chapel Hill, N.C., 1960), 40–71; for opposed points of view that do not really refute Sellers, see Robert McColley, *Slavery and Jeffersonian Virginia* (Urbana, Ill., 1964) and David Brion Davis, *The Problem of Slavery in the Age of Revolution, 1770–1823* (Ithaca, N.Y., 1975).

21. The ritual of adhering to the association is described in *Va. Gaz.* (R), Nov. 4, 1774. I have dated the event as occurring on the first possible Caroline County court day after the Virginia convention.

22. On the history of increasing concern with the individual as the focus of real meaning that has accompanied the rise of mass, cosmopolitan culture, see Richard Sennett, *The Fall of Public Man* (New York, 1976). One does not have to agree with Sennett on all points to accept the reality of the trends he seeks to interpret. For an earlier analysis—more speculative and very technical, yet rich with insights—see Thomas Luckmann, *The Invisible Religion: The Problem of Religion in Modern Society* (New York, 1967 [orig. publ. Freiburg, Germany, 1963]).

23. Robert Honyman, Journal, MS, Mar. 16, 1780, Library of Congress.

24. [Anburey], *Travels*, II, 407; Schoepf, *Travels*, II, 36. The persistence of traditional values centering on the family "lineage" is strongly argued in Henretta, "Mentalité," *WMQ*, 3d Ser., XXXV (1978), 19, 29–30, but the possible effects upon the social ethos caused by large-scale movement in pursuit of these values is not discussed.

25. Cited in John B. Boles, *The Great Revival, 1787–1805: The Origins of the Southern Evangelical Mind* (Lexington, Ky., 1972), 14; Bishop [William] Meade, *Old Churches, Ministers, and Families of Virginia* (Baltimore, 1966 [orig. publ. Philadelphia, 1857]), I, 420. See also Conway, *Edmund Randolph*, 165.

26. Meade, *Old Churches*, I, 301, 486, II, 162. For the reorganization and decline of the vestries, see Eckenrode, *Separation of Church and State*, 147.
27. The decline of public spirit was most forcefully asserted in a much-applauded set of literary sketches first published in 1803 (see William Wirt, *The Letters of the British Spy, to Which Is Prefixed a Biographical Sketch of the Author*, intro. by Richard Beale Davis [Chapel Hill, N.C., 1970], 191–194). The private correspondence of the period is interspersed with lamentations of the perceived declension.
28. R[ichard] Garrettson, "An Account of the Revival of the Work of God at Petersburg in Virginia," *Arminian Magazine* (London), XIII (1790), 306. For the vestry's prohibition, see Meade, *Old Churches*, I, 441–442.
29. Meade, *Old Churches*, I, 372, II, 47, I, 242, II, 47.
30. Mill Swamp Baptist Church, Isle of Wight County, Recs., July 2, 1774.
31. On the subject of bodily controls and relaxation of controls, see Douglas, *Natural Symbols*, 93–112; also Victor W. Turner, *The Ritual Process: Structure and Anti-Structure* (Chicago, 1969). Mathews, *Religion in the Old South*, 41–42, draws attention with fine, sensitive commentary to the physical contact aspect of Separate Baptist meetings and rituals.
32. Daniel Hall in Lorenzo Dow, ed., *Extracts from Original Letters to the Methodist Bishops . . .* (Liverpool, 1806), 56; Thomas Sargent, *ibid.*, 58–59. The descriptions of forms of action are taken from Sargent's more detailed account of a camp meeting in Maryland.
33. Richard R. Beeman, ed., "Trade and Travel in Post-Revolutionary Virginia: A Diary of an Itinerant Peddler, 1807–1808," *VMHB*, LXXXIV (1976), 181, 183; Farish, ed., *Journal of Fithian*, 183; Jones, *Present State of Virginia*, ed. Morton, 84. For examples of the courthouse as a place for preaching appointments, see Clark *et al.*, eds., *Journal of Asbury*, I, 403, 434, 449, 511, II, 13, 14. This is an appropriate place to enter a reservation concerning the admirable account of major transformations given in Mathews, *Religion in the Old South*. The strong dominance of evangelicalism in southern religion is persuasively demonstrated, but insufficient attention is given to the fact that religion did not have such complete dominance in social life. In the larger sphere, evangelical norms had to compete with aggressive worldly styles and values that could neither be suppressed by, nor assimilated into, the modes of piety.
34. St. George Tucker, ed., *Blackstone's Commentaries: With Notes of Reference to the Constitution . . . of the United States, and of the Commonwealth of Virginia . . .* (Philadelphia, 1803), V, Appendix, 20. (Note that the pagination of each volume is divided between Blackstone's text and Tucker's discourses on U.S. and Virginia legal developments.)

35. *Ibid.*, I, Appendix, 19, 387, 438. See also Morton J. Horwitz, *The Transformation of American Law, 1780–1860* (Cambridge, Mass., 1977), 10–30. On dissatisfaction with county government, see Richard R. Beeman, *The Old Dominion and the New Nation, 1788–1801* (Lexington, Ky., 1972), 30–33.

36. "Letters from William and Mary College, 1798–1801," note on party violence, 1799–1800, *VMHB*, XXIX (1921), 178. See also A. W. Patterson, *The Code Duello with Special Reference to the State of Virginia* (Richmond, Va., 1927).

37. The militia also became provincialized as it was distributed into U.S. brigades and divisions. See Hening, ed., *Statutes at Large*, XIII, 340–356, for the act of 1792. For a vivid representation of the 19th-century Virginia courthouse as a faintly ridiculous meeting place of bumpkins, see [John Pendleton Kennedy], *Swallow Barn, or a Sojourn in the Old Dominion* (Philadelphia, 1832), 199–200. The suggestion that political fulfillment must involve transcending the parochial scene and setting up for Congress is very clear in the sketch of Squire Meriwether (pp. 26–27).

38. The word "modernization" has been so much abused, and the categories that have described its progress (commercialization, industrialization, urbanization) have tended to be so mechanical, that it is used with hesitation. On the concept and its relationship to preindustrial commercialization in England, see E. A. Wrigley, "The Process of Modernization and the Industrial Revolution in England," *Journal of Interdisciplinary History*, III (1972–1973), 225–259.

A DISCOURSE ON THE METHOD

1. For a convenient initial reference on the nature of society, see Peter L. Berger and Thomas Luckmann, *The Social Construction of Reality: A Treatise in the Sociology of Knowledge* (Garden City, N.Y., 1966).

2. Social theorists have used the word "action" in various ways. I hope that I may escape the perplexities of this situation by using it to connote the aspects of behavior that are meaningful to participants. For a judicious critique of Weber's concept of action and a modified formulation that accords with the approach I have adopted, see Alfred Schutz, *On Phenomenology and Social Relations*, ed. Helmut R. Wagner (Chicago, 1970).

3. The relationship between observers' ("experience-far") and participants' ("experience-near") categories is explored in Clifford Geertz, "On the Nature of Anthropological Understanding," *American Scientist*, LXIII (1975), 47–48.

4. *Virginia Gazette* (Purdie and Dixon), Oct. 18, 1770, supp. The Scripture reference in the report of the service is incorrect. It appears to be a very free rendering of Psalm 62:7.

5. Jack P. Greene, ed., *The Diary of Colonel Landon Carter of Sabine Hall, 1752–1778* (Charlottesville, Va., 1965), I, 286–292. On the colonel's relationship with his son and daughter-in-law and his performance as father and grandfather, see *ibid.*, 310, 314. In a few places I have departed from the editor's reading of the manuscript as the requirements of sense have given cause.

6. The striking of bargains implicit in much of social life is given extended theoretical treatment in Peter M. Blau, *Exchange and Power in Social Life* (New York, 1964).

7. See Berger and Luckmann, *Social Construction of Reality*, 149–152.

8. Landon Carter's ineptitude has been sensitively analyzed and contrasted with the successful authority styles of other gentlemen planters in Gerald W. Mullin, *Flight and Rebellion: Slave Resistance in Eighteenth-Century Virginia* (New York, 1972). Mullin develops and applies a concept of role-performance, which deserves the closest attention of ethnographic historians. *Ibid.*, 19–33, 63–72.

9. The importance that narrative and the interpretation of episodes have assumed in the work of such leading social historians as E. P. Thompson has misled one distinguished historian into celebrating a revival of *traditional* narrative history. See Lawrence Stone, "The Revival of Narrative: Reflections on a New Old History," *Past and Present*, LXXXV (1979), 3–24. It is important, therefore, to stress that the role advocated for narrative in this discourse has nothing to do with the kind of outlines of "rise and fall" that have provided the narrative framework for traditional history. See June Philipp, "Traditional Historical Narrative and Ethnographic History" (unpubl. paper).

10. The diary refers interchangeably to Mangorike Will, Willy, and Billy. There are also references to "Billy the foreman" and to "Billy" unqualified. That Mangorike Will was a slave trusted with responsibility is made clear by a later entry that he will be put in charge of a quarter in place of an unsatisfactory overseer, who is to be dismissed. Greene, ed., *Diary of Landon Carter*, I, 168, 308, 483, 551, II, 742, 773, 1141.

11. Metaphors are among the most important forms of "models" in systems of everyday knowledge. "Models" as used in social science are usually elaborate metaphors. In the latter case, however, it is essential that the comparison necessarily present in the metaphor be scrutinized and controlled as precisely as possible. I have throughout reserved the term "metaphor" for the constructs in the minds of past actors, and the term "model" for those to be employed by the investigating historian. For a thoughtful historical-anthropological discussion of the "metaphors" in the culture of·alien peoples and the "models" employed by historians as social scientists, see Greg Dening, *Islands and Beaches: Discourse on a Silent Land, Marquesas, 1774–1870* (Melbourne and Honolulu, 1980), 86–94. For a fine application of the concept by a historian, see Charles E. Rosenberg, "Flor-

ence Nightingale on Contagion: The Hospital as Moral Universe," in Rosen-berg, ed., *Healing and History: Essays for George Rosen* (New York, 1979), 116–136.

12. On definition of the situation, see Erving Goffman, *The Presentation of Self in Everyday Life* (Woodstock, N.Y., 1973), 15–27.

13. Greene, ed., *Diary of Landon Carter*, II, 940–941. The significance of the pa-triarchal metaphor in this reported encounter is increased when it is noted that the passage immediately following it (evidently written at the same time) de-scribes an attempted reconciliation between Landon Carter and a daughter who had married without his consent. Carter examines his decisions and his feelings in the matter explicitly in terms of the dual aspects of Judaeo-Christian divine fatherhood—an imperative to punish transgressors for their offenses, and an imperative to show forgiveness and mercy.

14. Two recent works deserve particular mention for their treatment of Anglo-American perceptions of fatherhood and the social-cultural system. The power of the metaphor in religious feeling and the formation of personalities is finely treated in Philip Greven, *The Protestant Temperament: Patterns of Child-Rearing, Religious Experience, and the Self in Early America* (New York, 1977). The per-vasiveness of the metaphor as a mediator of social relations is a central theme in Eugene D. Genovese, *Roll, Jordan, Roll: The World the Slaves Made* (New York, 1974).

15. Richmond County, Va., Criminal Trials, [1710]–1754. Microfilm record most kindly made available by the Virginia State Library, Richmond.

16. The important concept of "typification" was developed by the phenomenologist Alfred Schutz. See Schutz, *On Phenomenology*, ed. Wagner, 138.

17. This crucial concept is defined extensively in use in Berger and Luckmann, *Social Construction of Reality*, 61, 173–174, and *passim*.

18. For a sustained theoretical discussion of the use of the human body as a cos-mological reference system, see Mary Douglas, *Natural Symbols: Explorations in Cosmology*, 2d rev. ed. (New York, 1973). This work is highly suggestive in its discussion of relationships between forms of social communication, intensities of concern for boundary maintenance, and modes of viewing the world.

19. The dangers of becoming so fascinated with the rituals and customs of the past as to lose sight of power relations have been forcefully denounced in Elizabeth Fox-Genovese and Eugene D. Genovese, "The Political Crisis of Social History: A Marxian Perspective," *Journal of Social History*, X (1976–1977), 205–220.

20. A convenient set of illustrations of both settings and roles highly structured by paired oppositions may be found in Mary Douglas, ed., *Rules and Meanings: The Anthropology of Everyday Knowledge, Selected Readings* (Harmondsworth, Mid-

dlesex, 1973). See especially J. C. Faris, "'Occasions' and 'Non-Occasions'" (pp. 45–59); P. Bourdieu, "The Berber House" (pp. 98–110); and R. Hertz, "The Hands" (pp. 118–124). With the subject of oppositional pairs, the "structuralist" system of Claude Lévi-Strauss rears its head. This author deems it prudent not to take a position here with regard to the intense controversies surrounding that theorist.

21. Quoted in Lawrence W. Levine, *Black Culture and Black Consciousness: Afro-American Folk Thought from Slavery to Freedom* (New York, 1977), 17.

22. See Dening, *Islands and Beaches*, 86–94.

ABOUT THE ILLUSTRATIONS

Figures I and II. Engravings made by Theodore de Bry (1590), after watercolor paintings by John White, an Englishman who accompanied the first abortive expedition to settle "Virginia" in 1587. The newcomers were struck by the distinctive hunting-gathering-gardening economy of the native inhabitants. Internecine warfare called for the palisading of the Indian "towns," as the English called them. See Stefan Lorant, ed., *The New World: The First Pictures of America* . . . (New York, 1946), 30, 31, 185–275. Courtesy the Virginia State Library.

Figure III. Detail from John Smith's map of Virginia (1612). The great adventurer came to know the Indians' territory well, but he transposed it into a European perspective when he represented it on a map. See *A Map of Virginia. With a Description of the Countrey* . . . (Oxford, 1612). Courtesy The Colonial Williamsburg Foundation, Inc.

Figure IV. The Thornton map of Virginia (c. 1725). The invaders' occupation has remade the landscape. Counties reveal an English way of apportioning territory. All save four of these jurisdictional units had imported names. The places of settlement shown are almost entirely the seats of leading families (appropriately connoted by little framed houses) along the river frontages. Courtesy The Colonial Williamsburg Foundation, Inc.

Figure V. The "Salt" map (1683). We see an English pattern of fenced enclosures and the humble houses of tenants who work the soil and owe rent to a landlord. Courtesy the Trustees of the William Salt Library and Sir Michael Salt of Shillingstone, Dorset. Photograph by Peter Rogers.

Figure VI. This surveyor's plat from Charles County, Maryland (c. 1697) is happily enriched with sketches of the structures that occupied the space at the crossroads, which had been set apart for public purposes. Courtesy the Maryland Hall of Records. Photograph courtesy the St. Mary's City Commission.

Figure VII. Benjamin Henry Latrobe came to Virginia in 1796 with a view to settling there. This drawing was made and laconically captioned on March 13, 1798, after Latrobe had already entered sharp protests against slavery in his journal. See Edward C. Carter II *et al.*, eds., *The Virginia Journals of Benjamin Henry Latrobe, 1795–1798* (New Haven, Conn., 1977), II, 225, 359. Courtesy The Papers of Benjamin Henry Latrobe, Maryland Historical Society, Baltimore, Maryland.

Figure VIII. Sketch of Westover by J. S. Glennie (1811). This early drawing from the journal of a Scottish traveler shows a double pair of symmetrically placed dependencies contributing to the central dignity of the mansion itself. From the J. S. Glennie Journal, May 8, 1811. Courtesy The Andre deCoppet Collection, Princeton University Library.

Figure IX. The College of William and Mary (c. 1740) was set in a formal garden and (by the 1750s) was dignified on either side by grand flanking buildings: the president's house and the Brafferton Indian school (not shown here). The artist and the engraver of the Bodleian plate from which this figure is extracted are not known. Courtesy The Colonial Williamsburg Foundation, Inc.

Figure X. The Capitol was an architectural representation of the British constitution as adapted for use in the colonies. In the upper story of the west wing was the grand chamber where the King's Council sat as the upper legislative house, and where the lower house waited on the king's representative (the governor or lieutenant governor) for the opening of sessions and for the giving or withholding of assent to bills at the session's conclusion. Immediately below in the west wing was the hall in which governor and council sat as the General Court, the highest judicial body in the colony. In the corresponding hall on the opposite side, in the east wing, sat the elected representatives of the counties and boroughs as the House of Burgesses. The gallery joining the two wings was designed for conferences between the Council and the Burgesses on disputes over the form and substance of bills. The square form of the south faces of the two wings reveals that the plate was prepared after the Capitol had burned down in 1747 and been rebuilt. Courtesy The Colonial Williamsburg Foundation, Inc.

Figure XI. St. Peter's Church, New Kent County (dated 1701). This was one of many dignified brick churches that began to replace rougher wooden structures about 1700 and during the early decades of the eighteenth century. Courtesy The Colonial Williamsburg Foundation, Inc.

Figure XII. Mill Creek (or Mauck's) Meeting House (exterior). This barnlike structure is said to date from the colonial era. It may have been erected by German Baptists near the Shenandoah, rather than by Separate Baptists. Nevertheless, it provides images of the contrast between popular evangelical forms of close association and the formal hierarchalism of Anglican liturgical community. See Harold Wickliffe Rose, *The Colonial Houses of Worship in America Built in the English Colonies before the Republic, 1607–1789, and Still Standing* (New York, 1963), 519–521. I am indebted to Dr. Dell Upton for further advice on the provenance of this building. Courtesy the H. Wickliffe Rose Papers, Yale University Library.

Figure XIII. Mill Creek (Mauck's) Meeting House (interior). Courtesy the H. Wickliffe Rose Papers, Yale University Library.

Figure XIV. The pulpit of Aquia Church, Stafford County (dated 1757). This grand example of the form of pulpit found in the parish churches of the established Church of England displays a clear intention to elevate authority and to impose decorum. Courtesy the H. Wickliffe Rose Papers, Yale University Library.

Figure XV. Patrick Henry, posthumous portrait by Thomas Sully, oil painting (1815). An idealized likeness of the man raised above his generation—in its general estimation—by his ability to communicate in popular style a passion for a world reshaped in truly moral order. Courtesy The Colonial Williamsburg Foundation, Inc.

Figure XVI. Philip Dawe, *The Alternative of Williamsburg*, mezzotint (London, 1775). Armed patriots compel recalcitrant merchants to sign articles of "Association" declaring they will not import British goods. The "alternative" is the cask of tar and the bag of feathers suspended from the scaffold behind. Courtesy The Colonial Williamsburg Foundation, Inc.

Figure XVII. The wearer of the uniform of the king's Virginia forces is George Washington, as portrayed in an oil painting by Charles Willson Peale in 1772—that is, during the period between Washington's retirement from active service as a regular officer in the time of the French and Indian War, and his acceptance of the command of the Continental Army. Courtesy the Washington/Custis/Lee Collection, Washington and Lee University, Virginia.

Figure XVIII. The osnaburg (canvas) hunting tunic (with Indian tomahawk and long Kentucky rifle) appears clearly in this sketch by Baron Ludwig von Closen of one of the self-consciously American troops known as "shirtmen" or "riflemen." Courtesy the Library of Congress. Photograph courtesy The Colonial Williamsburg Foundation, Inc.

Figure XIX. Old Pohick Church, oil painting (c. 1834) attributed to John Gadsby Chatman. Many Virginians in the nineteenth century had a deep sense of living among the ruins of a more glorious past. Photograph courtesy Walter H. Miller & Company, Inc., Williamsburg, Virginia.

Figure XX. Camp meeting, lithograph (c. 1835) after painting by A. Rider. Popular evangelical forms of religious expression had become altogether ritualized by the Age of Jackson. Courtesy The New-York Historical Society, New York City.

Figure 1. Queens Creek, York County. Photograph by the author.

Figure 2. *Landon Carter*, attributed to Charles Bridges. Courtesy the Reverend T. Dabney Wellford and Mr. R. Carter Wellford. Photograph courtesy The Colonial Williamsburg Foundation, Inc.

Figure 3. *The Tobacco House*, from G. Melvin Herndon, *William Tatham and the Culture of Tobacco* (Coral Gables, Fla., 1969), 29. Photograph courtesy The Colonial Williamsburg Foundation, Inc.

Figure 4. York River view, looking northwest toward West Point, Virginia, [March 1797], watercolor by Benjamin Latrobe. (Quotation from Hugh Jones, *The Present State of Virginia from Whence Is Inferred a Short View of Maryland and North Carolina*, ed. Richard L. Morton [Chapel Hill, N.C., 1956], 73.) The low-lying forest-and-swamp terrain and the landscape made by the orientation of plantations to rivers and shipping appear very clearly in this sketch. The fine Georgian mansion on the left was the great house of the Airy Plains estate of Henry Banks, Esquire. Courtesy The Papers of Benjamin Henry Latrobe, Maryland Historical Society, Baltimore, Maryland.

Figure 5. The Governor's Palace, from the Bodleian plate (see note to figure IX). A model of symmetry set up in Williamsburg, 1710–1720. Courtesy The Colonial Williamsburg Foundation, Inc.

Figure 6. *The Plantation* (c. 1825), artist unknown. Vines (and laurels?) enclose the garden as well as festooning one of the trees. The architecture of the house clearly reveals this to be of comparatively late date. The form is more "intensive" and "closed" with the flanking dependencies drawn in and incorporated as supporting lateral elements of the mansion house itself. See discussion in chapter 13, p. 305. Courtesy The Metropolitan Museum of Art. Gift of Edgar William and Bernice Chrysler Garbisch, 1963.

Figure 7. Based on a 1742 surveyor's plat, this plan of the Carter family seat at Shirley shows the orientation of the great house to the river landing place and the disposition of outbuildings to make a court designated by the mansion and its two flanking dependencies. This cluster was set beside a "park," with garden and orchard included. Less dignified workplaces and the village-like "great quarter" where the slave community was located were kept at a greater distance. The original plat by Sackvil Brewer is owned by Mr. and Mrs. Hill Carter of Shirley plantation, and is photographically reproduced in Catherine M. Lynn, "Shirley Plantation: A History" (M.A. thesis, University of Delaware, 1967), 63. Drawn by Richard J. Stinely.

Figure 8. A panel at the foot end of a raised marble tomb located outside Christ Church, Lancaster County, immediately behind the altar. The monument is to Colonel Landon Carter's father, Robert "King" Carter (1663–1732) and shows clearly that eschatological symbolism of the body's corruptibility persisted into the second quarter of the eighteenth century. There are two earlier representations of the same icon on tombs in Bruton churchyard, Williamsburg. Photograph by the author.

Figure 9. Schematic rendition of part of York County. The cartographic industry of French artillery officers during the Revolutionary War provides a unique basis for visual presentation of the pattern of watercourses, trees, great houses (plantation complexes), common planters' scattered farms, clustered slave dwellings, and community facilities. By 1781 in areas such as this, the planters were evidently dependent on manuring and were pressing hard on woodland resources. Based on the "Carte de la Campagne de la Division aux Ordres du Mis. de St. Simon en Virginie depuis le 2. 7bre. 1781. jusqu-a la Reddition d'Yorck le 19. 8bre. même année" (original in the Ayer Collection, #238, Newberry Library). Drawn by Richard J. Stinely.

Figure 10. Christ Church, Lancaster County (exterior). The liturgical east end is seen from outside the churchyard wall. This house of worship built c. 1730 at Robert "King" Carter's expense at the end of an avenue leading from his great house, Corotoman, was designed as a memorial to the great landowner's father, John Carter (d. 1669). Photograph by the author.

Figure 11. Christ Church, Lancaster County (interior). The design conforms remarkably to the specifications indicated by Christopher Wren for "auditory" churches. See the discussion on pp. 61–63. Photograph by the author.

Figure 12. Plan of Christ Church, Lancaster County. Drawn by Benjamin Hellier.

Figure 13. Diagram of mid-eighteenth-century Virginia buildings that illustrate in comparative view the social statements and level of investment represented by each. The great house is Sabine Hall (measuring approximately 60 by 42 feet); the church is Christ Church (71 by 69); the courthouse is that of King William County (50 by 49); the common planter's dwelling is Pear Valley (21 by 16); and the log slave cabin stands on the River View property in St. Mary's County, Maryland (18 by 17). Drawn by Cary Carson and Benjamin Hellier.

Figure 14. Plan of Bacon's Castle (1665). The sketch illustrates the disposition of living spaces, hearths, and entrances in a large hall-and-parlor house of the "pre-Georgian" seventeenth century. Drawn by Cary Carson and Benjamin Hellier.

Figure 15. *The Old Plantation*, watercolor by unknown artist (c. 1800). This painting was found in South Carolina without any records or even clear internal evidence to establish its provenance. The scene depicted could be located anywhere from the Susquehanna to the Caribbean. The nature of the action has also eluded definite categorization. Clearly the artist was impressed by the solemnity of the dance-ritual, as communicated in the seriousness of the participants' facial expressions. After long and frequent scrutiny and careful analysis of the component elements I have arrived at a tentative hypothesis that it shows a double wedding, that the kerchiefed dancers are matrons, and that this stage of the ritual will culminate in their draping the scarves they display over the shoulders of the two décolleté young women, whom I take to be brides. The two men in white I presume to be grooms (third and fourth figures from the left), and the two older men (second left, third right) perhaps fathers of the brides—although the hand of one of them resting on the presumed bride's bosom hardly lends support to this speculative theory. If this is a wedding, then the carved stick may be a more visibly African ancestor of the broomstick used in slave marriage ceremonies recorded later in the century. See Eugene D. Genovese, *Roll, Jordan, Roll: The World the Slaves Made* (New York, 1974), 479. Courtesy the Abby Aldrich Rockefeller Folk Art Center, Williamsburg, Virginia.

Figure 16. Hanover Courthouse (c. 1735). On the green in front of this handsome building Elkanah Watson witnessed a Virginia wrestling match (see p. 98). Inside, Patrick Henry delivered his legendary denunciation of the royal legislative veto and of the greed of the clergy in the Parsons' Cause (see p. 145). Behind the camera stands the ordinary where the young patriot, not yet a stern moralist, is reported to have kept bar and played his fiddle (see p. 268). Courtesy the Virginia State Library.

Figure 17. Billiards in Hanover Town, Virginia, [November 1797], pen and ink drawing by Benjamin Latrobe. Dress reveals plainly and bearing shows subtly that consciousness of rank ordering in society was not eliminated by common engagement in an absorbing contest. Courtesy The Papers of Benjamin Henry Latrobe, Maryland Historical Society, Baltimore, Maryland.

Figure 18. The College of William and Mary, west end of the chapel (c. 1740). Detail from the Bodleian plate (see note on figure IX). Courtesy The Colonial Williamsburg Foundation, Inc.

Figure 19. Bruton Parish Church, Williamsburg. The tower was part of the extensive rebuilding completed in 1715. The octagon and the steeple were added in 1769. Courtesy The Colonial Williamsburg Foundation, Inc.

Figure 20. Norborne Berkeley, baron de Botetourt (1718–1770), governor of Virginia from 1768 to 1770, life-size marble statue. The leaders of Virginia society grieved at the end of the rapprochement between colony and parent country that Botetourt's governorship had accomplished. The General Assembly commissioned this memorial to stand in the courtyard of the colonial capitol. Later it was transferred into the keeping of the college he had patronized. Courtesy The College of William and Mary. Photograph courtesy The Colonial Williamsburg Foundation, Inc.

Figures 21 and 22. Panels in the pedestal of the Botetourt statue. Words and imagery convey the sorrowful sense of a moment of imperial reconciliation (perhaps now passed with the governor's death) that his lordship's brief vice-regal reign had instituted. Courtesy The College of William and Mary. Photographs courtesy The Colonial Williamsburg Foundation, Inc.

Figure 23. *Peyton Randolph*, engraver unknown. From Sidney Hayden, *Washington and His Masonic Compeers* (New York, 1905), 260. Photograph courtesy The Colonial Williamsburg Foundation, Inc.

Figure 24. The Grand Master's Chair, Williamsburg Lodge of Free Masons (c. 1760). Both the craftsmanship incorporated in this fine chair and the opulence of the Williamsburg Freemasons were signs of the advance of cosmopolitan culture in the colonial capital. See Wallace B. Gusler, *Furniture of Williamsburg and Eastern Virginia, 1710–1790* (Richmond, Va., 1979), III. Courtesy Williamsburg Masonic Lodge #6, Williamsburg, Virginia.

Figure 25. Thomas Jefferson's instructions concerning his tombstone, June 24, 1826, Thomas Jefferson Papers, Library of Congress, Washington, D.C. The Greek quotation is from Anacreon and may be translated: "And lie we shall and must/ A little dust/ Of bones uncemented" (J. M. Edmonds, ed. and trans., *Elegy and Iambus . . . with the Anacreontea*, Loeb Classical Library Edition [London, 1931], Ode 32, lines 9–10). By 1882 the original tomb had been so mutilated by souvenir collectors that Congress deemed it appropriate to provide for the erection of a new monument, which when completed in 1883 was more than twice the height originally specified by Jefferson. Courtesy the Library of Congress.

Figure 26. Christ Church, Lancaster County, pulpit (c. 1730). Such furnishings were regular features of the colonial parochial churches. They communicated powerful images of hierarchy and the descent of authority from on high. Photograph by the author.

Figure 27. "Bunn, the blacksmith, at a Campmeeting near Georgetown" (artist's caption), pen sketch by Benjamin Latrobe, [6 August 1809]. The artisan-preacher stands on a platform of planks roughly roofed against the weather. The tears on his face connote an appeal for the sharing of personal feelings rather than a formal exercise of superior learning and authority. When his time is up, or when he is emotionally spent, the preacher will be relieved by one of those seen seated behind. Courtesy The Papers of Benjamin Henry Latrobe, Maryland Historical Society, Baltimore, Maryland.

Figure 28. The ascent of learning (a variant of the iconography of "The Choice of Hercules"), engraved in 1799 from a design by Charles Fenton Mercer, a young Virginian. The device was prepared for the American Whig Society of the College of New Jersey (now Princeton University). It shows a youth (apparently not the young Hercules) being directed onto the arduous path of study that leads upward to the temple of virtue, and away from the downward road of ease. Fellow scholars perform academic exercises on the left. See the discussion on p. 289. Courtesy the Seeley G. Mudd Manuscript Library, Princeton University.

Figure 29. Diagram contrasting the openness of the earlier planters' houses (above) with the closed off, comparatively inaccessible living space of later designs. See the discussion on pp. 72 and 305. Drawn by Cary Carson and Benjamin Hellier.

Figure 30. Diagram showing the relationships of one of Landon Carter's slaves, Simon the oxcarter. Drawn by Richard J. Stinely.

Figure 31. Elevation of Sabine Hall, reconstructed as it was in 1766. The caption is a quotation from Isaac Ware, trans., *The Four Books of Andrea Palladio's Architecture . . .* (London, 1738), i. Drawn by Benjamin Hellier.

INDEX